The Effect of D&O Insurance on Managerial Risk Taking

Maximilian K.P.
Gaber

The Effect of D&O Insurance on Managerial Risk Taking

intersentia

METRO

Ius Commune Europaeum

Maximilian K.P. Gaber

The Effect of D&O Insurance on Managerial Risk Taking

Intersentia Publishing Ltd.
Sheraton House | Castle Park
Cambridge | CB3 0AX | United Kingdom
Tel.: +44 1223 370 170 | Email: mail@intersentia.co.uk

ISBN 978-1-78068-348-5
D/2015/7849/119
NUR 827

British Library Cataloguing in Publication Data. A catalogue record for this book is available from the British Library.

PREFACE

Although I wrote this thesis, finalizing it would not have been possible without the guidance, good will and continuous assistance of some that I owe great thanks to. The process from having an idea to expressing it in a book could not have taken place without having met these people.

I remember very well the meeting I had with Prof. Hildegard Schneider, currently dean of the law faculty, about the possibilities of writing a Ph.D. at Maastricht University. I had many ideas, not all fit for a decent research topic, but Hildegard Schneider was a great listener nonetheless. Supporting my willingness to write a Ph.D., she kindly referred me to Prof. Michael Faure.

The first meeting with Prof. Michael Faure who later became my supervisor was astonishing and eye-opening to me. Being a person with charisma, his remarks and suggestions contain the perfect notions of directness, politeness and motivation. I am grateful to have had the opportunity of working with him. His insights and intuition keep surprising me even after the finalization of the book. His steady support and good will were an essential ingredient to expressing my thoughts in written words.

Dr. Niels Philipsen has been invited to be my co-supervisor. I came to highly appreciate his tranquillity and thoroughness. For the guidance of my progress, he has been an indispensable complement to Michael Faure. His detailed remarks and questions on previous drafts demonstrate that he spared no effort in making this thesis happen.

The assessment committee was composed of Prof. Hildegard Schneider (chair), Prof. Kid Schwarz, Prof. Anthony Ogus and Prof. Jac Rinkes. Since their specialities range from comparative law, company law, law and economics to insurance law, I am very thankful for their mutually positive feedback.

Obviously, my surroundings have been very understanding and supporting in respect to my work on the Ph.D. thesis. I would not want to miss the enjoyable moments and constructive discussions I experienced with fellow Ph.D. students that I met during my research at Maastricht University.

Furthermore, I owe my accomplishments to people of the Institute for Transnational Legal Research Metro and Maastricht University that worked in the background. In this regard, I want to express my thanks to Yleen Simonis and Marina Jodogne.

In the later stages of my doctoral studies, I was working at the law firm RESOR NV in Amsterdam. Although the work load at Amsterdam law firms such as RESOR NV can be overwhelming, I am indebted to Prof. Jako van Hees for his recommendations on how to best finalize a Ph.D. thesis while working. Furthermore, besides the joyful moments I had at RESOR NV, I am indebted to the coaching efforts, skills and knowledge of my colleagues. The skills I developed because of them had definitely an impact on the quality of the thesis.

Needless to say, I deeply appreciate that my family continuously supported me through all the times of the Ph.D. project. Finally, I express my highest gratitude to my partner Nadine. She was not only understanding for when I had to work on the thesis in the middle of the night or at weekends. She also encouraged me to pursue my aim and to work hard for the Ph.D. Without her everlasting support, this project would not have been possible.

Leiden, March 2015

CONTENTS

ABBREVIATIONS

AG	*Aktiengesellschaft* (German public corporation)
AktG	*Aktiengesetz* (Statute regarding German public corporations)
AO	*Abgabengesetz* (German Tax Act)
CA	1985 Companies Act (England)
BGB	*Bürgerliches Gesetzbuch* (German Civil Code)
BGH	*Bundesgerichtshof* (German Federal Supreme Court)
BV	*Besloten vennootschap* (Dutch private corporation)
BW	*Burgelijk Wetboek* (Dutch Civil Code)
CAR	Cumulative Abnormal Return
CDDA 1986	Company Directors Disqualification Act 1986 (England)
CEO	Chief Executive Officer (managing director)
CFO	Chief Financial Officer
CJEU	Court of Justice of the European Union
DCGK	*Deutscher Corporate Governance Kodex* (German Corporate Governance Code)
Del. C.	Delaware Code (Civil Code of Delaware)
D&O insurance	Insurance for D&O risk
D&O risk	D&O risk is the sum of managerial liability risk and indemnification risk
EBITDA	Earnings Before Interest, Taxes, Depreciation and Amortization
EU	European Union
Fw	*Faillissementswet* (Dutch Bankruptcy Code)
GmbH	*Gesellschaft mit beschränkter Haftung* (German private corporation)
GmbHG	*Gesetz betreffend die Gesellschaften mit beschränkter Haftung* (Statute regarding German private corporations)
Hof	*Gerechtshof* (Dutch court of appeal)
HR	*Hoge Raad* (Dutch Supreme Court)
IA 1986	Insolvency Act 1986 (England)
Inv 1990	*Invorderingswet* (Dutch Tax Act)
IPO	Initial Public Offering
LLC	Limited Liability Company (Delaware)
Ltd.	Private *Limited* Company by shares (England)

M&A	Mergers & Acquisition
NV	*Naamloze vennootschap* (Dutch public corporation)
OLG	*Oberlandesgericht* (German court of appeal)
ROA	Return on Assets
Rb.	*Rechtbank* (Dutch court of first instance)
SEC	Securities and Exchange Commission (USA)
Side-A	Insurance for the managerial liability risk
Side-B	Insurance for the indemnification risk
Side-C	Insurance for losses of the corporation arising from a managerial liability claim
SME	Small and Medium-sized Enterprise
SOX	Sarbanes-Oxley Act
StGB	*Strafgesetzbuch* (German Penal Code)
UG	*Unternehmensgesellschaft* (less common legal form of a German private corporation)
UK	United Kingdom
USA	United States of America

Chapter 1

INTRODUCTION

1.1. Background

Risk taking in business contributes to innovation. Yet, excessive risk taking is associated with corporate failure and even economic crises.[1] The impact of risk taking on society may be best symbolized as a two-edged sword.

On the one hand, society in Europe depends on entrepreneurs and managers daring to embrace risks. Next to reinforcing economic growth, managers of SMEs offer almost two thirds of all available jobs.[2] Society has to promote an entrepreneurial culture.[3] Furthermore, managers of multinational corporations should be encouraged to take risks.[4] However, the stigma of failure and accompanying detriments, such as liability, could deter people from becoming managers or entrepreneurs.[5]

On the other hand, the recent economic crises turned the spotlight on those managers that take excessive risks.[6] For instance, the meltdown of Lehman Brothers is associated with the aggressive business style at the top management level.[7] In this context, many believe that managerial opportunism in connection with empire building, exorbitant management fees and sub-prime rated security trades are partly responsible for the crises.[8]

In this regard, risk taking affects society positively as well as negatively. The economy has to carefully balance these effects. According to law and economics theory, the liability of managers could deter managers from taking excessive risks (called managerial

1 Braun and Latham 2009, p. 260. According to The Economist 12 March 2010, "*Even when executives began to understand the scale of the risks they were taking, they kept taking on business rather than walk[ing] away from deals. Board directors were unaware for several months in 2007 that Lehman had breached its risk-appetite limit.*"

2 According to the European Commission, Annual Report on SMEs 2012/2013, p. 11, "*[p]roviding the right conditions in which SMEs can flourish is paramount for ensuring a sustained recovery and achieving prosperity for all EU citizens.*"

3 "*Entrepreneurial culture ... refers to the pro-active behaviour towards risk taking ventures and innovation of the entrepreneurs.*" See: European Commission, Annual Report on SMEs 2012/2013, p. 11.

4 Marks 1999, p. 694; Posner 2007, p. 441.

5 Semadini 2008, p. 557.

6 E.g. Laeven and Levine 2009, p. 259; Ferguson 2010, 'Inside Job'.

7 Valukas 03-03-2010, p. 2-3.

8 E.g. Hagendorff and Vallascas 2011, p. 1079-1080; Fahlenbrach and Stulz 2011, p. 12.

liability).[9] Still, complex (and possibly harsh) liability rules may chill the manager's willingness to seize risks that are beneficial to society. Insurance for managerial liability (called Directors' & Officers' insurance or D&O insurance), the less prominent affiliate to liability, may be equipped with the necessary tools to both prevent opportunism and promote efficient risk taking by the manager. In fact, a properly functioning D&O insurance system may more elegantly incentivize adequate managerial risk-taking than for example, direct regulation of managerial activity (e.g. disqualification) or the adoption of harsher liability rules.[10] These considerations serve as the foundation to analyse the social desirability of D&O insurance.

The next section will outline the purpose of this thesis. Section 1.3 will turn to the methodology and section 1.4 will introduce the structure of the thesis. Section 1.5 will raise some caveats.

1.2. Purpose of the thesis

This thesis will answer the research question: *How does D&O insurance affect managerial risk taking?*

To do so, the thesis will develop hypotheses on the D&O insurance market and apply these to the actual market. It will seek to highlight topics that have not yet been fully appreciated. Finally, the thesis will recommend alterations to enhance the benefits of D&O insurance and point to future research possibilities.

When analysing the research question, three issues will be highlighted in this thesis.

First, this thesis will observe that smaller corporations usually lack D&O insurance[11] and, under some circumstances, D&O insurance becomes difficult to re-insure.[12] This thesis will explain the occasional absence of D&O insurance and re-insurance and develop possible solutions to this problem.

Secondly, academic discussion of D&O insurance does not yet fully appreciate the fact that D&O insurance also insures the indemnification risk. When a corporation agrees to indemnify the manager for his liability risk, the manager is covered. Still the indemnifying corporation often insures the risk of having to indemnify the manager (called indemnification risk).[13] This thesis will identify some possible reasons why a principally risk neutral firm would desire insurance for that risk.

Thirdly, Baker and Griffith fear that insurers cannot positively influence managerial risk taking.[14] This thesis will show that insurance seems to alter the risk-taking of the

9 Kraakman 2009, p. 35. Empirical analysis, e.g. in the area of car insurance, shows that liability has a deterrence effect. See: Harrington and Danzon 2000, p. 305.

10 Shavell 2004, p. 257; Polinsky and Shavell 1993, p. 256; Kraakman 1984, p. 870–871; Kraakman et al. 1993, p. 1736; Harrington and Danzon 2000, pp. 304–305.

11 E.g. Advisen Report 2013, p. 9.

12 E.g. Berger et al. 1992, pp. 253–254; Doherty and Smetters 2005, pp. 375–376; Culp and O'Donnell 2009, pp. 430–431.

13 E.g. Bishop 1966, p. 103; Baker and Griffith 2009, pp. 760–762.

14 Baker and Griffith 2009, p. 831.

manager. Specifically, the effect of the insurer's settlement practice will be analysed. Yet, a change of risk-taking does not necessarily mean that managers take excessive risks. Some observations actually suggest that an insured manager rather takes into account creditors' interests. This thesis advocates a limited publication of the corporate D&O insurance policies. Such publication could signal valuable information to market participants and possibly enhance the positive effects of D&O insurance.

1.3. Methodology

The research question of how D&O insurance affects managerial risk taking will be answered by applying three approaches: a law and economics analysis, a comparative law analysis and an empirical review. These three approaches will be applied to the research question for the following reasons.

A law and economics analysis reveals the extent to which managerial risk taking is influenced by liability rules and how liability insurance changes the incentive structure of the liability system. In turn, it predicts how a change of liability insurance could alter managerial risk taking.[15] This analysis will be heavily based on the work of law and economics scholars such as Kraakman and Shavell.

A comparison between legal systems enables the best practices of very fragmented national liability regimes and D&O insurance markets to be identified. An analysis of the USA represents a good start to discuss D&O insurance, because the first profitable D&O insurance was developed there.[16] Since it has been argued that the US D&O insurance system works inefficiently,[17] the US system will be compared to three EU Member States, namely the UK, Germany and the Netherlands.[18]

A review of empirical studies demonstrates the level of impact that some factors have on the demand for D&O insurance, the supply of D&O insurance and the effect of D&O insurance on the manager. Furthermore, it provides evidence with respect to the feasibility of the law and economics hypotheses that this thesis will formulate.[19]

1.4. Structure

These three approaches will be embedded in the thesis according to the following structure. The first four chapters 2 to 5 will outline the law and economics theory on D&O insurance. Chapters 6 to 9 will apply the hypotheses of the previous chapters to the comparative analysis, as well as to the empirical findings. Chapter 10 will summarize the findings.

15 Polinsky and Shavell 1993, p. 256; Kraakman 1984, p. 870–871; Kraakman et al. 1993, p. 1736.

16 Plück and Lattwein 2004, p. 187–189.

17 Baker and Griffith 2009, p. 831.

18 The EU's legal system of managerial liability is very fragmented. Due to the fragmentation, a universal analysis of the D&O insurance in the EU is impossible. See: Gerner-Beuerle et al. 2013, p. viii.

19 De Groot 1975, p. 419–421; Doane and Seward 2011, pp. 15–17, 551–552; Bain and Engelhardt 2014, pp. 358–359. For more information on errors with respect to the approval or rejection of the null-hypothesis, see: Doane and Seward 2011, pp. 344–347.

The deterrence effect of liability will be outlined in Chapter 2. It will identify three managerial liability rules, (i) tort liability, (ii) bankruptcy liability and (iii) internal liability. Chapter 3 will outline the effect of risk bearing and general liability insurance on risk taking. Chapter 4 will point to hurdles to the proper handling of risks by insurers. These concepts serve as the basis for an understanding of D&O insurance.

Chapter 5 will develop hypotheses on the effect of D&O insurance on managerial risk taking. It will apply the framework of insurance of chapters 3 and 4 to the three liability rules identified in Chapter 2. The attitudes of managers, shareholders and insurers towards managerial liability will be outlined, also taking into account liability rules in which the standard of care is uncertain.

Equipped with this theory, the subsequent chapters turn to D&O insurance practice. Chapter 6 will compare the national managerial liability rules of the USA, the UK, the Netherlands, and Germany. The procedural requirements and the national standards of care will be compared. The chapter will further analyse legal limitations to indemnifying the manager. Chapter 7 will review empirical studies, most of them conducted in Canada. The hypotheses formulated in Chapter 5 will be applied to these studies. Chapter 8 will discuss the actual wording of D&O insurance policies. Public surveys on D&O insurance and D&O insurance contracts of the USA, the UK, the Netherlands and Germany will be analysed and compared.

Chapter 9 will outline divergences between the hypotheses of Chapter 5 and practice. It will answer the research question, recommend best practices and point to possibilities of future research. The final Chapter 10 will summarize the findings.

1.5. Caveats

Some caveats are in order.

First, this thesis is concerned with an economic approach to the law. It formulates its hypotheses and arguments on the basis of economic considerations. The author realizes that applying this (economic) approach may ignore considerations of ethics, equity and justice.

Secondly, to focus on the research question, the discussion is limited to managerial liability. Liability rules of the firm, the entrepreneur or the officer (also called non-executive board members or outside managers) in most cases do not directly affect the risk taking behaviour of managers. Thus, the thesis will refrain from discussing these rules.

Thirdly, it must be kept in mind that the findings of the empirical studies are only comparable to a certain extent because their methodologies differ. Furthermore, this thesis is unable to provide exhaustive and empirically validated evidence on the effect that the D&O insurance has on managerial risk taking in the four countries. Empirical studies on the D&O insurance market in the USA, the UK, the Netherlands and Germany are yet to be published. Still, this thesis will provide an indication about the current status on the effect of D&O insurance on managerial risk taking.

Fourthly, the overall discussion remains on the male prefix for reasons of simplicity and is not intended to imply any discrimination.

Chapter 2

MANAGERIAL LIABILITY

2.1. Introduction

To answer the research question on the effect of D&O insurance on managerial risk taking, let us first begin with outlining the liability of corporate managers (managerial liability).

The different liability rules will be grouped into two categories. The first category includes liability rules that protect parties that are external to the firm (external liability). The second category refers to internal liability rules.

Tort liability is an external liability rule that that can deter injurers (e.g. managers) from harming victims and that can induce firms to internalize costs.[20] However, when the assets of the manager are insufficient to entirely compensate the victim, his incentive to take care is weakened (judgement-proof problem). One solution to this problem is called vicarious liability where the manager's principal, his superior, could instead be held liable for the misconduct of the manager. The optimal effect of vicarious liability is subject to the condition that the principal can control the manager. When the principal cannot sufficiently control the manager, managerial liability may be an adequate additional deterrence next to vicarious liability.[21] These issues will be outlined in section 2.2.

When the principal is a corporation, its assets are limited pursuant to the concept of limited liability. In this regard, the assets of the principal can be (or can become) insufficient to entirely compensate the victim (e.g. in the vicinity of insolvency). In that case, managerial liability as additional liability to vicarious liability is introduced.

Furthermore, voluntary creditors may desire a right to sue the manager, especially in the vicinity of insolvency.[22] The reason is that the manager may take desperate measures when he fears to lose his job. Here, managerial liability may also adequately deter misbehaviour.[23] Because these liability actions of victims and voluntary creditors can usually only be lodged in the vicinity of insolvency or during bankruptcy proceedings, the following will refer to these liability rules as bankruptcy liability. Section 2.3 will be devoted to these considerations.

20 Shavell 2004, p. 177; Harrington and Danzon 2000, p. 279.
21 Kraakman 2008, p. 134.
22 Kraakman et al. 2009, p. 134.
23 Carney 1999, p. 684.

The second category of liability refers to internal liability rules. When ownership and control is separated, agency costs between shareholders and managers arise.[24] The liability of the manager is one of many (and probably less important) tools that deters the manager from bad performance. A corporation may even choose to change the scope of managerial liability (referring to the indemnification of the liable manager). Whether indemnification should be allowed has been controversial.[25] Section 2.4 will discuss internal liability and will sketch the scholastic view on indemnification.

These considerations will provide the necessary context with respect to managerial liability. The next two chapters will turn to the insurance market in general and to the obstacles of insurance. Chapter 5 will turn to D&O insurance.

2.2. Tort liability

The classic model of accident law is developed by Calabresi,[26] Shavell[27] and Coase.[28] First, this section will introduce strict and negligence liability.[29] Secondly, it will turn to the relationship of firm and consumer where the firm is held liable for defective products it sold (product liability). Thirdly, the general inability of the manager to be held liable will be discussed. Afterwards, the section will turn to vicarious liability (subsection 2.2.4) and agent liability (subsection 2.2.5).

2.2.1. Injurer liability to victims

This subsection introduces the classic model of accident law. It turns to strict liability and negligence. This subsection also considers actions of the victim (bilateral case). Finally, this subsection deals with the levels of activity.

Expected damage without liability – The classic model of accident law assumes that there are two parties, an injurer and a victim. Further, the harm caused is pecuniary.[30] The injurer causes damage to the victim. For example, consider a unilateral case where the injurer has a steel factory that pollutes the air.[31] According to the classic model, the occurrence of damage arises probabilistically and with a clearly defined severity. The

24 Posner 2007, p. 441.
25 Marks 1999, p. 704.
26 Calabresi 1961, pp. 499–500.
27 Shavell 1980, p. 1.
28 Coase 1960, pp. 1–2.
29 Next to the basic forms of strict liability and negligence liability, scholars also studied the effects of strict liability with a defence of contributory negligence, negligence liability with a defence of contributory negligence and comparative negligence. Where appropriate, this chapter will refer to these additional liability rules. For more information see: Shavell 2004, pp. 184–189, 201–203.
30 Shavell 2004, p. 177–178; Shavell 1980, pp. 2–3, Posner 2007, pp. 167–169; Schäfer and Müller-Langer 2009, p. 5; Cooter and Ulen 2012, pp. 198–201.
31 Posner 2007, pp. 167, 178; Schäfer and Müller-Langer 2009, p. 5; Cooter and Ulen 2012, pp. 201–203. When the victim cannot influence the amount of damage at all (for example damage arising from pollution), it is not socially optimal for the victim to take care. See: Shavell 2004, pp. 178, 203.

multiplication of probability and severity equals the expected damage. The model further assumes that both the injurer and the victim desire to maximize utility and are risk neutral.[32] In other words, a damage of EUR 100 with a probability of occurrence of 10% equals an expected damage of EUR 10. The person that bears this damage will interpret the uncertain payment of EUR 100 as a certain payment of EUR 10 (this amount resembles his negative utility of having to breath dirty air).[33]

Liability rules (strict v. negligence liability) – Liability is a legal tool to compensate the victim for the damage and is paid by the injurer. If the occurrence of the damage is dependent on the acts of the injurer, liability will have a certain deterrence effect on the injurer. There are two kinds of liability rules, negligence liability and strict liability.[34]

To begin, the classic model of accident law assumes that the expected damage is solely dependent on the injurer's level of care. If he exercises more care, expected damage will decline (e.g. the injurer installs better air filters). The social optimum would be to minimize the sum of costs, being the cost of care and the expected damage. Where the costs of taking care plus the marginal decrease of overall costs related to the expected damage are lowest, social optimum is arrived.[35] Let us consider an example outlined in Graph 1.

Graph 1[36]

Level of care	Expected loss	Overall cost
EUR 0	15,00% of EUR 100	EUR 15
EUR 3	10,00% of EUR 100	EUR 13
EUR 6	8% of EUR 100	EUR 14

When zero care is exercised, the expected damage is 15% times EUR 100, EUR 15. The overall cost is 15 EUR. When the cost of taking care is 3 EUR and therefore the expected damage decreases to EUR 10, the overall cost is EUR 13. Where the costs of taking care are high (say 6 EUR) and the marginal decrease of expected loss declines (expected damage is 8% times EUR 100, being EUR 8), the overall costs would increase again (here EUR 14). As a result, the social optimum is likely to involve some expected damage and not the highest possible level of care.[37]

Under strict liability, the injurer will have to compensate the victim, disregarding the level of care taken. Thus, the injurer's costs equal overall costs. To minimize his own costs, he will choose a medium level of care (EUR 3) leading to social costs of EUR 13.

32 The assumption on risk neutrality will be relaxed in the subsequent chapter.

33 Shavell 2004, p. 178; Posner 2007, pp. 167–168; Schäfer and Müller-Langer 2009, p. 5; Cooter and Ulen 2012, pp. 198–201.

34 Shavell 2004, p. 177; Posner 2007, pp. 167, 178; Schäfer and Müller-Langer 2009, p. 3; Cooter and Ulen 2012, pp. 201–202, 205–207; Harrington and Danzon 2000, p. 281.

35 Shavell 2004, p. 178; Posner 2007, pp. 167–168; Schäfer and Müller-Langer 2009, p. 5; Cooter and Ulen 2012, pp. 200–203.

36 Shavell 2004, p. 179.

37 Shavell 2004, pp. 178–179; Posner 2007, p. 168; Schäfer and Müller-Langer 2009, pp. 5, 6.

Under negligence liability, the court sets a level of due care (e.g. the court determines which air filters to use). The classical model of accident law assumes that this level of due care equals the socially optimal level of care.[38] The injurer will consequently adapt his level of care to the set level of due care. The injurer will have no incentive to exercise a much higher level of care than the one set by courts, because it would lead to additional costs. Additionally, taking less than due care, means being held liable, whereas taking due care means escaping liability. Both rules result in a social optimum. However, the injurer bears the costs of the strict liability rule, whereas the victim faces the costs under negligence (e.g. the victim will have to breath the filtered but still somewhat dirty air). Furthermore, regarding the negligence rule, the costs (i) to seek the efficient level of care in the first place and (ii) to establish the level of care in court need to be considered.[39]

Bilateral case – When the victim can influence the occurrence of the accident, also his level of care has to be considered. For example, consider a case where a victim fails to look down the street when crossing it and is hit by a car. This illustration refers to a bilateral accident case. In the bilateral version, the social optimum is derived from the sum of the levels of care of both parties and the resulting expected damage. Although one party might adapt his level of care to the behaviour of the other, there will be an equilibrium of care, where neither party is willing to change his behaviour. Under strict liability, the injurer will have an optimal level of care, whereas the victim will exercise no care (e.g. the car driver is always liable). In such a case, a victim's level of care that is zero will lead to a social cost that is higher than optimal. With negligence liability the injurer will exercise due care to escape liability (e.g. the driver observes the speed limit). To avoid damage, the victim will also take care (e.g. looking down the street). Such a situation results in an optimal level, when the level of due care equals the optimum.[40]

Next to negligence liability in a bilateral case, scholars have also pointed to the socially beneficial effects of strict liability with the defence of contributory negligence. Under this rule, the injurer is only strictly liable for the entire loss, when the victim's level of care was at least equal to the victim's due level of care (e.g. the car driver is strictly liable provided that the victim looked down the street). When the injurer is able to show in court that the victim' negligence was a contributory factor (e.g. he did not look down the street), the injurer (partly) escapes his obligation to compensate the victim.[41]

Level of activity – Whereas the level of care represents the precautions taken, when engaging in an activity, this section will analyse to what extent the level of activity will influence the social optimum. Considering the unilateral case, where the victim has no influence on the expected damage, the model assumes that an increase of activity will

[38] The next chapter will relax that assumption.

[39] Shavell 2004, pp. 180–182; Schäfer and Müller-Langer 2009, p. 6; Cooter and Ulen 2012, pp. 217–222.

[40] Shavell 2004, pp. 182–187; Schäfer and Müller-Langer 2009, p. 9; Cooter and Ulen 2012, pp. 204–205.

[41] Shavell 2004, p. 184–185; Posner 2007, pp. 172–177; Schäfer and Müller-Langer 2009, pp. 18–19; Cooter and Ulen 2012, pp. 208–211. Furthermore, scholars analysed the effects of a negligence rule with the defence of contributory negligence and a comparative negligence rule. In this classical model, where the parties adhere to the level of care, these other rules are superfluous. See: Shavell 2004, pp. 186–187; Posner 2007, p. 175; Golobardes and Pomar 2009, p. 46.

lead to a proportional decrease of expected damage (taking into account the additional utility of the injurer). Social optimum equals the utility derived from exercising the activity minus costs of care and expected damage.[42]

Without a liability rule, the injurer will increase his activity level as long as he obtains some additional utility from it. He will not take the expected damage into consideration because it is externalized. With strict liability, the injurer will behave according to the social optimum. He will adapt his activity and care level to it (e.g. produce less steel and install filters). After all, he will have to bear the costs of expected damage, disregarding his care. As a result, he will only engage in more activity, if the additional utility exceeds the costs of care and expected damage. When the negligence rule is applied, the injurer will escape liability, when he takes due care. As a result, he can increase the level of activity within the limits of due care. As long as the injurer lives up to that level of care, he will not be deterred from engaging in a level of activity that is potentially socially excessive.[43]

This defect of the negligence rule is important when the damage has high severity (e.g. the polluted air causes untreatable cancer). When damages are disastrous even when taking due care, a measure to decrease the activity level should be chosen. Theoretically, the court could set a level of activity. To do so, it would need to acquire exact knowledge about the utility increase that is experienced by the activity. Furthermore, the court would need to find out the actual level of activity from the injurer. Because in reality this is impossible, the strict liability rule is chosen for cases of high severity.[44]

When additionally the victim's level of activity is taken into account, the legal system needs to decide whether to expose the victim or the injurer to the expected loss. When the injurer's activity creates disastrous risks (keeping dogs of a vicious breed) and the activity of the victim is part of ordinary life (taking a walk), strict liability with a defence of contributory negligence should be adopted. When the injurer engages in an activity that is commonly accepted (playing football), negligence liability would be appropriate.[45]

2.2.2. Firm liability to consumers (product liability)

When injurers are firms, the relationship to the victim is at least two dimensional. The victims can be either strangers to firms or their customers. When they are strangers, the same analysis as above will apply. This subsection will focus on the relationship

42 Shavell 2004, pp. 193–194; Posner 2007, p. 178; Schäfer and Müller-Langer 2009, p. 9; Cooter and Ulen 2012, pp. 211–213.

43 Shavell 2004, pp. 195–197; Schäfer and Müller-Langer 2009, pp. 12–13; Cooter and Ulen 2012, pp. 211–213.

44 Shavell 2004, pp. 197–199; Schäfer and Müller-Langer 2009, pp. 12–13; Cooter and Ulen 2012, pp. 211–213.

45 Shavell 2004, pp. 199, 202–203; Schäfer and Müller-Langer 2009, p. 15; Cooter and Ulen 2012, p. 213. For a formal description, see: Harrington and Danzon 2000, pp. 279–280.

firm-consumer.[46] This subsection will further analyse how liability changes the firm's incentive to induce its employee to take optimal care.[47]

When considering the firm's potential change in behaviour, the consumer's perceived risk of the bought product must be taken into account. The consumer's utility derived from a product must exceed the product's market price plus the perceived expected defect of the product. When information is perfect, the consumer desires a product that functions properly and thus has the desire to pay a price that incorporates the firm's costs to minimize product defects. When the consumer knows perfectly the risks of malfunctioning attached to a product, no liability rule would be needed.[48]

When the consumer does not have all the information to estimate the actual expected damage, he will either over- or underestimate (or randomly correctly estimate) the risk attached to the product. A firm that will take care is not rewarded by the purchase behaviour of its consumers. As a result, a firm under competition will choose to take no (or less) care, in order to offer the product more cheaply. The cost of expected damage of defect will therefore be externalized and is borne by the consumer. In this regard, a liability rule of product defects may serve as a tool to internalize these costs.[49]

With liability, the firm will design rewards and punishments to induce employees and managers to reduce the risk of causing harm. The price of the firm's products partly reflects its ability to induce optimal behaviour of the employee and manager.[50]

2.2.3. *Liability of the firm's manager and the judgement-proof problem*

Instead of firm liability, one may call for personal liability. However, personal liability may fail to provide appropriate incentives at all levels of the firm. Moreover, the activity that caused the damage is likely to have been conducted in teams. In such a scenario, it might be difficult to assess the individual's level of culpability. Finally and most importantly for the purposes of this thesis, personal liability does not incorporate the judgement-proof problem that most of the agents are exposed to.[51]

The agent's assets may be insufficient to pay for the full damage. His incentive to reduce risk by taking care is limited to the expected loss of his assets. Any remaining expected damage is ignored by the agent. A personal liability rule would not deter the injurer for damage that surpasses his assets. He is judgement-proof in relation to the remaining damages. As a result, the injurer would choose levels of care and activity that

46 Shavell 2004, pp. 207–212; Posner 2007, pp. 182–183; Schäfer and Müller-Langer 2009, pp. 31–32; Cooter and Ulen 2012, pp. 225–226.
47 Polinsky and Shavell 1993, p. 240.
48 Shavell 2004, pp. 212–214; Posner 2007, pp. 182–183; Schäfer and Müller-Langer 2009, pp. 31–32; Cooter and Ulen 2012, pp. 225–226.
49 Posner 2007, pp. 182–183; Schäfer and Müller-Langer 2009, pp. 31–32; Cooter and Ulen 2012, pp. 225–226. Alternatively, firms may use warranties to signal to the consumer that they incorporated due levels of care. See: Shavell 2004, pp. 220–222.
50 Polinsky and Shavell 1993, p. 240.
51 Oded 2011, p. 274; Shavell 2004, pp. 230–231; Cooter and Ulen 2012, pp. 240–242.

are socially excessive. The judgement-proof problem is made worse by an increased disparity between injurer assets and expected damage.[52]

Particularly, the injurer's incentives to lower risks are diluted, when these risks remain higher than his assets. Furthermore, the judgement-proof problem may arise when the injurer has opportunities to shield assets.[53]

One solution to the judgement-proof problem is vicarious liability. Under vicarious liability, a party is held liable that is able to effectively monitor the injurer. Such a party is called the principal or *respondeat superior*.[54] This solution will be the topic of the next subsection.

Four other solutions to the judgement-proof problem were suggested. The first solution entails a minimum asset requirement. Only parties with sufficient assets may engage in particular dangerous activities. Although it ensures adequate possibilities for the victim's recourse, it excludes poor parties. Furthermore, the asset requirement gives rise to high monitoring costs in order to control the injurer to retain a sufficient amount of assets.[55]

A second solution is criminal liability. The judgement-proof injurer may be deterred from particular actions by introducing criminal, particularly non-pecuniary sanctions against him. The concept of criminal liability can also be linked to the concept of vicarious liability, holding a party other than the injurer criminally liable.[56]

A third possibility is the direct regulation of the party's risk-taking behaviour. The regulation would prohibit or set requirements for the engagement in certain activities (for example that milk has to be pasteurized). Still, the more technical the activity, the more difficult it is to regulate and monitor that activity.[57]

The fourth approach is liability insurance. The insurer's ability to control the judgement-proof problem will be discussed in subsection 3.2.5. Insurance might in some cases be prohibited because of an alleged breach of public order. Particularly, this argument emerges with regards to insuring criminal sanctions.[58]

2.2.4. Vicarious liability

The concept of holding the firm liable for activity engaged in on its behalf by natural persons has been linked to the theory of vicarious liability. "*'Vicarious liability' is the absolute liability of one party – generally the legal 'principal' – for [the] misconduct of another party – her 'agent' – the actor whose activities she directs.*"[59]

If the principal can monitor the agent's level of care, vicarious liability induces the principal to compel the agent to exercise optimal care, because that will decrease the expected damage payments of the principal.[60]

52 Shavell 2004, pp. 230–231; Cooter and Ulen 2012, pp. 240–242.
53 Shavell 2004, p. 231; Kraakman et al. 2009, pp. 116–117.
54 Shavell 2004, p. 232; Kraakman 2008, in: Faure 2009, pp. 134–136.
55 Shavell 2004, p. 232; Wittman 1977, pp. 193–194.
56 Shavell 2004, p. 232; Polinsky and Shavell 1993, pp. 239–240.
57 Shavell 2004, p. 232; Wittman 1977, pp. 193–194; Stone 1980, pp. 17–19; Cooter and Ulen 2012, pp. 238.
58 Shavell 2004, p. 230-232; Kraakman 2009, p. 137.
59 Kraakman 2008, p. 134.
60 Shavell 2004, p. 233; Kraakman 2008, p. 135; Sykes 1984, pp. 1236–1237.

The theory of vicarious liability is subject to the principal-agent theory. The principal-agent theory applies to a situation, where the welfare of one party (the principal) depends upon actions taken by another party (the agent). It assumes that there is an information asymmetry between the principal and the agent and seeks to recommend solutions to the issue of "*motivating the agent to act in the principal's interest rather than simply in the agent's own interest.*"[61]

If the principal cannot monitor the agent's level of care, the principal may use other measures to induce the agent to take care. He can create either positive incentives by offering him the prospect of being discharged, or negative incentives such as demotion and legal action. In this context, the agent could be held personally liable. The question is whether it is socially desirable to hold the manager liable when the corporation is already held liable.[62] Indeed, it has been argued that these measures will generally not induce the agent to choose the optimal level of care.[63] In this regard, another solution could be to extend firm liability. However, extended liability on the firm does not improve its ability to control the agent. Further, when the firm has to pay more than simply the damage caused, the product prices rise.[64]

Irrespective of whether the principal can observe and control the agent's level of care, the principal is likely to reduce the agent's participation in, and level of, risky activity.[65]

There are benefits to vicarious liability. First, personal liability, absent vicarious liability, may lead to undesired results. The firm can externalize costs and shield its assets by ways of the personal liability of the agent. The only cost firms would have to carry is the wage expense of offsetting agents' expected liability costs.[66] Secondly, a firm, when risk neutral has a comparative advantage to bear risk over a risk averse manager.[67] Thirdly, principals may be more knowledgeable about the risk than agents.[68] Fourthly, principals may be better able to monitor agents than the courts.[69] Fifthly, vicarious liability may treat the problem of 'multiple agents'. That is, an outside victim that faces extreme costs in determining the agent who allegedly caused the damage, may save these costs by holding the principal liable instead. The principal in turn may be in a better position than the victim to locate and discipline the relevant agent.[70] Sixthly, a vicariously liable principal may be better able to rationally handle the risk than an irrational agent.[71]

Put in more general terms the benefits are often described as twofold. First, without a judgement-proof problem, vicarious liability makes sense, when the principal is better

61 Kraakman et al. 2009, p. 35; cf. Foss et al. 1999, p. 635; Sykes 1984, pp. 1233–1234.
62 Polinsky and Shavell 1993, p. 239.
63 Shavell 2004, p. 233; Sykes 1984, p. 1237; Kraakman 2008, pp. 137–140.
64 Polinsky and Shavell 1993, p. 255.
65 Shavell 2004, p. 233.
66 Kraakman 2008, p. 135.
67 Fischel and Bradley 1985, p. 285; Sykes 1948, pp. 1235–1236; Kraakman 2008, p. 136. The concept of risk aversion will be discussed in Chapter 3.
68 Kraakman 2008, p. 136.
69 Kraakman 2008, p. 136.
70 Oded 2011, p. 274.
71 Kraakman 2008, p. 137; cf. Wagner 2009, p. 381; cf. Cooter and Ulen 2012, pp. 230–233; Stone 1980, p. 23.

able to monitor agent risk-taking (first condition).[72] Secondly, vicarious liability internalizes externalities provided that the principal is more solvent than the agent (second condition).[73] The social welfare of vicarious liability increases as the disparity between the agent's assets and the amount of damage grows.[74] Subsection 2.2.5 will discuss a situation in which the principal is unable to induce efficient risk taking (cf. first condition). Section 2.6 on bankruptcy liability will turn to the issue when the principal is (or becomes) insolvent (cf. second condition).

2.2.5. *Agent liability when the principal cannot perfectly monitor*

Imposing vicarious liability on principals that are unable to monitor agents is unlikely to mitigate damage.[75] The deterrence effect of monitoring is limited by the amount of assets that the agent has. When the harm brought about by the firm is much higher than the highest penalty that the firm can impose on the agent, then the agent's incentives to reduce the risk generally will be too small. As a result, the level of care of the agent will be inadequate. To induce an appropriate level of care, the state could impose a financial penalty, possibly additionally encouraged by a prison sentence in case the penalty is left unpaid.[76]

Secondly, there are offsetting effects in case the agent's misconduct is difficult to detect and the principal has a considerable advantage over outsiders in monitoring. The information received through monitoring may increase the probability to be held liable under vicarious liability. On the one hand, monitoring may mitigate expected liability costs by disciplining agents. On the other hand, the principal might discover misconduct when monitoring, for which it will be held strictly liable. As a result, the principal might rationally avoid monitoring to reduce the risk of being held strictly liable.[77]

Other actors may also be able to monitor the agent. For example, senior managers within the firm may be better able to supervise employees. In these cases, the secondary liability of the manager may serve as a backstop for vicarious liability.[78]

The law may hold other influential actors liable beyond the group of top managers and the firm, such as outside directors, lawyers, accountants or auditors. Broadening the group of liable actors is called the gatekeeper strategy. Such a strategy is designed to augment potentially inadequate levels of liability imposed on the firm. The personal liability of these actors may partially offset the inadequacy of vicarious liability.[79]

72 Kraakman 2008, p. 135; Shavell 2004, p. 233; Sykes 1984, pp. 1238–1239.

73 Kraakman 2008, p. 135; Shavell 2004, pp. 231–232.

74 Kraakman 2008, p. 135.

75 Shavell 2004, p. 234–235; Polinsky and Shavell 1993, p. 240; Sykes 1984, pp. 1237–1238.

76 Inherent to this suggestion is the assumption that the state is better able to collect fines than the firm. See: Polinsky and Shavell 1993, p. 240.

77 Kraakman 2008, p. 138; Shavell 2004, p. 234–235. To counteract this problem scholars have suggested liability regimes that motivate the principals to optimally monitor and set precautionary measures. For more information, see: Kraakman 2008, p. 142–144.

78 Kraakman 2008, p. 144; Stone 1980, p. 17.

79 Kraakman 2008, p. 144.

2.3. Bankruptcy liability

The assets of most firms are limited to the amount that the firm owns. The assets of the firm's owners remain separate from corporate assets. In this regard, the firm can only be held liable to a limited extent, called limited liability. Limited liability changes the deterrence effect of vicarious liability. Leebron,[80] Easterbrook,[81] Posner[82] and Blumberg[83] contributed significantly to understanding the concept of limited liability and its effects on voluntary creditors and victims (also called involuntary creditors). The following will first explain why limited liability is introduced in the first place. Subsection 2.3.2 will analyse how limited liability creates obstacles to the effectiveness of vicarious liability to protect victims.

Subsection 2.3.3 will outline the agency costs created through the introduction of limited liability and borne by the voluntary creditor. Subsection 2.3.3 will discuss the effects that mitigate the costs of limited liability.

Managerial liability may be one of the tools to mitigate the costs of limited liability on victims (subsection 2.3.2). Subsection 2.3.6 will explain under which circumstances personal liability is desired to protect voluntary creditors.

2.3.1. Benefits of limited liability

When assuming zero transaction costs, contracting parties would prefer the firm's unlimited liability over limited liability. With unlimited liability, the firm has a greater recourse to assets and thus a lower risk of default. In turn, a creditor would award a firm's unlimited liability by decreasing the interest rate on the loan and further requiring less (strict) covenants. The firm's shareholders benefit from lower interest rates as their return increases. In such a scenario, limited liability would lead to a higher risk of default, higher interest rates and more generally higher borrowing costs.[84]

However, with the introduction of transaction costs, lenders are uncertain about the firm's risk-taking. Creditors may increase borrowing costs to a point, where the firm's owners prefer to finance their projects without debt capital. Limited liability creates a state of the world where the worst possible state of the world is known to all investors. Limited liability restricts creditors of the corporation to making claims against the separate patrimony.[85] Creditors do not need to investigate relevant information about all the shareholders' securities and are able to focus their diligence on the corporation itself. It limits creditor's costs of investigating the riskiness of the corporation.[86] Such a clear-cut balance sheet simplifies debt financing and bankruptcy proceedings.[87] Unlimited

80 Leebron 1991, pp. 1590–1594.
81 Easterbrook 1990, pp. 415–416.
82 Posner 2007, pp. 424–427, 431–435.
83 Blumberg 1985, 'Limited Liability and Corporate Groups', The Journal of Corporation Law, pp. 574–577.
84 Carney 1999, p. 67; Kraakman et al. 2009, p. 10.
85 Kraakman et al. 2009, p. 9–11; Posner 2007, pp. 424–426.
86 Polak 2011, p. 2; Kraakman 2009, pp. 6–8, 9–10; Carney 1999, p. 676.
87 Leebron 1991, pp. 1590–1594; Kraakman et al. 2009, pp. 9–11.

liability does not provide this kind of certainty.[88] Studies suggest that limited liability firms have a higher risk of bankruptcy than their unlimited counterparts, but also seem to have higher growth rates.[89]

Secondly, the concept of limited liability shields the owner against claims by the contracting parties of the firm. It is a tool to increase the attractiveness to invest in a firm.[90] The liability is limited to the amount the owner has provided as original investment. When additional debt is raised, he will not face further liabilities. Limiting liability to the amount invested decreases the investor's cost to monitor.[91]

Thirdly, under unlimited liability the costs of collecting judgements would be high. A firm's creditors would seek to collect from wealthy investors. The wealthy investors would in turn have recourse to less wealthy shareholders to be provided with (probably incomplete) compensation. In this regard, the costs of collection are high when there are a large number of small investors. These collection costs would weaken both the deterrence and compensation function of owner liability. Under limited liability, the creditors may simply turn to one entity, the firm.[92]

2.3.2. Vicarious liability when the firm's assets are limited

The benefits of vicarious liability may diminish in connection with limited liability. Principals may make use of legal forms that embody limited liability (such as corporations) to mitigate the impact of vicarious liability. Shareholders may intentionally undercapitalize or move assets to minimize potential tort liability.[93] For example, they may assign high-risk production processes to thinly capitalized subsidiaries, in order to externalize the costs of tort.[94]

Under an efficient liability regime, actors consider the full cost of their actions. Similar to the judgement-proof problem,[95] limited liability externalizes part of these costs, which could be regarded as a subsidy for risk taking behaviour. "*While corporations generate positive as well as negative externalities, there is no way to measure the balance of these externalities under a regime of limited liability.*"[96]

Generally, the externalization that results from limited liability creates the problem that firms make excessively risky decisions.[97] Some argue that limited liability substantially limits victim's opportunities to bring claims.[98]

88 Carney 1999, p. 676; Kraakman et al. 2009, p. 10.

89 Carney 1999, p. 678.

90 Kraakman et al. 2009, pp. 9–11; Posner 2007, pp. 424–425. When the shareholder is only liable for the amount invested, his remaining wealth can be devoted to other corporations. In this regard, limited liability enables the diversification of the shareholder's portfolio. See: Carney 1999, p. 677–678.

91 Leebron 1991, p. 1590–1594; Carney 1999, p. 670; Posner 2007, pp. 424–425.

92 Carney 1999, p. 674; Leebron 1991, p. 1611.

93 Kraakman et al. 2009, p. 120; Posner 2007, pp. 424–425; Carney 1999, p. 668; Leebron 1991, p. 1609.

94 Kraakman 2008, p. 140; Posner 2007, pp. 424–425.

95 Wagner 2009, p. 394; Shavell 2004, pp. 230–231; Cooter and Ulen 2012, pp. 240–242.

96 Carney 1999, p. 665.

97 Carney 1999, p. 678. The next section will further analyse the positive effects of limited liability. Posner 2007, p. 426.

98 Kraakman et al. 2009, p. 9–11; Posner 2007, p. 426; Leebron 1991, p. 1626; Carney 1999, pp. 685–686.

2.3.3. *Agency costs created through limited liability*

According to Kraakman, the following agency problems between the firm and the voluntary creditor arise when adopting a system of limited liability.

Ex ante, i.e. before contracting, the debtor firm may lie about its assets to get a (better) contract. *Ex post*, i.e. after contracting, the firm may alter the risks. Limited liability aggravates these problems. Limited liability creates an incentive for shareholders to engage in activities to the detriment of creditors.[99]

First, shareholders may take out corporate assets to their own benefit. Such asset dilution harms creditors because there are fewer corporate assets available to satisfy their claims.[100]

Secondly, shareholders may be interested in increasing corporate risk-taking. For example, they may take assets used for low-risk activities and put them to use for high-risk activities, which is called asset substitution. The upside of the risk-taking is exclusively borne by the shareholders, but the downside is disproportionately borne by the creditors.[101]

Thirdly, shareholders may desire to increase borrowing. They are able to realize more capital when being provided with capital from new creditors. However, the old creditor's ability to satisfy their claims from the corporate assets is mitigated because the old creditor has to share these assets with the new creditors. The old creditors, who originally agreed to the terms of lending on the basis of the full ability to satisfy their claims from the corporate assets, are now worse off. This effect is called debt dilution.[102]

2.3.4. *Effects that mitigate the costs of limited liability*

However, several aspects mitigate the costs of limited liability.

First, when insolvency threatens, managers may have incentives that are in conflict with the shareholders' interests. Close to insolvency, shareholders seek to remove assets from the firm. However, in the course of reorganisation, creditors could become the new equity holders after reorganisation. To remain appointed manager of the new shareholders, the manager may support such a reorganisation by retaining (or possibly raising) firm assets. In this regard, the manager's interests are rather aligned with those of the creditors and in contrast to shareholder's interests.[103] Generally, the better the alignment of interests between shareholders and managers, the higher the risk is that the manager also contributes to harming the creditors.[104] In accordance with this line of thought, when the alignment is under-developed (for example in large corporations), the manager is less likely to harm creditors.[105]

99 Kraakman et al. 2009, p. 116; Posner 2007, p. 425.
100 Kraakman et al. 2009, p. 116.
101 Kraakman et al. 2009, pp. 116–117; MacMinn and Garven 2000, pp. 541–544; Posner 2007, p. 425; Leebron 1991, p. 1594.
102 Kraakman et al. 2009, p. 117; MacMinn and Garven 2000, pp. 541–544; Posner 2007, p. 425.
103 Carney 1999, p. 681; Posner 2007, p. 441; Kraakman et al. 2009, p. 135.
104 Kraakman et al. 2009, pp. 117–118; Posner 2007, p. 441.
105 Kraakman et al. 2009, p. 135; Posner 2007, p. 440–443.

Secondly, unsecured contract creditors may risk losing some of their assets in the case of vicarious liability. To prevent such a loss, contract creditors may ask the debtor to carry vicarious liability insurance. In this regard, the cost of limited liability may be sufficiently internalized.[106]

Thirdly, in closely-held corporations, shareholders invest significantly in the corporation and they seek to protect that investment. These shareholders are incentivized to insure against the loss of that investment.[107]

Fourthly, shareholders may be interested to tie themselves to the interests of the creditors, in order to decrease the cost of debt capital. The firm and the creditors agree to covenants. These covenants may include that the shareholder waives his right to dividends, agrees to not make significant asset transactions, or agrees to not increase borrowing.[108] There are three reasons, why one should not regulate these protective measures. First, protection of the creditor may lead to too little risk-taking by the firm. Secondly, the interests of creditors will be too divergent to protect these in one universal and static rule of regulation. Thirdly, the desired protection will probably change over time. If so, it would have to be re-negotiated. Legally fixed restrictions are difficult to re-negotiate.[109]

2.3.5. Limited liability and victims

The degree of limited liability could be lessened to the benefit of tort victims.[110] Generally, there are four approaches to do so.

First, the shareholders may be held liable for actions that are inconsistent with the legal personality. According to the doctrine of 'piercing the corporate veil' shareholders are held liable when there is a misrepresentation of third parties, a commingling of assets, or inadequate capitalization of the firm.[111]

Secondly, as a substitute to shareholder liability, involuntary creditors could assume a priority status in bankruptcy systems. Such a measure would shift some risk from the involuntary to the voluntary creditors. Although it might increase monitoring by the voluntary creditors, it is questionable whether voluntary creditors have a competitive advantage over shareholders to monitor for this kind of risk.[112]

Thirdly, as another substitute to shareholder liability, contract creditors could become subject to unlimited liability. In this regard, contract creditors are not only liable to the amount of the debt capital provided but instead have to contribute additional capital in case the debtor is in distress. It has been suggested that large creditors may be in a position to monitor the firm for adequate capitalization and adjust interest rates to

106 Carney 1999, p. 681.
107 Carney 1999, p. 681.
108 Kraakman 2009, p. 118; Posner 2007, p. 426.
109 Kraakman 2009, p. 119; Posner 2007, p. 426.
110 Kraakman et al. 2009, pp. 9–11, 120; Posner 2007, p. 426; Leebron 1991, p. 1626; Carney 1999, pp. 685–686.
111 Carney 1999, p. 681; Posner 2007, pp. 438–440; Boyd and Ingberman 1994, p. 898; Rao et al. 1996, p. 66; Kraakman et al. 2009, p. 121.
112 Carney 1999, p. 683; Kraakman et al. 2009, pp. 120–121.

incentivize such capitalization.[113] However, after the last financial crises, scholars adopted a less optimistic and more balanced approach when analysing the extent to which the bank is better able to monitor a corporation than the corporate shareholder.[114]

Fourthly, to the extent that the previous approaches lead to inefficient solvency, the manager could be held personally liable. In this regard, corporate managers are best able to monitor themselves.[115] Similarly, agents that are very solvent and knowledgeable should rather bear personal liability. In this regard, it reverses the original argument in favour of vicarious liability.[116] The liability of managers for corporate torts could protect tort victims against under-capitalized firms rather than against judgement-proof agents.[117] However, managers may be inefficient risk bearers and face uninsurable reputation costs.[118]

When the manager is held personally liable, the firm may be willing to indemnify him. Such a measure would incentivize high-risk decision-making that is in the interest of the corporation. The law may prohibit indemnification to augment potentially inadequate levels of liability imposed on the firm.[119]

2.3.6. Managerial liability with respect to voluntary creditors

With respect to voluntary creditors, the firm and the creditor negotiate on particular actions that are owed to one another.[120] When negotiating, the creditor takes into account the risk of non-performance of the firm. In credit arrangements, such a risk resembles the risk of the firm's default on its payment obligations.[121]

However, the incentives of shareholders and managers to make value-decreasing transactions to the detriment of creditors become stronger, when the firm is close to bankruptcy. Furthermore, corporate vicarious liability may not deter managers, "*when these managers are trapped in an end game and take desperate measures to avoid bankruptcy.*"[122]

Restrictions could be introduced that require managers to act in the interests of creditors rather than shareholders, when the corporation is close to bankruptcy. Moreover, third parties may be recruited as monitors who, under certain circumstances, are able to rescind transactions that were made shortly before bankruptcy and were to the detriment of creditors.[123]

113 Carney 1999, p. 683; Leebron 1991, p. 1643.
114 For example see Acharya 2013, pp. 1–3.
115 Kraakman 2008, p. 137.
116 Kraakman 2008, p. 144; Sykes 1984, p. 1236.
117 Kraakman 2008, p. 144; Kraakman 1984, p. 869; Sykes 1984, p. 1236.
118 Carney 1999, p. 684; Sykes 1984, pp. 1235–1236.
119 Kraakman 2008, p. 144; Pillai and Tractenberg 1981, p. 106; Polinsky and Shavell 1993, p. 254. A similar argument has been provided by Kraakman 1984, p. 866.
120 Shavell 2004, p. 291–292; Posner 2007, pp. 424–427.
121 Carney 1999, p. 675; Posner 2007, pp. 424–427.
122 Kraakman 2008, p. 137.
123 Kraakman et al. 2009, p. 120; Cabrillo and Depoorter 1999, 'Bankruptcy Proceedings', in: Bouckaert and De Geest (eds.), *Encyclopedia of Law and Economics, Volume V. The Economics of Crime and Litigation*, Cheltenham, Edward Elgar, 2000, p. 271.

There are two major categories of managerial liability. First, managers are tempted to commit securities fraud, when they expect to lose their jobs in corporate bankruptcy. Personal liability may deter these actions.[124]

Secondly, the manager may be held liable for net increases in losses to creditors resulting from the board's negligence or fraud, when the firm is (almost) insolvent.[125] However, when the manager considers the creditor's interests rather than the shareholder's interests anyway (which is the case in a big firm where shareholding is dispersed, see next section), such liability would be likely to over-deter the manager. Furthermore, in small firms in which the manager has a major equity stake, such a rule will render a meaningless deterrence, because the manager-owner has no more assets at his disposal than the assets already assigned to the firm (judgement-proof problem).[126] Criminal liability or disqualification may be another measure, which leads to deterrence.[127] Especially as disqualification may represent an adequate deterrence for manager-owners with limited assets.[128]

Thirdly, the corporation may be faced with the last period problem. When the corporation has to decide between two alternatives, where both lead to insolvency, the corporation rationally chooses the one that contributes to a higher expected return. The last period problem might incentivize excessive risk taking by the manager and possibly delay the bankruptcy. A personal liability action may ensure socially efficient risk taking in the vicinity of insolvency.[129]

2.4. Internal liability

The theory of internal liability is based on the principle of a separation of ownership and control. Important contributions in this field have been published by among others Posner,[130] Kraakman[131] and Jensen and Meckling.[132] Subsection 2.4.1 will outline the concept of the separation of ownership and control. Internal liability is one of six corporate governance tools (subsection 2.4.2). Subsection 2.4.3 will be devoted to internal liability tools. These tools can be subdivided into a standard of competence (subsection 2.4.4) and measures that deter related party transactions (subsection 2.4.5). Subsection 2.4.6 will turn to the arguments that ask for either an optional or a mandatory regime of internal liability (which also serves as a basis for the later discussion on indemnification).

124 Carney 1999, p. 684; Kraakman 2008, p. 137.
125 Kraakman et al. 2009, p. 135; Kraakman 2008, p. 144.
126 Kraakman et al. 2009, p. 135; Polinsky and Shavell 1993, p. 240.
127 Kraakman et al. 2009, p. 137; Polinsky and Shavell 1993, p. 240.
128 Kraakman et al. 2009, p. 137. On other sanctions, see: Cabrillo and Depoorter 1999, p. 264.
129 Boyd and Ingberman 1994, pp. 896–898; Easterbrook 1990, pp. 415–416; Carney 1999, p. 679. Regarding a dissenting opinion, see Suen 1995, pp. 633; Rao et al. 1996, p. 66: "*If the last period problem is defined as an expected cost of a firm with positive cash flows, the incentive to take excessive risk may be offset by the long term loss.*"
130 Posner 2007, pp. 424–425.
131 Kraakman et al. 2009, pp. 9–11.
132 Jensen and Meckling 1976, pp. 305–311.

2.4.1. *The separation of ownership and control*

When equity investors are invited to the firm, the firm's ownership and control, originally held by one person, is divided and passed to the shareholder and the manager respectively.[133]

A corporation may seek to invite equity investors to the firm, next to financing a corporation by raising the amount of debt,[134] because investors do not receive interest on their investment, neither do they account for the risk of default. Instead the potential financial benefit of the firm is shared among them, as share dividend and appreciation of the share value. Additionally the costs of capital decrease because transaction costs to draw up a sophisticated loan contract become obsolete.[135]

The separation of ownership and control might be beneficial because of three reasons: (i) it enables investors to diversify and change their portfolio due to fewer monitoring requirements and transferable shares, (ii) it enables an increased use of the economies of scale, and (iii) it leads to more specified and skilled managers.[136]

Usually, the relationship between shareholders and managers is regarded as a principal-agent problem. When shareholders are not affiliated with the corporation, because of public trading and diversification, they are less likely to effectively control managers. The manager, seeking to maximize personal utility,[137] might abuse the lack of monitoring to his own benefit.[138] In general, the manager could act in contrast to the shareholder's interests due to two reasons. On the basis of the seminal contribution of Jensen and Meckling 1976, scholars argue that the manager could either steal from the corporation or shirk responsibility and work.[139] The concept of 'stealing' refers to the fact that the managers might not have the incentive to do so. In other words, there is a conflict of interest between the manager and other parties (among which the shareholders take a prominent role). Regarding 'shirking', the manager may lack the ability to do so (incompetence of the manager). This issue refers to a situation in which the managerial skills are below a standard that is expected by the shareholders.[140]

2.4.2. *Corporate governance*

To limit the costs of the separation of ownership and control, six tools were proposed, being (i) business failure, (ii) the market for corporate control, (iii) direct managerial financial incentives, (iv) corporate governance oversight, (v) shareholder empowerment,

133 Marks 1999, p. 694; Posner 2007, p. 440–442.
134 Posner 2007, pp. 424–425; Leebron 1991, pp. 1590–1594; Kraakman et al. 2009, pp. 9–11.
135 Posner 2007, pp. 424–425; Marks 1999, pp. 694–695.
136 Marks 1999, p. 694; Posner 2007, p. 441.
137 Marks 1999, p. 696; Posner 2007, p. 441.
138 Posner 2007, p. 441; Marks 1999, p. 696; Kraakman 2008, pp. 137–138; Polinsky and Shavell 1993, p. 256.
139 Jensen and Meckling 1976, pp. 305–311.
140 Marks 1999, p. 698; Kraakman et al. 2009, p. 79; Pacces 2011, p. 314.

and (vi) managerial duties. Many of those tools rely on actors other than the shareholders.[141]

First, business failure eliminates incompetent managers. His incentive to manage the firm well is strong because he fears unemployment when the firm becomes bankrupt. Without additional measures to eliminate conflicts of interest, a market solely dependent on business failure is not efficient.[142]

Secondly, even without any shareholder control, the manager is forced by takeover pressure to maximize share price. Incompetent managers and misbehaving managers will be removed through the takeover process. However, some critics question the correlation between share price and managerial performance.[143]

Thirdly, the manager is rewarded for good performance. Such measures treat the problem of conflicting interests, but not the competence issue. Performance is usually measured by way of share performance. A common reward scheme is a pre-defined bonus payment or the manager's participation in the share value development. As the manager's participation in shareholding increases, his interests align with the interests of the shareholders. Due to the participation, he would directly experience his potential under-performance. To raise share value, it is in his interest to avoid the waste of production factors and mistakes.[144]

Fourthly, a loose group of measures are directed at the structure and procedures of the board of directors. The managers are appointed and dismissed by the (representatives of) the shareholders according to their preference. Furthermore, (secured) lenders may exert oversight over the manager. Another measure is gate-keepers liability, imposing liability on third parties.[145]

Fifthly, the cost may be mitigated by increasing the power of shareholders. But as the shareholder is provided with a greater say in the firm, the original advantages of the separation of ownership and control are diminished. In addition, excessive empowerment may lead to a situation, in which a minority shareholder may be able to control the corporation against the will of majority shareholders and management.[146]

Sixthly, the manager is deterred from bad performance by ways of personal liability rules.[147] In general, these legal liability rules are perceived to be less important in corporate governance than the other tools mentioned to protect the interests of shareholders as a class.[148] The reasons are that (i) the wide scope of liability restricts their

141 Posner 1974, pp. 178–181; Kraakman 2009, p. 35; Marks 1999, p. 698.

142 Posner 2007, p. 441; Marks 1999, pp. 698–699.

143 Marks 1999, p. 699–703; Posner 2007, pp. 442–443.

144 Kraakman 2009, pp. 14–16; Posner 1974, pp. 184, 185; Marks 1999, pp. 707–708.

145 Kraakman 2008, pp. 58–62, 145; Marks 1999, pp. 705–707; Posner 2007, pp. 427–431. A prominent tool of corporate oversight is the existence of supervisory board members that lack any executive power, called outside directors. However, many consider the appointment of outside managers by executive managers as mutual back-scratching. The executive manager simply invites a befriended manager from another firm to become outside manager under the condition that the befriended manager does him the same favour. Many policy considerations are directed as to increase the independence and power of outside directors. See: Marks 1999, pp. 705–707.

146 Marks 1999, pp. 708–709; Posner 2007, pp. 442–443.

147 Marks 1999, p. 703; Kraakman et al. 2009, pp. 79–81.

148 Kraakman 2009, p. 78; Pacces 2011, p. 314–316; Fischel and Bradley 1985, p. 283.

application to relatively extreme cases and (ii) indemnification, insurance and hurdles pursuant to procedural law reduce the scope of liability. A major role of internal liability is to deter large one-shot frauds.[149] The following section will analyse these liability rules. Chapter 5 will outline the effect of indemnification and insurance on liability rules.

2.4.3. *Constraint strategy: internal liability*

The constraint strategy in the form of liability rules should deter bad performance, that is incompetence ('shirking') and conflicts of interest ('stealing'). Generally, there are two approaches to enforce liability, direct enforcement by the government and private rights to claim. The government enforcement includes rules on insider trading and other specific requirements.[150]

Regarding private rights to claim, usually lawyers are provided with incentives through lawyer fees to litigate cases in which directors violate their duties. In such a system "*someone other than shareholders (that is attorneys) provides the enforcement mechanism (the shareholder is just a nominal presence).*"[151] The duty of loyalty and the duty of care belong in this category. The duty of loyalty can be loosely attributed to deterrence against conflicts of interest. The duty of care will deter incompetence.[152]

The threat of internal liability encourages the manager to publish information. With a liability rule, the shareholder can signal liability by holding the manager liable for the fact that the shareholders received less information than was available about corporate conduct.[153]

2.4.4. *Standard of competence: duty of care*

Hard-edged rules to constrain incompetence are purely suited to protecting the interests of the shareholders. More effective tools to constrain incompetence are the appointment and removal of the manager. Appointment and removal are cheaper to design, monitor and enforce compared to constraint measures.[154] Still, a very broad duty requires managers "*to take reasonable care in the exercise of their office*".[155]

Some view the duty of care as a protection against corporate malpractice. According to Kraakman, such an analogy ignores that the lack of reasonable care of the corporate management is a lot more difficult to pinpoint than malpractice of doctors or auditors. Violation of the duty of care is subject to negligence or gross negligence. The manager

149 Fischel and Bradley 1985, pp. 283, 287.

150 Marks 1999, p. 703; Kraakman et al. 2009, pp. 79–81.

151 Marks 1999, p. 703; Kraakman et al. 2009, pp. 79–81.

152 Kraakman et al. 2009, p. 79–81; Marks 1999, p. 703; Gerner-Beuerle et al. 2013, p. xi. Also see: Pacces 2011, p. 314: "*While appropriate legal rules can possibly contain the diversion of the firm's surplus once it is produced (stealing), no legal mechanism can substitute for the suboptimal exercise of business judgment over the production of the same surplus (shirking).*"

153 Lawless et al. 1997, pp. 210–212.

154 Kraakman et al. 2009, p. 78; Pacces 2011, p. 314–316; Sykes 1984, p. 1238; Posner 2007, pp. 441–442.

155 Kraakman et al. 2009, p. 79.

has to be given enough discretion, in order to take risks that are necessary and desired. Furthermore, it is questionable whether the judge is in a better position to evaluate managerial performance than other actors (regarding the judge's hindsight bias and the potential of legal error).[156]

2.4.5. Duty of loyalty and other measures to deter related party transactions

Related party transactions are either transactions in which related parties deal with the corporation (such as self-dealing and managerial compensation) or transactions in which related parties appropriate corporate value (such as taking corporate opportunities and trading in the corporate shares).[157]

The duty of loyalty is "*a fairness standard that requires judges to determine ex post whether shareholders – as a class or as a minority – are worse off as an outcome of a related party transaction.*"[158]

Besides the duty of loyalty, some policy-makers prohibit loans between the corporation and the manager. Further, third party employment contracts of managers can be prohibited or non-compete rules can be introduced. It will guarantee that the manager only takes into account the interests of his firm. Thirdly, insider trading is regulated.[159]

Regulation of insider trading refers to two categories. One is the prophylactic restriction on short term trading and the second is a direct ban on trading on material inside information. Especially, the second category is widely adopted in many jurisdictions. It is questionable whether the direct ban increases efficiency.[160] Some empirical studies suggest that more prohibitive jurisdictions correlate with public stock price information and market liquidity. Other studies conclude that direct bans fail to control insider trading.[161] Some, such as Manne, go as far as to call insider trading an efficient form of incentive compensation.[162] Manne further argues that "*the argument for a strong positive relationship between market efficiency and insider trading has proved to be very robust.*"[163]

2.4.6. Optional or mandatory regime of internal liability (indemnification)

Some argue that the internal liability regime should be optional rather than mandatory. Under the opt-out regime, the lawmaker would introduce duties that would be optimal for most firms. Corporations who wish to take other deterrence measures are still allowed

156 Kraakman et al. 2009, p. 79; Marks 1999, p. 703; Gerner-Beuerle et al. 2013, p. xi; Kraakman et al. 1994, p. 1769.

157 Kraakman et al. 2009, p. 153; Posner 2007, pp. 440, 441, 453; Marks 1999, pp. 703–705.

158 Kraakman et al. 2009, p. 173.

159 Kraakman et al. 2009, pp. 169, 170. These prohibitions might also prohibit loans that represent an *ex ante* indemnification payment for potential bankruptcy liability. Bainbridge 1999, p. 774; Posner 2007, p. 449.

160 Bainbridge 2000, pp. 772–773.

161 Kraakman et al. 2009, pp. 170–173; Posner 2007, pp. 449–450.

162 Manne 2006, p. 168.

163 Manne 2006, p. 169.

to opt-out from the duties, for example in their corporate charters. Such a regime is based on the view that a firm is a nexus of contracts designed to minimize agency costs.[164]

Proponents of the opt-out regime stress that the same set of duties is unlikely to be optimal for every corporation. In an efficient market for securities, corporations are forced to adopt provisions that are efficient. Corporations with inefficient rules and duties would have a depressed share price and would eventually be taken over.[165]

Scholars who propose mandatory regimes point to market failure. They argue that the market is not efficient because of information asymmetry. Such asymmetry can only be cured by a mandatory duty to disclose information which is enforced by the liability rule. Without disclosure of information, efficient charter provisions are unlikely (referred to as a catch-22).[166]

Further, market forces may not be strong enough to induce optimal charter provisions. A charter amendment would have a great impact on the manager's financial position. Still, a change of the manager's financial position would affect corporate assets only marginally. When a charter amendment has only negligible effect on the corporate financial position, it would be neglected by the market.[167]

Other authors argue that managerial duties represent a public good. Even though the duties have a small effect on each individual, the sum of the costs resulting from not taking due care is socially inefficient.[168]

Mandatory regimes may also be necessary due to the lack of sophistication of shareholders. Furthermore, mandatory duties may protect other societal goals such as distributive goals.[169]

2.5. Conclusion

This chapter has sought to outline and summarize the existing literature on managerial liability. Managerial liability can be divided into three groups, (i) tort liability, (ii) bankruptcy liability, and (iii) internal liability.

Tort liability rules are aimed at reducing (the costs of) accidents. Liability allocates (some of) the costs of damage to the injurer. The injurer is deterred from engaging in dangerous activities and will take precautionary measures (also called care). Similarly, the firm may be held liable for defective products. Product liability internalizes otherwise externalized costs. Under strict liability, the injurer bears the risk of expected loss and in turn the victim could choose too high levels of activity. The opposite is the case under negligence

164 Marks 1999, p. 704; Kraakman 1984, p. 858, 864, 865; Bebchuk 1989, p. 1822. According to this view, the organisation of firms is based on a nexus of contracts, which is merely a special kind of market contracting. The difference with market contracting lies mainly in the continuity of association of owners of capital, labour, land and so on. See: Foss et al. 1999, p. 636 and Cooter and Ulen 2012, p. 26.

165 Marks 1999, p. 704; Kraakman 1984, p. 859.

166 Marks 1999, p. 704; Lawless et al. 1997, p. 210–212.

167 Marks 1999, p. 705; Bebchuk 1989, p. 1838.

168 Marks 1999, p. 705; Kraakman et al. 1993, p. 1743.

169 Marks 1999, p. 705; Bebchuk 1989, p. 1839.

liability, the victim bears the risk and the injurer may choose high levels of activity. To optimally distribute damage when both parties should take some care, strict liability with a defence of contributory negligence could be adopted. However, neither of these liability forms can control the activity level.

Generally, the lawmaker should avoid liability for the actions of the manager that were carried out on behalf of his firm. The most important reason to do so is the judgement-proof problem. The injurer does not have enough assets at his disposal to pay the entire damages. In that case, the deterrence effect of personal liability would be too low and hence inefficient. To cure the judgement-proof problem, law and economics theory offers five solutions, (i) minimum asset requirements, (ii) criminal liability, (iii) direct regulation of the activity, (iv) liability insurance, and (v) vicarious liability of the injurer's principal. Vicarious liability is a solution when the principal has sufficient assets and can easily monitor the injurer. To cure the problem of high costs of monitoring, liability of the injurer as additional action to vicarious liability was proposed.

Secondly, although limited liability is generally beneficial, also to creditors, its advantages crumble in the vicinity of insolvency. The manager may pay too much attention to shareholders and remove assets from the firm to their benefit. Besides, managers that fear unemployment might take desperate measures to avoid bankruptcy. Bankruptcy liability could deter the manager from actions that harm the victim and the voluntary creditor. The victim and the voluntary creditor could hold the manager liable, besides holding the firm vicariously liable, when the firm's assets are insufficient.

Where bankruptcy liability does not deter enough, one can introduce criminal liability or the disqualification sanction.

The third group refers to the internal liability of the manager. Internal liability should reduce costs that arise from the separation of ownership and control. Internal liability is one of the tools of corporate governance (and probably a less important one) that seek to prevent two situations. First, the manager may not be as skilled as expected (incompetence). Secondly, he may abuse his position to his own benefit and to the detriment of shareholders (conflict of interest). The duty of care should deter incompetence but still has to grant the manager enough discretion to take risks that are necessary and desired. The duty of loyalty can be loosely attributed to a fairness standard that will reduce conflicts of interest. Moreover, an internal liability claim could be used by a shareholder to signal that the shareholder received less information than was available about corporate conduct.

The corporation's habit to opt-out from the internal liability regime has been viewed suspiciously. Arguments in favour include that the corporation should know best and is also induced to behave efficiently. Opponents of such an opt-out possibility point to an alleged market failure of the system. Without liability, the manager has no incentive to provide the market with sufficient information about the firm's performance. Without that information, outside investors make wrong investment decisions.

With these considerations in mind, the following two chapters will take a closer look at insurance. Chapter 5 will synthesize these observations and develop a general theory on D&O insurance.

Chapter 3

RISK BEARING AND INSURANCE

3.1. Introduction

To understand the role of D&O insurance on managerial risk taking, this chapter will outline the economics of general liability insurance.

The purpose of insurance for the victim but also for the injurer is to "*allocate and spread the risks of losses [...], so that those who are risk averse do not bear them [...].*"[170]

In this regard, the demand for insurance is usually explained by the attitude of risk aversion. Section 3.2 will outline the concept of risk aversion. In this section, the focus will be on insurance for risk averse injurers, also called liability insurance because of two reasons. First, the insurer pays for the injurer's actions so that the injurer will not have to pay damages when found liable. In that sense, liability insurance changes the incentive structure of the liability system. Secondly and as a consequence of the first aspect, it has to be asked whether and in how far liability insurance is socially desirable. Under some circumstances, one may seek a prohibition of insurance or generally require everyone to carry insurance, in order to ensure social optimality.[171]

Risk neutral parties in principle do not desire insurance. Chapter 5 will describe how far risk neutral parties, such as firms owned by well-diversified shareholders, may also desire insurance.

Insurance can be supplied when the insurer is able to apply the law of large numbers. According to seminal contributions, such as those of Calabresi,[172] the law of large numbers states that the relative frequency of an outcome will resemble more closely the corresponding probability of the outcome, when trials were repeated a large number of times.[173] The insurer can either transfer the liability risk to an insurer or share the risk with other mutual injurers (risk sharing). These matters will be discussed in section 3.3.

170 Shavell 2004, p. 257; Cooter and Ulen 2012, p. 237; Harrington and Danzon 2000, p. 283; Schäfer and Müller-Langer 2009, p. 33.

171 Shavell 2004, p. 257; Cooter and Ulen 2012, pp. 223–224; Harrington and Danzon 2000, p. 289.Wagner 2009, pp. 397–398.

172 Calabresi 1961, pp. 499–553.

173 Wagner 2009, p. 382; Berliner 1985, pp. 314, 318; Faure et al. 2013, p. 225.

As will have been explained in section 3.2, the liability risk may be uninsurable and/ or insurance may be socially undesirable. A general note on these issues will return in section 3.4.

This chapter will identify numerous obstacles to a proper functioning of the insurance system. The purpose of Chapter 4 is to explain the most pressing obstacles, namely the uncertainty of the risk, an ambiguity of parties, adverse selection, moral hazard and general issues of the insurance industry. Chapter 5 will apply the considerations of chapters 2, 3 and 4 to formulate hypotheses on D&O insurance.

3.2. Demand for insurance

The demand for liability insurance is explained by the general attitude that people are risk averse to a varying degree (subsection 3.2.1). Seminal works on risk bearing have been published by Mossin, Shavell and Calabresi.[174] Subsection 3.2.2 will outline the effect of risk aversion on the injurer and victim in a situation in which no insurance is available. The following subsection 3.2.3 will turn to a situation where insurance is available taking into account insurance for strict liability as well as insurance for negligence liability. Subsection 3.2.4 will outline the demand for insurance when the level of care under negligence liability is uncertain. As extensions to this general discussion, the judgement-proof problem (subsection 3.2.5), administration costs (subsection 3.2.6) and contract interpretation and litigation (subsection 3.2.7) will be introduced.

3.2.1. Risk aversion

Risk aversion describes an attitude of dislike of (pure financial) risks. A risk-averse person would rather make certain payments than to take a risk. Generally, he prefers certain outcomes over uncertain ones. Even more so, a risk-averse person would not enter into a gamble that may even be in his favour. For instance, he would avoid a gamble where he has a 49% chance of losing $1000 and a 51% chance of winning $1000. A person is risk averse when the marginal utility of money declines for him as his wealth increases. For such a person, utility reduction when losing money is higher than the utility increase when gaining the same amount of money.[175]

Risk-aversion is particularly relevant when the damage would be substantial in relation to the person's assets and accordingly would disastrously affect the person's utility. When however the occurring damage is small relative to his assets, he would show a risk-neutral attitude towards that risk. Generally, parties such as firms with many assets will experience risk neutrality for medium sized risks. This situation changes in cases in which the expected loss greatly surpasses the firm's assets.[176]

174 Mossin 1968, pp. 553–568; Shavell 1982, pp. 120–132; Calabresi 1970, 840 p.

175 Shavell 2004, p. 258; Wagner 2009, p. 378–379; Schäfer and Müller-Langer 2009, p. 33. Models have been introduced that enhance the predictability of demand for insurance. For a descriptive model, see: Machina 2000, p. 52.

176 Shavell 2004, p. 259; Wagner 2009, p. 378.

In this regard, the firms are also treated as risk-neutral when they are held by well-diversified shareholders. The attitude of well-diversified shareholders does not necessarily need to reflect the risk attitude of the managers of the firm. To the degree that managers might be risk averse, the behaviour of the firm may reflect risk aversion, too. According to Wagner, indeed most firms are risk averse.[177]

A risk-averse person would desire full insurance for a risk that he bears as long as the premium is actuarially fair. A premium is actuarially fair, when the premium equals the expected damage of the risk. For instance, say the occurring damage would amount to $1000 and the probability of occurrence is 10%. The expected damage would be the product of probability multiplied by damage being $100. The actuarially fair premium would in this case be $100.[178] Section 4.3 will outline shortcomings to the general model of risk aversion and provide extensions to that general model (biases).

The function of social welfare as defined in the previous section 2.2 will be enhanced in this chapter. Here, social welfare refers to a function of all individuals' expected utilities. The expected utility equals "*the sum over all possible outcomes of the probability of each outcome multiplied by its utility*".[179] Next to the observations of the previous section 2.2 on the benefits of individuals when conducting some activity and costs of individuals by ways of prevention and damages incurred, this chapter takes into account the parties' expected utility. Thus, a socially desirable solution also includes a treatment for the risk aversion of victims and injurers. In other words, in an ideal world the injurer should be relieved from the liability risk that creates risk aversion. The same applies for victims.[180]

3.2.2. *A liability system without insurance*

Assume a system in which injurers are faced with liability and there is no insurance for either the injurer or the victim. In effect, the consequences are the same as sketched in section 2.2. However, the effects of these liability rules on risk bearing differ.[181]

Under strict liability, the victim will be covered for any damage by the injurer. The injurer bears the risk. Such a bearing of risk creates a socially undesirable outcome when the injurer is risk averse. When risk averse, the injurer would be more cautious than desired. Strict liability of risk averse injurers may lead to excessive care taking of the injurer. The injurer may also be discouraged from engaging in the activity at all. One solution to excessive care and too low activity levels may be to reduce the damages that the injurer would be liable to pay. In this regard, the damages paid would be less than the losses borne by the victim. The loss would thus not be fully internalized.[182]

177 Shavell 2004, p. 259; Wagner 2009, p. 379.
178 Shavell 2004, p. 259; Cooter and Ulen 2012, pp. 237–238; Harrington and Danzon 2000, p. 287.
179 Shavell 2004, p. 259.
180 Shavell 2004, p. 259; Harrington and Danzon 2000, p. 283.
181 Shavell 2004, p. 260; Harrington and Danzon 2000, pp. 279–282.
182 Shavell 2004, p. 260; Schäfer and Müller-Langer 2009, pp. 9–10, 37–38; Harrington and Danzon 2000, p. 283.

Under the negligence rule, injurers do not bear any risk, as long as they adhere to the due level of care (without the courts making errors). In this case, the risk averse injurer does not bear any risk, as long as he takes due care. He neither exercises excessive care nor is he discouraged from engaging in the activity. However, in case damage occurs, notwithstanding due care having been taken, the victim bears the losses. If the victim is risk averse, such a situation is socially undesirable.[183]

Without insurance, strict liability is more desirable when the injurer is less risk averse than the victim. Negligence liability is better in cases where the victim is less risk averse than the injurer.[184]

3.2.3. *A liability system with insurance*

With the availability of insurance that is priced at the actuarially fair premium, there is demand for accident insurance and liability insurance. Under negligence rules, risk-averse victims would desire accident insurance. Under strict liability, the risk-averse injurer would desire liability insurance.[185]

Strict liability – When the insurer pays for the damages accrued by the injurer under strict liability, the injurer loses his incentive to take care. Without taking due care, the original goal of accident law to reduce accidents is endangered. The insurer in this case needs to effectively deter the injurer from taking too much risk. In other words, the insurer needs to observe the injurer's level of care. For instance, the fire insurer inspects the insured injurer's house to detect whether fire extinguishers were purchased and correctly installed.[186]

If the insurer is able to perfectly observe due care, the injurer seeks to purchase full coverage and this coverage is offered at an actuarially fair price. The insurer would simply decrease or increase the insurance premium to the expected damage that the injurer faces. When the expected damage increases due to a lower level of care, the insurance premium rises too. Because it would be too expensive for the injurer to pay the higher premium, the injurer would in turn increase his level of care. Such increase in care again leads to a decrease in the insurance price.[187]

Furthermore, full coverage means that the risk aversion of the injurer is perfectly treated. Insurance, when taking care is observable, leads to a social optimum. It is thus socially desirable. Without insurance, the injurer is worse off because he bears the risk of being held strictly liable and victims would be just a well off.[188] Section 4.5 will turn to the question of how far insurance is desirable, when taking care is not observable by insurers. It will discuss how far an inability to observe may lead to moral hazard.

183 Shavell 2004, p. 261; Harrington and Danzon 2000, p. 283.
184 Shavell 2004, p. 261; Schäfer and Müller-Langer 2009, p. 34.
185 Shavell 2004, p. 261; Cooter and Ulen 2012, pp. 236–237; Schäfer and Müller-Langer 2009, p. 34.
186 Shavell 2004, p. 262; Cooter and Ulen 2012, pp. 237–238.
187 Shavell 2004, p. 262; Cooter and Ulen 2012, p. 237; Schäfer and Müller-Langer 2009, p. 33.
188 Shavell 2004, p. 262; Harrington and Danzon 2000, p. 283; Schäfer and Müller-Langer 2009, p. 34.

Negligence liability – In a perfectly functioning negligence liability system, injurers take due care. Changes in risk attitude do not alter the level of care taken. A risk averse injurer simply wants to take due care more strongly than his risk neutral counterpart.[189]

He does not desire insurance. After all, he does not bear any risk provided he takes due care. Insurance would cost too much. The basic model without liability insurance is thus socially ideal. Victims purchase accident insurance for their losses. Liability insurance is not undesirable but there is effectively no market for it, because no insurer will purchase it. It is cheaper for the injurer to take due care, rather than to take no care and to pay for increased insurance premiums.[190]

3.2.4. Uncertain negligence liability and insurance

The negligence liability system does not function perfectly, when "*there is a risk of findings of negligence due to errors in the negligence determination or to [the] inability of injurers to control perfectly their levels of care.*"[191] In such a case, there is a chance that the injurer is held liable even though he took due care (error) or he was unable to take due care (inability). This chance creates a risk that the injurer bears. The injurer develops risk aversion for this risk. As a result, the injurer would desire liability insurance for the portion of the liability risk that represents the chance of error or inability. The desired insurance coverage will not cover the entire liability risk. It is still cheaper for the injurer to take care which eliminates the greatest portion of the liability risk. Liability insurance "*tends not to compromise deterrence*".[192] As insurance assumes the risk of error and inability, the injurer is relieved from that risk. As a treatment to the injurer's risk aversion, such partial liability coverage is socially desirable.[193] In this regard, "*the demand for liability insurance and its effect on social welfare depend critically on the information available to courts and to insurers.*"[194]

The considerations of the previous subsection on the observability of the insured injurer's level of care by the insurer apply *mutatis mutandis*. Section 4.5 will discuss how far the insurer's inability to observe may lead to moral hazard.

3.2.5. The judgement-proof problem and insurance

The injurer's assets may be insufficient to pay for the full damage. He is judgement-proof in relation to the remaining damages. His insufficient wealth has implications for the effectiveness of liability insurance.[195]

189 Shavell 2004, p. 264; Wagner 2009, p. 380.
190 Shavell 2004, pp. 264–265; Schäfer and Müller-Langer 2009, p. 34.
191 Shavell 2004, p. 265. Also see: Cooter and Ulen 2012, pp. 217–220, 220–222.
192 Shavell 2004, p. 265.
193 Shavell 2004, p. 265; Harrington and Danzon 2000, p. 284.
194 Harrington and Danzon 2000, p. 283.
195 Shavell 2004, pp. 230–231, 275; Cooter and Ulen 2012, pp. 240–241.

First, the incentive for a potential victim to purchase insurance is increased. After all, the fact that assets of the injurer are insufficient means that the victim will be unable to collect his damages from the injurer in the case where the injurer is found liable.[196]

Secondly, the incentive for injurers to purchase insurance is dulled. When they are judgement-proof without insurance, they have to pay less than full damage. When an injurer who owns $8000 faces a liability of $100000 with a probability of 10%, he would have to pay an actuarially fair premium of $10000 to receive insurance. The actuarially fair premium surpasses his wealth. As a consequence, he could simply avoid insurance. In general, a risk-averse judgement-proof person would buy partial or no insurance. His purchase decision depends on the size of his assets relative to the damage, the probability of the damage and his degree of risk aversion.[197]

Such an outcome is socially undesirable. Although the judgement-proof person desires no insurance, he still bears risk. Such risk bearing creates risk aversion. However, the victim will not bear more risk as he purchases accident insurance for the remaining damage that cannot be collected from the injurer because of him being judgement-proof.[198]

When the judgement-proof problem creates disastrous social outcomes,[199] one may regulate insurance. One may either require everyone to purchase insurance (examples are car insurance or health care insurance) or prohibit the purchase of insurance altogether. Compulsory insurance works like a tax and induces decreased levels of activity. As a consequence, it achieves general (meaning for all persons) but no specific (in other words at the individual level) deterrence.[200] In general, "*a prohibition against coverage might be beneficial (and superior to requiring coverage), but only if liability insurers are unable to observe levels of care. The potential social benefits of doing this might outweigh the disadvantages.*"[201] The insurer's inability to observe will be a topic of the section 4.5 (moral hazard).

3.2.6. *Administration costs and insurance*

The victim might be *uncertain*, whether the claim against the injurer is successful. To decide whether to claim, the victim weighs the costs that arise from starting an action, called administration costs, against the damages arising from the accident.[202]

Administration costs refer to the costs to establish the injurer's actual level of care. In this regard, not only do liability trials need to be considered, but also settlements. To achieve a settlement, timely and costly negotiations are put into practice.[203]

196 Shavell 2004, p. 275; Cooter and Ulen 2012, p. 240.

197 Shavell 2004, p. 275; Wagner 2009, p. 395; Harrington and Danzon 2000, pp. 287, 289.

198 Shavell 2004, p. 276; Cooter and Ulen 2012, pp. 240–241.

199 The judgement-proof problem could create disastrous social outcomes because injurers bear high levels of uninsured risk. See: Shavell 2004, pp. 275–276. Also see: Cooter and Ulen 2012, pp. 240–241; Harrington and Danzon 2000, p. 290.

200 Harrington and Danzon 2000, p. 290; Wagner 2009, pp. 397–398.

201 Shavell 2004, pp. 276, 278; Cooter and Ulen 2012, pp. 223–224; Harrington and Danzon 2000, p. 289.

202 Shavell 2004, pp. 280–282; Cooter and Ulen 2012, pp. 223–224.

203 Shavell 2004, pp. 280–282; Harrington and Danzon 2000, p. 285.

Because of administration costs, the victim or consumer might overuse or under-use the liability regime compared to the social optimum. If that is the case, this might be an argument for subsidy or regulation of the liability regime. One could think of specialized, small scale courts to lower trial costs. Further, class actions or legal aid programs might do the same. Another supportive program might be the introduction of an insurance system that functions as an arbiter between the two parties and is able to allocate the costs efficiently.[204]

3.2.7. Contract interpretation, litigation and insurance

Court rulings have a great impact on the insured risk. Not only do they decide on the individual liability case, but they also establish precedents for future related liability risks. The ruling influences the size of other liability risks. In this regard, a change of the size of the risk by un-anticipated changes in law and social norms endanger the correctness of the *ex ante* estimation of the risk. Furthermore, because liability depends on social norms and legal standards, losses among policyholders are positively correlated.[205]

The duration of time between the estimation of the underwritten risk and the actual occurrence of a claim correlates with a higher risk that "*un-anticipated information about hazards or new legal standards will shift the distribution of expected loss for all outstanding policies.*"[206]

Naturally, the insurer seeks to limit the outflow of capital resulting from cases in which the insured injurer is held liable. One measure is the additional litigation over terms in the insurance contracts. If the interpreting court finds that a policy does not cover the injurer with respect to the particular liability case, the insurer is freed from its promise to pay for the liability of the insured injurer. The litigation over contractual terms is "*more likely in the event of large claims involving multiple policyholders.*"[207] Another measure is the settlement of the claim out of court. Settling however does not convey information as to whether the due care was met.[208]

3.3. Supply of insurance

Calabresi,[209] Borch,[210] Erlich and Becker[211] and Joskow[212] are some of the leading scholars regarding risk distribution and risk management. The ability to distribute risks and become risk neutral is derived from the law of large numbers and its characteristics

204 Shavell 2004, pp. 286–287; Cooter and Ulen 2012, pp. 242–243; Harrington and Danzon 2000, p. 285. The reader is also referred to Schäfer and Müller-Langer 2009, pp. 35–36 on ambiguity.

205 Harrington and Danzon 2000, pp. 285, 291; Cooter and Ulen 2012, pp. 242–243.

206 Harrington and Danzon 2000, p. 291. Also see: Baluch et al. 2011, pp. 130–132.

207 Harrington and Danzon 2000, p. 293.

208 Harrington and Danzon 2000, pp. 284, 294; Cooter and Ulen 2012, p. 224.

209 Calabresi 1961, pp. 499–500.

210 Borch 1962, pp. 424–425.

211 Ehrlich and Becker 1972, pp. 623–625.

212 Joskow 1973, pp. 327–328.

will be discussed in subsection 3.3.1. The subsequent two subsections will relate the law of large numbers to the functioning of insurance (subsection 3.3.2) and risk sharing (subsection 3.3.3). The effectiveness to apply the law of large numbers has limitations (subsection 3.3.4). In order to cure these limitations, risk bearers follow a method called the subdivision of risks (subsection 3.3.5). This section will end with a comparison between insurance and risk sharing (subsection 3.3.6).

3.3.1. The law of large numbers

The relative frequency of an outcome will resemble more closely the corresponding probability of the outcome, when the trials are repeated a large number of times. According to Wagner, "*[t]he law of large numbers says that, in repeated, independent trials, with the same probability of a particular outcome in each trial, the actual incidence of that particular outcome will converge more closely with the probability of that outcome as the number of trials increases*".[213]

An illustration to this law is the rolling of a dice. The probability of each of the six outcomes (where the outcome can be 1, 2, 3, 4, 5, 6) is one sixth. The expected value of rolling a dice is 3.5. It is highly unlikely to correctly predict the outcome when the dice is rolled once (or a few times) and it is impossible to receive an outcome of 3.5 when rolling the dice once. However, when the dice is rolled, say 30000 times, is it reasonable to predict that each outcome (1 through to 6) will have more or less occurred 5000 times, which equals one sixth of the trials. The average expected value of such a trial will be close to 3.5. This effect is called pooling or risk spreading.[214]

3.3.2. The law of large numbers and insurance

Let us assume that the insurer would sell insurance for this game. The insurer would charge an actuarially fair premium that is equal to the expected value, being 3.5, in exchange for the promise to pay either outcome (which is 1 through to 6). When selling a single contract it is pure chance whether the insurer gains or loses from the transfer of the risk. However, when the insurer sells 30000 insurances for the rolling of a dice, all outcomes are likely to occur 5000 times and the expected value will be around 3.5. "*The risks have canceled each other out.*"[215]

3.3.3. The law of large numbers and risk sharing

Similar to the example of rolling a dice, a risk bearing party may choose to share his risk with others, in order to make use of the law of numbers. A common example is a risk sharing agreement for the possibility of a nuclear accident. Let us assume that a nuclear accident costs the owner EUR 10 000 000. The probability attached to the occurrence is

213 Wagner 2009, p. 382. Also see: Berliner 1985, pp. 314, 318.
214 Wagner 2009, pp. 382–383; Berliner 1985, pp. 314, 318; Faure et al. 2013, p. 225.
215 Wagner 2009, p. 383. Also see: Berliner 1985, pp. 314, 318.

0.1%. Thus the expected loss is EUR 10 000. Let us further assume that this risk is exogenous and that the loss, when occurring, is higher than the individual assets could ever be. Additionally, the individual only owns one nuclear facility. It is reasonable to think that the individual is not able to compensate and manage the magnitude of such an accident.[216]

To solve this issue, individuals in the same business could share this risk, without the need to involve a third party. That means that, if a nuclear facility of one of these members breaks, the pool of the group compensates that individual.[217]

3.3.4. Limits to the law of large numbers

Consider the example of rolling a dice once again. Applying the law of large numbers, the insurer may reasonably expect a fair spread of an almost equal amount of outcomes of the numbers 1, 2, 3, 4, 5, 6. The insurer will not worry, when the outcome of one insured dice rolling is 6. In the end, he will also expect a 1 to occur. Both events cancel each other out. The risk that only sixes will occur is mitigated, which is called relative risk. "*[A] large pool reduces the risk associated with every single policy (called relative risk).*"[218]

Still, the effect of spreading does not make it more probable that the expected loss will occur (which is 3.5 in the example). Moreover, spreading makes it more probable that the insurer is faced also with a lot of sixes and ones. Any 6 or 1 that occurs is a divergent from the expected loss of 3.5. In this regard, pooling increases "*the degree to which a possible outcome may diverge from [an] aggregate expected loss (so-called absolute risk).*"[219]

Because of the absolute risk, it may be idealistic to assume that the insurer is able to perfectly eliminate risks by creating large pools. After pooling, the insurer bears a residual risk that features a combination of low probabilities and high stakes.[220]

Next to the absolute risk, the insurer is faced with the problem that the original assumptions may not hold true. Most risks are neither similar nor independent to each other. Furthermore, the created pool may not be large enough to eliminate the relative risk.[221] With respect to the illustration of risk sharing among operators of nuclear facilities, the risk sharing possibility may be lessened because not enough operators can be invited to the pool.

When the risks are different from each other, the insurer needs to adapt its policy to each individual risk.[222] Section 4.4 will turn to the problem, when the insurer is unable to differentiate its policy to each individual risk (adverse selection).

216 Wagner 2009, p. 382; Berliner 1985, p. 318; Faure 2004, pp. 471–472.
217 Faure et al. 2013, pp. 166–168; Faure 2004, pp. 471–472.
218 Wagner 2009, p. 383. Also see: Berliner 1985, p. 318.
219 Wagner 2009, p. 383.
220 Wagner 2009, p. 383; Berliner 1985, p. 319.
221 Wagner 2009, p. 383; Berliner 1985, p. 319.
222 Loubergé 2000, in: Dionne, Handbook of Insurance, p. 13; Berliner 1985, p. 319.

3.3.5. *Subdivision of risks*

Even without the law of large numbers and the resulting pooling, insurers may be able to insure single events. When the insurer underwrites such a single event, the insurer is unable to make use of the spreading effect. The risk corresponding to the event cannot be cancelled out by other independent but similar risks.[223]

An example of insurance of highly unlikely (and maybe impossible) events is the insurance for sighting the Loch Ness monster. A Scottish Whiskey distillery once offered to pay £1 million to any person who is able to find the Loch Ness monster. The Scottish Whiskey distillery was exposed to the risk that a person would actually be able to find the monster and wanted to buy insurance for that risk. The insurer Lloyd's agreed to insure that risk. The insurance was sold for a premium of £ 2500. Within Lloyd's, independent underwriters assumed each 7.5% of the risk in their books. Lloyd's divided the risk among the group. This approach is called co-insurance.[224]

Another tool of division would be to transfer part of the risk to a third party. Such practice has been given the name re-insurance. Furthermore, to increase the capacity of the ultimate risk bearer, insurers and other entities may pull together and contribute to a common pool. For example, in Germany the pharmaceutical industry is faced with large risks. As one insurer is unable to insure these risks, the entire Pharma industry contributes to a mutual Pharma-Pool.[225] Section 4.2 will consider issues and solutions to the concept of risk division in more detail (cf. risk uncertainty).

3.3.6. *Comparison between insurance and risk sharing*

Insurance resembles a relationship between the insurer being a third party and the insured injurer. In risk sharing the injurers are both insured and insurer, and no third party is necessary.[226]

Risk sharing can be established by either requiring an advance payment of the members to a common fund or by ways of an *ex ante* risk sharing agreement (the latter being called risk sharing institutions or mutuals).[227]

The interests of insurer and insured are not necessarily congruent. The insured may seek to externalize costs to the insurer. The insurer, as a profit-maximizing firm, may limit or deny coverage and possibly overcharge premiums. By ways of risk sharing the injurers are both providers and recipients of insurance. The conflict of interest between both parties is mitigated accordingly.[228]

The risk-sharing agreement creates a situation in which each member monitors the other members in order to mitigate the mutual risk and thus the required payments to

223 Wagner 2009, p. 383; Berliner 1985, p. 319.

224 Wagner 2009, pp. 383–384; Berliner 1985, pp. 319, 324.

225 Wagner 2009, pp. 383–384; Faure 2004, pp. 473–474.

226 Faure et al. 2013, p. 166; Harrington and Danzon 2000, p. 292; Faure 2004, pp. 474–475. Also compare to: Berliner 1985, pp. 322–323.

227 Faure et al. 2013, p. 167; Harrington and Danzon 2000, p. 292; Faure 2004, pp. 474–475.

228 Faure et al. 2013, p. 167; Harrington and Danzon 2000, p. 292; Faure 2004, pp. 474–475.

the pool. "*Mutuality is established usually when the members are subject to similar safety rules, exposed to a comparable level of liability and is usually formed in highly technical industries.*"[229] The reason is that the individual members usually have more expertise and precise knowledge about the risk to be insured than any third party (such as an insurer) would ever have.[230]

The pool also has advantages over insurance, in case the risk is not entirely quantifiable.[231] This issue of risk uncertainty will return in section 4.2.

3.4. Insurability and desirability of liability insurance

Having outlined the demand for and supply of insurance, this section will provide a general outline on insurability (subsection 3.4.1) and the economic feasibility of the insurance system (subsection 3.4.2). The section will also serve as a link to the next chapter, which will be devoted to offering solutions to obstacles which have already been outlined and to those which are to be outlined as obstacles of the insurance system.

3.4.1. Insurability

From the foregoing, it can be deduced that the insurability of risks is anything but a hard concept. Insurability is a matter of degree and consequently based on the decision of the insurer whether or not to assume the risk. Often the risk is estimated by extrapolating past experience to future expectancy. Such estimation is naturally based on the assumption that the future will behave similarly to the past.[232]

When the insurer is able to adjust its premium to the outcomes, slight divergences of the actual outcomes from the *ex ante* expected outcomes can be cured. Obviously, the higher the divergences and the smaller the ability to adjust the premium, the less robust is the possibility of insuring a specific risk.[233]

Furthermore, premiums are usually not priced actuarially fair. Premiums are instead higher than the expected damage, called 'loading'. Such loading may result from the fact that the insurer is not risk neutral.[234] Another reason may point to the administration costs, profits, underwriting expenses, and taxes or costs of capital.[235]

It has been argued that insurability is first and foremost a matter of price. When the premium is too high, the injurer is unwilling to pay the price. Anything can be insured, provided that the parties agree on the price. The premium's price can change over time and so can the insurability of the risk.[236] Problems to estimation and premium loading

229 Faure et al. 2013, p. 167; Faure 2004, pp. 474–475.
230 Faure et al. 2013, p. 167; Faure 2004, p. 474.
231 Faure et al. 2013, p. 167; Harrington and Danzon 2000, p. 292; Faure 2004, pp. 474–475.
232 Wagner 2009, p. 399–401; Berliner 1985, pp. 321–322; Berliner 1985, pp. 322–323.
233 Wagner 2009, p. 399–401; Berliner 1985, p. 325.
234 Harrington and Danzon 2000, p. 283; Hogarth and Kunreuther 1989, p. 20–29.
235 Faure et al. 2013, p. 166–168; Cooter and Ulen 2012, p. 237; Harrington and Danzon 2000, p. 292.
236 Wagner 2009, p. 401; Arrow 1971, p. 141; Cooter and Ulen 2012, pp. 239–240; Harrington and Danzon 2000, p. 295.

in general and uncertainty about an underwritten risk in particular will be thoroughly discussed in sections 4.2 and 4.6.

3.4.2. *Economic feasibility of the liability insurance system*

Taking into consideration compensation and risk spreading alone, accident insurance is economically more feasible than liability insurance.[237] However, the liability insurance system must be regarded as a measure to also induce an efficient deterrence on the insured injurer.[238]

Comparing both accident insurance and liability insurance, the loading of the premiums is much greater for liability insurance. Still, additional costs of liability insurance may be also attributable to its deterrence function.[239]

Some courts hold the injurer liable because the injurer is supposed to be more able to obtain insurance than the victim. Liability insurance is in this case cheaper than accident insurance. The liability insurer fulfils the role of the least-cost avoider. The concept of *least-cost avoider* refers to a situation, where one of the parties will bear lower costs to entirely eliminate an expected damage than the other one. The obligation to compensate the loss will be strictly distributed to the party that has the lowest costs avoiding the event.[240]

However, according to some, "*feedback effects between liability insurance coverage and litigation have produced socially excessive levels of litigation and costs*"[241] The expanding liability increases the demand for liability insurance which in turn leads to additional litigation.[242]

3.5. Conclusion

This chapter outlined the economics of general liability insurance that serve as a foundation for analysing the effect of D&O insurance on managerial risk taking. The following will summarize under what circumstances the injurer desires insurance and how insurance can be supplied.

Demand for insurance is usually explained by risk aversion. Risk aversion describes an attitude of dislike of risk. It means that the utility reduction when losing money is higher than the utility increase when gaining the same amount of money. People are risk averse

237 Regarding the concept of accident insurance, see subsection 3.2.3.

238 Harrington and Danzon 2000, p. 302. Also compare to: Kraakman 1984, p. 859. A similar reasoning is provided by Privileggi et al. 2001, pp. 181–185.

239 Harrington and Danzon 2000, p. 302. In this regard, some questioned the efficiency of (the insurance of) strict product liability. See: Harrington and Danzon 2000, p. 302; Cooter and Ulen 2012, pp. 237–238.

240 Harrington and Danzon 2000, p. 304; Shavell 2004, p. 189; Cooter and Ulen 2012, pp. 237.

241 Harrington and Danzon 2000, p. 304–305, summarizing Syverud 1994, pp. 1629–1654 and D'Arcy 1994, pp. 163–181.

242 Harrington and Danzon 2000, p. 305. For further information on the interdependence between litigation and insurance see: Cooter and Ulen 2012, p. 242–243.

to a varying degree depending on the person's wealth and the magnitude of the risk. It is socially desirable to treat risk aversion, in order to maximize social utility. Section 4.3 and Chapter 5 will point to other reasons, next to risk aversion, that explain the demand for insurance. It will explain why firms that are owned by well-diversified shareholders and thus less risk averse may desire insurance nonetheless.

Strict liability and negligence liability differ in their impact on risk aversion. Under strict liability, the injurer internalizes all costs. The injurer is exposed to the entire risk. Under negligence liability, the injurer bears no costs provided he takes due care. When taking due care, any damage which occurs is borne by the victim. Only the victim bears a risk.

According to Shavell, it is socially inefficient, when a party that is risk averse is exposed to risk. To allocate the risk to someone that can bear it, insurance is offered. Under negligence liability an injurer that bears no risk will not desire insurance. Under strict liability the injurer bears the risk and, if risk averse to the risk, he will desire insurance.

Insurance may change the insured injurer's incentive to take care. The injurer does not have to pay for damages any more. He might act less carefully and engage more in the dangerous activity. As a response, the insurer has to observe the injurer. Section 4.5 will turn to the problem that the insurer may not be able to observe the injurer (moral hazard).

When the level of care with respect to negligence liability is uncertain, injurers may be willing to purchase partial insurance. Uncertainty refers to two situations. First, the due level of care may be incorrectly established (error) and/or secondly, the injurer may be unable to take the required level of due care (inability). These uncertainties could create a risk which the injurer bears. When the injurer is risk averse to that risk, the injurer desires liability insurance. However, he will only insure the portion of the liability risk that corresponds with the risk of error or inability. Partial insurance of liability usually tends not to compromise deterrence. The injurer is still liable for acts that courts correctly establish and that he is able to control.

The injurer sometimes does not have enough assets to pay a liability claim. The injurer is judgement-proof. When the injurer is judgement-proof, his incentives to buy insurance are dulled. The lawmaker may choose to either make insurance compulsory or prohibit insurance. When the insurer is unable to observe the judgement-proof insured injurer, a prohibition of liability insurance is necessary.

Administration costs may lead to a situation where the victim starts a liability action too soon or not soon enough. A well-functioning insurance system and the insurer's ability to settle may mitigate these costs.

Supply of insurance is explained by the law of large numbers. The law of large numbers enables a spreading of risks. The law of large numbers only functions properly when there is a large number of risks that are similar but independent to each other. Section 4.4 will turn to the problem, when the risks are different to each other and the insurer is unable to adapt its policy to each individual risk (adverse selection).

Risk sharing (also called pools) may be more beneficial than insurance because no third party needs to become involved. The insurer aims for profit maximization which risk sharing usually does not. Moreover, risk sharing injurers could be in a better position to reduce and monitor the risk than the insurer because of their technical expertise.

There is no clear boundary between an insurable and an uninsurable risk. Whether or not to insure is a value judgement of the insurer. (Un)certainty surrounding the risk greatly affects the premium price. The injurer may find the requested premium excessive. The issue of insurability will return in section 4.6.

Chapter 4

OBSTACLES TO RISK BEARING AND INSURANCE

4.1. Introduction

The previous chapter outlined the economics of risk bearing and insurance. It showed that the insurance system is confronted with numerous obstacles. This chapter will discuss the most pressing issues and offer solutions.

The previous chapter discussed the idea that the question of whether a risk is insurable depends on the insurer's ability to deal with uncertainties. Uncertainty of risks will be the topic of section 4.2.

The previous chapter further described the classical model of accident law in which demand for insurance can be explained by the risk aversion of injurers (and victims). Insurance in turn would be offered by risk neutral parties (insurers or pools). These risk attitudes do not always correspond to the actual attitudes observed, as shown by behavioural studies. These studies may enable a more accurate prediction of the behaviour of injurers, victims and insurers (or pools). The studies will be outlined in section 4.3.

It was assumed in the previous chapter that each injurer bears a similar and independent risk. However, the size of the liability risk depends on the individual injurer and can differ to a high degree.[243] The insurer may be unable to observe the differences of the individual risks. Due to the inability to observe, the insurer may adversely select only those injurers that bear a higher than estimated risk. This problem is called adverse selection and will be discussed in section 4.4.

The previous chapter argued that the insurer needs to monitor the insured injurer so that the injurer's incentive to reduce accidents remains the same once he is insured. However, the ability to monitor the insured injurer may be limited. If that is the case, the injurer may be less inclined to reduce accidents. This problem is called moral hazard. Moral hazard and solutions to it will be outlined in section 4.5.

Finally, this chapter will turn to three issues that have already been mentioned in the previous chapter regarding insurability and desirability of insurance. First, there is the issue of insurance policy distribution. Secondly, there is the phenomenon of insurance cycles. Thirdly, the insurance premium is usually loaded due to administration costs. Section 4.6 will turn to those issues.

243 Loubergé 2000, p. 13.

The next chapter will apply the considerations of this and the previous two chapters to the concept of D&O insurance.

4.2. Risk uncertainty

This section will analyse a situation in which the risk cannot be clearly defined. The risk is uncertain. Uncertain risks were analysed by Ellsberg[244] and later developed by Einhorn and Hogarth.[245] This section will be structured as follows. First, the uncertain risk will be related to certain risks. Secondly, the uncertain risk's features of probability and magnitude will be discussed. Thirdly, the risk assessors' attempts to deal with uncertainties will be analysed. Fourthly, the functioning of the pool under uncertainty will be outlined.

4.2.1. Classification of uncertain risks

When a risk is uncertain, it can still be approximated. When approximation of a risk is impossible, one speaks of ignorance. To explain the relationship between uncertainty and ignorance, an illustration by Gardenfors and Sahlin 1982 is useful.

"Consider Miss Julie who is invited to bet on the outcome of three different tennis matches. As regards match A, she is very well-informed about the two players [...] Julie predicts that it will be a very even match and a mere chance will determine the winner. In match B she knows nothing whatsoever about the relative strengths of the contestants [...] Match C is similar to match B except that Miss Julie has happened to hear that one of the contestants is an excellent tennis player although she does not know anything about which player it is, and that the second player is indeed an amateur so that everyone considers the outcome of the match a foregone conclusion."[246]

Match A corresponds with certain risks, match B refers to ignorance, and match C entails uncertainty about the risks. In a state of ignorance no distribution of occurrences can be ruled out. Uncertainty is the state between ignorance and certain risk.[247]

4.2.2. Identification of uncertainty

A risk is calculated by multiplying probability times magnitude.[248] Uncertainty about the risk can either amount to an uncertain probability variable (paragraph 4.2.2.1), an uncertain magnitude variable (paragraph 4.2.2.2), or uncertainty about both variables (paragraph 4.2.2.3).

244 Ellsberg 1961, pp. 643–646.

245 Einhorn and Hogarth 1986, pp. 225–227.

246 Einhorn and Hogarth 1986, p. 229, citing: Gärdenfors and Sahlin 1982, pp. 361–362.

247 Einhorn and Hogarth 1986, p. 229, citing: Gradenfors an Sahlin 1982, pp. 361–362.

248 Wagner 2009, p. 382; Shavell 2004, p. 259; Cooter and Ulen 2012, pp. 237–238; Harrington and Danzon 2000, p. 287.

(4.2.2.1) The probability is calculated by looking at past experience on the frequency of the risk's occurrences. Ideally, the frequency is derived from a proper data set that incorporates a large number of past occurrences related to the same kind of risk. The frequency of observed losses equals their probability, if the data set is big enough (the law of large numbers).[249] The estimation becomes better, the more is known about the nature of the occurrence, the higher the probability of occurrence, the longer the period that the occurrence has been observed (for example by ways of statistics), and the higher the amount of observable occurrences that relate to the assessed risk. The more clearly these elements are defined, the better the approximation of the size of the risk becomes.[250]

To illustrate, there could be a risk of a satellite accident, in which the satellite might burn while it heads off into the sky. The magnitude of the risk of burning is clear. The damage equals the value of the satellite plus accompanying costs. However, the probability of such an event is uncertain. The risk of burning has not materialized in the past often enough, to attach a probability to that event.[251] Thus, the assessment becomes difficult with respect to the probability.[252]

(4.2.2.2) Regarding magnitude, there are two uncertainties, the issue of quantification, and the issue of similarity.

First, the magnitude must be quantifiable. This might be extraordinarily difficult in some areas, for example for non-pecuniary loss, emotional distress or foregone earnings. If there is a risk of a broken arm, there is physical damage. Besides, the individual might not be able to pursue his profession and suffers emotional distress. After all, there is no objective price tag to emotional distress or foregone earnings.[253]

Secondly, the risk has to have a universal character, in order to use it for future estimations. To cite the example of the broken arm again, the consequent damage must always be the same. Such an assumption is clearly far-fetched. To name but a few possible divergences, the arm could be broken in different ways and different locations, which will make a difference in the healing process. Furthermore, the ability of the patient to pursue his profession will be impaired differently, relating to the nature of that profession.[254]

(4.2.2.3) Some risks entail uncertainty toward both variables. For example, risks relating to catastrophes are often categorized as such. The exact occurrence of an earthquake in time and location is very hard to predict by seismologists (uncertain probability). Furthermore, the consequential damages arising from the earthquake can vary to a high degree.[255] The assessment of the worst case is especially important. Another example is the risk assessment with respect to nuclear energy facilities. The design basis accident refers to the worst case that risk assessors can think of *ex ante*, in order to design the

249 Wagner 2009, p. 382; Berliner 1985, pp. 314, 318; Faure et al. 2013, p. 225.
250 Berliner 1985, pp. 313–319.
251 Kunreuther et al. 1993, p. 73.
252 Einhorn and Hogarth 1986, p. 225–226.
253 Shavell 2004, pp. 240–247; Wagner 2009, p. 381–382.
254 Shavell 2004, pp. 236–249; Wagner 2009, p. 381–382.
255 Kunreuther et al. 1993, p. 73.

nuclear facilities. These facilities are then supposed to withstand the occurrence of the worst case. Because the probability is uncertain, every facility was built, according to that worst case prediction. However, the nuclear accident in Fukushima, Japan shows that the *ex ante* estimated worst case did not incorporate the magnitude of a tsunami of such size hitting the facilities.[256]

4.2.3. *Assessment of uncertainty*

The risk assessor is faced with the difficult task of approximating these uncertainties.[257] Still, irrespective of the lack of data, he is able to make projections from a small sample, according to principles of probability theory. These principles enable the risk assessor to make a fairly accurate projection from a relatively small sample.[258]

To do so, he makes an educated guess on the probability (e.g. based on previous experiments), which he calls null-hypothesis. He will then use the observed sample to approve or disprove the null-hypothesis. If the outcomes of the sample correspond to the null-hypothesis for more than 99% (called highly significant amount), he is fairly certain that his educated guess approximates to reality.[259]

Problems with this method are the correlation and the endogeneity of factors with the null-hypothesis. This is because of the following. When 99% correlates with a factor that is inherent to the whole sample, the approval of the null-hypothesis was established only on first sight. To solve this problem, the risk assessor can make use of dummies and regressions. He inserts factors in the calculation, of which he knows that they correlate with either the null-hypothesis or the sample only. It will guarantee that the significant approval (or disapproval) is still existent (also called robust) when these dummies and regressions are included.[260]

4.2.4. *The pool or risk sharing*

Applying the law of large numbers, a pool or a group that shares the risk pursuant to a risk sharing agreement has a greater capacity to compensate damage than the individual members by themselves. When only the magnitude is known, the pool has to have at least an amount of assets that equal actual damage. The actual damage is divided among the number of pool members. That amount is paid by the pool members upfront.[261]

256 Kunreuther et al. 1993, p. 73. For more information on nuclear accidents, see: Hirano et al. 2012, pp. 1–2; Faure and Fiore 2008, pp. 288–290.

257 Einhorn and Hogarth 1986, p. 227; De Groot 1975, pp. 2–3.

258 De Groot 1975, pp. 6, 419, 437; Doane and Seward 2011, pp. 15–17. On the determination of a reliable sample size, see: Doane and Seward 2011, pp. 374–276; Bain and Engelhardt 2014, pp. 160–162.

259 De Groot 1975, p. 419–421; Doanne and Seward 2011, pp. 15–17, 551–552; Bain and Engelhardt 2014, pp. 358–359. For more information on errors with respect to the approval or rejection of the null-hypothesis, see: Doanne and Seward 2011, pp. 344–347.

260 De Groot 1975, pp. 173, 369, 439, 498, 507; Doanne and Seward 2011, pp. 15–17, 745, 560–561; Bain and Engelhardt 2014, pp. 177–178, 186, 389–395. For implications with regressions, see: Doanne and Seward 2011, pp. 528–531.

261 Faure and Hartlief 2001, pp. 69–70; Faure et al. 2013, pp. 166–168; Harrington and Danzon 2000, p. 292.

When neither the magnitude nor the probability of the risk is known, the pool is able to make use of the *ex post pro rata* liability scheme. When the magnitude turns out to be higher than estimated, the members could be obliged to pay the remaining amount to the pool when the damage occurs. The payment of each member corresponds to his share in the pooled risk.[262] This arrangement eliminates the problem of potentially faulty risk assessment when dealing with uncertain risks. Needless to say, if the wealth of the sum of the members is too small to build up sufficient capacity, the pool does not survive.[263] Moreover, "*mutual insurers* (read: pools) *are less able than stock insurers* (read: insurers) *to raise external capital following large losses, which would increase the capital that mutuals need to hold ex ante.*"[264]

4.3. Ambiguity aversion and biases

The previous chapter discussed the concept of risk aversion. It has been assumed that the probability distribution of the risk is certain. Furthermore, it has been assumed that the individual rationally calculates the risk.[265] In subsection 4.3.1, these assumptions will be relaxed, in order to incorporate less rational, subjective and emotional views of the individual.[266] As will be shown, the context of the risk is highly important for the individual. Subsection 4.3.2 will deal with the fact that the individual often does not have all the information that is necessary to estimate the risk's features. Subsection 4.3.3 will attempt to incorporate the previous two sections and offer a model to better predict the individual's choice behaviour when dealing with uncertain risks, which is called the ambiguity model. Subsection 4.3.4 and 4.3.5 will introduce two more peculiarities of choice behaviour, being the competence bias and decision-making under scrutiny.

Once the aspects that depart from the concept of risk aversion have been outlined, this section will turn to the individual's attitude toward ambiguity. In subsection 4.3.6, the relationship between risk attitude (aversion and neutrality) and ambiguity attitude will be focused at. Consequently, the limitations to offering insurance (subsection 4.3.7) and possible solutions (subsection 4.3.8) will be dealt with.

4.3.1. The context of the risk

Individuals are highly affected by emotions and this puts a heavy weight on information that has an emotional context. Furthermore, the individual can assess a situation better, when it is easy to imagine.[267] This subsection will first introduce the concept of framing,

262 Faure and Hartlief 2001, pp. 69–70; Faure et al. 2013, pp. 166–168. Although some insurance policies provide for retro-active premium adjustments through dividends or assessments on policyholders, these provisions are difficult to enforce when the insured injurer knows more about the risk than the insurer. See: Harrington and Danzon 2000, p. 292.

263 Faure and Hartlief 2001, pp. 69–70; Faure et al. 2013, pp. 166–168.

264 Harrington and Danzon 2000, p. 292.

265 Einhorn and Hogarth 1986, p. 226.

266 Slovic 1999, pp. 689–690.

267 Kahneman and Tversky 1973, pp. 208–209. For more information, see: Binder et al. June 2005, pp. 905–906.

in which a particular use of language alters the individual's approach to risk. Secondly, the individual's confusion between frequency and probability is focused on, called the theory of gambler's fallacy. Paragraph 4.3.1.3 will deal with the fact that individuals make faults when comparing two bets, because the decision for the second bet is influenced by the decision of the first bet (called common consequence effect).

(4.3.1.1) Kahneman and Tversky 1981 provide an illustration of the strong impact of emotions and words. In this study, the word 'to save' led to a different response than the word 'to die' even though the expected loss calculations were equal. The original problem is worded as follows: "*Imagine that the U.S. is preparing for the outbreak of an unusual Asian disease, which is expected to kill 600 people. Two alternative programs to combat the disease have been proposed. Assume that the exact scientific estimate of the consequences of the programs are [sic] as follows:*"

There were two groups that received a slightly different text. Group I read: "*If program A is adopted, 200 people will be saved. If program B is adopted, there is a 1/3 probability that 600 people will be saved, and a 2/3 probability that no people will be saved.*" The alternatives presented to group II were: "*If program C is adopted, 400 people will die. If program D is adopted, there is a 1/3 probability that nobody will die, and a 2/3 probability that 600 people will die.*"[268]

Stochastically, both texts from group I and II are the same. However, 72% of group I preferred option A, while 78% of group II preferred option D. This outcome is contradictory to the model on risk attitude for two reasons.[269]

First, all options bear the same expected loss of 400 dead people. Thus, they are the same and no option should be preferable to the other. Nonetheless, respondents do prefer one option over another. Secondly, the options A, C and the options B, D share a similarity because the magnitude and probability variables are equal. Thus, even if the first remark does not hold, the respondents of group I and II should either prefer option A and C, or B and D. However, they do not. This outcome is not affected by the respondent's education or intelligence.[270]

According to Kahneman and Tversky 1981 this finding shows that the framing or wording of the risk has a major effect on the applicant's choice.[271] It further provides insights about the individual's tendency to avoid simple calculations of expected loss (multiplying probability by magnitude). Especially, the feature of probability seems to be difficult to grasp for an individual.[272]

(4.3.1.2) The previous considerations already imply one important feature, namely that the individual refers to frequency, when he makes an estimation about a risk's probability. This is an already well-known bias called gambler's fallacy. The gambler's fallacy has

268 Kahneman and Tversky 1981, pp. 453–458.
269 Kahneman and Tversky 1981, pp. 453–458.
270 Kahneman and Tversky 1981, pp. 453–458.
271 Kahneman and Tversky 1981, pp. 453–458. For an overview of descriptive models that formalize this and other outcomes, see: Starmer 2000, pp. 338–340.
272 Kahneman and Tversky 1981, p. 453–458.

been observed in the casinos of Monte Carlo for games where each trial is independent from the previous one (such as roulette). At those games, the fallacy is observed at tables where the frequency of events is below the probability of the events. Many players believe that a past frequency that is below probability has to be levelled out in the future by a frequency that is above the probability. So they think, the future bet is more likely to be awarded.[273]

(4.3.1.3) Also known as common consequence effects, the following phenomenon is illustrated by Allais 1953. Imagine that respondents have to decide during two experiments between two options respectively. Regarding the first question, the respondent has to decide between option A ($1 million with 100% probability) and option B ($5million with 10%, $1million with 89%, $0 with 1%). Regarding the second question, the respondent has to choose between option C ($1million with 11%, $0 with 89%) or option D ($5 million with 10%, $0 with 90%). The model on risk aversion teaches us that the individual either chooses A and C or B and D, referring to their risk attitude. In contrast to that prediction, respondents preferred option A and D.[274]

Allais explained that the respondents do not calculate their utility but rather estimate their chances. In the first question, the $1million is for sure. Thus, the respondents take the sure thing. In the second question, the respondents are lured by the similarity of the probabilities. The reward between the chance to receive $1million and $5million is very different, but the individual perceives the probability to be almost the same, 11% looks pretty similar to 10%. Thus, they take the chance to win $5mln.[275]

4.3.2. *The availability heuristic*

To better understand the dealing with probability, Kahneman and Tversky 1973 undertook several studies and developed the theory of the availability heuristic. According to this heuristic, individuals view information that they remember easily as more important than information that comes to mind later. "*That associative bonds are strengthened by repetition is perhaps the oldest law of memory known to man. The availability heuristic exploits the inverse form of this law, that is, it uses strength of association as a basis for the judgment of the frequency. [...] [H]e estimates frequency or probability by the ease with which instances or associations could be brought to mind.*"[276]

The authors first looked at the application of available information. In the test, respondents had to seek words in word-puzzles. The respondents were quick and fairly accurate in combining correct words. The respondents were able to construct and retrieve available information. Furthermore, the assessment of availability remained accurate without the need to actually construct or retrieve words from the puzzle. During the subsequent tests, respondents judged the frequency of events higher, when these events

273 Barron and Leider 2010, 'pp. 117–120.
274 Starmer 2000, pp. 346–349, citing: Allais 1953, pp. 503–505.
275 Starmer 2000, pp. 346–349, citing: Allais 1953, pp. 503–505.
276 Kahneman and Tversky 1973, p. 208. For more information, see: Binder et al. June 2005, pp. 905–906.

were remembered more easily. For example, the respondents overestimated the frequency of the names of famous artists in lists of names of which they only read the first part.[277]

A contrario to this logic, the authors argue that events that are difficult to remember will receive a low probability. This consideration is proved by their study. In fact, if the events are not easy to remember or the context of the event remains vague in memory, the respondent estimated the event as highly unlikely or even impossible.[278]

Similarly, the estimation of probability can be altered externally by, for example, one-sided media coverage or entertainment. When a respondent perceives a particular event in the near past, he thinks that the probability of that event to happen again is fairly high. According to the authors, "*many must have noticed an increase in the subjective probability that an accident or malfunction will start a thermonuclear war after seeing a movie in which such an occurrence was vividly portrayed.*"[279]

4.3.3. The ambiguity model

Einhorn and Hogarth 1986 propose a model to describe the individual's deviation from the model on risk attitude due to uncertain risks.[280] Their model, called the ambiguity model, is based on the model on risk attitude. According to Hogarth and Kuenreuther 1989, the ambiguity model is merely a slight deviation from the generally correct outcome of the model on risk attitude.[281]

The ambiguity model takes into account the individual's subjective judgement of a risk. It basically relies on two factors, the first being an approximated number of the risk and the second being a degree of ambiguity toward the estimation. Both variables are added up. This approach is called anchoring-and-adjustment process. Let us consider these two factors in more detail.[282]

First, the ambiguity model is applied for uncertain risks. The uncertainty refers to either the probability variable (example: satellite accidents), the magnitude variable (example: broken arm) or both variables (example: earthquake). The uncertain risk is approximated through different tools of probability theory and stochastic theory. The outcome is a numerical representation, which serves as an estimation of the risk. This variable is also called anchor. Thus, Einhorn and Hogarth call this process of estimation the anchoring strategy.[283]

Secondly, the individual is given the opportunity to imagine an increase or decrease of the estimated anchor. The individual adjusts the first estimated anchor-risk incorporating his own experience, expertise and common knowledge. The degree of adjustment corresponds to the degree of ambiguity that the individual faces. The outcome of this process is reflected by a variable, called the adjustment variable.[284]

277 Kahneman and Tversky 1973, pp. 208–212.
278 Kahneman and Tversky 1973, p. 229.
279 Kahneman and Tversky 1973, p. 230; Hogarth and Kunreuther 1989, p. 8.
280 Einhorn and Hogarth 1986, pp. 226–227.
281 Hogarth and Kunreuther 1989, p. 6.
282 Einhorn and Hogarth 1986, p. 230; Hogarth and Kunreuther 1989, pp. 6–12.
283 Einhorn and Hogarth 1986, p. 230; Hogarth and Kunreuther 1989, pp. 6–12.
284 Einhorn and Hogarth 1986, p. 231; Hogarth and Kunreuther 1989, pp. 6–12.

Some aspects of their study need to be highlighted. Regarding losses, the ambiguity preference increases as the anchor probability increases. This might even result in an ambiguity preference for high probability losses. Further, an individual is ambiguity averse for small probability losses. The overestimation of small risks and underestimation of high risks, described in this ambiguity model, enables a formal description of flight and car insurance. Risks that are assessed to be low such as flight accidents usually go hand in hand with a high ambiguity aversion. Where risks are assessed to be fairly high such as car accidents, individuals experience ambiguity preference.[285]

Interestingly, studies showed that ambiguity aversion has a different impact on insurers. Insurers seem to have a higher ambiguity aversion than individuals. Possible reasons of increased ambiguity aversion will be explained by the next two sections.[286]

4.3.4. Subjective competence

Heath and Tversky 1991 introduced the theory of competence bias. According to this theory, the individual considers a bet differently, when he thinks he is knowledgeable about that bet. The important factor is his perception of competence. It does not matter if the knowledge is indeed existent (or correct). For example, consider bets that have an equal and independent probability distribution (for example rolling a dice or flipping a coin). In these experiments, any subjective perception on competence is deemed to be faulty.[287]

However, as their experiments showed, the individual is more willing to make a bet, when the individual thinks he is competent. Trusting his competence, he is willing to raise the intake to a higher amount than the model on risk aversion would predict. The authors argue that such willingness arises from peer group dynamics. Whenever the decision to trust one's own competence turns out to be right, the individual is able to receive credit for his knowledge. When the opposite takes place, the individual can attribute the failure to chance.[288] Heath and Tversky conclude that "*[c]ompetence or expertise, therefore, helps people take credit when they succeed and sometimes provides protection against blame when they fail. Ignorance or incompetence, on the other hand, prevents people from taking credit for success and exposes them to blame in case of failure.*"[289]

4.3.5. Scrutiny

Another interesting and much cited study was published by Curley et al. 1986.[290] In their study, the authors primarily focus on the other-evaluation hypothesis, also later cited as decision-making under scrutiny.[291]

285 Hogarth and Kunreuther 1989, pp. 27–29.
286 Hogarth and Kunreuther 1989, pp. 27–29; Kunreuther et al 1993, p. 73.
287 Heath and Tversky 1991, pp. 5–7.
288 Heath and Tversky 1991, pp. 7–9.
289 Heath and Tversky 1991, p. 8.
290 Curley et al. 1986, p. 233.
291 Kunreuther et al. 1993, p. 77.

In such a scenario, the individual has to make a decision under uncertainty, while knowing that this decision will be evaluated by others afterwards. When the individual needs to choose while having the later scrutiny in mind, he tends to choose the alternative that he perceives to be the best justifiable decision. The best justifiable decision is likely to be a decision that revolves around a non-ambiguous rather than an ambiguous option.[292]

The authors interpret this finding as follows: "*A possibility is that subjects do so because they evaluate decisions on the basis of decision outcomes, and not on the basis of the decision process. Accordingly, they anticipate that their own decisions will be so evaluated, and choose the non-ambiguous option to avoid the outcome of losing with an ambiguous bag...*"[293]

4.3.6. Comparison of the previous approaches to ambiguity

The manner on how the individual perceives the risk plays an essential role with respect to the theories on the availability heuristic and the contexts of the risk.[294] For instance, media coverage may make individuals more accustomed to one set of risks ignoring other risks.[295] When the frequency is very low and the individual does not remember similar events in the past, the probability is regarded to be close to zero. He is likely to ignore the risk.[296] Subjective competence leads to ambiguity preference.[297] Scrutiny leads to increased ambiguity aversion.[298]

Furthermore, ambiguity to a particular risk alters the individual's demand for insurance. Ambiguity preference can decrease the demand and ambiguity aversion can increase the demand. Ambiguity preference might be so strong as to diminish insurability. As outlined above, ambiguity preference is observable for high probability losses, such as car accidents. Ambiguity aversion might in turn be so powerful that individuals over-insure. The individual develops a high ambiguity aversion for risks that have a low probability, such as flight insurance.[299]

4.3.7. Limits to insurability

The classical model of insurance is altered by ambiguity. This subsection will first look at the insurance market when the demand is ambiguous about the risk, and secondly, when the supply is ambiguous about the risk.

292 Curley et al. 1986, pp. 231–232.
293 Curley et al. 1986, p. 253.
294 Kahneman and Tversky 1981, pp. 453–458.
295 Kahneman and Tversky 1973, p. 230; Hogarth and Kunreuther 1989, p. 8.
296 Hogarth and Kunreuther 1989, pp. 27–29.
297 Heath and Tversky 1991, pp. 5–9.
298 Curley et al. 1986, p. 253.
299 Hogarth and Kunreuther 1989, pp. 27–29.

First, ambiguous individuals still desire insurance provided that the insurer takes into account the mechanisms of ambiguity aversion and preference. First, it has been shown that individuals are ambiguity averse with respect to low-probability risks. In this regard, the insurer could tailor the risks in such a manner that each part of the risk would have a low probability of occurring, in order to increase demand. A danger of this technique is that the probability could become too low. If the probability is so low that the individual ignores the risk altogether, the insurer has destroyed demand. Secondly, when the individual's perception of competence proves to be wrong or when the individual's competence is less developed than another person's competence, the ambiguity preference decreases and might even turn to aversion. To make use of this fact, the insurer could confront the individual with reports from apparently more competent individuals, such as expert opinions, in order to sell the policy.[300]

Secondly, Hogarth and Kuenreuther hypothesize that increased ambiguity aversion of insurers can be partly explained by the competence bias and decision-making under scrutiny.[301]

The insurance underwriter may think that his competence to understand the risk is lower than the individual's competence. Because of this perception, the underwriter may imagine a worse outcome than the individual which in turn leads to a higher ambiguity aversion of the insurer.[302]

The increased ambiguity aversion could also be explained by the fact that the underwriter is scrutinized by superiors. When the individual is assumed to underwrite on his own behalf, he does not have to justify his decisions. On the other hand, the underwriter has to justify the policy which he has granted.[303]

According to another line of reasoning, unlike the pool's mechanism regarding *ex post pro rata* compensation payments, the insurer is generally not able to adapt the premiums *ex post*.[304] The insurer fears to wrongly estimate the risk *ex ante*.[305]

As a response, the insurer includes an additional amount in the premium that incorporates the uncertainty. The premium becomes loaded. When the premium is too loaded, the premium's price could surpass the individual's willingness to pay for insurance. The risk becomes uninsurable.[306] A common example to illustrate uninsurability is the nuclear energy insurance industry. Because of the high ambiguity related to nuclear energy, such as radiation and contamination, insurability turns out to be difficult.[307]

300 Kahneman and Tversky 1973, p. 230; Hogarth and Kunreuther 1989, p. 30; Curley et al. 1986, p. 253. These findings do not reflect reality absolutely, because of administration and brokerage costs. The marginal costs of these factors may lead to a situation, where additional risks cannot be borne anymore. See: Berliner 1985, pp. 318–321.

301 Hogarth and Kunreuther 1989, pp. 20–29; Arrow 1951, p. 421; Friedman and Savage 1948, p. 279; Loubergé 2000, p. 52.

302 Hogarth and Kunreuther 1989, pp. 27–29.

303 Hogarth and Kunreuther 1989, pp. 27–29.

304 Harrington and Danzon 2000, p. 292; Faure and Hartlief 2001, pp. 69–70; Faure et al. 2013, pp. 166–168.

305 Berliner 1985, pp. 313–319; Einhorn and Hogarth 1986, pp. 228–229.

306 Berliner 1985, pp. 313–319; Einhorn and Hogarth 1986, pp. 228–229.

307 Hogarth and Kunreuther 1989, pp. 30–32.

4.3.8. *Solutions such as partial coverage and third party involvement*

To eliminate uninsurability, the previous chapter introduced the principle of subdividing risks. The mechanism to subdivide risks makes use of either the relationship between the individual and the insurer or between the insurer and another party.

Regarding the first relationship, subdivision takes place in the form of (1) exclusions, (2) deductibles, (3) retentions, (4) upper limits and (5) co-insurance.[308]

First, exclusions exclude from the policy certain activities that the individual engages in. Secondly, with the introduction of a deductible, a minimum amount of magnitude is determined, below which the individual is not covered by the insurer. Thirdly, when retentions are used, the insurer only covers a proportion of the risk, the residual proportion remains with the individual. Fourthly, a coverage limit determines the maximum amount of magnitude, above which the insured individual has no coverage. Finally, co-insurance refers to a tailoring of the original risk to proportions that the insurer is willing to bear, as outlined in the example of Lloyd's insurance for the potential discovery of the Loch Ness monster.[309]

Regarding the second relationship, possible solutions are (1) pooling, (2) re-insurance and (3) the application of portfolio theory.[310] First, the insurer could choose to establish a pool of capital among other insurers. The benefits and limitations of such an insurer-pool are the same as outlined above in relation to pools for individuals. Being a member of such an insurer-pool, the insurer is supported by a strong financial buffer and can make use of the *ex post pro rata* liability arrangement.[311]

Secondly, the insurer can seek re-insurance. A re-insurer is rather able to apply the law of large numbers. To cope with ambiguity, the re-insurer, in turn, might also want to subdivide the risk in accordance to the just outlined tools of retention, exclusion, deductible, upper limit or co-insurance.[312]

Thirdly, the original risk is not regarded solely, but has to be considered in relation to other risks. The inter-relation between risks enables the insurer to assess the risk more accurately and build up its capacity. The insurer uses the tools of diversification, hedging and, more generally, portfolio theory.[313]

4.4. Adverse selection

When the insured risks are different to each other (also referred to as the heterogeneity of risks), the insurer needs to adapt its policy to each individual risk.[314] When the insurer

308 Harrington and Danzon 2000, pp. 284–285; Cooter and Ulen 2012, p. 238.
309 Wagner 2009, p. 382; Faure and Hartlief 2003, p. 73; Cooter and Ulen 2012, p. 238.
310 Cooter and Ulen 2012, p. 238; Doherty 1980, pp. 405–406.
311 Faure and Hartlief 2003, pp. 73–78; Wagner 2009, pp. 383–384.
312 Faure et al 2013, pp. 224–236; Wagner 2009, pp. 383–384.
313 Doherty 1980, pp. 405–406; Markowitz 1952, pp. 77–79.
314 Loubergé 2000, p. 13; Berliner 1985, p. 319.

is unable to adapt its policy to each individual risk, the insurer is exposed to the problem of adverse selection. This section will be structured as follows. First, seminal work will be the focus, and considerations on adverse selection will be outlined. Secondly, this section will look at the consequences of adverse selection. To mitigate the problem of adverse selection, the insurer can let the individual self-select his policy (subsection 4.4.3), apply experience rating (subsection 4.4.4), encourage declarations (subsection 4.4.5) and categorize the risk (subsection 4.4.6).

These tools to treat the inability to observe are not always applicable. Risk categorization might be hampered because of legal constraints, such as laws that prohibit discrimination (subsection 4.4.7). Furthermore, competition can endanger the effective use of risk categorization (subsection 4.4.8).

4.4.1. The advent of the concept of adverse selection

The concept of adverse selection is based on two cumulative conditions. First, the class of insured individuals is heterogeneous: some face a higher risk than others. Secondly, the insurer is unable to distinguish the different risk classes without costs before underwriting. As a result, the insurer requires every individual to pay the same premium. This treatment is beneficial to the individual who bears more risk than average and is detrimental to the individual who is exposed to less risk that average. In a Pareto efficient market, however, the individual who is exposed to a smaller risk should benefit to be incentivized to avoid costs. The academic discussion focuses on this dilemma.[315]

The seminal contribution of Akerlof in 1970 described the issue of adverse selection by illustrating the market of second-hand cars.[316] He shows that the prices are higher than the corresponding quality of cars would, under normal conditions, suggest. He further demonstrated how far deciding against an employee with an ethnic background is rational. When assuming a statistical correspondence between ethnic background and quality of education, ethnicity serves as an indicator for dis-functionality in the future job. To treat this issue, Akerlof asked for some reliable forms of trustworthiness and suggests establishing objective standards by third party authorities, such as diplomas by high schools or quality checks for cars.[317] His contribution on adverse selection is based on the seminal work of Arrow 1963 which identified adverse selection for the supply of medical care.[318]

Similar considerations were made by Crocker and Snow 2000, who state that the competitive pressure between insurers induces each insurer to attract the group that bears the smallest risk.[319]

315 Loubergé 2000, p. 13; Berliner 1985, p. 319.
316 Akerlof 1970, pp. 492–495.
317 Akerlof 1970, pp. 492–495.
318 Arrow 1963, pp. 941–969.
319 Crocker and Snow 2000, pp. 247–249.

4.4.2. *Consequences of adverse selection*

Because every individual is different with respect to features and activities, no risk borne by an individual is the same. A group that shares a risk will not be entirely homogeneous, but heterogeneous. Similarly, the risks that will be transferred to the insurer are not entirely the same. To simplify the divergence of risks in a heterogeneous group, Rothschild and Stiglitz 1976 distinguished between two groups of individuals that are similar in the kind of risk, but different in the probability and severity of the loss they insure. The class of individuals that have a small risk are called good risks, and the class of individuals that bears a high risk are called bad risks.[320]

Heterogeneity does not lead to adverse selection, when the pool or insurer effectively monitors the heterogeneous group. When monitoring becomes impossible, heterogeneity might lead to adverse selection. The rationale is the following.

To be profitable in a competitive environment, an insurer desires to underwrite the good risks and deny cover for the bad risks. However, it is assumed that the difference of both risks cannot be identified before underwriting. To be profitable, the insurer needs to find a premium that takes into account both risks, which means that the good risk pays a higher premium than would be appropriate to his risk class and the bad risk pays less. This concept is called pooling of risks.[321]

Such a method leads to adverse results for the good risk, the bad risk, and the insurer. First, if the good risk finds out that he pays a higher premium than would be appropriate to his risk class and this additional amount is used to subsidize the bad risk, he is likely to leave the insurer. Bearing the risk himself or pooling the risk with other good risks might be less costly. Secondly, the bad risk would pay a premium that is lower than his corresponding size of the risk. That means that such insurance over-compensates the bad risk's risk aversion. Thirdly, the insurer in turn is left with the bad risk that pays a premium that is too low. The insurer would have an unprofitable business. In the extreme, there would be no equilibrium in the market and the risk would become uninsurable.[322]

4.4.3. *Self-selection*

According to Rothschild and Stiglitz and also to Spence,[323] one solution to the problem that the insurer has no knowledge whatsoever about the different risk classes, is that the insurer offers different sets of policies. When the insurer is able to offer a set of policy contracts, such as one policy that corresponds to partial coverage and one policy that corresponds to full coverage, the choice of the individual will give an indication of the individual's risk class.[324]

According to their theory, the good risk purchases partial coverage, whereas the bad risk buys full coverage. The rationale is the following. The good risk chooses to partially

320 Rothschild and Stiglitz 1976, pp. 634–636.
321 Crocker and Snow 2000, pp. 247–249.
322 Rothschild and Stiglitz 1976, pp. 634–638; Priest 1987, pp. 1524–1525.
323 Spence 1978, pp. 427–429.
324 Spence 1978, pp. 427–429.

cover, because it is cheaper for him to only transfer part of the risk and to self-insure for the remaining risk.[325] Furthermore, the bad risk faces a higher risk aversion because he bears a higher risk. Because of the higher degree of risk aversion, the bad risk prefers full coverage rather than the good risk.[326]

4.4.4. *Experience rating*

The section on self-selection concluded that good risks are covered partially, whereas bad risks receive full coverage. Such a result is not beneficial for the good risk. They are constrained to partial insurance. The method of experience rating relaxes this constraint. Regarding experience rating, the above mentioned model that is based on a one-period contract needs to be extended to a multi-period contract. In a multi-period contract, the contractual relationship of the insurer and the individual survives the occurrence of losses. An example might be automobile insurance or health insurance. The rationale of experience rating is that the partially covered good risk receives full coverage later on for a premium that is lower than the bad risk's premium.[327]

Above it was assumed that the bad risk desires full coverage. *A priori*, when an individual chooses partial insurance, the insurer identifies such an individual as a good risk. To counteract the possibility that a bad risk chooses partial insurance and thus offsets the insurer's calculation, experience rating can also be used. When the insurer later on notices that a partially covered individual bears more risk than estimated, the insurer increases the premium (and if desired also decreases the coverage) to the standards of the bad risk. However, such a mechanism requires full commitment of the insured bad risk. Full commitment means that the bad risk individual has no possibility to switch in period two or later to another insurer. Full commitment is necessary, because otherwise the insurer will not be able to induce an adaptation of the policy that is to the detriment of the individual.[328] Subsection 4.4.8 will deal with the issue on how to categorize risks when there is no full commitment, which means that the individual can freely choose to drop out of an insurance contract.

4.4.5. *Self-selection, experience rating and declaration*

A more elaborate model of self-selection is provided by Dionne.[329] His model considers self-selection with respect to a multi-period contract.

The individual is asked to estimate his own risk and declares that risk to the insurer. As long as the individual's losses stay within a certain range of the declared risk, he will

325 Dionne et al. 2000, p. 193; Ehrlich and Becker 1972, p. 623–624; Winter 2000, p. 162.

326 Dionne et al. 2000, p. 193. The success of self-selection is based on certain condition, being (i) that the bad risk has a higher risk aversion than the good risk, (ii) that the insurer pursues a pure Cournot-Nash strategy and (iii) that there is a sufficient number of bad risks to find a market equilibrium. For more information, the reader is referred to Rothschild and Stiglitz 1976, pp. 633, 639–645.

327 Loubergé 2000, p. 16; Cooter and Ulen 2012, p. 238; Cooper and Hayes 1987, pp. 211–213; Harrington and Danzon 2000, pp. 284–285.

328 Loubergé 2000, p. 16; Cooper and Hayes 1987, pp. 211–213.

329 Dionne et al. 2000, pp. 192–195.

pay the corresponding premium. In other words, the actual frequency and magnitude of the occurring losses has to stay within that pre-defined deviation from the *ex ante* calculated probability and magnitude. When the individual's frequency of losses is only negligibly deviant from the declared risk over a certain amount of time, the premium stays unaltered. However, if the damage deviates to a high degree from the declared risk, the individual is required to pay a penalty premium. The deterrent effect of a possible penalty premium incentivizes the individual to declare properly.[330]

Furthermore, the mechanism of reporting can be introduced. The individual is given the possibility to report a (potentially) high deviation before the occurrence of the event to the individual. When properly reporting, he can escape the penalty premium. The insurer is willing to allow reporting and abstain from asking for penalty payments because the insurer is able to properly classify the individual before the occurrence of the event.[331]

However, when the insurer bases its policy structure solely on the reporting mechanism, the insurer bears the problem of under-reporting. The bad risk might be incentivized to under-report occurrences in order to be considered a good risk. As a wrongly perceived good risk, he might enjoy a cheaper premium.[332] A solution to under-reporting will be outlined in subsection 4.5.6 when considering auditing.

4.4.6. *Risk categorization*

Self-selection is based on the assumption that the insurer has no information about the heterogeneity of the risk. This section deals with the tool of risk categorization that assumes imperfect information, instead of no information. The insurer might be able to identify and observe variables that correlate with the insured risk. If that is the case, the insurer can adapt the policy to the size of the correlating risks and in this regard classify each risk. This method is called risk categorization.[333]

Hoy provides the example of auto-mobile insurance and categorization based on gender. Let us assume that there is a relationship between the probability of car accidents and distances driven. Further, let us assume that males drive longer distances on average than females. As a result, if the insurer cannot observe the distances driven, sex might be used to imperfectly categorize the risk class. According to this example, males will be attributed to a high risk class and females to a low risk class. For some incidences this categorization will be misclassified, males driving small distances and females long ones, but on average, it will hold.[334]

330 Dionne et al. 2000, pp. 196–197, 199–202; For background information, see: Cooter and Ulen 2012, pp. 238–239.

331 Dionne et al. 2000, pp. 199–202.

332 Dionne et al. 2000, pp. 199–202.

333 Hoy 1982, p. 321; Dionne et al. 2000, pp. 233–234; Berliner 1985, p. 319; Wagner 2009, p. 387. A relationship between statistical variables and the insured risk has been suggested already by Akerlof 1970, pp. 492–495.

334 Hoy 1982, p. 321.

Furthermore, empirical studies by Dionne et al. showed that categorization can effectively eliminate adverse selection. In this regard, an appropriate risk categorization is also a substitute for the need for self-selection.[335]

4.4.7. Discrimination and risk categorization

Although risk categorization may be efficient, equity considerations may be incompatible with proper risk categorization.[336]

For example, on average women live longer than men. In this regard, women could be attributed to a risk class of long living individuals and men to a risk class of shorter living individuals. Although some men might live longer, a statistical categorization based on sex approximates different risk classes. Differentiation of the risk classes would be efficient for the purpose of risk categorization. Crocker and Snow claim that if gathering discriminatory information is costless, its use will nonetheless benefit everyone (i.e. men and women alike). If it benefits bad risks and good risks alike, there is no economic reason not to discriminate.[337]

However, since 2011, the Court of Justice of the EU (CJEU) prohibited the discrimination (read: categorization) based on sex. According to the CJEU, the right of equality between men and women outweighs the economic benefits of categorization.[338]

4.4.8. Limits to control/adapting the policy

The tools of experience rating and risk categorization do not take into account the competitive pressure. When there is competition, the individual is not fully committed to the insurance. Full commitment means that the bad risk individual has no possibility to switch in period two or later to another insurer.[339] Subsequent paragraphs will deal with the introduction of competition, where commitment is relaxed. It will consider semi-commitment and no commitment.

Semi-commitment – When the individual is able to re-negotiate the policy, but not to terminate the contractual relationship, one speaks of semi-commitment. In a scenario of semi-commitment, the insurer has two possibilities to discriminate the good from the bad risks. The first possibility is called highballing and the second is lowballing.

Highballing is based on the tool of self-selection. In the first period, both premiums (for the good risk and the bad risk) are loaded with an additional amount. In the second period, the individual wants to re-negotiate. In these negotiations, the insurer can use the additional profits that arose from the loaded premiums of period one to offer a

335 Dionne et al. 2000, pp. 233–234.
336 Wilson 1977, p. 168.
337 Crocker and Snow 1986, pp. 321–323.
338 CJEU C-236/09. For further information see: De Baere and Goessens 2011, pp. 347–352; Caracciolo di Torella 2011, pp. 59–60.
339 Dionne et al. 2000, pp. 192–202; Loubergé 2000, p. 16; Cooter and Ulen 2012, pp. 238–239.

discount in period two. The policy of period one subsidizes the policy of period two. The good risk is provided with a discounted premium in the second period.[340]

In the strategy of lowballing, the insurer will make a loss in the first period, but profits from subsequent periods. It is thus the perfect opposite to the procedure of highballing.[341]

No commitment – When the individual has no commitment to the insurer, for example when there are high numbers of similar insurance products that compete with each other, he could leave the insurer for another insurer at any time. Such a scenario would mean that experience rating and subsequent risk categorization would not survive. When the individual comes to know of the fact that the insurer loaded the premium at any period, he could terminate the contract.[342]

However, when the insurer knows more of the individual than he does of himself, the insurer could adapt the policy to the known information in later periods. This information enables experience rating and risk categorization, subject to the condition that the information remains confidential with the insurer. If the individual came to know of that information, he would turn to another insurer that had not accrued the relevant information yet. In other words, when it can be concluded that experience rating and subsequent risk categorization is Pareto-efficient and the insurance market is competitive, the private information of the insurer should be protected.[343]

4.5. Moral hazard

When the insurer is unable to adapt its policy to the conduct and features of the individual, the individual might be incentivized to alter his risk after taking out insurance. This tendency is referred to as moral hazard.[344] The theory of moral hazard is based on the seminal contributions of Arrow 1963,[345] Pauly 1968,[346] Spence and Zeckhauser[347] and Shavell.[348]

This section is structured as follows. First, it will analyse the emergence of the theory of moral hazard. Consequently, this section will outline the extent to which the insurer is able to mitigate the detrimental effects of moral hazard by collecting information about the insured (subsection 4.5.2) and by attempting to control the behaviour of the insured (subsection 4.5.3). The most prominent solution to moral hazard is the adaptation of the premium (subsection 4.5.4). However, there are problems regarding the premium adaptation (subsection 4.5.5). To supervise whether the individual lives up to his

340 Loubergé 2000, p. 16; Dionne et al. 2000, p. 213–220; Cooter and Ulen 2012, pp. 238–239.
341 D'Arcy and Doherty 1990, p. 146.
342 Nilssen 1990, pp. 641–645; Dionne et al. 2000, pp. 216–217.
343 Nilssen 1990, pp. 641–645; Dionne et al. 2000, pp. 216–217, 235–236.
344 Shavell 1979, p. 541.
345 Arrow 1963, pp. 961–962.
346 Pauly 1968, p. 531; Pauly 1974, pp. 44–45.
347 Spence and Zeckhauser 1971, pp. 380–381.
348 Shavell 1979, p. 541.

promises, the insurer audits the individual (subsection 4.5.6). Partial coverage as an inferior solution to premium adaptation will be discussed in subsection 4.5.7.

4.5.1. *Emergence of moral hazard*

According to Shavell, "*moral hazard refers ... to the tendency of insurance protection to alter an individual's motive to prevent loss*".[349] Let us consider this definition more closely.

As explained in the previous chapter, insurance may change the insured injurer's incentive to take care. Because the injurer does not have to pay for damages any-more, he might act less carefully and engage more in a dangerous activity. As a response, the insurer will have to monitor the injurer.[350]

However, according to Shavell, moral hazard can never be so high as to reject insurance altogether.[351] The insurer simply has to respond to the issue of moral hazard by way of imperfect monitoring.

4.5.2. *Treatment of imperfect knowledge and risk categorization*

To be provided with some level of information, the insurer might choose to observe other risks or features that are more easy or less costly to observe.

Signals may be used that correlate with the insured risk to discover risk changing behaviour. A signal is information that does not need to have any causal relation with the insured risk. The signal is informative, if it correlates with the risk. According to Holmström, an observation of a signal always adds to the proper estimation of the risk, however less correlated the signal may be. The value of the signal then depends on the costs that are attached to acquire and to administer the signal's information.[352]

In the previous section, the insurer used the mechanism of self-selection and risk categorization. Bond and Crocker 1990 link the problems of moral hazard and adverse selection to the tool of risk categorization. The scholars distinguish between categorization of exogenous characteristics, such as sex, race, age and endogenous characteristics, such as the choice to buy a fast car or start smoking. Whereas the first aspects can only be observed by the insurer, the second aspect can also be influenced by the individual. To illustrate, an individual cannot change his age but he can choose to start smoking. The characteristics that can be influenced by the individual were termed correlative products.[353]

Correlative products can be further divided into variables that have a causal link to the insured risk or merely a statistical link. A causal link exists between the choice to smoke and the state of one's health. Medical evidence shows that smoking negatively

349 Shavell 1979, p. 541.
350 Pauly 1974, p, 47–48; Shavell 1979, p. 541–546; Kraakman et al. 2009, p. 35; Shavell 2004, pp. 262–263.
351 Shavell 1979, pp. 541–546; Harrington and Danzon 2000, p. 284.
352 Holmström 1979, pp. 83–88.
353 Bond and Crocker 1991, p. 178.

correlates with health. The purchase of a fast car, however, has a merely statistical correlation with a higher risk of putting one's life in danger.[354]

Because the individual is able to choose the consumption of these correlative products, the choice indicates their level of mitigation effort and their risk class.[355]

When the insurer is able to observe the consumption, it can indirectly classify the insured individual.[356]

4.5.3. *Treatment of imperfect control*

According to Shavell, the insurer has two alternatives to control the insured individual, adapting the premium or partial coverage.[357] These two alternatives have a different impact on the insured individual and the insurer.

First, a change of the premium should be preferred over partial coverage. The reason is that the first tool perfectly treats the individual's risk aversion, whereas the second tool only partially covers and thus partially treats risk aversion. In this regard, partial coverage is inferior to premium adaptation.[358]

Secondly, the two alternatives differ as to when they can be exercised. Partial coverage and premium adaptation can be applied before the occurrence of the loss. However, after occurrence of the loss, only partial coverage can be used. The insurer is unable to adapt the premium retrospectively after the occurrence of the loss.[359]

4.5.4. *Adaptation of the premium*

When the individual is likely to experience multiple losses while he is insured, the premium can be adapted according to past experience.[360] The measure can be linked to the model of penalty payments.[361] The discount for the good risk is subsidized by the penalty payment. Such a potential discount on the premium will incentivize the individual to mitigate the risk.[362] However, when the mechanism of penalty payments is applied too strictly, the policyholder will have to pay a higher premium too often. He is over-deterred. When the opposite is the case, he is under-deterred.[363]

The premium can be adapted due to the individual's consumption preferences. As outlined by Crocker and Snow, the insurer may be able to observe a change in the consumption of correlative products. If so, the insurer can adapt the premium accordingly.[364]

354 Bond and Crocker 1991, p. 178.
355 Bond and Crocker 1991, p. 178.
356 Bond and Crocker 1991, p. 178, 179.
357 Shavell 1979, p. 541.
358 Shavell 1979, p. 541; Shavell 2004, pp. 262–263.
359 Shavell 1979, p. 550, 553–554; Pauly 1974, pp. 47–48; Cooter and Ulen 2012, p. 238.
360 Rubinstein and Yaari 1983, p. 75.
361 Rubinstein and Yaari 1983, pp. 86–92.
362 Rubinstein and Yaari 1983, p. 93.
363 Winter 2000, p. 177.
364 Bond and Crocker 1991, pp. 178–179.

An enhanced risk categorization (of correlative products) can contribute to the correct adaptation of the premium. The use of partial coverage as an inferior solution can be limited to cases, where risk categorization does not deliver the possibility to classify risks.[365]

4.5.5. *Problems with premium adaptation*

There are three issues regarding an effective premium adaptation. First, for experience rating to work, the consequences that are attached to an occurrence of loss must be revealed quickly to renegotiate the contract for the next period. If the consequences are unknown for some time, because the revelation is delayed by, for example, ongoing court proceedings, adaptation is hampered for that period of time.[366] Secondly, as outlined in the previous section, experience rating in a competitive environment is only feasible when the information stays confidential.[367] Thirdly and also discussed before, risk categorization may violate ethical norms.[368]

4.5.6. *Monitoring implementation through random audits*

The adaptation of the premium has to be supported by audits. First, this subsection will deal with the reason for an audit. Secondly, it will discuss the difference between constant auditing and random audits. Thirdly, the differences in the costs of auditing will be outlined.

Reasons for audit – The reasons for audit are twofold. First, the audit should guarantee that only bad risks are confronted with the requirement to pay a penalty premium. An individual, experiencing a loss, may have taken all preventive measures, but nonetheless had bad luck. To ask for a penalty premium in such a situation would lead to adverse incentives.[369]

Secondly, an audit may solve the issue of under-reporting already outlined. An individual might be interested to lie about the loss, in order to get a discount premium. An audit that verifies the report undermines such conduct.[370]

Occurrence of the audit – The audit can take place regularly or randomly. First, in Townsend 1979, the assumption is made that audits always take place, when the individual reports a claim. Consequently, the individual has the certainty of being audited. When the audit reveals that the loss does not fall within the insurance policy, the individual has to pay for the audit, plus the losses already occurred from the risk. If the individual does not know about the scope of the insurance policy, he weighs off the

365 Bond and Crocker 1991, pp. 178–179.
366 Fudenberg and Tirole 1990, p. 1279.
367 Nilssen 1990, pp. 641–645; Dionne et al. 2000, pp. 216–217, 235–236.
368 Wilson 1977, p. 168.
369 Townsend 1979, pp. 276–283.
370 Townsend 1979, pp. 276–283; Cooter and Ulen 2012, pp. 238.

costs of the verification process with the cost of the damage. If the former is lower, he files the claim.[371]

When audits occur on a random basis, the individual still faces the threat of being audited, which induces him to keep filing honest claims.[372] Random audits are regarded as more efficient than regular audits, because random audits are executed less often and random audits induce a risk (and a corresponding risk aversion) upon the individual that the insurer might audit.[373] Additionally, the insurer can introduce a penalty for false reporting and a reward for truthful reporting, which aggravates risk aversion.[374]

Evasion – Bond and Crocker 1997 introduced the concept of evasion. The individual files a higher claim that is more difficult to disapprove by the insurer. The insurer is faced with the aggravated cost to cover the claim or to engage in costly auditing. The insurer's response can incentivize non-evasion by using two methods. First, the insurer entirely covers claims that would be cheap to monitor, thus incentivizing the filing of those claims. Secondly, the insurer only partially covers the claims that are related to costly verification. In other words, it settles claims that are difficult to audit.[375]

4.5.7. *Partial coverage*

Next to adapting the premium, the insurer can partially insure the individual. Whereas premium adaptation is exclusively an *ex ante* measure, partial coverage can be used *ex post* as well as *ex ante*.[376] Partial coverage refers to the tools exclusion, deductible, retention, co-insurance and upper limit, already discussed above.[377]

According to Winter 2000, the individual is incentivized to reduce the risk's probability, when the partial coverage takes the form of a retention (a proportion of the loss is paid by the individual) or a deductible (the individual pays losses below a certain amount).[378]

When the policy includes an upper coverage limit, the individual bears the loss that surpasses the insured upper limit of damage. Such policy inclusion incentivizes the individual to reduce the risk's magnitude. A similar effect should be observable regarding a progressive retention (the proportion of the risk that remains with the insured individual grows with the increase of the loss which occurred).[379]

371 Townsend 1979, pp. 265–268.
372 Townsend 1979, pp. 265–268.
373 Loubergé 2000, p. 14.
374 Border and Sobel 1987, pp. 525–527; Mookherjee and Png 1989, pp. 402, 406.
375 Townsend 1979, p. 266; Bond and Crocker 1997, p. 240.
376 Loubergé 2000, p. 13.
377 Cooter and Ulen 2012, p. 238; Harrington and Danzon 2000, pp. 284–285; Wagner 2009, p. 382; Faure and Hartlief 2001, p. 73–78.
378 Winter 2000, p. 162; Loubergé 2000, p. 13; Harrington and Danzon 2000, p. 287.
379 Winter 2000, p. 167; Loubergé 2000, p. 13; Harrington and Danzon 2000, p. 287.

4.6. Insurance industry

This section will focus on three additional aspects essential to the understanding of the insurance system. The first aspect deals with the marketing and distribution of insurance policies. The second aspect refers to insurance cycles. The third aspect relates to the loading of the premium.

4.6.1. *The supply of insurance policies*

In imperfect markets, an individual who desires insurance is exposed to costs to find the appropriate insurer.[380] There are two approaches to distribute insurance to the individual.

The first approach refers to direct writing. The insurer markets, tailors and advises the individual directly. The insurer depends on mass marketing, the use of employee sale agents and exclusive agents. The second approach points to independent agencies. The individual will be approached by independent marketing agencies or insurance brokers. Studies in the property-liability insurance market suggest that direct writing is more efficient than an independent agency. The reason is that the direct writing decreases underwriting costs and cuts out the middleman.[381]

The existence of independent agencies is not completely understood, but it has been suggested that they can compete over direct writing because they can provide a better quality of service in a market which is not transparent. Other scholars regard independent agencies as a short term phenomenon, which will be eaten up by direct writers in the long run.[382]

In a non-transparent and competitive market, an independent agency might have a niche when individuals subjectively regard them as impartial. When the individual is unable to exhaustively comprehend the supply of policies, the independent agent might support him to find the proper policy. In this regard, the independent agent might be perceived as more trustworthy than an insurer.[383]

4.6.2. *Insurance cycles*

The D&O insurance industry is exposed to insurance cycles. These cycles incorporate a regular and gradual alternation from a soft market to a hard market. Perfectly soft markets lead to an insurance which has a low premium and a full coverage. Hard markets feature high premiums and partial coverage.[384]

To explain the cycle phenomenon, it has been argued that the premium price alters with the available interest rates on the market. When the insurer receives a good interest rate by hedging on the financial market, the originally risk neutral insurer may develop

380 Regan and Tennyson 2000, pp. 709–712.
381 Joskow 1973, p. 41.
382 Regan and Tennyson 2000, pp. 718–722.
383 Regan and Tennyson 2000, pp. 718–722.
384 Harrington and Niehaus 2000, pp. 657–659; Harringon and Danzon 2000, pp. 295–296.

a risk attitude that corresponds to risk preference. When the insurer increasingly desires to assume risks, it seeks to sell more insurance and in this regard offers more favourable policies. In contrast, capital shocks and capacity constraints, such as financial crises, lead to hard markets.[385]

Other scholars argue that the cyclical behaviour of the market is the result of moral hazard and adverse selection. During a soft market phase the issues of moral hazard and adverse selection are neglected. After a period of increased underwriting, claim reporting increases too. With the growth of reporting, the insurer is exposed to moral hazard and adverse selection. As a response, the insurer limits the policies and asks for higher premiums. Such a response leads to hard markets. According to this explanation, the cyclical behaviour of the market is simply an industry-wide adaptation of the policies to a previously unmonitored problem of moral hazard or adverse selection.[386]

4.6.3. *Loading of premiums*

This chapter has discussed additional costs that are included in the required premium relating to the administration costs, safety loadings, and penalty payments. Administration costs refer to costs to deal with ineligible claims or negotiations in and out of court.[387] Safety loadings generally compensate the insurer to assume uncertain risks.[388] Penalty payments are included to enable the insurer to effectively monitor the insured individual, as outlined above.[389]

Another loading, not yet discussed, refers to the loading related to the insurer's expenses. The insurer is an entity aiming to maximize utility. When assuming the risk, the insurer seeks to ask the highest possible premium. As a result, these premiums are not calculated at an actuarially fair premium, but include a considerable margin for profit.[390]

When the relevant insurance market is perfectly competitive, the profit margin shrinks. Still, even under perfect competition, the premium is loaded due to costs that arise from the internal organisation of the insurer. These organisation costs entail costs, such as marketing costs and the employee's salary.[391]

As the above has shown, the degree of premium loading has a negative correlation with the degree of insurability. The loading can be so high that it eliminates the insurability of the risk.[392]

385 Priest 1987, pp. 1529–1532; Cooter and Ulen 2012, pp. 239–240; Harringon and Danzon 2000, pp. 298–300.

386 Cooter and Ulen 2012, p. 240; Harringon and Danzon 2000, pp. 297–298.

387 Shavell 2004, pp. 280–287; Harrington and Danzon 2000, p. 285.

388 Berliner 1985, pp. 313–319; Einhorn and Hogarth 1986, pp. 228–229; Borch 1960, p. 163.

389 Dionne et al. 2000, pp. 199–202.

390 Faure et al. 2013, pp. 166–168; Harrington and Danzon 2000, p. 292; Faure 2004, pp. 474–475.

391 Faure et al. 2013, pp. 166–168; Cooter and Ulen 2012, p. 237; Harrington and Danzon 2000, p. 292.

392 Faure et al. 2013, pp. 166–168; Wagner 2009, p. 399–401; Berliner 1985, p. 325.

4.7. Conclusion

This chapter has discussed obstacles essential to the understanding of risk bearing and insurance. It has dealt with risk uncertainty, ambiguity aversion, adverse selection, moral hazard, and general issues of the insurance industry. Let us revisit these in turn.

When the insurer cannot exactly estimate the risk because the probability and magnitude is uncertain, the risk assessor has no choice but to approximate the risk. Because of its *ex post pro rata* compensation mechanism, a pool may be better able than an insurer to deal with the uncertainty.

The above further explained that people usually over-estimate low probability risks (e.g. the risk of a flight accident) and underestimate high probability risks (e.g. the risk of a car accident). When the risk's probability is too low, however, people tend to ignore the risk entirely (e.g. the risk of an earthquake). When an individual thinks he is competent in dealing with a certain risk, he is likely to prefer to take that risk. Scrutiny by superiors leads to increased risk aversion. Interestingly, an insurer seems to be more averse to uncertainties than an individual. To compensate for the uncertainty aversion, the insurer will tend to ask for a higher premium. The premium may be so high that the risk bearing individual is unwilling to pay for insurance. The risk becomes uninsurable. A subdivision of the risk (also called partial coverage) mitigates the exposure to the entire risk. This tool may overcome uninsurability.

Adverse selection deals with the issue that good risks self-insure and bad risks pay a premium that is lower than it should be. To treat adverse selection, the insurer has several tools at his disposal. Either (i) the individual reveals his risk class himself when selecting his policy, (ii) the insurer is able to classify the risk due to its past experience with the insured individual, or (iii) the insurer is able to categorize the risk class according to correlating factors. Some may disapprove of risk categorization because of equity concerns (e.g. discrimination/categorization based on sex).

To evade the revelation of his risk, a bad risk may choose the policy that is intended for the good risks (e.g. wrong self-selection) and/or to under-report losses (e.g. ineffective experience rating). Furthermore, in a competitive environment the insurer cannot induce the insured bad risk to pay a higher premium, because the bad risk can simply leave the insurer for another one that offers better conditions. To verify proper self-selection and reporting, the insurer can audit the insured individual. Moreover, induced premium adaptations remain possible, when the insurer has an information advantage over the insured individual about the insured risk (e.g. confidential information).

Moral hazard reflects a situation in which the individual may take more risk once he is insured. When the premium does not adapt to a risk increase, it is under-priced. To treat moral hazard, the insurer needs to monitor the individual's risk taking. To observe changes in the risk taking behaviour, the insurer applies the same tools that treat adverse selection. The insurer controls the individual by adapting the premium to his risk taking. The insurer verifies its choice of adapting the policy by audits.

Audits can be costly and the insured individual may under-report. In that case, the insurer incentivizes proper reporting by covering losses entirely that are cheap to audit and by settling the losses that are costly to audit. However, when the actual revelation of the loss which has occurred is delayed for some time by, for example, on-going court proceedings, adaptation is hampered for that time. Furthermore, when monitoring is too costly or impossible, the insurer has the inferior solution to partially cover the risk. This solution is inferior because partial coverage is unable to fully treat the risk aversion of the individual.

The insurance policy can be distributed either by the insurer or by an insurance broker. Although a distribution by brokers increases costs, brokers may provide more trustworthy advice than the insurer (or at least risk bearers see it that way). Furthermore, the individual does not only pay for the expected loss that is insured (actuarially fair premium), but also for penalties, insurer's organisation costs, safety and administration costs, as well as the insurer's profit margin. These additional costs, and the willingness and the capacity of the insurer to insure, change over time (referring to insurance cycles).

The analysis of these obstacles is essential to understand D&O insurance which will be the topic of the next chapter.

Chapter 5

D&O INSURANCE

5.1. Introduction

This chapter will provide a theoretical analysis on how D&O insurance may affect managerial risk taking.

According to the classic model of accident law, managerial risk taking is influenced by liability. Section 5.2 will (i) revisit the liability rules, (ii) analyse whether negligence or strict liability should be adopted, and (iii) in how far the manager is risk averse. For the purpose of this thesis, the risk of the manager to be held liable is called liability risk.

Law and economics theory provides that risks should be allocated to risk neutral entities, so that risk-averse individuals do not have to bear them.[393] Risk neutral entities are usually firms held by well-diversified shareholders or insurers. Besides insuring the liability risk, the risk could be transferred from the risk-averse manager to the firm (called indemnification). In this regard, the question arises as to how far a salary increase or insurance are substitutes for indemnification. These considerations will be discussed in section 5.3.

Under negligence liability, the injurer only desires insurance (or another form of compensation), when the level of care is uncertain. Section 5.4 will argue that efficient risk taking by the manager is threatened when the level of care is uncertain. The shareholder or creditor may identify a chance by filing unsound claims. Fearing to be held liable, the manager may be discouraged from taking risks that are in the interest of the corporation (and possibly society). The manager desires compensation (being either indemnification, insurance or a salary increase) for bearing that additional risk of uncertainty.

However, Shavell,[394] Kraakman[395] and others[396] pointed to the question of to what extent compensation by way of indemnification or insurance is socially desirable. Section 5.5 will review their arguments.

Law and economics theory in principle provides that risk neutral entities (such as a risk neutral firm) do not desire insurance. However, already in 1966 Bishop pointed to

[393] For the same reason Bishop advocates insurance for managerial liability. See: Bishop 1966, p. 95.

[394] Polinsky and Shavell 1993, pp. 239–242.

[395] Kraakman 1984, pp. 857–858; Kraakman et al. 1993, pp. 1733–1737.

[396] Fishel and Bradley 1985, pp. 261–263: Oesterle 1983, pp. 513–517.

the fact that insurance is mostly sold to risk neutral corporations but not to the risk averse managers who benefit.[397] Section 5.6 will look at reasons that could explain why the corporation desires insurance. The section will argue that corporations desire insurance when the insurer is better able (i) to monitor the manager than the corporation (insurance for the liability risk) and/or (ii) to mediate on internal conflicts in the corporation (insurance for the risk of having to indemnify the manager who is liable).

Chapter 3 explained that in order to insure risks, insurers make use of the law of large numbers and the subdivision of risk. Section 5.7 will outline how to insure the D&O risk. For the purpose of this thesis, 'D&O risk' is a generic term that refers to the managerial liability risk and the indemnification risk collectively.

It is probable that the insurer observes the insured manager (section 5.8) and controls the insured manager (and possibly the corporation), as will be outlined in section 5.9. If monitoring is not possible, the insurer may choose to partially cover the risk, which is outlined in section 5.10. Section 5.11 will provide some general remarks on the D&O insurance industry.

The subsequent chapters on D&O insurance practice will evaluate the extent to which these hypotheses apply to the actual D&O insurance market.

5.2. Managerial liability revisited

In this section, the manager is assumed to adhere to the due level of care. Section 5.4 will relax this assumption. This section will revisit the scope of internal liability in subsection 5.2.1 and external liability (including tort liability and bankruptcy liability) in subsection 5.2.2. Subsection 5.2.3 will outline differences between negligence liability and strict liability. Subsection 5.2.4 will analyse how far these liability rules affect the risk attitude of the manager.

5.2.1. Internal liability

Internal liability is supposed to deter the manager from engaging in particular activities.[398] First, there is a risk of related party transactions. Secondly, there is a risk of a decrease of corporate value due to managerial incompetence.[399]

Section 2.4 introduced two internal liability rules, the duty of loyalty and the duty of care. The duty of care will deter incompetence. Still, the duty of care grants the manager enough discretion to take risks that are necessary and desired.[400] The duty of loyalty can be loosely attributed to a fairness standard that can reduce conflicts of interest.[401]

397 Bishop 1966, p. 103.
398 Kraakman et al. 2009, pp. 79–81; Marks 1999, p. 703; Pacces 2011, p. 314.
399 Posner 1974, p. 178–183; Gerner-Beuerle et al. 2013, p. ix-xiii; Marks 1999, p. 703; Kraakman et al. 1993, p. 1736.
400 Kraakman 2009, p. 78; Pacces 2011, p. 314–316; Posner 2007, pp. 441–442.
401 Kraakman et al. 2009, p. 153; Posner 2007, pp. 440, 441, 453; Marks 1999, pp. 703–705.

The tool of internal liability is beneficial to the corporation when internal liability increases corporate value. Internal liability increases corporate value when one of two alternatives occur. Either "*the prospect of the suit deters misconduct, ... or the suit ... yields a positive recovery net of all costs that the corporation must bear as a consequence of a suit.*"[402] Subsections 5.4.4 and 5.5.2 will analyse the circumstances in more detail.

5.2.2. *External liability*

As outlined in subsection 2.2.3, personal liability under tort law fails to provide appropriate incentives when individuals acting on behalf of the firm, such as the manager, are judgement-proof.[403] Vicarious liability is a solution when the principal has sufficient assets and can easily monitor the manager. To cure problems of high costs of monitoring and insufficient assets of the firm, liability of the manager as additional action to vicarious liability was proposed. Let us review these two problems in turn.

Tort liability – There are several reasons as to why the firm is unable to monitor the manager. A manager may reasonably believe that he will not be sanctioned by the firm because the harm cannot be attributed to him. In that case, internal sanctions must be raised to compensate for the chance that the harm cannot be attributed to the manager.[404]

Furthermore, when the harm brought about by the firm is much higher than the highest penalty that the firm can impose on the manager, then the manager's incentives to reduce the risk generally will be too small. As a result, the level of care of the manager would be inadequate. To induce an appropriate level of care, one could introduce a liability claim to be brought by an external party.[405] Furthermore, the state could impose a financial penalty which could be additionally encouraged by a jail term in case the penalty is left unpaid.[406]

When fines are not high enough to induce the manager to take optimal care, the state can penalize divergent behaviour by ways of imprisonment. The social costs of imprisonment must not be too high though. When the tool of imprisonment is applied, "*the optimal level of liability on the firm will turn out to be the harm plus the social cost of imprisonment less the private disutility of imprisonment (and any fines that are imposed)*".[407]

Bankruptcy liability – The personal liability of the manager may also cure the problem of insufficient assets of the firm (referred to as bankruptcy liability).[408] Furthermore, bankruptcy liability could deter the manager from engaging in desperate

402 Kraakman et al. 1993, p. 1736.
403 Oded 2011, p. 274; Shavell 2004, pp. 230–231; Cooter and Ulen 2012, pp. 240–242.
404 Polinsky and Shavell 1993, p. 256.
405 Stone 1980, p. 17.
406 Inherent in this suggestion is the assumption that the state is better able to collect fines than the firm. See: Polinsky and Shavell 1993, p. 240.
407 Polinsky and Shavell 1993, p. 241.
408 Kraakman 2008, p. 144; Kraakman 1984, p. 869.

measures to avoid bankruptcy.[409] Where bankruptcy liability does not deter enough, one can introduce criminal liability or the disqualification sanction.[410]

5.2.3. *Negligence liability v. strict liability revisited*

Some scholars argue that the costs of taking care might differ for injurers. A due level of care that sets a universal standard somewhere in the middle might be inefficient. The universal due level of care might incentivize high risk injurers and low risk injurers to take an inefficient level of care. In this regard, some argue that strict liability has an advantage over negligence liability.[411]

An efficient liability rule needs to incentivize a proper level of care and to take into account the individual risk classes of injurers.[412] To do so, courts sometimes develop different standards of due care that correspond to the risk type of the individual manager and/or firm. For instance, experts need to adhere to a higher standard than lay people.[413]

It is argued that the imposition of fines should rather be designed in the form of negligence liability than strict liability. In contrast to strict liability, the fact that a manager can entirely escape liability under negligence rather induces him to take due care.[414] Further, the threat of imprisonment can be used to induce managers to take more care without having to actually imprison anyone.[415]

5.2.4. *Managerial risk attitude*

The manager desires to be compensated for any liability risk he bears.[416] Bishop argued that the level of risk exposure is one of many topics that will be considered when the manager and the firm negotiate on the terms of employment. The manager and the firm mutually agree on the risks and rewards attached to taking the job, one of which is the size of the liability risk.[417] According to Kraakman, the manager is able to negotiate

409 Kraakman 2008, p. 137.

410 Kraakman et al. 2009, p. 137; Kraakman 2008, p. 144; Polinsky and Shavell 1993, p. 240. On other sanctions, see: Cabrillo and Depoorter 1999, p. 264.

411 Schäfer and Müller-Langer 2009, p. 24–27.

412 However, it might be unrealistic and also undesirable that law makers and courts, not trained in business and economics, retain the power to set an individualized level of care. Instead, it is probable that most standards incorporate two features, first a pre-defined universal level of care, and secondly an *ex post* evaluation of the circumstances.

413 Schäfer and Müller-Langer 2009, p. 25. Generally, Bishop argued that an adaptation of the liability rule is a simpler method to incentivize adequate risk taking than the use of insurance. See: Bishop 1966, p. 111.

414 Polinsky and Shavell 1993, p. 252. When managerial tort liability takes shape in the form of negligence liability and the manager takes due care, the firm must be held strictly liable "*for the full harm when an accident occurs in order for the price to reflect expected accident costs.*" See: Polinsky and Shavell 1993, p. 253. A similar argument has been provided by Kraakman 1984, p. 875.

415 Polinsky and Shavell 1993, p. 253.

416 Bishop 1964, p. 839; Bishop 1966, p. 96; Polinsky and Shavell 1993, p. 241; Fischel and Bradley 1986, p. 285.

417 Bishop 1966, p. 101.

adequate compensation because the manager has (i) sufficient information, (ii) the bargaining power to require compensation (iii) enough personal assets.[418] Compensation is provided by a combination of an increased salary, indemnification or insurance.[419] It is probable that he is not compensated for liability claims that are based on illicit managerial behaviour (similar to a breach of the duty of loyalty).[420]

When the manager is exposed to the risk of penalties, he desires compensation for bearing the risk. This compensation could take the form of a salary increase.[421] Although the firm has to pay higher wages, it is in the firm's interest to introduce penalties, provided that it is unable to discipline the manager otherwise. The reason is that through the introduction of fines the manager takes optimal care and expected harm falls. With it the prices of the firm's products should fall. Such a situation is optimal, when the decreased expected harm plus the salary premium is less costly than a system without additional personal liability.[422]

Risk-averse managers tend to take more care than risk neutral managers, which provides a boost to the deterrent effect of managerial liability. In turn the more risk averse the manager is, the less harsh the sanctions attached to the relevant liability rule have to be. Furthermore, for risk-averse managers a negligence rule is preferable to strict liability in terms of risk allocation. Under negligence liability the manager exercises due care and there is no risk of liability (provided that the level of care is certain).[423] It renders risk aversion and corresponding demand for compensation obsolete. When not bearing any liability risk, the manager does not have to be compensated by the firm.[424]

5.3. Compensating the liable manager when the level of care is certain

To compensate the manager against the liability risk, he can be indemnified, insured or paid.[425] Early scholarship regarded insurance and indemnification as alternatives and substitutes to each other.[426] From a risk allocation perspective, indemnification by the

418 Kraakman 1984, p. 871.

419 Bishop 1964, p. 839; Bishop 1966, p. 97; Kraakman et al. 1993, p. 1746.

420 Kraakman et al. 1993, p. 1747. They argue that the manager does not have the bargaining power to ask for compensation of liability suits when they are filed because the manager clearly stole from the firm. See: Kraakman et al. 1993, p. 1747. It remains questionable whether a firm would be willing to support the manager's participation in a cartel by indemnifying him for liability actions that arise out of this participation.

421 In this regard, the level of liability imposed on the firm should be reduced so that firm liability plus managerial liability equal the harm. See: Polinsky and Shavell 1993, p. 241.

422 Polinsky and Shavell 1993, p. 241. A similar reasoning is made by Kraakman 1984, p. 880.

423 Polinsky and Shavell 1993, p. 254.

424 This is an *a contrario* argument based on Polinsky and Shavell 1993, p. 241; Fischel and Bradley 1985, p. 285.

425 Bishop 1964, p. 839; Bishop 1966, p. 97; Kraakman et al. 1993, p. 1746. These considerations ignore differences in managerial salary, such as bonus payments, option plans, or reward payments in the form of corporate shares. As will be seen in section 7.6, the form of managerial salary affects the D&O insurance purchase decision significantly. See: Core 1997, p. 81, 82.

426 Bishop 1966, p. 92; Polinsky and Shavell 1993, p. 254; Fischel and Bradley 1985, p. 283.

firm is possible when the firm has a risk neutral attitude (subsection 5.3.1). This section will further outline indemnification (subsection 5.3.2) and insurance (5.3.3).

5.3.1. *Risk attitude of the firm*

Firms are risk neutral when they are held by well-diversified shareholders. The application of portfolio theory enables a well-diversified shareholder to ignore corporate specific risks,[427] such as managerial liability risks.[428] The risk neutrality of the firm is subject to two qualifications. First, to the degree that managers are risk averse, the behaviour of the firm may reflect risk aversion.[429] Secondly, many firms are not held by well-diversified shareholders. If the shareholders are not able to diversify, risk neutrality cannot be assumed. Usually, small and medium sized enterprises, whose shares are not traded in public, are held by non-diversified shareholders. According to Wagner, indeed most firms are risk averse.[430]

Scholars argue that a firm held by well-diversified, risk neutral shareholders has a competitive advantage over a firm held by non-diversified, risk averse shareholders.[431] When a firm is averse to a known risk, it seeks to actively reduce the risk and in turn accrues costs in doing so. A firm that is risk neutral to a known risk accepts the risk and hedges against it. When the risk neutral firm benefits the same way from hedging but accrues lower costs, the firm retains more assets than its non-diversified counterpart. In this regard, the former firm is of higher value to investors.[432]

5.3.2. *Indemnification*

A risk neutral firm has a comparative advantage to bear risk over a risk-averse manager.[433] Risk-averse managers will evaluate projects with a risk-averse bias. Salary premiums and career prospects only partially offset this risk-aversion, even if the manager is under high competitive pressure.[434] When assuming the risk from the risk-averse manager, the firm can encourage the manager to evaluate projects according to their actual present net value.

Indemnification further has a comparative advantage over salary premiums. The reasoning goes as follows. The firm has the choice to either assume the liability risk by way of indemnification or compensate the manager for the liability risk in the form of an increased salary. When the manager is indeed risk-averse the disutility of the risk-averse manager to bear the risk is higher than the potential disutility of the risk neutral firm to

427 Loubergé 2000, pp. 21–22. This assumes perfect information symmetry. Furthermore, it assumes no contracting cost, no bankruptcy cost, no externalities, nor convex tax schedules, which would lead to diverging interests between the corporation and general society. See: Paetzmann 2008, pp. 184–185.
428 Sykes 1984, pp. 1235–1236.
429 Shavell 2004, p. 259; Wagner 2009, p. 379.
430 Wagner 2009, p. 379.
431 MacMinn and Garven 2000, pp. 541–544; Loubergé 2000, pp. 21–22.
432 MacMinn and Garven 2000, pp. 541–544; Loubergé 2000, pp. 21–22.
433 Fischel and Bradley 1985, p. 285; Sykes 1984, pp. 1235–1236.
434 Kraakman 1984, p. 864.

assume the risk. When the manager is compensated in the form of a salary premium for bearing the risk, the salary premium has to equal his disutility. In this regard, the costs to indemnify the manager are less than paying him the salary premium.[435] In other words, it is cheaper for a firm to indemnify the manager than to raise his salary. If this conclusion holds true, indemnification is more cost-effective than a salary raise.

Another reason for indemnification may be that the shareholders think that the scope of internal liability too harshly restricts managerial risk taking. Indemnification could incentivize risk taking.[436] It is likely that the shareholder's willingness to incentivize greater risk-taking is related to the shareholder's risk attitude. In this regard, risk-neutral shareholders would ask for more risk-taking than risk averse shareholders. As a result, it is more likely that indemnification is observed in corporations, where shareholders are well-diversified, than in corporations that are held by non-diversified shareholders.[437]

With respect to corporate governance, indemnification undermines the shareholder's ability to reduce agency costs by holding the manager liable. Bishop has the same concern: "*We make a monkey out of the stockholders remedy, if the money simply travels in a circle from the insiders' pockets to the corporation's treasury and back to the insiders' pockets.*"[438] Similarly some argue that indemnification is provided by the firm to the manager without the shareholders knowing about it, or at least without them caring enough to change the practice. The effects of indemnification on managerial performance may not be big enough to justify the costs attached to prohibiting indemnification and the costs of shareholders to actively pursue a strategy of holding the manager liable.[439]

The opposite position is assumed by Kraakman. According to Kraakman, indemnification could also mitigate agency costs. Without indemnification, the necessary salary increases to compensate for liability risks add another dimension of complexity to the issue of monitoring. When indemnifying, this additional complexity is eliminated.[440] Similar to this reasoning, indemnification has been regarded as "*an extreme business judgement rule with a logic transcending the idea of limited scope of court review.*"[441]

5.3.3. *Indemnification more likely than insurance*

There are possibly two reasons why the manager is more likely to be indemnified than personally insured, being that it saves transaction costs and litigation costs.

Bishop raised the question whether the manager should only be able to insure personally.[442] When indemnification is prohibited, the corporation has to increase the manager's salary. With the salary premium, the manager could pay for D&O insurance.[443]

435 Cf. Fischel and Bradley 1985, p. 285; Kraakman 1984, pp. 864, 865.
436 Marks 1999, p. 704; Kraakman 1984, p. 859.
437 This argumentation is based on the illustrations of Marks 1999, p. 704 and Kraakman et al. 2009, pp. 116–117.
438 Bishop 1964, pp. 843–844.
439 Bishop 1964, p. 844; Bishop 1966, p. 97.
440 Kraakman 1984, p. 865.
441 Kuykendall 1998, p. 466.
442 Bishop 1966, p. 112.
443 Bishop 1966, pp. 103, 113; also compare to Fischel and Bradley 1985, p. 285.

There are three points of interest about such reasoning. First, the transaction cost of finding an appropriate insurer and negotiating an adequate policy is borne by the manager. These costs have to be compensated by the firm as well. Secondly, the manager's risk aversion may increase the disutility that arises from the transaction costs which in turn increases the salary premium. By way of indemnification, these transaction costs are saved.[444] Thirdly and similar to the effect of a salary increase, the involvement of an insurer could add another dimension of complexity to effective corporate governance by the shareholders.[445]

Furthermore, indemnification of internal liability suits may save litigation costs and time.[446] The dispute is simply settled internally by the corporation. When the manager is personally insured (instead of indemnified), the shareholders, the insurer and the manager have to work out their dispute openly and accrue litigation costs. When indemnified, the corporation as a mediator between the two can quickly settle the claim.[447]

Due to these reasons, indemnification would have an advantage over insurance. These arguments do not hold any-more, though, when the insurer is better able to monitor the manager than the shareholders are, and also in a better position to settle claims than the corporation.

5.4. Uncertain negligence liability

This section relaxes the assumption that the level of care is certain. Uncertainty about due care influences the manager, the shareholders and the creditors.

The manager might be exposed to the chilling effect (subsection 5.4.1) and the judgement-proof problem (subsection 5.4.2). Subsection 5.4.3 will outline which of the three compensations, being a salary increase, indemnification or insurance is sought by the manager.

When the level of care is certain, the shareholders and creditors probably know the scope of the negligence rule. In this context, the shareholders and creditors would only file claims when the liability rule is actually breached.[448] However, when the level of care is uncertain, the claimants might claim on other occasions also, which will be outlined in subsection 5.4.4.

5.4.1. The chilling effect and reputation costs

Managerial liability may undesirably deter the manager from taking beneficial but risky decisions.[449] The manager may be held liable due to a mistake or simply because the

444 This argument is based on the reasoning of Oesterle 1983, p. 570.
445 Similar arguments have made by Kraakman 1984, p. 865; Fischel and Bradley 1985, p. 291.
446 Pillai and Tractenberg 1981, p. 105.
447 Oesterle 1983, p. 572.
448 For background information, see Chapter 2 and Shavell 2004, pp. 264–265.
449 Carney 1999, p. 684.

liability rule is too complex, ambiguous or novel.[450] Furthermore, "*bold decisions may misfire and seem negligent or worse in hindsight.*"[451] According to Kraakman, "*lucrative business projects of borderline legality may be worth the wager to the firm even though they impose legal risks on managers.*"[452] The manager could develop risk aversion to this risk.[453]

The manager may even be chilled from taking risks. The chilling effect refers to an over-deterrence of the injurer, where the predefined level of care is too high.[454] Uncertainty aggravates the chilling effect.[455] For instance, some argue that the Sarbanes-Oxley Act chills managerial risk taking.[456]

To prevent the chilling effect, the risk to be held liable should be allocated to a more efficient risk bearer, such as the corporation or an insurer.

Furthermore, the manager faces disastrous reputation costs.[457] Unlike shareholders, the manager is unable to diversify his sources of income. In fact, he is induced to employ all his abilities to the better working of the firm that employed him and may even be prohibited from working for other firms (e.g. non-compete requirements).[458] The loss of the manager's reputation is unlikely to be insurable.[459]

5.4.2. *The judgement-proof manager*

When the manager's assets are insufficient to pay the full damage of the victim, he is judgement-proof in relation to the remaining unpaid damages.[460] The manager's assets may be insufficient because first, the liability risk has a low probability and a high magnitude[461] and secondly, the impact of managerial activity may be amplified by the corporate assets that the manager employs when engaging in the activity. According to Shavell, the incentive for judgement-proof injurers to purchase insurance is dulled.[462] The corporation of the manager on the other hand is more likely to purchase D&O insurance because it is willing to do so in the context of assembling the managerial

450 Bishop 1966, p. 98; Kraakman 1984, p. 864. In the words of Shavell, the chance of legal error or inability to take care creates a risk that the manager bears. See: Shavell 2004, p. 265; Polinsky and Shavell 1993, p. 254.

451 Kraakman 1984, p. 864.

452 Kraakman 1984, p. 865.

453 Shavell 2004, p. 265; Polinsky and Shavell 1993, p. 254.

454 Schauer 1978, pp. 685–789; De Geest 2012, p. 291–293.

455 De Geest 2012, p. 291–293.

456 Bargeron et al. 2010, pp. 34–35. "*... by increasing the role of independent directors in corporate governance and expanding/criminalizing their liability for corporate misdeeds, SOX discourages directors from approving risky investments that are costly to monitor. In addition, SOX requires chief executive officers (CEOs) and chief financial officers (CFOs) to certify their companies' financial statements and imposes criminal liability for knowing or willful violations of this provision.*" See: Bargeron et al. 2010, p. 35.

457 Paetzmann 2008, p. 192.

458 Wagner 2009, p. 379: Kraakman 2009, p. 170.

459 Bishop 1966, p. 106; Carney 1999, p. 684.

460 Shavell 2004, p. 230–231; Cooter and Ulen 2012, pp. 240–242.

461 Bishop 1966, p. 95; Pillai and Tractenberg 1981, p. 102; Baker and Griffith 2007, 'Predicting Corporate Governance Risk', pp. 494–496; Bishop 1964, p. 834.

462 Shavell 2004, p. 275; Wagner 2009, p. 395; Harrington and Danzon 2000, pp. 287, 289.

compensation package. The next subsection 5.4.3 will outline the compensation package in more detail.

5.4.3. *Compensation: salary increase, indemnification or insurance*

The manager may not desire compensation for adhering to the level of care of which he is certain (provided that the shareholders are satisfied with the level of risk taking). The manager simply avoids any corresponding liability risk by adhering to the level of care that is certain.[463] In this regard, the compensation is likely to include only partial coverage for the uncertainty surrounding the due level of care.[464] Compensation is provided by a salary premium, indemnification or insurance.[465] As outlined above, when the manager is risk averse, indemnification is more likely than a salary increase (and possibly more likely than insurance).

However, bankruptcy liability gives rise to demand for insurance irrespective of the corporate indemnification efforts. The scope of indemnification is limited to the size of corporate assets. In bankruptcy, the corporate liabilities surpass the corporate assets.[466] When the indemnifying corporation is in the vicinity of bankruptcy, the indemnified manager remains subject to damage arising from liability. To eliminate the remainder of the liability risk, it is likely that the manager desires insurance. Furthermore, insuring this bankruptcy liability could also protect creditors against under-capitalized firms.[467]

It is probable that the relevant D&O insurance is purchased by the corporation instead of the manager because a corporate purchase is cheaper. A well-diversified corporation with many managers provides the insurer with a ready-made pool of risks. Moreover, transaction costs to find an appropriate insurer and to negotiate an adequate policy are reduced when a corporation negotiates for its managers, in contrast to a situation in which each liability risk has to be negotiated by the respective manager.[468]

5.4.4. *Ignorance about due care*

According to Shavell, a victim might overuse or under-use the liability system compared to the social optimum, because of administration costs.[469] More specifically, the victim, the voluntary creditor and the shareholder may feel deceived by the manager or misread

463 Kraakman et al. 1993, p. 1746. According to Shavell 2004, pp. 264–265, non-ambiguous actions entail intentional behavior. These actions are usually not covered by insurance. If the shareholders are dissatisfied with risk taking and want to increase risk taking, the shareholders can indemnify the manager for a higher amount.

464 Shavell 2004, p. 265; Kraakman et al. 1993, p. 1746. Uncertainty refers to errors of courts and the injurer's inability to take care. See: Shavell 2004, p. 265. Also see: Cooter and Ulen 2012, pp. 217–220, 220–222.

465 Polinsky and Shavell 1993, p. 254.

466 Bucy 1990, p. 326.

467 Kraakman 2008, in: Faure 2009, p. 144; Kraakman 1984, p. 868–869.

468 Sykes 1984, p. 1236.

469 Shavell 2004, pp. 280–282.

the manager's intentions.[470] Although objectively adhering to the level of care, the manager is held liable by (one of) these parties. Increased claiming creates an additional layer of uncertainty, imposing a risk on the manager. This uncertainty risk is further increased when it remains dubious whether the court will award the requested damages. The manager desires to be compensated for bearing that risk.[471] The costs of the compensation are borne by the corporation (meaning all the corporate shareholders), while the amount of compensation paid when the claim has been successful exclusively belongs to the claimant.[472]

Under a derivative suit,[473] the shareholder may file a claim at any time that the expected benefit of the claim is higher than the total litigation costs to bring a claim. The shareholder who makes this claim only holds a small fraction of the corporate shares. The expected benefit and total litigation costs borne by this shareholder are divided by the fraction of shares that the shareholder holds.[474] Because of his limited fraction of shares, the shareholder does not necessarily care whether the claim increases corporate value.[475]

Furthermore, the liability system could empower individual shareholders to influence the corporate strategy. The prospect of being held liable could induce the manager to publish more information about the corporation.[476]

When there is an overuse or under-use of the managerial liability system, the subsidy or regulation of the system is proposed by Shavell and others, such as specialized small scale courts to lower trial costs, class actions, legal aid programs or insurance.[477] Kraakman et al. 1993 suggest however "*that a variety of regulatory devices-notably, relying on the corporate board, the trial court, or the corporate charter to screen derivative suits-cannot, as they are presently administered, fully correct the distorted litigation incentives...*"[478] Section 5.6 will further analyse the ability of D&O insurers to administer an efficient liability regime.

5.5. Limits to compensating the manager

After having recognized the role of indemnification and insurance, scholars turned to the question of to what extent compensation is socially desirable. Generally, insurance or indemnification should not be prohibited when a prohibition "*does not necessarily*

470 This argument is based on the arguments made by Posner 1974, pp. 179–180; Kraakman 1984, p. 859; Polinsky and Shavell 1993, p. 240; MacMinn and Garven 2000, pp. 542–544.

471 Polinsky and Shavell 1993, p. 241; Fischel and Bradley 1985, p. 285. Also compare to: Harrington and Danzon 2000, p. 285.

472 Fischel and Bradley 1985, p. 285.

473 Under a derivative suit, the shareholders as a group sue the management on behalf of the corporation for a breach of duties. See: Cahn and Donald 2010, pp. 601–603, 607–608.

474 Bishop 1966, p. 94; Kraakman et al. 1993, p. 1741.

475 Fischel and Bradley 1985, p. 292; Kraakman et al. 1993, pp. 1735–1736.

476 Marks 1999, pp. 696, 698–709; Kraakman 2009, pp. 36, 39, 115; Lawless et al. 1997, p. 112. By way of the liability system, a minority shareholder may be able to control the corporation against the will of the majority of shareholders and management. See: Marks 1999, pp. 708–709.

477 Shavell 2004, pp. 286–287; Harrington and Danzon 2000, p. 285.

478 Kraakman et al. 1993, p. 1737.

provide enough deterrence to offset the greater costs that it imposes on regulated firms."[479] To further analyse this trade-off, this section will propose restrictions to compensation with respect to external liability (tort liability and bankruptcy liability) in subsection 5.5.1 and limits in the area of internal liability in subsection 5.5.2.

5.5.1. Limits to compensate external liability

Compensation should be prohibited when the personal liability of the manager is essential to induce an optimal level of care.[480] When compensation is prohibited, one speaks of absolute personal liability.[481] Positively formulated, risk transfer should be allowed, "*if absolute personal liability does not contribute to deterrence, or if its contribution – however great – is offset by the costs imposed on innocent firms and managers.*"[482] Polinsky and Shavell 1993 argue that the manager may be compensated subject to the condition that the sum of managerial liability and firm liability equal the harm. Compensation should be allowed if it "*will properly balance the beneficial effect of reducing risk against the detrimental effect of diluting the incentive to take care.*"[483] The following will distinguish between liability suits brought by victims and by voluntary creditors.

Indemnification against suits brought by victims is socially beneficial when it "*can force the firm and its shareholders to internalize the expected liability costs that undercapitalization would otherwise impose on tort victims*".[484] The implementation of personal liability rules that can be compensated or shifted is socially desirable when (i) it reduces the chance of over-adoption or under-adoption of liability rules and (ii) it allows managers to select the optimal strategy with respect to compensation, self-insurance and firm activities.[485]

Kraakman argues that indemnification should be prohibited, however, when the sanction that corresponds to the liability rule is unable to sufficiently deter a firm's wrong-doings. The sanction is unable to adequately deter the firm when the firm is judgement-proof.[486] In other words, Kraakman seeks to prohibit a situation in which the expected loss that would have been borne by the manager is externalized through indemnification to a judgement-proof firm. Being judgement-proof, the firm's incentives to take care are limited to the expected loss of its assets. Any remaining damage is ignored by the firm.[487] The remaining damage would either be borne by the manager or the claimant.[488]

479 Kraakman 1984, p. 866.

480 Kraakman 1984, p. 859. A similar reasoning is provided by Privileggi et al. 2001, pp. 181–185.

481 It has been argued that absolute liability is likely to serve as an effective control over organizational conduct. See: Kraakman 1984, p. 859.

482 Kraakman 1984, p. 862.

483 Pillai and Tractenberg 1981, p. 106; Polinsky and Shavell 1993, p. 254. A similar argument has been provided by Kraakman 1984, p. 866.

484 Kraakman 1984, p. 870.

485 Bishop 1964, p. 839; Kraakman 1984, p. 874.

486 Kraakman 1984, p. 868.

487 Compare to subsection 2.2.3.

488 Section 9.2 will develop these considerations and apply it to the D&O insurance market.

However, insurance of the judgement-proof firm for the risk to indemnify may be less intrusive than a prohibition of indemnification.[489] Insurance of a judgement-proof firm is only effective, when insurers are able to sufficiently monitor the judgement-proof firm.[490] The ability of the insurer to monitor will be discussed in section 5.6 and 5.9.

With regard to suits brought by voluntary creditors, an indemnification may increase the costs to attract debt capital. Consider for example that shareholders may have an interest to incentivize an elevated use of debt capital for risky projects and indemnify the manager for that reason.[491] When the creditor knows that indemnification is used to increase managerial risk taking to the creditor's detriment, he will increase the interest rate,[492] and the shareholder needs to off-set the rewards of indemnification against the increase of costs of debt capital.[493] In this regard, the effect of indemnification is already regulated due to the offsetting increased costs of debt capital.

However, when the creditor is ignorant about the indemnification, insurance of the indemnification risk and/or of external liability could function as a signal. This signal could be used by the creditor to correctly price the cost of debt capital. This consideration will be further examined in subsection 5.6.3.

5.5.2. *Limits to compensate internal liability*

Compensation may endanger the original goal of liability to guarantee corporate value.[494] As explained above, internal liability increases corporate value when either "*the prospect of the suit deters misconduct, ... or the suit ... yields a positive recovery net of all costs that the corporation must bear as a consequence of a suit.*"[495] The costs associated with an internal liability suit are (i) the litigation costs (time and money) and (ii) the compensation costs that firms face to induce managers to stay in office. The second kind of costs refer to the already mentioned insurance premiums, indemnification payments or salary raises.[496]

The claim may not deter misconduct for the following reason. As explained in subsection 5.4.4, the shareholder claims when the expected benefit of the claim is higher than the litigation costs of bringing a claim. When the prospect of filing does not relate to misconduct but to expected benefits, the claim is not always brought when misconduct occurs. A claim can only deter the manager when shareholders commit themselves *ex ante* to sue any-time that misconduct occurs. Without such commitment the deterrence

489 For background information, see: Oesterle 1983, p. 570; Shavell 2004, pp. 276, 278.

490 Compare to subsection 3.2.5.

491 The shareholders are able to benefit from the risky decision, if successful. Still the creditors bear the costs, if unsuccessful. See: Kraakman 2008, p. 144. MacMinn and Garven 2000, pp. 541–544. In their contribution, the considerations of risky investments to the cost of creditors were made to explain corporate insurance, not indemnification. Here, this rationale is applied to indemnification.

492 In this regard, the interest rate refers to the cost borne by the corporation to attract debt capital. See: Carney 1999, p. 67; Kraakman et al. 2009, p. 10.

493 An argumentation based on the illustrations of Marks 1999, p. 704; Kraakman et al. 2009, pp. 116–117 and MacMinn and Garven 2000, pp. 541–544.

494 Marks 1999, pp. 696, 698–709; Kraakman 2009, pp. 36, 39, 115; Lawless et al. 1997, p. 112.

495 Kraakman et al. 1993, p. 1736.

496 Kraakman et al. 1993, p. 1738.

function is mitigated.[497] The manager does not bear the costs of liability (he is compensated for it) and even if the claim is coincidentally brought when misconduct occurred, the manager does not link the claim to his misconduct. In this regard, the signalling effect proposed in section 2.4.3 is eliminated.[498] However, D&O insurance may be able to reawaken the lost signal, as will be proposed in the next section.

Further, the suit may not yield a positive recovery net of all costs. The reason is that any return of the claim is offset by an indemnification payment to the manager or higher D&O insurance premiums at a later stage.[499] Also the salary has already been negotiated when the shareholder decides to file a claim.[500]

Because of this issue, Kraakman et al. propose to award attorney fees only when the suit increased corporate value.[501] Regarding the deterrence function, they propose that the court awards attorney fees any time that the claim has a high likelihood of adequately deterring the manager. The likelihood is not determined mathematically but rather builds on the observations of the court.[502] The proposal eliminates the incentive to bring claims without merit and mitigates the use of insurance funds and forces claimant's attorneys to reject settlements. If the proposal does not yield the socially desirable risk taking, D&O insurance has to be limited or prohibited.[503] The authors suggest that a claim under this proposal leads to a partial payment by the D&O insurer but also affects the manager (by ways of dismissal or demotion).[504]

5.6. Corporate demand for D&O insurance

Usually demand for insurance is explained by risk aversion.[505] However, risk aversion does not explain why a risk neutral firm would desire insurance.[506] Being risk neutral, the firm can bear the risk itself.[507] Similarly Kraakman et al. argue that corporations cannot gain in any systematic sense when they recover costs from liability insurers. The insurance premium simply increases with an increased amount of internal liability

497 Kraakman et al. 1993, p. 1743.

498 Some argue that the shareholder can signal liability by holding the manager liable for the fact that the shareholders received less information than was available about corporate conduct. See: Lawless et al. 1997, pp. 210–212.

499 Kraakman et al. 1993, pp. 1736, 1741.

500 Kraakman et al. 1993, p. 1743.

501 Kraakman et al. 1993, pp. 1762–1766. They further suggest possibilities to calculate the increase of corporate value. For a more general discussion of the effect of fees, see: Harrington and Danzon 2000, p. 304.

502 Kraakman et al. 1993, p. 1763.

503 Kraakman et al. 1993, p. 1767.

504 Kraakman et al. 1993, p. 1768.

505 Shavell 2004, p. 261; Cooter and Ulen 2012, pp. 236–237; Schäfer and Müller-Langer 2009, p. 34.

506 Indeed, it could be argued that the firm is not risk neutral at all, but risk averse. See: Shavell 2004, p. 259; Wagner 2009, p. 379. If that is the case, the corporate demand for insurance can be simply explained by risk aversion. Insurance would be a tool to treat risk aversion of the corporation and/or the corporate shareholders. Because it treats risk aversion, D&O insurance may contribute to a better diversification of the shareholders' investment and more generally a more efficient securities market.

507 For differing opinions and more information, the reader is referred to Cabrillo and Depoorter 1999, pp. 261–264; for further reading, see: Warner 1977, pp. 337–338; MacMinn and Garven 2000, p. 542.

suits.[508] Yet, corporate D&O insurance can be explained by its additional beneficial effects on the liability system. The firm desires insurance when the insurer can substitute the shareholders for their monitoring role, outlined in subsection 5.6.1. Furthermore, the firm may desire insurance to mediate internal corporate conflicts, outlined in subsection 5.6.2. Subsection 5.6.3 will analyse in how far D&O insurance can function as a signal to voluntary creditors.

5.6.1. Shareholders' demand for insurance due to better monitoring

Section 5.3 explained that indemnification is more likely than insurance when it saves transaction costs and litigation costs. Yet, insurance may be desired when it is able to settle more cheaply.

In this context, it is probable that the well-diversified shareholders of the corporation refrain from actively engaging in settlements, because the use of financial markets (selling the corporate shares or diversifying the risk) is more cost effective. It is cheaper to diversify that firm specific risk and free-ride on the settlement endeavours of other involved parties (such as other shareholders, disinterested outside managers, gatekeepers etc.). However, when there is no-one that represents the corporation in settlements and the need to reduce litigation costs is essential, the assignment of a proxy, such as an insurer, to settle the claim may be an alternative.

More generally, Oesterle,[509] Mayers and Smith,[510] Holderness,[511] and Skogh[512] suggest that insurers may substitute the shareholder for its monitoring role. According to these scholars, the insurer is able to offer the same or better monitoring services than the shareholder to a lower cost.

According to Mayers and Smith, "*insurance firms develop a comparative advantage in processing claims because of scale economies [sic] and gains from specialization. ... [They] are low-cost suppliers of these services*" which they call real-service efficiencies.[513]

Specifically with respect to D&O insurance, Holderness hypothesizes three monitoring possibilities of the insurer. First, during the process of underwriting, the insurer observes the corporate features that are associated with a claim and classifies them. The insurer might suggest alterations to the corporate risk exposure or explicitly exclude particular events.[514]

In the second step, the insurer makes the policy subject to conditions. Actions that are likely to lead to opportunistic managerial behaviour, such as resistance to takeovers and targeted share repurchases are prohibited. Further, when a qualifying action of one of the managers was not properly reported by either of the managers, no manager will be

508 Kraakman et al. 1993, p. 1746; Paetzmann 2008, p. 188.

509 Oesterle 1983, p. 572.

510 Mayers and Smith 1982, p. 285.

511 Holderness 1990, pp. 115–116.

512 Skogh 1999, pp. 526, 527–529."*Purchases may be motivated by: low-cost claims administration services provided by insurers, assistance by insurers in assessing the value of safety and maintenance projects, improvements in the incentives to undertake investments in safety and maintenance projects [...].*"

513 Mayers and Smith 1990, p. 23. Also compare to: Harrington and Danzon 2000, p. 286.

514 Holderness 1990, pp. 118–119, citing Wyatt Company Survey, pp. 47–48.

insured. Moreover, the loss of insurance is a valuable signal to capital markets participants that corporate governance mechanisms in that specific corporation are inadequate.[515]

Thirdly, the insurer assumes an essential role during litigation. Holderness distinguishes between the aspect of investigating the truth and the communication to the victim. Regarding the first aspect, the insurer has an advantage over judicial, corporate or external investigations, because they can complement a timely, efficient, independent and harsh approach. Regarding the second aspect, the insurer develops an information advantage, which offers great resources for the lawyer to defend the corporation.[516]

5.6.2. *Insurance for the risk to indemnify a liable manager (mediation)*

Up to section 5.5, this chapter focussed on indemnification and insurance as alternatives and substitutes.[517] Further, it has been argued that compensation should be prohibited when the sanction insufficiently deters a firm's wrongdoings (often that is the case when the firm is judgement-proof).[518] Yet, there may be situations in which corporate insurance for the risk to indemnify the liable manager may be less intrusive than an outright prohibition. Furthermore, insurance for the risk to indemnify may enhance corporate value, when the insurer can signal the degree of managerial risk taking.[519]

Insurance would cover the indemnification payments any time a shareholder sues an indemnified manager. The economic desirability of such insurance has been questioned.[520] It has been argued that insurance for the risk to indemnify embodies a "*hidden ... farcical triangle*".[521] Shareholders do not benefit from indemnification insurance because (i) "*to the extent that insurers cannot anticipate firm-specific liability costs, some firms gain and others lose from insured recoveries*"[522] and (ii) "*when shareholders weigh insurance costs against expected recoveries ex ante, they will prefer to bar suits that cost the insurance pool more than they recover on behalf of individual corporations*".[523] The insurance premium simply increases with an increased amount of indemnification payments.[524]

Yet, besides treating risk aversion of non-diversified shareholders,[525] insurance of the risk to indemnify the liable manager may be beneficial because of three reasons.

515 Holderness 1990, pp. 119–120.
516 Holderness 1990, pp. 120–123.
517 Bishop 1966, p. 92; Polinsky and Shavell 1993, p. 254; Fischel and Bradley 1985, p. 283.
518 Cf.. Oesterle 1983, p. 570; Shavell 2004, pp. 276, 278.
519 To reiterate, it is essential to distinguish between two kinds of insurance. First, there is insurance that insures liability risks. Secondly, there is insurance as outlined in the previous paragraph that insures the risk to indemnify the liable manager. See: Bishop 1966, p. 110.
520 Bishop 1966, pp. 103, 107, 110; Oesterle 1983, pp. 571–573; Kraakman et al. 1993, p. 1746 and the footnotes 35 and 95.
521 Oesterle 1983, p. 571.
522 Kraakman et al. 1993, footnote 35.
523 Kraakman et al. 1993, footnote 95. This argumentation assumes a derivative suit.
524 Kraakman et al. 1993, p. 1746.
525 Bishop 1966, p. 110; Oesterle 1983, p. 572. The risk aversion of the victim is applied to the risk aversion of a non-diversified shareholder. See: Shavell 2004, pp. 264–265.

First, the insurer may be better able to mediate between the claimant (shareholder or victim) and the firm. In usual circumstances, the firm is controlled by the manager.[526] It may be unwise to let a manager mediate a conflict for which he allegedly is (partly) responsible. Even if indemnified, he probably remains defensive when dealing with such a claim. In this regard, the insurer could substitute the manager in his role to impartially represent the firm, when the manager has a conflict of interest.[527] The insurer may function as an arbiter between the claiming shareholder and the firm that effectively and swiftly handles conflicts.[528] Well-diversified shareholders may appreciate the insurer's ability to settle claims quickly and soothe conflicting shareholder interests.

Secondly, it has been argued that the signalling effect of a shareholder suit as proposed in section 2.4.3 is eliminated when the claims are not always brought whenever misconduct occurs.[529] *A contrario*, a claim could sufficiently signal misconduct when the claim is indeed always brought when misconduct occurs. It has been argued that a claim is brought when (i) the expected benefit is higher than (ii) the total litigation costs to bring a claim.[530] When indemnification is insured, the insurer may have the ability to mitigate litigation costs by his settling efforts (see point (ii)). The question remains whether the insurer incentivizes shareholders to only (and always) bring a claim when misconduct occurs (see point (i)). Here, one may think of a system where the insurer pays higher settlement amounts whenever the claim has a high likelihood of adequately deterring the manager. Similar to the reasoning of Kraakman et al.,[531] the likelihood would not be (entirely) determined mathematically but would rather build on the observations and case-by-case analysis of the insurer. Yet, a court and an insurer probably take into account entirely different factors when deciding whether and to what extent to compensate.[532]

Thirdly, the premium of that insurance might sufficiently signal insufficient corporate governance mechanisms.[533] In this case, the shareholder can simply avoid investing in corporations where internal conflicts are signalled by the insurance. This signalling effect is subject to three heavy qualifications, being (i) the policy takes into account differences between corporate governance mechanisms, (ii) the insurance policy is publicly available to function as a signal and (iii) the shareholder makes use of that signal.

526 Marks 1999, p. 694 and Posner 1974, p. 179.

527 A similar argument was made by Finch 1994, pp. 890–891. She argues that the insurance has an advantage over indemnification because the insurer is rather impartial (in comparison to the indemnifying corporation).

528 Shavell 2004, pp. 286–287. The reader is also referred to Schäfer and Müller-Langer 2009, pp. 35–36 on ambiguity.

529 Kraakman et al. 1993, p. 1743. For the origin of the signalling hypothesis, see Lawless et al. who argue that the shareholder can signal liability by holding the manager liable for the fact that the shareholders received less information than possible about corporate conduct. See: Lawless et al. 1997, pp. 210–212.

530 Bishop 1966, p. 94; Kraakman et al. 1993, p. 1741.

531 This argumentation has been inspired by the proposal provided by Kraakman et al. 1993, p. 1763.

532 Harrington and Danzon 2000, pp. 284–285; Bishop 1964, p. 843; Oesterle 1983, p. 581; Kraakman et al. 1994, p. 1769; Kuykendall 1998, p. 574.

533 A similar reasoning has been provided with respect to insuring the liability risk by Holderness 1990, pp. 119–120.

5.6.3. *D&O insurance as signal to voluntary creditors*

D&O insurance may strengthen the interests of voluntary creditors.

This chapter argued that, when the creditor is ignorant about the indemnification, insurance of the indemnification risk and/or of external liability may function as a signal.

This is the case when the liability insurer is able to differentiate between firms that bear a high risk (of external liability and/or of indemnification) and firms that do not.[534] The insurer could adapt its premium accordingly. A firm bearing a higher risk can only insure against a higher premium. When the creditor knows about the differences in policy prices (for instance because of the legal requirement to publish such information), the insurance policy may function as yet another signal for well-functioning firms. This signalling hypothesis is subject to three heavy qualifications, being (i) the insurer is able to differentiate risks, (ii) the insurance policy is known by the creditor to function as a signal and (iii) the creditor actually uses that information.

In this regard, the corporate insurance can provide a signal to the creditor about the firm's asset sufficiency and/or the firm's monitoring ability. The insurance policy could indicate how far the corporation assumes excessively risky projects and/or is undercapitalized. Such information is essential to the creditor to correctly price the debt capital.[535] Moreover, the insurer may be more solvent than a bankrupt firm to compensate a claim. Insurance guarantees the solvency of the debtor.[536]

5.7. Supply of insurance

Insurance is not the only possibility to deal with the D&O risk. As outlined in Chapter 3 and 4, risks can be shared in pools. Subsection 5.7.1 will outline why it is unlikely that the D&O risks bearers create a risk-sharing arrangement (or pool).

Furthermore, the previous sections have already explained how far the manager only desires partial coverage. When the risk that is to be insured is uncertain, the insurer tends to prefer partial coverage over full coverage, which will be explained in subsection 5.7.2.

5.7.1. *Supply by ways of insurance rather than pooling (risk sharing)*

As explained in section 3.2, the risk should be allocated to a risk neutral entity, such as an insurer or a risk sharing pool. One might expect a high amount of pools, where

534 In principle, the same argument should apply when managers directly insure their liability risk. However, as will be shown in later chapters, the D&O insurance is usually purchased by the firm. Furthermore, with respect to the costs of debt capital, the creditor is probably rather interested in the risk exposure of the firm (i.e. risk of default) than the risk exposure of the manager. In accordance with these considerations, subsection 5.6.3 focusses on the ability of insurers to differentiate between firms (instead of the insurer's efforts to categorize between managers).

535 MacMinn and Garven 2000, p. 543.

536 Bishop 1966, p. 110; MacMinn and Garven 2000, p. 543; Skogh 1999, p. 527.

managers share the managerial liability risk. However, there are two reasons why risk sharing is less likely.

First, it has been argued that a risk neutral corporation will compensate the manager for bearing the liability risk. In this regard, the risk is already allocated to an entity who can bear it. The manager does not have to bother to find others that are willing to share the risk with him.[537]

Secondly, the reason why this risk is insured rather than shared (by pooling or risk sharing) may relate to competition policy considerations.[538] When managers agree on a pooling of risk that in large part correlates with the risk of making business, it is difficult to clearly separate such a pooling agreement from cartel-like arrangements. Indeed, when managers collectively agree to share the risk of managerial liability, managers may collude to the detriment of their shareholders to shirk and steal from their corporations as a group. Having become risk neutral through pooling, managers may rather exploit their position. Moreover, the threat of being replaced by another manager is reduced, when managers know each other from risk sharing and collectively agreed to abuse their power for their own utility-maximizing purposes.

5.7.2. Excessive premiums and partial risk transfer

The D&O insurer may have trouble in calculating the D&O risk[539] and may become ambiguous about the risk. According to section 4.3.7, the effect of ambiguity aversion is even stronger on insurers than on individuals. When ambiguous, the insurer may ask for excessive premiums.[540] The requested premiums for insurance may be so loaded that the manager or shareholder is unwilling to pay the amount.[541] To limit the ambiguity, partial coverage of the insured D&O risk is proposed.[542] Partial coverage could rather facilitate the predictability of the risk as the maximum insurance amount would be restricted to the upper limit.

Partial coverage refers to deductibles, retentions, limits, and co-insurance.[543] To increase capacity, the insurer could turn to re-insurance, pooling, or financial markets. Section 5.10 will deal with partial coverage.

5.8. Measures to combat adverse selection

The insurer's instruments to distinguish risk classes are self-selection, experience rating, and risk categorization. Let us revisit these three methods in turn.

537 Indeed, it has been argued that risk neutral corporations ask for insurance because of additional benefits (monitoring and mediating). If these benefits could be offered for a cheaper price by a pool, risk sharing may be more likely than insurance.

538 For example, on competition policy considerations regarding environmental risks, see Faure and Hartlief 2001, pp. 74–76.

539 Kraakman et al. 1993, footnote 35.

540 Bishop 1966, pp. 110–111, 114.

541 Faure et al. 2013, pp. 166–168; Cooter and Ulen 2012, p. 237; Harrington and Danzon 2000, p. 292.

542 Bishop 1966, pp. 110–111.

543 Harrington and Danzon 2000, p. 285; Cooter and Ulen 2012, p. 238.

5.8.1. *Self-selection*

According to self-selection, the good risk will purchase partial coverage, whereas the bad risk obtains full coverage. The rationale to do so is the following. The good risk chooses to partially insure, because it is cheaper for him to only transfer part of the risk and to self-insure the remaining risk.[544] The bad risk bears a higher risk and thus faces a higher risk aversion. Because of the higher risk aversion, the bad risk desires full coverage more than the good risk.[545] For the risk averse manager or non-diversified risk averse shareholders self-selection is a practical tool.

For a risk neutral corporation, self-selection is less sensible at first sight because it does not desire a risk allocation. However, it could be argued that the more this group requires the additional benefits that the insurer offers (e.g. monitoring and mediating), the more insurance this group is willing to buy. If the insurer can predict what kind of corporation desires monitoring and/or mediation, the insurer could offer different policies (e.g. self-selection). In this regard, the insurer may offer one policy that excludes insurance for the liability risk (only insuring the risk to indemnify) and another policy that includes it. When a corporation purchases the first policy, the insurer would know from the purchase that the corporation wants the insurer to monitor the manager but cares less about mediation. As a consequence, the insurer can differentiate the risk classes between those that desire insurance for the indemnification risk and those that do not. The insurer could in turn price the premium according to the policy.

5.8.2. *Experience rating*

In experience rating, the insurer observes the actual frequency and severity of the claims after underwriting and adapts the policy accordingly.[546] Experience rating might be difficult for managerial liability, because managerial liability claims are characterized by timely and costly periods in court and out-of-court.[547] These features hamper the timely adaptation of the policy.[548] Furthermore, the D&O policy is re-negotiated often[549] and competitive.[550] To effectively rate on experience in a competitive market, the private information of the insurer should be protected.[551] It will be outlined in Chapter 8 whether

544 Dionne et al. 2000, p. 193; Ehrlich and Becker 1972, pp. 634–643; Loubergé 2000, p. 162.

545 Dionne et al. 2000, p. 193. A successful treatment of adverse selection by self-selection is subject to certain conditions, being (i) that the bad risk has a higher risk aversion than the good risk, (ii) that the insurer pursues a pure Cournot-Nash strategy and (iii) that there is a sufficient number of bad risks to find a market equilibrium. For more information, the reader is referred to Rothschild and Stiglitz 1976, pp. 633, 639–645.

546 Loubergé 2000, p. 16; Cooter and Ulen 2012, p. 238; Cooper and Hays 1987, pp. 211–213; Harrington and Danzon 2000, pp. 284–285.

547 Harrington and Danzon 2000, p. 285; Shavell 2004, pp. 280–282.

548 Fudenberg and Tirole 1990, p. 1279.

549 LaLone 2004, p. 2; Baker and Griffith 2007, 'The Missing Monitor', p. 1820.

550 For example, see Marsh 24-09-2013.

551 Dionne et al. 2000, p. 210–223.

the re-negotiations enable the insurer to rate the insured manager (and possibly the corporation) according to experience.

5.8.3. *Risk categorization*

In risk categorization, the insurer applies its knowledge on correlating factors to evaluate the liability risk. It might be difficult or impossible to observe the level of care of the manager. However, it may be simpler to observe the correlating factors of the underlying risks such as corporate performance and the risk of bankruptcy.[552]

A categorization of risk classes can be strengthened by an ongoing risk assessment[553] and a confidential settlement practice.[554] Ongoing declarations might also show a change of factors that correlate with the level of care.[555] To verify these declarations, the insurer might choose to audit the manager (and possibly the corporation).[556]

Regarding internal liability, outside signals that indicate power struggles, such as prior claims, take-over attempts, or the existence of a big majority shareholder that is non-diversified could be correlating factors.[557] Indicators to bankruptcy liability may be high debt/equity ratios and risky investment decisions. A scrutiny of the financial statements should reveal the factors. Chapter 7 will thoroughly discuss factors that correlate with the D&O insurance.

5.9. Moral hazard and imperfect control

Bishop 1966 argued that it is essential to preserve the deterrence effect of the liability rules once the manager is insured.[558] Moral hazard deals with the problem that the insured manager takes less care once being insured.[559] The insurer may also be confronted with the moral hazard of a claimant shareholder. The claimant shareholder may seek to recover a higher amount in settlement than the corporation paid as premium.[560]

To deal with moral hazard, the insurer can adapt the premium. When the penalty load of the premium is high enough, the insured individual is deterred from further increasing the risk.[561]

552 On the publishing requirements of corporations, see: Kraakman et al. 2009, p. 124. For more information, see: The International Financial Reporting Standards Foundation. The reader is also referred to section 6.2.

553 Bond and Crocker 1991, pp. 178, 179; Hoy 1982, p. 321; Dionne et al. 2000, pp. 233–234; Berliner 1985, p. 319; Wagner 2009, p. 387. A relationship between statistical variables and the insured risk has been suggested already by Akerlof 1970, pp. 492–495.

554 Townsend 1979, p. 266; Bond and Crocker 1997, p. 240.

555 Dionne et al. 2000, p. 199–202; Bond and Crocker 1991, p. 178.

556 Townsend 1979, pp. 265–268.

557 A similar reasoning is made by Oesterle 1983, p. 526.

558 Bishop 1966, p. 110.

559 Shavell 1979, p. 541.

560 Bishop 1966, pp. 103, 107, 110; Oesterle 1983, pp. 571–573; Kraakman et al. 1993, p. 1746 and the footnotes 35 and 95.

561 Oesterle 1983, p. 526; Shavell 2004, p. 262. With regards to the insurance for the risk to indemnify, see Kraakman et al. 1993, p. 1746.

In line with the reasoning of section 3.2.3,[562] the adaptation of the premium seems to be a proper measure to control the moral hazard of the manager, provided he pays for the insurance himself.

When the premium is borne by the corporation (which it often is), the manager or claiming shareholder would not be directly affected by an adaptation of the premium. It is questionable whether the corporation would pass on an increased premium to the manager (by way of a lower salary) or shareholder (by way of a lower dividend).[563]

In this regard, Bishop raised the question whether the manager should only be able to insure personally and insurance bought via the corporation should be prohibited.[564] Scholars have a similar sentiment with respect to insurance for the risk to indemnify.[565] However, a change in the scope of coverage and the extensive use of settlements may be more sensible and less intrusive to induce a change of managerial behaviour than an outright prohibition.[566] This consideration will return in the next section on partial coverage.

5.10. Partial coverage

When monitoring is impossible or too expensive, the insurer can limit its exposure to moral hazard by ways of partial coverage.[567] Partial coverage is an inferior measure to deal with moral hazard compared to monitoring.[568] However, partial coverage may indirectly affect risk taking. Let us first turn to the inferiority argument and secondly outline the controlling effects of partial coverage.

The impact of the monitoring and mediating efforts of the insurer is limited to the degree of risk assumption.[569] Probably, there is a breaking point at which the firm is unaffected by the monitoring efforts. When the insurer does not assume enough risk, the monitoring efforts by the insurer have no effect. If that breaking point is reached, monitoring by the insurer becomes effective.

The insurer may indirectly influence managerial risk taking by excluding particular actions from the coverage.[570] The prospect to further exclude activities can function as a deterrence against wrong declarations.[571] Secondly, partial coverage increases the importance of settlements. When the insurer has an information advantage, the manager (and possibly the corporation) first turns to the insurer for advice. Such advice is often the first step in settling the claim under conditions that are unilaterally imposed on the manager and victim by the insurer. The insurer's dominant role when settling could be

562 Shavell 2004, p. 262; Cooter and Ulen 2012, p. 237; Schäfer and Müller-Langer 2009, p. 33.
563 A similar reasoning has been provided by Bucy 1990, p. 342.
564 Bishop 1966, p. 112.
565 Bishop 1966, pp. 103, 107, 110; Oesterle 1983, pp. 571–573; Kraakman et al. 1993, p. 1746 and the footnotes 35 and 95.
566 Oesterle 1983, p. 526; Holderness 1990, pp. 118–123; cf. Bishop 1966, p. 113.
567 Bishop 1966, p. 98.
568 Shavell 1979, p. 553.
569 Shavell 1979, p. 553.
570 Holderness 1990, pp. 118–123.
571 Dionne et al. 2000, pp. 199–202.

used to incentivize and deter particular behaviour.[572] Thirdly, an adaptation of the coverage influences the manager more directly than a premium increase, when the corporation pays for the insurance.[573]

5.11. Insurance industry

Because the liability system is fairly complex, it is likely that independent agencies distribute insurance policies. Furthermore, insurance purchasers (i.e. firms) may rather trust independent agencies than insurers. The purchasers may fear that insurers take advantage of their superior information with respect to the scope of the insurance policies which are offered.[574] Chapter 8 will analyse how far cycles of the D&O insurance market are observable.[575] Regarding the premium's loading, the insurer is likely to ask an additional amount for costs that arise with respect to the settlement practice especially, a safety loading due to the risk's uncertainty,[576] and penalties as a response to adverse selection and moral hazard.[577] Furthermore, the premiums are likely to be higher in markets, in which the competition in the D&O insurance market is low. When competition among D&O insurers is high, the premium is likely to drop.[578]

5.12. Conclusion

Chapter 2 outlined the managerial liability risk in relation to internal liability, tort liability and bankruptcy liability. This chapter analysed to what extent these risks are allocated and what effect such an allocation would have. This chapter outlined (i) the relationship between the liability risk and managerial compensation, (ii) the limitations to managerial compensation, (iii) the corporate demand for D&O insurance and its effects, and (iv) the supply of D&O insurance. Let us consider these aspects in turn.

(i) For risk-averse managers a negligence rule is preferable to strict liability in terms of risk allocation. Under negligence liability the manager exercises due care and there is no risk of liability. The imposition of fines (or possibly imprisonment) boosts the incentive to take due care. With the absence of liability risk, compensating the manager is not required.

Yet, the level of care of the negligence rule may be uncertain. Managerial liability may undesirably deter the manager from taking beneficial but risky decisions, when the level of care is uncertain. The manager may be chilled to take risks. In this regard, the risk to

572 Holderness 1990, pp. 118–123.

573 In general, under negligence liability, the injurer only insures for the uncertainty and not for the entire liability risk. See section 3.2.4 and Shavell 2004, p. 265.

574 Regan and Tennyson 2000, pp. 718–722; Joskow 1973, p. 41.

575 Harrington and Niehaus 2000, pp. 657–659; Harrington and Danzon 2000, pp. 295–296.

576 Küpper-Dirks 2002, p. 74. More generally, on uncertainty, see: Faure et al. 2013, pp. 166–168; Harrington and Danzon 2000, p. 292; Faure 2004, pp. 474–475;.

577 Cooter and Ulen 2012, p. 240; Harrington and Danzon 2000, pp. 297–298. For more information, the reader is referred to subsections 4.4.5, 4.5.4 and 4.5.6.

578 Faure et al. 2013, pp. 166–168; Cooter and Ulen 2012, p. 237; Harrington and Danzon 2000, p. 292.

be held liable should be allocated to a more efficient risk bearer, such as the corporation or an insurer. An increased amount of ill-founded claims creates an additional layer of uncertainty, increasing the risk that the manager bears.

To avoid the liability, the manager and his corporation may negotiate his level of risk exposure as one of the terms of employment. The manager will seek compensation from the firm by (a combination of) an increased salary, indemnification or insurance. Except for bankruptcy liability, the manager would desire to be indemnified.

Indemnification is offered because of the following reasons. A firm, when risk neutral has a comparative advantage to bear risk over a risk-averse manager. Because of the differences in risk attitude, it is cheaper for a firm to indemnify the manager than to raise his salary. Secondly, managerial risk-taking can be incentivized by indemnifying him. Thirdly, indemnification can simplify the relationship between the shareholders and the manager and in this sense decrease agency costs. Indemnification is more likely than insurance when indemnification saves transaction costs (finding and negotiating the insurance policy) and litigation costs (simplified settlements).

(ii) However, compensation for the uncertainty risk is subject to certain limitations.

With respect to external liability, the manager may be compensated provided that the sum of managerial liability and firm liability equals the harm. Indemnification should be prohibited, when the expected loss that would have been borne by the manager is externalized through indemnification to a judgement-proof firm. Being judgement-proof, the firm's incentives to take care are limited to the expected loss of its assets. Any remaining damage is ignored by the firm. However, when insurers are able to sufficiently monitor the judgement-proof firm, insurance for the risk to indemnify may be less intrusive than a prohibition of indemnification.

With regards to suits brought by voluntary creditors, the possibly detrimental effect of indemnification should already be regulated due to offsetting the increased costs of debt capital. However, when the creditor is ignorant about the effect of indemnification, the price of debt capital may be incorrect. Insurance may signal the effects of indemnification to the creditor who is in turn able to price debt capital correctly.

When the prospect of filing correlates to the shareholder's or victim's expected benefit and the expected benefit does not always correlate to the actual occurrence of managerial misconduct, the claim is not always brought when misconduct occurs. It has been argued that a claim can only deter the manager when shareholders commit themselves *ex ante* to sue whenever that misconduct occurs. Without such commitment the deterrence function is mitigated. The manager does not bear the costs of liability (he is compensated for it) and even if the claim is coincidentally brought when misconduct occurred, the manager does not link the claim to his misconduct. In this regard, the signalling effect proposed in subsection 2.4.3 (e.g. filing a claim to induce the manager to disclose corporate specific information) is eliminated. However, D&O insurance may be able to re-awaken the lost signal.

(iii) According to classic insurance theory, a risk neutral entity does not desire insurance. A risk neutral corporation may desire insurance, nonetheless, for the insurer's ability

(i) to monitor the managers (when insuring the liability risk) and (ii) to mediate internal corporate conflicts (when insuring the indemnification risk).

Regarding monitoring, the insurer may (i) suggest alterations to managerial risk taking or explicitly exclude particular events, (ii) make the policy subject to conditions and (iii) assume an essential role during litigation (complementing a timely, efficient, independent and harsh approach while building on private knowledge). The loss of insurance may be a valuable signal to capital markets participants that corporate governance mechanisms in that specific corporation are inadequate.

Insurance for the indemnification risk raised suspicion. Yet, besides treating any risk aversion of non-diversified shareholders, the insurance could be socially desirable because of three reasons. First, the insurer may substitute the manager, who is exposed to a conflict of interests, in his role to represent the firm impartially. Secondly, the insurer may have the ability to mitigate litigation costs by its settling efforts and could adequately deter the manager by paying higher settlements whenever the claim has a high deterrence effect on the manager (building on case-by-case analysis of the insurer). Thirdly, the premium of that insurance may signal internal conflicts that give rise to high indemnification payments.

Under restricted conditions, corporate insurance can provide a signal to the voluntary creditor about the firm's asset sufficiency and/or monitoring ability.

Chapter 6 will analyse the managerial liability rules in the USA, the UK, the Netherlands and Germany, to reveal to what extent the rules are uncertain. Chapter 7 will review empirical evidence to discover to what extent the hypotheses of demand, as outlined, are observable in practice.

(iv) The risk is probably insured rather than shared by risk-sharing agreements due to competition policy concerns. When the liability rules are complex, independent distribution agencies probably exist to mediate between demand and supply. Partial coverage should precede full coverage, when the level of care is uncertain. To combat adverse selection of the D&O risk, the insurer would offer different policies (self-selection) and screen the potential manager and the corporation (risk categorization). The policy would continuously be adapted according to the insurance history (experience rating). The insurer may be exposed to moral hazard when the adaptation of the premium is not big enough to communicate inefficient risk taking. Still, the adaptation of the coverage may be a sufficient signal. According to Holderness 1990, regular risk differentiation before and during the period of insurance and the insurer's ability to influence the compensation payment in settlement, contribute to a mitigation of moral hazard.

Chapters 7 and 8 will further look at the insurer's ability to observe and control the manager (and possibly the corporation). Chapter 9 will deal with deviations between the hypotheses of this chapter and D&O insurance practice.

Chapter 6

NATIONAL MANAGERIAL LIABILITY RULES

6.1. Introduction

The preceding four chapters provided a theoretical foundation about the effect of D&O insurance on managerial risk taking. Chapter 2 outlined the scope of managerial liability. Chapters 3 and 4 explained the major issues of insurance. Chapter 5 hypothesized how the D&O insurance would be structured in theory. The following chapters are intended to present evidence that suggests as to what extent D&O insurance influences managerial risk taking.

This chapter will outline the extent to which the national liability rules in the EU and the USA create liability risk and to what extent corporations are able to compensate the manager for bearing that risk in the form of indemnification.

The USA represents a good start to discuss the liability risk, because the first profitable D&O insurance was developed there.[579] According to various authors, the US D&O insurance system works inefficiently.[580] The following chapters will seek to illustrate the status of D&O insurance in the EU.

However, the EU's legal system of managerial liability is very fragmented. Due to the fragmentation, a universal analysis of the D&O insurance in the EU is impossible.[581] To circumvent this issue, this thesis will outline the status of three EU Member States. The three Member States are chosen due to their relative differences regarding the purpose of managerial liability and the scope of the D&O coverage in these countries. These countries are the United Kingdom, the Netherlands, and Germany.

To structure this chapter, section 6.2 will set managerial liability in the context of national views on corporate governance and stakeholder protection. Section 6.3 will identify the liability rules of the systems and outline procedural requirements to bring a liability action. Section 6.4 will analyse the standard of care of these rules. Section 6.5 will discuss to what extent these rules create risk and how far the manager may be averse to that risk.

579 Plück and Lattwein 2004, pp. 187–189.

580 Baker and Griffith 2007, 'Predicting Corporate Governance Risk', pp. 487–490; Baker and Griffith 2007, 'The Missing Monitor', pp. 1795–1801; Baker and Griffith 2009, 'How the Merits matter', pp. 755–763.

581 Gerner-Beuerle et al. 2013, p. viii.

It has been suggested in subsection 5.3 that the corporation could indemnify the manager for the liability risk. Section 6.5 will outline the legal limitations in the countries with respect to corporate indemnification. Section 6.6 will outline how far the manager and/or corporation desires insurance due to the regulation of indemnification.

Consequently, Chapter 7 will provide empirical evidence to check the validity of the hypotheses of Chapter 5. Chapter 8 will explain how far responses to uncertainty, adverse selection, or moral hazard can be identified in the policy. Chapter 9 will point to unresolved problems of the D&O insurance market, answer the research question on how far D&O insurance affects managerial risk-taking, and point to solutions.

6.2. Managerial liability in a legal context

This section will briefly sketch the purpose that liability rules are supposed to fulfil in the four legal systems. This section will outline the respective national approaches to corporate governance (subsection 6.2.1), the role of the manager (subsection 6.2.2), the external relationships of the manager (subsection 6.2.3), and the protected interests in bankruptcy (subsection 6.2.4). Subsection 6.2.5. will introduce some statistics on the topic of managerial liability.

6.2.1. Corporate governance

As explained in section 2.4.2, internal corporate governance entails the appointment right of the manager, constraint measures and reward strategies. Unlike the hypotheses of section 2.4.2, these tools are, in some legal systems, not exercised by the corporate shareholders, but by a separate corporate supervisory entity, represented by non-executive members.[582]

Each legal system incorporates that supervisory entity by either applying a one-tier or a two-tier board structure. Executive members are responsible for the daily business and assume the management. Non-executive members supervise whether the executives act in the interest of the corporation.[583] The distinction can be of interest because of two concerns.

First, the make-up of the board structure has enormous influence on the understanding of which person is responsible for what. This allocation of responsibility is legally set in stone under the two-tier structure.[584]

Secondly, if managerial liability claims can only be brought by the corporation (read: by non-executive board members), the formal distinction of the two-tier board structure increases the effectiveness of managerial liability.[585]

582 Kraakman et al. 2009, pp. 56–58; Marks 1999, pp. 705–707.
583 Gerner-Beuerle et al. 2013, p. viii; Cahn and Donald 2010, pp. 300–302.
584 Gerner-Beuerle et al. 2013, p. viii; Kraakman et al. 2009, pp. 56–58.
585 Gerner-Beuerle et al. 2013, p. viii; Kraakman et al. 2009, pp. 56–58.

Delaware (the most prominent Corporation State Law of the USA) and the UK have a one-tier board structure. Germany adopted the two-tier board structure approach. In the Netherlands, both structures are possible.[586]

In Delaware, any shareholder may bring an internal liability claim against the manager. In Germany and the UK, managerial liability is subject to the condition that the shareholders who sue have to represent a certain amount of shares. In the Netherlands, the manager can only be held liable by the corporation, which is usually represented by the executive board or, under exceptional circumstances, by the supervisory board. These considerations are further outlined in the next section.[587]

6.2.2. *The role of the manager*

The actions of the manager reflect the interests of the corporation. The interests of the corporation are not commonly defined. Whereas some legal systems regard the corporate interest as equal to the shareholder's interest (shareholder model), other systems incorporate additional interests (stakeholder model), such as the interests of employees and the interest of corporate continuity. In the EU, the countries adhering to a stakeholder model require the corporations to involve employees in the decision-making process.[588]

Kraakman suggests that the UK, fundamentally, and the US, to a lesser extent, adhere to the shareholder model. Germany and the Netherlands rather adhere to the stakeholder model. Especially in Germany, the employees' interests are protected because employee representatives have a voice in the corporate decision-making process.[589] Thus, one might observe more rules protecting interests other than the shareholder's interests in the Netherlands and Germany. This consideration will be further outlined in the next section.

6.2.3. *External relationship*

Under the external relationship, section 2.3 introduced the dilemma of the manager that is torn between the interests of the shareholders and the interests of the creditors. Kraakman et al. states that "*the more successful the various strategies ... in aligning managers' interests with shareholders', the stronger will be the managers' incentives to act in a way that may benefit shareholders to creditors' expense.*"[590] The term creditor refers to voluntary creditors, involuntary creditors, and the state.

To ensure that voluntary creditors are able to determine the interest rate to the cost of capital correctly, most legal systems ask for publication of corporate financials. All

586 Cahn and Donald 2010, pp. 300–302; Kraakman et al. 2009, pp. 56–58. For the Netherlands, see Article 2:129a BW regarding the NV and Article 2:239a BW regarding the BV.

587 Gerner-Beuerle et al. 2013, p. viii.

588 Gerner-Beuerle et al. 2013, p. viii; Cahn and Donald 2010, pp. 300–302; Kraakman et al. 2009, pp. 56–58. According to Gerner-Beuerle et al. 2013, p. viii, the often-applied division between common law and civil law countries is not that crystallized with regards to managerial liability.

589 Gerner-Beuerle et al. 2013, p. viii; Cahn and Donald 2010, pp. 300–302; Kraakman et al. 2009, p. 56–58.

590 Kraakman et al. 2009, p. 118.

observed countries require 'public corporations' to disclose financials. 'Private corporations' in the USA are only partially required to publish financials. In the other observed countries, private corporations are also required to publish financial data. Furthermore, the EU countries ensure the correctness of the financials by the possibility of holding the auditor liable.[591]

To hold the corporation accountable for the damages which occur, the corporation is usually vicariously liable, based on tort law, for these accidents. When the corporation is solvent, the manager is usually, notwithstanding some very narrow rules in Germany and in the Netherlands,[592] not held directly liable. Consequently, the liable corporation can discipline the relevant manager.[593]

The state might regard some corporate actions to be enormously conflicting to society as a whole. As a result, some countries, such as Germany introduce criminal law rules against the corporation or leading corporate personnel.[594] Furthermore, Germany and the Netherlands protect the payment of particular taxes or social security contributions by holding the manager liable.[595] The next section will further outline the rules.

6.2.4. *Protected interests in bankruptcy*

When insolvency threatens, the manager might pay too much attention to the exploiting interests of the shareholders. Furthermore, managers that fear unemployment might take desperate measures to avoid bankruptcy. Bankruptcy liability could deter the manager from these actions.[596]

The scope of managerial liability has to be determined carefully to avoid managerial over-deterrence. The countries adhere to different approaches to managerial liability. First, the standard of care may have a differing degree of leniency. Secondly, the liability rule may only be used when the corporate debt/assets ratio is sufficiently low or a managerial decision has a high potential impact on this ratio. Thirdly, the rule may only be used by a particular individual, such as the bankruptcy administrator.[597]

The degree of leniency relates to the state's opinion on an efficient scope of the standard of care. The debt/asset standard will guarantee that the manager knows, when exactly there is a shift of the managerial duty from the shareholders toward the creditors. The administrator requirement guarantees a solution to the general free riding and collective action problem of the group of creditors toward an insolvent corporation.

591 Kraakman et al. 2009, pp. 11–12, 123–129. Public corporations are corporations that have freely transferable shares. Freely transferable shares permit the firm to remain in business when the identity of the owners changes. This characteristic maximizes the liquidity of shareholdings and enables the shareholders to diversify their share portfolio. In private corporations the transferability of shares is restricted.

592 Regarding Germany, see Thümmel 1998, pp. 137–140. Regarding the Netherlands, see Van Schilfgaarde 2006, pp. 156–158.

593 Kraakman 2008, p. 136.

594 Thümmel 1998, pp. 133–136; Gietl 2010, p. 1005.

595 Regarding Germany, see Thümmel 1998, pp. 133–136. Regarding the Netherlands, see Van Schilfgaarde 2006, pp. 154–156.

596 Carney 1999, p. 684; Kraakman 2008, pp. 137, 147.

597 Kraakman et al. 2009, pp. 82–87; Gerner-Beuerle et al. 2013, pp. xvii, 240.

Individual creditors might attempt to recover most assets from the insolvent corporation to the detriment of the remaining creditors (free riding). Furthermore, a creditor may dislike bearing the costs to hold the manager liable to the benefit of all (collective action).[598]

Whereas the US and the UK have a lenient approach to bankruptcy liability, Germany introduces strict standards, also incorporated in criminal law. The Netherlands adheres to a more balanced approach between the two extremes. These differences might also be explained by the different manners of corporate capitalization. Whereas the corporations in the US and the UK are mostly funded by equity capital, German corporations assume a great deal of debt capital.[599]

The degree of leniency will be discussed in section 6.4 on the scope of managerial liability. The debt/asset standard and the administrator requirement will be discussed in the next section 6.3.

6.2.5. Statistics of liability

To provide a general view on managerial liability, this section will outline some statistics on managerial liability of the USA, the UK, the Netherlands, and Germany.

USA – Most actions in the US against the director are lodged on the basis of securities law. On average, 212 securities law claims arise per year. For smaller firms, most claims are based on employment related issues, which are usually not within the scope of D&O insurance policies.[600] In *Morrison et al v National Australia Bank Ltd et al*, the Supreme Court held that a legal action can only be brought by investors that traded in the territory of the USA. Extraterritorial financial deals, even if having a domestic impact, do not qualify for a suit.[601]

Some studies suggest that the risk to be sued via a securities law claim is 2% for an average public corporation in the USA in any given year, with an average settlement amount of $24 million in 2005. The median settlement amount between 1993 and 2003 fluctuated between $4 and $6 million.[602]

The UK – Claims are virtually always settled. 32% of the claims arise from employees and 21% of the claims originate from the shareholders and the competitors. The claims are filed on the basis of wrongful termination of employment, domestic market activities, discrimination, dishonesty/fraud, and financial reporting.[603]

598 Kraakman et al. 2009, pp. 82–87; Gerner-Beuerle et al. 2013, pp. xvii, 240.

599 Kraakman et al. 2009, pp. 82–87.

600 Baker and Griffith 2010, pp. 22–23; Cornerstone Research 2013, p. 4; Foster et al. 2007, pp. 2–4; Racioppo 2013, pp. 16–18.

601 Bradford and Bole 2013, p. 5.

602 Baker and Griffith 2007, 'Predicting Corporate Governance Risk', p. 498; Baker and Griffith 2007, 'The Missing Monitor', p. 1801; Foster et al. 2007, pp. 2–4; Racioppo 2013, p. 16–18.

603 Finch 1994, pp. 897–905; Baxter 1995, p. 546–556.

The Netherlands – The court admitted a liability claim, in which the liable parties and most of the claimants were not Dutch. This claim was previously denied by a US-American Court.[604] The number of Dutch claims against the manager seems to be on the rise.[605]

A major amount of claims derive from a widened scope of bankruptcy liability and an increase of the amount of insolvencies due to the financial crises. More important for the claimant than the success of the claims seems to be the signalling function of liability suits. The manager seeks to prevent liability because he fears reputation costs. In the end, 80% of the claims are not successful. Of the successful claims, 70% are settled. The amount of claims covered by the insurer increased by 30% in 2009 in relation to 2008. Three-quarters of these claims are bankruptcy liability claims, whereas the majority of claims that are finally admitted to the court are internal liability suits. According to Weterings, bankruptcy administrators are more likely to hold the manager liable, when they know that the managers are insured for liability.[606]

Germany – In 2004, 10% of the covered liability claims equalled an amount of damages of more than EUR 2 billion.[607] Two thirds of the claims are brought by the corporate supervisory board.[608]

Since 2000, the amount of claims has increased dramatically. The reason for the dramatic increase is threefold. First, in the past, it was difficult for the shareholder to represent enough equity in the firm to bring a claim (10% requirement in the public corporation (*Aktiengesellschaft*, AG) and majority requirement in the private corporations (*Gesellschaft mit beschränkter Haftung*, GmbH). Now the AG requirement is 1%. Secondly, shareholders apparently thought that it was inappropriate to hold their own manager liable. In the last years, the claim culture changed.[609] Thirdly, legal changes in 1995, corresponding to the second *Finanzmarktförderungsgesetz* (roughly translated: Law to the Development of the Financial Market), and the fall of corporate empires invoked a feeling of managerial blameworthiness,[610] and nurtured claims, mostly against big multinationals.[611]

6.3. Managerial liability

The previous section showed that the national view on managerial liability rules originates from more general views on the function that corporations are supposed to

604 Sullivan and Durrant 2013, p. 628; Bradford and Bole 2013, p. 5; Court of Appeal Amsterdam NJ 2012/355.

605 Walters and Verhille 2009, p. 14; Wijnhoven 2009, p. 28. However, the Advison report by Bradford and Bole 2013 (p. 5) does not observe an increased claiming in the Netherlands.

606 Weterings 2010, pp. 163, 169–170.

607 Thümmel 1998, pp. 165, 161–165; Hendricks 2004, pp. 9–11.

608 Bradford and Bole 2013, p. 5.

609 Thümmel 1998, pp. 161–165.

610 For more information, see Gesetz zur Kontrolle und Transparenz im Unternehmensbereich (roughly translated: Law for the Control and Transparency of Enterprises) and the corporate voluntary implementation of the Deutsche Corporate Governance Kodex (German Corporate Governance Code). Also see: Thümmel 1998, pp. 161–165; Werder and Bartz 2013, pp. 885–886.

611 Thümmel 1998, pp. 161–165, citing: BGH DB 1997, 1068.

fulfil in society. This section will identify the different rules in the legal systems. Furthermore, attention is paid to the parties that may bring a suit and under which procedural circumstances the suit is admissible. To do so, it will define the term 'manager' (subsection 6.3.1), distinguish between internal claims (subsection 6.3.2), external claims (subsection 6.3.3), claims in bankruptcy (subsection 6.3.4), and claims pursuant to public law (subsection 6.3.5).

Section 6.4 will outline the precise standard of care of each liability rule that has been identified in this section.

6.3.1. The manager

The term of manager as used does not have a universal definition. To make comparison possible, this section will outline the scope of the term manager in the USA, the UK, the Netherlands and Germany.

The USA – The US-American Corporation Law is enforced at the state level and not at the federal level. The most prominent Corporation State Law of the USA is the law of Delaware. Most US-American corporations are established in Delaware, even though they might have their business elsewhere. The corporation is managed by or under the direction of a board of directors.[612] Principally, managerial liability suits seek to hold the director liable.[613]

The UK – A private company limited by shares and a public company are co-ordinated by the managing director.[614] Next to the *de jure* managing director, there are *de facto* directors and shadow directors. *De facto* directors are in control of the company's affairs without properly being appointed to office. Any management resolution of the *de facto* director has to be approved by the general meeting of shareholders.[615] Possibilities to hold the *de facto* director liable are wider than for the *de jure* director, when it appears that the *de facto* director's resolution has not been approved.[616] Shadow directors are individuals that give 'directions or instructions' to the managing director, which the individual is 'accustomed to follow'.[617] Shadow directors need to adhere to the same duties and rules as managing directors.[618]

The Netherlands – Pursuant to the Dutch Civil Code (*Burgelijk Wetboek*, BW), the executive board is charged to manage the corporation.[619] The executive board does not

612 Cahn and Donald 2010, p. 17. Delaware Corporate Law, Title 8, Chapter 1, Subchapter IV, §141.
613 Baker and Griffith 2010, pp. 24–25.
614 Cahn and Donald 2010, p. 134; Brough 2005, p. 63.
615 Plant and Prior 2000, p. 304.
616 Plant and Prior 2000, p. 304.
617 Cahn and Donald 2010, pp. 341–342.
618 Cahn and Donald 2010, pp. 341–342.
619 Van Schilfgaarde 2006, pp. 1–7, 37, 55–59; Artt. 2:129, 2:239 BW. A Dutch corporation (vennootschap) that has legal personality and limited liability, is either the *besloten vennootschap* met beperkte aansprakelijkheid (BV) or the *naamloze vennootschap* (NV).

only render day-to-day business decisions, but also determines long-term goals and the strategy to be followed. The executive board has board members (*bestuurders*). Besides a board member, an informal manager (*feitelijk bestuurder*) is any person next to the board member that solely or with others determines the management of the corporation, as if he/she was a board member.[620]

Germany – The representation and management of the GmbH and AG is exercised by the manager (*Geschäftsführer*) or executive board (*Vorstand*) respectively.[621] An informal manager is any person that factually and substantially manages the firm as if he were a formal manager. The informal manager does not have to substitute the formal manager to qualify as an informal manager.[622]

6.3.2. *Internal liability*

This section will look at the parties that may bring a internal liability suit and under which procedural circumstances the internal liability suit is admissible.

USA – Under Corporation State Law, a shareholder can sue the manager for a breach of duty either pursuant to a derivative or a direct action. Under a derivative action, the shareholder makes a claim on behalf of the corporation. To be admissible, the claim has to be verified by the board of directors. The board can also refuse the claim, except in cases that the shareholder proves a wrongful refusal, such as in a situation of a conflict of interests. In a direct action, the shareholder sues on his own behalf. In 2000, 80% of the claims based on an alleged infringements of the duties, were direct shareholder class actions. One shareholder is sufficient to bring the claim. Class actions are admissible.[623]

A shareholder can also sue the manager pursuant to the Securities Exchange Act 1995, which is federal law. Any investor may bring a claim in case managerial public statements are regarded as false or misleading *ex post*.[624]

General EU view – Regarding the shareholder's ability to bring a claim, many legal systems have the condition that a certain amount of shareholders have to vote in favour of a liability claim, in order to be admissible. In a model of dispersed ownership, dispersed owners will find it difficult to restrain the management by ways of a liability claim. Furthermore in a situation of controlling v. minority shareholders, minority shareholders will have problems to enforce their interests. Moreover, some countries "*require the shareholder to advance the costs of the proceedings and impose the litigation risk on them*

620 For the purpose of liability, see Van Schilfgaarde 2006, pp. 153–154, 157–158; HR NJ 1998, 269 and the Note of J.M.M. Maeijer to court case HR NJ 1998, 170.

621 §6, §35(1) GmbHG; §76, §78 *Aktiengesetz* (AktG). A German corporation (Gesellschaft) that has legal personality and limited liability, is either the Gesellschaft mit beschränkter Haftung (GmbH), the Aktiengesellschaft (AG), or the Unternehmensgesellschaft (UG). See: Hemmer and Wüst 2012, pp. 158–168. A popular alternative to mitigate the power of capital owners is the GmbH & Co. KG.

622 Gietl 2010, p. 972.

623 Baker and Griffith 2009, pp. 27–30.

624 Baker and Griffith 2009, p. 45.

[which] aggravates the collective action problem."[625] Under these systems, shareholders are deterred from bringing an action. The EU study on Directors' Duties and Liabilities 2013 states that of the three EU countries observed, the Netherlands deters shareholders the most to bring an internal liability action, followed by Germany and the UK.[626]

The UK – To bring an internal claim, the shareholder can either bring a direct action or a derivative claim. Under a direct action, the shareholder has to show personal interest. Personal interest is regarded as an interest that is distinct from the general shareholder's interest to recover a loss of investment. Instead, the shareholder must show that a personal duty is owed to him and that this duty is breached, which led to a personal loss, irrespective of the loss to the shareholders as a class.[627]

Under a derivative action, the shareholders as a group sue the management on behalf of the corporation for a breach of duties. Under previous legal requirements, only the majority of shareholders could bring such a claim. With the change of the Companies Act 2006, any shareholder may bring a claim. The court reviews the claim and has discretionary power to allow it or not.[628] According to the EU study on Directors' Duties and Liabilities 2013, "*the court will consider many factors, including the costs of litigation, the time involved and the impact on the relationship between the shareholders, company, and directors. In addition, courts will consider whether the [managerial] act was authorised or ratified, or is likely to be authorised or ratified.*"[629]

The Netherlands – Internal liability (*interne bestuurdersaansprakelijkheid*) is based on the principle of accountability of the manager that is owed to the general meeting of shareholders, the supervisory board, and the works council. The liability rule will be brought by the corporation. The corporation is represented by the executive board. When the board cannot represent the corporation because of a conflict of interest, Art. 2:9 BW is to be read in conjunction with 2:129(6) BW or 2:238(6) BW, which means that the supervisory board, instead of the board, represents the corporation to file the claim.[630]

Internal liability can be invoked by a minority shareholder, but such a claim is subject to very strict conditions.[631]

The minority shareholder can also start an *enquête* procedure.[632] In such a procedure, a specialized court (*ondernemingskamer*) scrutinizes the dealing of the corporation.

625 Gerner-Beuerle et al. 2013, p. xvii.

626 Gerner-Beuerle et al. 2013, p. 202. Please note that this study does not thoroughly discuss the legal context of private corporations. Instead, it focuses on public corporations. Estonia and Luxembourg are at the same level as the Netherlands according to this study.

627 Gerner-Beuerle et al. 2013, p. A 887, citing: Johnson v. Gore Wood and Co. 2002.

628 Cahn and Donald 2010, pp. 601–603, 607–608; Sec. 260(3) CA 2006; Sec. 263(2) CA 2006; Foss v. Harbottle (1843).

629 Gerner-Beuerle et al. 2013, p. A 889.

630 If the corporation does not have a supervisory board, the general meeting of shareholders resolves the resolution, unless the articles of association provide otherwise. See: Art. 2:129(6) or 2:239(6) BW.

631 Supreme Court (Hoge Raad, HR) NJ 2006, 659.

632 To be admitted, the minority shareholder has to represent 10% of the outstanding shares or 250.000 EUR of the share's nominal value. See: Gerner-Beuerle et al. 2013, p. 199.

Among other aspects, the court analyses in how far the manager and shareholders adhered to their duties toward their corporation. The specialized court does not have the ability to hold the manager liable, but its wide powers to audit the corporation might lead to incriminating information against the manager. This information might at a later stage be used to hold the manager liable.[633]

Germany – The procedural requirements to hold the manager liable differ between the GmbH and the AG. Regarding the GmbH, to hold the manager liable, a resolution of the management, a resolution of the general meeting of shareholders or a resolution of the supervisory board have to be rendered to this effect. A resolution of the general meeting of shareholders is based on a relative majority.[634]

Regarding the AG, the same organs can bring a claim. Furthermore, a shareholder that has more than 1% of the outstanding shares or more than 100.000 EUR represented by the nominal share value of the shares he holds, may bring a claim.[635] To admit the claim of such a shareholder, the court also considers the general interest of the corporation and has to judge whether the claim would harm the corporate interests. If the claim would harm the corporate interest, the court has to deny the claim.[636]

Comparison – Due to the possibility of direct actions or security actions, it is fairly simple for a shareholder to sue under Delaware law or US law. The situation is more difficult in Germany and the UK. Next to a condition that the shareholder holds a certain amount of shares, the court is able to deny the claim, in order to protect the interest of the firm. It is most difficult to bring a claim in the Netherlands.

In Germany and the Netherlands, the supervisory board has far reaching powers to hold the manager liable.

6.3.3. *Managerial tort liability*

Tort liability entails a managerial standard of care to protect victims. Whereas vicarious liability of the corporation is the default rule, the scope of tort liability is limited.[637] The legal rules of the countries will be outlined below.

The USA – Creditors do not have a claim against the manager. There is no personal managerial duty owed to them.[638]

633 Van Schilfgaarde 2006, pp. 332–336; Art. 2:355 BW.

634 Thümmel 1998, pp. 137–140.

635 Gerner-Beuerle et al. 2013, p. 194; §148 AktG.

636 In this regard, the corporate interest reflects the interests of all stakeholders and not just the interests of the manager or the shareholders. See: Gerner-Beuerle et al. 2013, p. 202.

637 See subsection 2.2.5 and Shavell 2004, p. 232; Kraakman 2008, pp. 134–136, 144; Stone 1980, p. 17.

638 Rao et al. 1997, p. 64. Rao et al. 1997 further states at p. 55, footnote 3: "*Statutes in more than 28 states permit directors to take into account the interests of constituencies other than shareholders in discharging their duties. However, they have been widely criticized as encroaching upon the directors' fiduciary duty to the shareholders and the shareholder wealth-maximization objective.*".

The UK – External duties of managers are virtually non-existent provided that the corporation is solvent. In a situation of doubtful corporate solvency, the manager is bound to act in the interest of the firm taking into account the interests of creditors.[639] It has been suggested that it is not easy to bring an action on this basis.[640]

The Netherlands – Generally, voluntary or non-voluntary creditors may lodge a claim against the corporation of the manager.[641] As a second step, the corporation has the right of recourse to the manager.[642]

However, according to the case *Oosterhof*, *Ontvanger/Roelofsen* and *Tulip Air* before the Supreme Court (Hoge Raad, HR), a voluntary (and probably also an involuntary) creditor may hold the manager liable provided that he fulfils a set of very strict conditions, outlined in the next section.[643]

Germany – As a general rule, external liability by the creditor cannot be invoked directly against the director. The corporation compensates the victim for any wrongdoing by its employees, such as the director, according to §31 German Civil Code (*Bürgerliches Gesetzbuch*, BGB).[644] The corporation has the general right of recourse, when managerial misbehaviour that gave rise to the external liability claim also breached the duty of care or the duty of loyalty. In this regard, rules on indemnification are essential.[645]

There are exceptions to the general rule. One is called *Durchgriffshaftung*, based on §242 BGB, and is similar to a hole pierced in the corporate veil. Because such action holds the shareholders liable, further discussion is rendered meaningless. Another exception, only applicable for the AG, is the *Verfolgungsrecht*, according to §93(5) Public Corporation Statute (*Aktiengesetz*, AktG). Under limited conditions, the creditor can directly sue the manager for a failure of the corporation to perform a corporate obligation.[646]

Comparison – Regarding tort liability, all countries adhere to the general rule of vicarious liability. The USA and the UK only allow claims of the creditor against the manager in cases of corporate distress. Such an action is rarely admissible in court.

639 Gerner-Beuerle et al. 2013, p. A 884, citing: Colin Gwyer and Associates v. London Wharf [2002].

640 Gerner-Beuerle et al. 2013, p. A 884, citing: Facia Footwear v. Hinchcliffe [1998], p. 228: "*[t]he boundary between an acceptable risk that an entrepreneur may properly take and an unacceptable risk the taking of which constitute misfeasance is not always, perhaps not usually, clear cut...*".

641 Art. 7:661 BW.

642 Art. 7:661 BW. As the manager might also be an employee, he might be held liable by the corporation on the basis of Art. 7:611 BW, if the damage is the result of intentional or grossly negligent conduct of the employee. According to Van Schilfgaarde, this condition will be interpreted in the light of severe fault. See: Van Schilfgaarde 2006, pp. 148–149; HR NJ 2000, 6.

643 Art. 6:162; Van Schilfgaarde 2006, pp. 156–158; HR NJ 2000, 295; HR NJ 2006, 659; HR ECLI:NL:HR:2014:2628.

644 Hemmer and Wüst 2012, p. 162.

645 Thümmel 1998, pp. 137–140.

646 Palandt (eds.) 2010, §242, para. 71–74; Thümmel 1998, p. 26. When the manager also happens to be shareholder, the *Durchgriffshaftung* also strikes the personal assets of the manager.

In the Netherlands and in Germany, it is possible to bring a claim in the absence of corporate distress. However, the conditions for bringing a claim are very strict. Such a claim is regarded as an exception to the general rule of vicarious liability.[647]

6.3.4. *Managerial bankruptcy liability*

This subsection will look at the countries' laws on the topic of managerial bankruptcy liability. To reiterate, this subsection will look at the parties that may bring a claim against the manager and when such a claim may be brought to court.

The USA – When the corporation is approaching insolvency', for some courts the managerial duty shifts from the shareholder to the corporation and for other courts the duty widens to take into account the interests of the corporation next to the interests of the shareholders.[648] Even though the additional interests to be taken into account relate to the continuity of the firm, several courts allow claims by creditors, when the corporation is almost insolvent.[649] Still the point in time of this shift remains highly ambiguous.[650]

The claim may be brought by the bankruptcy administrator on behalf of the corporation.[651] Similar to the other countries, the creditor may only bring the claim, when he does so, on behalf of all creditors. He may not solely benefit personally from the claim.[652]

Furthermore, under strict conditions, the federal courts[653] allow creditors to bring a managerial liability claim on the basis of deepening insolvency.[654]

General EU view – The enforcement of the creditors' interests by ways of managerial liability is not very effective. In many situations in which creditors would seek to sue the manager, the bankruptcy administrator is entitled to sue the manager only. However, the bankruptcy administrator is deterred from holding the manager liable. According to the EU study 2013, this deterrence can be explained by the remuneration of the bankruptcy administrator, who does not benefit, when he sues the manager.[655] Furthermore, the manager of a bankrupt SME is often also a shareholder, which means that his personal assets are already in the corporation. Finally, the costs and duration of such a liability claim deter the relevant party from filing a claim.[656]

647 For more information, see e.g.: Kuchmann 2008, p. 114.
648 Kraakman et al. 2009, pp. 134–147; Rao et al. 1997, p. 64.
649 Rao et al. 1997, p. 65.
650 Rao et al. 1997, pp. 64–65.
651 Cohen 2001, pp. 383–384.
652 Cohen 2001, pp. 383–384.
653 Note: In the United States, there is a parallel system of federal courts and state courts. In the legal discussion on managerial liability in the USA, attention has been paid more to the state law of Delaware.
654 Sussman 2006, p. 794.
655 Gerner-Beuerle et al. 2013, p. 240.
656 Kraakman et al. 2009, p. 135.

The UK –There are three narrow liability actions of relevance, the misfeasance provisions,[657] the fraudulent and wrongful trading provisions.[658]

The misfeasance claim can be brought by the bankruptcy administrator, shareholder or creditor. The creditor's right to bring an action arises, when the company is in liquidation, but not previously when the company is insolvent. The beneficiary of a successful claim is the entire group of creditors. Because the costs of the creditor of bringing such a claim outweigh the benefits, virtually all misfeasance claims are made by the liquidator.[659]

The fraudulent trading provision is difficult to prove and thus gives way to the wrongful trading provision. The wrongful trading provision can only be invoked by the bankruptcy administrator.[660]

The Netherlands – The bankruptcy administrator has several tools at his disposal. He can hold the manager liable on the basis of Art. 2:138 or Art. 2:248 BW. Furthermore, he can hold the manager liable on behalf of the corporation on the basis of Art. 2:9 BW or on behalf of the collective creditors on the basis of Art. 6:162 BW. If the administrator decides not to hold the manager liable ex Art. 6:162 BW, an individual creditor has the right to do so, but only on behalf of the entire group of creditors.[661]

Germany – The most prominent rule is *Insolvenzverschleppung* (delayed bankruptcy). The rule is invoked by the bankruptcy administrator or the creditors for an amount that is equal to the damage borne by the creditors from the delayed bankruptcy.[662]

Under strict conditions, the manager is also liable in bankruptcy proceedings against creditors on the basis of tort law.[663]

Comparison – All countries provide the bankruptcy administrator with tools to hold the manager liable in formal bankruptcy. As mentioned before, the rules are subject to a different timing. One set of rules can be triggered, whenever the manager makes a decision that has a high impact on creditors. Another set of rules applies as insolvency approaches. A third set of rules is subject to the condition that the manager's corporation is formally bankrupt.[664]

Under strict conditions that may change, as will be seen in the next section, the creditors on behalf of all creditors can also bring a personal liability claim. A claiming culture of the creditors is virtually non-existent because it is unlikely that one creditor

657 Plant and Prior 2000, p. 305–306; Insolvency Act 1986, s 212.

658 Plant and Prior 2000, p. 305–306; Insolvency Act 1986, ss 213 and 214.

659 Plant and Prior 2000, p. 305–306; Insolvency Act 1986, s 212(3); Yukong Lines Limited v. Rendsbury Investment Corporation and Others (1997); Re Anglo French Co-Operative Society (1982); Mason v. Smith (1997); Re AMP International Limited (1996); Re D'Jan of London Limited (1993).

660 Plant and Prior 2000, p. 307.

661 Van Schilfgaarde 2009, pp. 172–173, 178–179; HR NJ 1983, 597; HR NJ 2005, 95.

662 Gietl 2010, p. 936.

663 Thümmel 1998, p. 26 citing: BGHSt 37, 106 (1990); BGH 109, 297 (1990).

664 Gerner-Beuerle et al. 2013, p. xvii.

wants to bear the costs, when the costs outweigh the benefits of the action (collective action problem).[665]

6.3.5. *Liability pursuant to public law (criminal law and tax law)*

The following will outline the countries' policies to hold the manager criminally liable or liable on the basis of corporate tax obligations.

The USA – In general, personal liability on the basis of federal criminal law is exceptional. State law may deviate.[666] Pursuant to the Delaware Code, title 6, §18–303(a), there is no personal liability on the manager for tax payments.[667]

The UK – The manager can be held liable under British criminal law.[668] There is no managerial liability for a failure to pay corporate taxes.[669]

The Netherlands – The tax authority may hold the manager liable, under conditions outlined in the next section.[670] The manager can also be held liable under criminal law.[671] However, in the context of the Dutch lawmaker's concern about a manager's fraud, far reaching criminal liability actions will be introduced in the near future.[672]

Germany – Under tax law, the manager can be held liable, when the taxes regarding corporate revenues, employees' salary or employees' social contributions are not paid.[673] Criminal law penalizes specific actions when the corporation declared bankruptcy.[674]

Comparison – In the USA, the UK and the Netherlands, the criminal sanctions are limited to cases of fraud and self-dealing. Under limited conditions, the manager might be held criminally liable for criminal wrongdoings of the corporation. Liability for tax obligations is found in the Netherlands and Germany, but not in Delaware or the UK.

Under German law, the manager has to take into account the far reaching criminal law provisions. These provisions are only applicable, when the corporation declared bankruptcy.

665 Kraakman et al. 2009, pp. 82–87; Gerner-Beuerle et al. 2013, p. xvii.
666 Gattuso and Proctor 2010.
667 Bendremer 2005, pp. 387–388.
668 Plant and Prior 2000, pp. 308–309; Companies Act 1985 s 458; Insolvency Act 1986, ss 206–211; CDDA 1986, ss 2–10, Sched 1; Statement of Insolvency Practice 4.
669 Anderson 2009, p. 15.
670 Van Schilfgaarde 2006, pp. 154–156; Art. 36 and 36a Inv.
671 Opstelten 27 June 2013, pp. 3, 4.
672 Opstelten 27 June 2013, pp. 3, 4; Opstelten 16 July 2014, p. 2.
673 Thümmel 1998, pp. 133–136.
674 Thümmel 1998, pp. 133–136; Gietl 2010, p. 1005.

6.4. Scope of managerial liability

After having identified the legal basis, the claimants and the point in time to sue in the last section, this section will explain the standard of care of these different rules. Similar to the previous section, this section will be structured per country between internal liability, external liability, bankruptcy liability and liability pursuant to public law.

6.4.1. *Internal liability*

This subsection will discuss the internal liability rules per country.

USA – As described above, the internal actions can be based on securities law or a breach of duties. Since 1995, under the Securities Exchange Act, the investor must prove that he made an investment loss due to a misrepresentation in connection with the purchase or sale of a security. Misrepresentation translates into a proof of a material false statement of the corporate leaders, where the corporate leader knew, or should have known, that the statement was false.[675] Next to usual damages, courts often decide to order punitive damages as well.[676]

Although the manager might not be skilled enough to detect false statements *ex ante*, he can be held liable for false statements *ex post*. The most the manager can do is to check whether he has no reason to believe that the statements are false and that the accountants making up the statements are experts and have no conflicting interests.[677]

Regarding the duties, the scope of the duty of care relates to the business judgement rule. Pursuant to the rule, a court presumes that the duty of care has not been breached, when a disinterested director did not engage in egregious mis-management.[678] The business judgement rule generally protects the manager from liability, when "*the [manager] of a corporation acted on an informed basis, in good faith and in the honest belief that the action taken was in the best interests of the [firm].*"[679] Thus, to meet the duty, the question is whether the decision failed to achieve success (which is not actionable) or constitutes serious mismanagement.[680]

The duty of loyalty will prevent self-dealing and mis-representation. To understand the standard of care regarding the duty of loyalty, the Delaware court attempts to grant some insights into a vague concept. In *Guth v. Loft*, the court held that the duty of loyalty "*demands of a corporate officer or director, peremptorily and inexorably, the most scrupulous observance of his duty, not only affirmatively to protect the interests of the corporation committed to his charge, but also to refrain from doing anything that would work injury to the corporation, or to deprive it of profit or advantage which his skill and ability might properly bring to it, or to enable it to make in the reasonable and lawful*

675 Baker and Griffith 2010, p. 45.
676 Thümmel 1998, p. 160; Schlechtriem 1991, p. 76.
677 Lipton 2007, pp. 21–22.
678 Cahn and Donald 2010, p. 370.
679 Gerner-Beuerle et al. 2013, p. xi.
680 Cahn and Donald 2010, p. 370.

exercise of its powers. The rule that requires an undivided and unselfish loyalty to the corporation demands that there shall be no conflict between duty and self-interest."[681] Still the court refrains from setting a standard of care that is pre-emptively fixed. Instead, the specific circumstances of the case are highly important. "*The occasions for the determination of honesty, good faith and loyal conduct are many and varied, and no hard and fast rule can be formulated. The standard of loyalty is measured by no fixed scale.*"[682]

Where it is shown by the claimant that the manager had a personal financial interest in a transaction, lacked independence, did not inform himself about all information that was reasonably available, failed to exercise the requisite level of care, or stood on both sides of the transaction, the business judgement rule loses some of its protective power in relation to the manager. To rely on the business judgement rule under these scenarios, the manager must meet the standard of entire fairness.[683]

The UK – Regarding internal duties, the duty of loyalty (also called fiduciary duty) requires the managing director to subordinate his interests to the corporate interests. He has to act in good faith, as a fiduciary, on behalf of the company, being the beneficiary, "*while exercising discretion with respect to a critical resource belonging to the beneficiary*". According to the enlightened shareholder model, the duty is primarily owed to the shareholder, but should also take into account interests of corporate reputation, employees, environment, community, suppliers, customers, long-term consequences, and fair treatment of all members. The manager shall apply independent judgement, exercise reasonable care, skill and diligence, and avoid conflicts of interest.[684]

According to the duty of care, "*the director... must exercise... the care, skill and diligence that would be exercised by a reasonably diligent person with ... the general knowledge, skill and experience that may reasonably be expected of a person carrying out such function ... and ... the general knowledge, skill and experience that the director has.*" The duty of care is examined *ex post* by the court according to the business judgement rule.[685]

The Netherlands – Pursuant to Art. 2:9 BW, each director is required to properly meet the duties of the board. Every director shall be liable with respect to mismanagement, unless a manager can show that he was not seriously blameworthy for the mismanagement and he did not refrain from taking measures to mitigate the damage.[686]

As the manager might also be an employee, he might be held liable by the corporation on the basis of Art. 7:611 BW, if the damage is the result of intentional or grossly negligent conduct of the employee. According to Van Schilfgaarde, this condition will be interpreted in the light of severe fault.[687]

681 Guth v. Loft, Inc. (1939), para 1.
682 Guth v. Loft, Inc., (1939), para 1. For more information, the reader is referred to para 7 and 8 of the case.
683 Altman and Raju 2005, p. 1474.
684 Cahn and Donald 2010, pp. 334–336.
685 Cahn and Donald 2010, pp. 334–336.
686 Van Schilfgaarde 2006, p. 147–151; Art. 2:9 BW; HR NJ 1997, 360.
687 Van Schilfgaarde 2006, p. 148–149; HR NJ 2000, 6.

Under strict conditions also an individual shareholder can bring a claim. The court held in *NOM/Willemsen* that "*the fact that the manager breached statutory provisions that are intended to protect an individual shareholder, will, in principle, suffice to bring a liability action.*"[688]

Germany – Internal liability, in general, is based on three cumulative conditions: breach of duty and fault. The management of the AG and GmbH have a similar required level of care.

The breach of duty is somewhat burdensome for legal discussion, because the German system knows many very narrow and specific duties, such as book-keeping, capital requirements, risk management, and publication of certain information. Generally, a failure of sufficient book-keeping represents a great liability risk.[689]

There is also a wider duty, similar to the other three legal systems. According to §43(1) Gesellschaft mit beschränkter Haftung Gesetz (GmbhG) and §93(1) AktG, the manager is required to exercise the level of care of a reasonable manager. His level of care entails the care of a reasonable business man, but also of a reasonable manager of capital. Furthermore, the manager has to adhere to the orders of the general meeting of shareholders, relating to the duty of loyalty, except when these orders endanger the corporate existence or the order to pay dividends would infringe §43(3) GmbHG.[690]

Regarding the general provision of §93(1) AktG, the management has a certain scope of judgement that incorporates business error or failure, which is similar to the business judgement rule.[691]

Fault is a fairly objective standard. A lack of experience or skill does not excuse the manager. He has to meet the standards of an administrator taking into account the financial continuity and sustainability of the firm. The fault of the manager is thus presumed. The manager can rebut that presumption, when he shows that he acted reasonably in good faith without fault.[692]

The supervisory boards of both, the AG and the GmbH, are required to hold the manager liable, when they know or should have known about eligible conduct. When they fail to do so, the supervisory boards can be held personally liable themselves.[693]

Comparison – Member States differ in how far they codify the manager's duties. Either Member States enforce general and less precise principles of conduct that managers are required to adhere to (i.e. the UK duty of care) or Member States stipulate very narrow and precise rules of specific managerial responsibilities (i.e. Germany's rules on book-keeping). Although these approaches appear to differ, in practice the manager is subject to a similar set of responsibilities and duties.[694]

688 HR NJ 2009, 21.
689 Küssel 2006, pp. 493–494.
690 Gietl 2010, p. 947.
691 Gietl 2010, pp. 941, 949.
692 Gietl 2010, pp. 941, 942, 949.
693 Thümmel 1998, pp. 137–140.
694 Gerner-Beuerle et al. 2013, p. xi.

In this context, the law is faced with two conflicting interests. On the one hand, it wishes to specifically codify responsibilities, in order to ensure legal certainty (such as Germany). As subsection 3.2.4 has shown, legal certainty is the main ingredient for an optimal economic effect of liability rules. This legal certainty can only be established by judicially developed rules that require time and the stakeholder's ability to access justice. On the other hand, the law desires to promote and enhance the economic development that arises from firms. Because of the flexible nature of development, too stringent rules have the effect of deterring innovation and firm growth. Too strict rules would not be able to take into account the numerous potential conflicts and duties arising from monitoring measures. As a result, an effective legal system has to find a balance between the two concepts.[695]

When considering the actual rules on liability, managers are generally subject to two duties or obligations, the duty of care and the duty of loyalty, which were outlined in turn. The former duty determines a standard to think and act reasonably in order to weigh risks and benefits. In this regard, the manager will be equipped with experience, skill, thoroughness, and the necessary corporate information. There are three elements to this, the standard of care, the burden of proof, and the business judgement rule. The standard of care relates to a set of substantial rules and principles that define misconduct. These rules differ in countries. So does the burden of proof. The burden of proof asks either the claimant or the director to prove the misconduct or the fulfilment of the duty respectively. The question of who bears the burden of proof is especially important, because the manager has a great information advantage over all other parties about the corporate conduct. The business judgement rule is based on the doctrine that a judge is not in the position to evaluate a business decision *ex post*, because, first, a judge does not have the skill, experience and firm knowledge, and secondly, an *ex post* evaluation is always burdened by a hindsight bias. According to Williamson and Eisenberg, a strict application of the duty would only lead to a discouragement of the manager to take entrepreneurial risks. The business judgement rule can offset the discretionary margin of the burden of proof.[696]

The duty of loyalty refers to the conflict of interests between the manager and the corporation. It relates to self-dealing and to taking corporate opportunities. In this regard, the manager must not compete with the corporation, must not accept benefits because of his position from third parties, and must not abuse his powers to his own advantage (direct conflict) or to the advantage of another party (indirect conflict). In the EU, the study of 2013 distinguishes the national duties of loyalty into three groups. The first group prohibits any conflict of interest, even if not directly making the corporation worse off, mostly represented by common law countries, like the UK. The second group prohibits transactions that are *de facto* to the detriment of the corporate interest. Germany and the Netherlands can be attributed to that second group. The third group does not have any duty of loyalty.[697] When applying this distinction to the US system, the USA is likely to be placed in the same group as the UK.

695 Gerner-Beuerle et al. 2013, p. xi.

696 Cahn and Donald 2010, p. 370–372; Gerner-Beuerle et al. 2013, p. xi.

697 Gerner-Beuerle et al. 2013, p. xi.

6.4.2. *Managerial tort liability*

As explained above, tort liability of the manager in the USA and the UK rarely leads to actionable suits from creditors. First, a claim is only actionable in times of corporate distress, just before bankruptcy. It is difficult to see, when this point in time arises. Secondly, the creditor has to share the damages awarded with all corporate creditors. Thirdly, the manager's duty of care is owed to the corporation and only peripherally to the creditors.[698] Thus, a successful liability claim in the USA and the UK is unlikely. The following will discuss the scope of the standard of care of the Dutch and German external liability rules.

The Netherlands – Pursuant to Art. 6:162 BW, the Supreme Court held in *Oosterhof* that the manager is liable, if he is personally and sufficiently severely blameworthy (*voldoende ernstig verwijt*) to have not fulfilled his corporate tasks. Thus, there are two conditions: blame can be attributed to the manager and this fault was sufficiently severe. The Supreme Court held that the fault is sufficiently severe, under the circumstances that the manager at the time of the contract's completion knew or should reasonably have known that the corporation will not be able to fulfil its contractual obligations.[699]

In *Ontvanger/Roelofsen*, the Supreme Court held that the manager can be held personally liable when he (i) acted on behalf of the corporation or (ii) allowed that the corporation infringed contractual obligations or the law. The manager can be held liable in cases where the manager's actions or failures to act were so unreasonable that the manager can be blamed personally for a serious fault.[700]

In *Air Tulip*, the Supreme Court held that under special circumstances, in addition to liability of the corporation, a manager can also be held personally liable. In order to assume such liability, it is required that the manager personally can be seriously blamed in relation to serious harm which occurred. Thus accepting the liability of a manager demands higher requirements than is generally the case. A high threshold for liability of a manager to a corporate creditor is justified because the actions that lead to the damage are principally actions of the corporation and because it is in the public interest that managers do not determine their scope of action to an undesirable extent by defensive considerations.[701]

Germany – The creditor can directly sue the manager of a public corporation for a corporate liability, when the public corporation is unable to fulfil the claim.[702] The claimant has to prove a mismanagement to meet the internal standard of care of §93(1) AktG, outlined in the section on internal liability.[703]

698 Kraakman et al. 2009, pp. 134–147.
699 Van Schilfgaarde 2006, pp. 156–158; Art. 6:162 BW; HR NJ 2000, 295.
700 HR NJ 2006, 259.
701 HR ECL:NL:HR:2014:2628, para. 3.5.2.
702 Thümmel 1998, pp. 137–140; §93(5) AktG.
703 Thümmel 1998, pp. 26, 137–140; Palandt (eds.) 2010, §242, para. 71–74.

Moreover, there are some hypothetical cases of external liability. First, the managerial action at first corresponded to his own and the corporate interest, but later only benefited him. The internal claim will not arise, because no breach of rules and duties were made at the time of the action. But external liability materializes later on. Secondly, the manager may be held externally liable, when the corporation is in the formation process (*Gründungsphase*). Thirdly, the manager could be held externally liable to cancel advanced negotiations.[704]

Comparison - Germany and the Netherlands sparsely equip a creditor to hold the manager liable. Similar to the USA and the UK, creditors are granted more rights, when the corporation is in a state of financial distress. The rules applicable during distress situations are further outlined in the next subsection.

6.4.3. *Managerial bankruptcy liability*

This section will look at the managerial bankruptcy liability, per country.

The USA - As insolvency approaches (vicinity of insolvency), the group of parties to which a managerial duty is owed expands. Next to shareholder interests, the manager has to ensure corporate continuity. In this regard, he owes a duty to creditors, employees and other parties interested in the corporation. As some courts believe in a shift of duties at insolvency, the Delaware courts regard the angle of duty to be expanded.[705]

The standard of care toward creditors is difficult to model. The court in *Geyer* held that when the corporation is in distress, the manager is required to "*a heightened duty of inquiry and a need ... to devote more time and attention to the corporation's affairs than is required when a corporation is financially healthy.*"[706] The court advises the manager to "*consider carefully, with the assistance of experienced business, financial and legal advisors, whether the line separating solvency from insolvency has been crossed or will be crossed as a result of a particular proposed transaction, and, if so, what the effect of the proposed transaction will be upon corporate creditors, as well as shareholders and the corporate entity itself.*"[707]

Furthermore, when the corporation is in deepening insolvency, the additional concurrence of debt or other actions that make a continuity of the corporation impossible can lead to the personal liability of the manager. The cases in which such action against the manager succeed, involve false statements of the manager about the financial health of the corporation.[708]

[704] Thümmel 1998, p. 157–159; Schlechtriem 1991, pp. 73–75.
[705] Bainbridge 2006, p. 347.
[706] Geyer v. Ingersoll Publ'n Co. (1992), p. 789.
[707] Geyer v. Ingersoll Publ'n Co. (1992), p. 789.
[708] Sussman 2006, p. 793.

The UK – Duties in bankruptcy translate to narrow liability rules. There are three liability actions of relevance, the misfeasance provisions,[709] the fraudulent trading provisions and the wrongful trading provisions.[710]

The misfeasance provisions enable the liquidator, shareholder or creditor to bring an action against the past or present director, when he "*has misapplied or retained, or become accountable for, any money or other property of the company, or been guilty of any misfeasance or breach of any fiduciary or other duty in relation to the company*".[711] Here, the equitable duties of good faith, to act in the best interest of the company, of skill and care, not to exceed power and authority, not to fetter discretion, and not to make a personal profit are to be mentioned. Because shadow directors are mentioned neither in the Insolvency Act nor in the Companies Act, Plant and Prior assume that they do not fall in the scope of these provisions. Instead, "*officers in relation to a body corporate, includes a director, manager or secretary*".[712] The decisive condition is whether the person exercises a supervisory level of control representing the company. The remedies the court awards amount to a loss that resulted from his breach of duty plus interest, as the court thinks just. The director is not able to set off any debt or claim he has against the company.[713]

Fraudulent trading is existent, "*if in the course of a winding up of a company it appears that any business of the company has been carried on with intent to defraud creditors of the company or creditors of any other person, or for any fraudulent purpose, ... the court on the application of the liquidator may declare that any persons who are knowingly parties to the carrying on of the business [in such a manner] are to be liable to make contributions (if any) to the company's assets as the court thinks proper*".[714] To be successful, there must be evidence of "*actual dishonesty involving, according to current notions of fair trading among commercial men, real moral blame*".[715]

Because this test is difficult to meet, an action brought by wrongful trading is more popular. According to that rule, the director or shadow director is liable when the company is in liquidation and when "*that person knew or ought to have concluded that there was no reasonable prospect that the company would have avoided going into insolvent liquidation...*".[716] Whether the knowledge test is met depends on the circumstances of the case, such as a company unable to meet liabilities, suppliers refusing to make deliveries, or a failure to prepare annual accounts in time for submission to shareholders. To ascertain, whether the director has failed to meet his duty, there is an objective and a subjective test. The objective test takes into account the standard of care of a reasonably skilled, experienced director that takes due care; also using already established standards of the English common law negligence rules. The subjective test looks rather at the actual

709 Insolvency Act 1986, s 212.
710 Insolvency Act 1986, ss 213 and 214.
711 Plant and Prior 2000, p. 305; Insolvency Act 1986, s 212(1).
712 Plant and Prior 2000, p. 305; Companies Act 1985, s 244.
713 Plant and Prior 2000, p. 305–306; Insolvency Act 1986, s 212(3).
714 Insolvency Act 1986, s 213(1) and (2).
715 Plant and Prior 2000, p. 306; Re Patrick & Lyon Limited (1933). Although the case is older, than the Insolvency Act, courts still use this test. See: Plant and Prior 2000, p. 306.
716 Insolvency Act 1986, s 214(1) and (2).

skills and experience of the director at hand. The bigger the company is, the more attention is paid to whether the objective test is met. It was held that the claim is barred by a time limit of six years between the act that constitutes wrongful trading and the liquidation procedure.[717]

The Netherlands – The bankruptcy administrator may bring a claim on the basis of art. 2:138 (or 248) BW, art. 2:9 BW, or art. 6:162 BW. The standard of care in relation to art. 2:9 BW is the same as already outlined above.[718]

According to art. 2:138(248) BW, the manager is liable for outstanding obligations that exceed the bankruptcy estate, when (i) he clearly did not fulfil his tasks decently and (ii) this non-fulfilment was an important cause of bankruptcy.[719] When he did not fulfil his obligations of sufficient book-keeping and of publication of the annual financial statement, the first condition is irrefutably met and the second condition is presumed to be fulfilled by law. In other words, it is a legal fact that the manager clearly did not fulfil his tasks decently. The presumption of the second condition can be rebutted by demonstrating that other circumstances were an important cause of bankruptcy.[720]

According to the Supreme Court on 14 January 1983, the bankruptcy administrator can also hold the manager liable on the basis of art. 6:162 BW on behalf of the collective creditors.[721] The standard of care regarding art. 6:162 was outlined above.[722]

Since 1 October 2012, a new liability rule has come into force for BV's. According to that rule, the board is jointly and severally liable to the corporation for a corporate deficit in corporate bankruptcy, when the board had known or reasonably should have known that a past dividend pay-out would lead to a situation of corporate bankruptcy.[723]

Germany – Regarding bankruptcy, the duty to file for bankruptcy in due time is the most important rule (*Insolvenzverschleppung*). The management has to file for bankruptcy within three weeks after the management knew or reasonably should have known that the corporation is either unable to fulfil payments (*Zahlungsunfähigkeit*) or over-leveraged (*überschuldet*). The action for a failure of timely filing for bankruptcy is brought by the bankruptcy administrator or the creditors for an amount that is equal to the damage borne by the creditors as a result of the delayed bankruptcy. When the inability to pay or over-leveraging is established by the court, the management is presumed to be at fault. The management can rebut this presumption by showing that they exercised the required level of care of a reasonable manager.[724]

Under certain circumstances, the manager is also liable in bankruptcy proceedings to creditors on the basis of tort law. According to two decisions of the Federal Supreme

[717] Plant and Prior 2000, pp. 306–308.

[718] Van Schilfgaarde 2006, pp. 156–158.

[719] Art. 2:138(1) BW: "*...indien het bestuur zijn taak kennelijk onbehoorlijk heeft vervuld en aannemelijk is dat dit een belangrijke oorzaak is van het faillissement*".

[720] Art. 2:138(2) BW conj. 2:10, 2:394. Also see: HR RvdW 2007, 1027 and HR NJ 1999, 318.

[721] HR NJ 1983, 597.

[722] HR NJ 2006, 259, HR ECLI:NL:HR:2014:2628, para. 3.5.2.

[723] Art. 2:216 BW.

[724] Gietl 2010, p. 934–940. The management is jointly and severally liable.

Court (Bundesgerichtshof, BGH), the manager is liable for a failure to act responsibly on behalf of the corporation.[725] The standard of care of the manager to protect external parties, based on tort liability, is difficult to capture. It is certain that the external standard of care is not equal to the internal standard of care. To infringe the external standard of care, the manager must do more than just violate his duties owed to the corporation and shareholders.[726] In the case of the Federal Supreme Court of 10 July 2012, the court held that the managerial action violates tort law, when the manager himself caused the harm by way of a forbidden action. Such a standard entails an active conduct. Omission to do something does not fulfil this standard. Other aspects are the causal link between harm and the managerial action, and the prohibition of that action.[727]

According to Gärtner, the courts found it difficult to establish an external duty of care of the manager, because the law does not protect a direct relationship between a corporate creditor and a corporate manager. Instead, the law focuses on an internal duty of care and the relationship between corporation and creditor.[728]

Comparison – Regarding bankruptcy, there are two main strategies that countries choose to follow. First, the country may require the manager to file for bankruptcy in a timely manner. Failure to do so leads to liability to an amount that equals the assets that are depleted because of the delayed filing. This method is applied in Germany (next to the action under tort liability outlined above). Secondly, the legal system may adopt a managerial duty to cease trading at the time that creditor's interests are at risk, such as the Netherlands, the UK, and the USA. The first measure is clear-cut and enhances legal certainty. The second measure is more relative. It enables trading of a balance sheet insolvent corporation, when there is a realistic chance to escape from bankruptcy proceedings. According to the EU study 2013, empirical research suggests that the second measure leads to a higher recovery rate.[729]

6.4.4. Liability pursuant to public law

Criminal liability only punishes individuals who engaged in serious misconduct. In general, objective fault and misconduct, necessary for civil liability, do not suffice for prosecution. Instead, each manager must be subjectively blameworthy (*mens rea*). In this regard, the general principle of guilt beyond reasonable doubt must be kept in mind.[730] The court has to be of the opinion that the defendant is guilty beyond a reasonable doubt. Such a high standard for prosecution is non-existent for civil liability (outlined in the previous three subsections) or tax liability. The following will outline the criminal and tax liability rules per country.

725 Thümmel 1998, p. 26 citing: BGHSt 37, 106 (1990); BGH 109, 297 (1990).
726 Gärtner 2013, p. 40.
727 Gärtner 2013, p. 39, para. 24, citing: BGH VI ZR 341/10.
728 Gärtner 2013, p. 40.
729 Gerner-Beuerle et al. 2013, p. xi.
730 Newman 1993, p. 979.

The USA – In general, personal criminal liability on the basis of federal criminal law is exceptional. State law may deviate.[731] However, managers were held criminally liable for fraud and self-dealing in the recent case of Enron.[732] Bendremer generally suggests that there might be personal liability on the grounds of equitable rules such as piercing the corporate veil.[733]

The UK – Criminal liability is also adopted under British law. Fraudulent trading might result in criminal sanctions, such as imprisonment, up to seven years, and/or a fine. The burden of proof is the same as for civil liability. Furthermore, malpractice, such as fraud, misconduct and misrepresentation, can be prosecuted. The director or shadow director can also be disqualified from taking up a management post for up to 15 years. In cases of disregard, imprisonment can be the result.[734] There is no managerial liability for a failure to pay corporate taxes.[735]

The Netherlands – The manager is subject to very restricted criminal sanctions only.[736] The tax authority can hold the manager liable on the basis of Art. 36 and 36a Dutch Tax Act 1990 (*Invorderingswet 1990*, Inv) for an amount that the corporation was obliged to pay as taxes, such as wage tax and revenue tax, and if the non-payment is a result of the negligent behaviour of the manager. If the corporation is unable to fulfil its tax obligations, every board member is entitled to inform the tax authority. If the tax authority has not been informed 14 days before the due date of the relevant tax, every board member is presumed to be negligent ex art. 36 and 36a Inv. To escape liability, each board member has to prove that he reasonably could not have contacted the tax authority 14 days before the due date and that the corporation's inability to fulfil tax obligations is not the fault of any board member who has been in office during the last three years.[737]

Germany – When the taxes for corporate revenues, employee's salary or employee's social contributions are not fulfilled and the manager acted intentionally or grossly negligent, the manager is personally liable for that amount, according to §§34, 69 German Tax Code (*Abgabengesetz*, AO). The same goes for the conduct of not declaring the due taxes in due time. Gross negligence is presumed by law.[738]

Criminal law penalizes specific actions of the manager when the corporation is financially distressed, such as wrongful book-keeping and accountancy, privileged relations to individual creditors, and interventions of third parties into the bankruptcy estate. Prosecution is restricted to the point in time that the corporation is bankrupt or unable to fulfil its obligations. According to §283 German Penal Code (*Strafgesetzbuch*,

731 Gattuso and Proctor 2010.
732 Lipman 2009, pp. 360–361; Van Aalten 2003, pp. 457–460.
733 Bendremer 2005, pp. 395–398.
734 Plant and Prior 2000, pp. 308–309; Companies Act 1985 s 458; Insolvency Act 1986, ss 206–211; CDDA 1986, ss 2–10, Sched 1; Statement of Insolvency Practice 4.
735 Anderson 2009, p. 15.
736 Compare to subsection 6.3.5.
737 Van Schilfgaarde 2006, pp. 154–156; cf. Art. 36 and 36a Inv.
738 Thümmel 1998, pp. 133–136.

StGB), the manager is held liable, in bankruptcy, for an impairment of assets, speculation and unreasonable expenses, dissipation of assets, to pretend to have rights or obligations, or destruction of account books.[739]

Comparison – This subsection showed that there are considerable differences among the four legal systems. Whereas the USA does not have direct liability actions against the manager based on criminal law (notwithstanding liability for corporate fault), Germany has very strict rules. In fact, many of the German cases of managerial liability in bankruptcy are based on criminal liability.[740] The UK criminal liability rules seem to seek a strong deterrence against fraudulent/wrongful trading. Dutch criminal sanctions are not as pronounced in relation to the other countries observed.

Federal US law and the UK do not have tax liability rules, whereas Germany and the Netherlands do. Indeed, the Netherlands imposes harsh rules for the non-fulfilment of particular taxes.

6.5. Application of the hypotheses of Chapter 5

The previous observations will be shortly summarized and linked to the hypotheses of Chapter 5. This section will first compare the observed managerial liability rules of the previous sections to the theoretical framework outlined in Chapter 2. Secondly, the section will turn to the question of how far the liability rules could create a risk aversion of the manager.

6.5.1. Liability rules in theory and in practice

Considering internal liability rules, the shareholder can claim most easily under American securities law. When the rules on the burden of proof work in his favour, a securities law claim can be lodged by one shareholder at any time that the share value drops dramatically. It is more difficult to bring a claim in the UK and Germany, where the shareholders have to show that it is in the interest of the corporation to file a claim, and hold a certain amount of shares. In fact, most internal liability claims in Germany are brought to court by the supervisory board. In the Netherlands, the shareholder can only lodge a claim against the manager under very strict conditions.

Subsections 5.2.1 and 5.4.4 argued that internal liability increases corporate value when one of two alternatives occurs. Either "*the prospect of the suit deters misconduct, ... or the suit ... yields a positive recovery net of all costs that the corporation must bear as a consequence of a suit.*"[741] Subsection 5.5.2 argued that when the prospect of filing does not relate to misconduct but to expected benefit and the manager does not bear the costs of liability (he is compensated for it), the manager does not link the claim to his misconduct.[742] The additional condition in the UK and Germany pursuant to which a

739 Gietl 2010, pp. 1006–1012.
740 Gietl 2010, pp. 1005.
741 Kraakman et al. 1993, p. 1736.
742 Kraakman et al. 1993, p. 1743.

claimant has to show that it is in the interest of the corporation to file a claim may (i) establish the necessary link between misconduct and the prospect of filing and (ii) increase corporate value. A claim under US securities law is not subject to similar conditions. The Dutch corporate governance tool to file an internal liability claim is very restricted in the first place. These restrictions do not necessarily have to be to the disadvantage of the Dutch corporate law because internal liability is perceived to be less important in corporate governance anyway.[743]

Regarding external liability, subsection 5.2.2 argued that vicarious liability is more likely than managerial liability.[744] In accordance to these considerations, external liability is non-existent in the USA and the UK, and has only limited application in the Netherlands and Germany.

When the corporation has high costs of monitoring the manager, the liability of the manager as additional action to vicarious liability was proposed.[745] The imposition of fines (or possibly imprisonment) may boost the incentive to take due care.[746] In this regard, the Netherlands presumes managerial liability when wage taxes and revenue taxes are not paid. The UK adopts criminal liability against fraudulent/wrongful trading and the USA only criminally punishes managers when the effects of their actions were disastrous (cf. Enron). In this regard, a major role of internal liability is to deter large one-shot frauds.[747]

Liability of the manager as additional action to vicarious liability was also proposed, when the corporation has insufficient assets.[748] As insolvency approaches, the manager might pay too much attention to shareholders' interests to remove assets from the firm.[749] In the USA and the UK, the risk of bankruptcy liability materializes when the corporation is near to insolvency which is before formal bankruptcy proceedings. In Germany and the Netherlands, a claim pursuant to bankruptcy liability can only be lodged during formal bankruptcy proceedings.

Where bankruptcy liability is not a sufficient deterrent, one can introduce criminal liability or the disqualification sanction.[750] In this regard, Germany resorts to criminal liability, possibly leading to imprisonment, for over-leveraging the corporation. In the Netherlands, managerial liability is presumed when the board failed to publish the corporate financial statements on time.

6.5.2. *Liability and risk aversion*

Subsection 5.2.4 suggested that a risk-averse manager desires compensation in the form of insurance, indemnification or a salary increase, when he has to bear risk.[751] When the

743 Kraakman 2009, p. 78; Pacces 2011, pp. 314–316; Fischel and Bradley 1985, p. 283.
744 Also see: Shavell 2004, p. 232; Kraakman 2008, pp. 134–136, 144; Stone 1980, p. 17.
745 Polinsky and Shavell 1993, p. 240, 256. A similar reasoning is made by Kraakman 1984, p. 880.
746 Polinsky and Shavell 1993, p. 240.
747 Fischel and Bradley 1985, pp. 283, 287.
748 Kraakman 2008, in: Faure 2009, p. 144; Kraakman 1984, p. 869.
749 Kraakman 2008, p. 137.
750 Polinsky and Shavell 1993, p. 240.
751 Bishop 1964, p. 839; Bishop 1966, p. 96; Polinsky and Shavell 1993, p. 241; Fischel and Bradley 1985, p. 285.

level of care is certain, the manager exercises due care and there is no risk of liability. However, an uncertain level of care creates risk.[752] The conditions and standards imposed by the liability rules differ per country. The previous subsection has shown that the procedural requirements to bring a claim differ to a great degree in the countries observed. Complexity of rules contributes to errors in establishing the actual standard of care in court (legal error).[753] Besides, the manager may lack sufficient oversight over all liability rules to adjust his care to the due level of care (inability).[754] In this regard, the standard of care corresponding to the rules may be uncertain.[755] This subsection will take stock of the extent to which the level of care depends on the rule, on the country and on the circumstances of each case.

Internal liability can be distinguished between a duty of care and a duty of loyalty. The standard of care relating to the duty of care is based on some variation of the business judgement rule in the countries observed, according to which the judge only marginally scrutinizes a particular business decision and only punishes severe faults of the manager. The standard of care relating to a duty of loyalty prohibits conflicts of interest between the manager and the corporation. In the UK and the USA, any conflict of interest is prohibited, even if not directly making the corporation worse off. Germany and the Netherlands prohibit transactions that are *de facto* to the detriment of the corporate interest.

The standard of care relating to external liability is based on the business judgement rule.

The standard of care with respect to bankruptcy liability is lenient in the USA and the UK. The manager does not meet the standard when the manager knew or should have known that a particular investment decision is likely to lead to bankruptcy. The standard is very strict in Germany (additionally penalized by criminal sanctions). When the manager does not file for corporate bankruptcy proceedings in due time, the standard of care is presumed to have been breached. The Netherlands adheres to a more balanced standard of care between the two extremes. The manager is liable for outstanding obligations that exceed the bankruptcy estate, when (i) he clearly did not fulfil his tasks decently and (ii) this non-fulfilment was an important contributory factor of bankruptcy.

The managerial liability rules are also subject to changes established by courts and by the state. The previous subsections have shown that some rules were established by the courts. In this regard, one can think of the external liability rules in Germany and the Netherlands. Furthermore, the state might seek to change, in some cases increase,[756] the level of deterrence relating to liability rules. Previous sections showed that the Dutch law maker considers the introduction of criminal sanctions against the manager.

These considerations suggest that the scope of the rules is highly complex. The complexity is likely to create risk aversion.[757] The manager may even be chilled to take

752 Shavell 2004, p. 265; Harrington and Danzon 2000, p. 284.

753 The chance of legal error or inability to take care creates risk that the manager bears. See: Shavell 2004, p. 265. Also see: Cooter and Ulen 2012, pp. 217–220, 220–222.

754 Bishop 1966, p. 98; Kraakman 1984, p. 864; Polinsky and Shavell 1993, p. 254.

755 Bishop 1966, p. 98; Kraakman 1984, p. 864; Shavell 2004, p. 265; Polinsky and Shavell 1993, p. 254.

756 Opstelten 16 July 2014, p. 2.

757 Shavell 2004, p. 265; Polinsky and Shavell 1993, p. 254.

risks (which means that the deterrence effect is too strong).[758] In this regard, the risk to be held liable should be allocated to a more efficient risk bearer, such as the corporation or an insurer. The manager will seek compensation by a combination of an increased salary, indemnification or insurance.[759] Subsection 5.3.3 argued that except for bankruptcy liability, indemnification is more likely than insurance when indemnification saves transaction costs (finding and negotiating the insurance policy) and litigation costs (simplified settlements).[760] The next section will analyse how far the four legal systems authorize corporations to indemnify a manager.

6.6. Corporate indemnification for managerial liability

Subsection 5.3.2 discussed the willingness of the corporation to take the entire liability risk or part of the liability risk from the manager by indemnifying him. The manager might either be indemnified before an eligible action or afterwards. Regarding the kind of indemnification, the shareholder can absolve the manager of any internal liability or refrain from bringing a claim based on internal liability (internally), but the shareholder can also compensate or absolve the manager of liability claims lodged by a creditor (involuntary and voluntary creditors, externally).

This section will outline the measures of the different countries. It will further consider legal limitations on the corporate ability to indemnify. This section will discuss the legal limitations of internal indemnification (subsection 6.6.1) and external indemnification (subsection 6.6.1). Indemnification for bankruptcy liability will be discussed in the subsection on external indemnification.

6.6.1. *Indemnification for internal liability*

The corporation may decide to indemnify the manager for claims that are based on internal liability actions. As shown above, in the Netherlands and Germany such actions are usually filed on behalf of the corporation. Reasons for indemnifying have been outlined in subsection 5.3.2. This section will shortly sketch the legal limitations of such an indemnification in the four countries.

The USA – The Delaware code authorizes a corporation to include in its charter a provision limiting or completely eliminating a director's personal liability for a breach of a fiduciary duty. It still prohibits an indemnification of liability (i) for a breach of the duty of loyalty, (ii) when the decision was not taken in good faith, (iii) when the action involved intentional misconduct, or (iv) a knowing violation of the law. The indemnification must further not limit the liability of the manager under federal law. The indemnification may

758 The chilling effect reflects, for example, the increased liability risk under the Sarbanes-Oxley Act in the USA. See: Bargeron et al. 2010, pp. 34–35.

759 Bishop 1964, p. 839; Bishop 1966, p. 96; Polinsky and Shavell 1993, p. 241; Fischel and Bradley 1985, p. 285.

760 Similar arguments have made by Kraakman 1984, p. 865; Fischel and Bradley 1985, p. 291; Oesterle 1983, p. 570, 572.

only encompass the director, not other employees or officers. Furthermore, Delaware permits indemnification, on the basis of a contract or a shareholder resolution, and these indemnifications are subject to the same limitations as those outlined in relation to the charter indemnification. The indemnification may be granted *ex ante*.[761] If the court sees fit, it may grant injunctive relief to the plaintiff by ways of its equitable powers that cannot be limited by the indemnification.[762]

Delaware authorizes the indemnification of the manager on the basis of a permissive indemnification. A permissive indemnification is granted *ex post*. It has to be authorized by the shareholders on a case to case basis.[763]

The UK – Pursuant to section 310 Companies Act 1985, any *ex ante* provision, whether pursuant to the articles of association or pursuant to a contract that indemnifies the director or shadow director from any breach of duties or claims arising from the internal relationship, is void.[764] This section was the result of the UK court decision in *Re City Equitable* of 1925 (Ch 407), in which the court held the directors *prima facie* negligent for their conduct and denied the manager the right to escape liability by invoking a provision in the articles of association that would have exempted them from any liability short of wilful neglect or default.[765]

Besides indemnification, equity rules serve as a relief from liability. The court has wide discretion. When the manager acted honestly and reasonably, he ought to be fairly excused from liability by the court, also taking into account all of the circumstances of the case. These small exceptions were introduced, because it was otherwise regarded as difficult to find responsible individuals that want to become a director.[766]

A rare example of relief is the case *D'Jan*. The judge acknowledged that the negligence was not gross at the time of the alleged misconduct.[767]

The Netherlands – There are two kinds of internal indemnifications, the *decharge* and the *vrijtekening*. The *decharge* (*kwijting*) requires a resolution of the general meeting to hold the manager harmless for any actions based on art. 2:9 BW. It is an *ex post* measure. The *decharge* does not encompass actions or omissions that were kept secret from the general meeting. Furthermore, a *decharge* only covers the relationship between the corporation and the manager on the basis of art. 2:9 BW. Claims based on other legal rules are not within the scope of a *decharge*.[768]

The *vrijtekening* (roughly translated: to sign off), being internal and *ex ante*, is an agreement between the corporation and the manager, in which the corporation promises not to hold the manager liable for future potential misconduct (a claim based on art. 2:9 BW). This agreement can be made by contract or via the articles of association.

761 Moskowitz and Effross 1992, pp. 909–910, 915; Delaware Code, title 8, §102(b)(7) (Supp. 1991).
762 Moskowitz and Effross 1992, p. 917.
763 Moskowitz and Effross 1992, pp. 905–906.
764 Companies Act 1985, s 310.
765 Baxter 1995, p. 541.
766 Baxter 1995, pp. 542–543; Companies Act 1985, s 727.
767 Baxter 1995, p. 542–543; Re D'Jan of London Limited (1993).
768 Eesthuis et al. 2011, p. 36; HR LJN BM2332; HR NJ 1990, 308.

Vrijtekening is not possible for intentional or grossly negligent conduct of the manager. It is questioned by some authors whether a *vrijtekening* would be upheld in court at all. They argue that the *vrijtekening* is contrary to the legally binding rule of art. 2:9 BW conj. Art. 2:25 BW or art. 3:40 BW, which condemns actions contrary to the *ordre public* and *bonos mores*. Furthermore, it is argued that a *vrijtekening* would be in clear contrast to the manager's duty of good faith and to adhere to the interest of the corporation.[769]

Germany – Thümmel distinguishes between three forms of internal indemnification, *Billigung pflichwidrigem Verhaltens*, *Verzicht auf Innenhaftungsansprüche*, and *Haftungsbeschränkung durch Vereinbarung*. The *Billigung* is an *ex ante* measure, in which the manager asks the shareholders for permission to take a specific decision. In this regard, the decision must be in accordance to the interests of the corporation. The shareholders give their permission by rendering a resolution of the general meeting (*Hauptverversammlung* or *Gesellchafter*). It has been suggested that the *Billigung* is not very practical because the manager is only exonerated for the decisions that he explicitly discussed in the general meeting. It is tenuous to think of every risk that may arise from a decision. Furthermore, to resolve a *Billigung*, the general meeting has to be called, which takes at least a month, and might have adverse affects for big corporations because a general meeting will be treated as a signal by the public.[770]

The *Verzicht*, an *ex post* measure, is again divided into two subcategories. The most important measure is the *Entlastung* (roughly translated: exoneration). The *Entlastung* takes place annually *ex post*. In a public corporation (*AG*) the *Entlastung* is only evidence that the shareholders trust the manager more or less. It does not exempt them from their ability to file an internal claim. In a private corporation (*GmbH*), the *Entlastung* exonerates the manager for all actions of the previous year provided that a shareholder should have known the actions by carefully scrutinizing all documents available.[771]

The second measure is the *Erlass* which is an agreement between the corporation and the manager, in which the corporation promises not to hold the manager liable for certain actions that are listed in the *Erlass*. In a public corporation (*AG*), such agreement can only be made three years after the particular claim could have been filed first. Furthermore, the majority of shareholders have to approve the *Erlass*, without the existence of a dissenting 10% minority (calculated from the amount of equity). In a private corporation (*GmbH*), the only condition for a valid agreement *(Erlass)* is a majority vote of the shareholders. However, the *Erlass* may not encompass actions that have been exercised after the court established bankruptcy of the corporation. The point in time that the corporation is deemed to be insolvent is determined *ex post* by the court.[772]

769 Hendrikse and Van den Heuvel 2009, p. 129; Eesthuis et al. 2011, pp. 36–37; see also: Van Schilfgaarde 2006, pp. 169–170; HR NJ 1967, 261.

770 Thümmel 1998, pp. 117–121; §37(1) GmbHG; §93(4):1 AktG; §123 AktG; OLG München NJW-RR 1997, 544.

771 Thümmel 1998, pp. 121–123; §120(1) AktG; §120(2):2 AktG; §46(4) GmbHG; BGH NJW 1959, 192; BGH WM 1976, 736 f; BGHZ 97, 382.

772 Thümmel 1998, pp. 122–124; §397 BGB; §93(4):3 AktG; BGH WM 1968, 114; BGH GmbHR 1998, 278.

The *Haftungsbeschränkung durch Vereinbarung* (roughly translated: a limit on liability via an agreement) aims at an *ex ante* exoneration of the manager. In private corporations, the *Vereinbarung* may include an exception of internal liability altogether, with the exception of internal misconduct and already outlined rules on liability in relation to bankruptcy. Such *Vereinbarung* requires a majority vote of the shareholders to be valid.[773]

Comparison – The rules on indemnification seem to differ to a high degree. Even within a system such as the German system, the rules of indemnification of the GmbH and the AG are very different. In general, it can be said that the UK has very strict rules to limit the extent of indemnity clauses. At the other end of the spectrum, the German GmbHG and the Delaware Corporation Law do not regulate the manner of indemnification much. In the Netherlands, *ex post* indemnification is authorized but *ex ante* indemnification is (probably) void. Relevant judgements in all jurisdictions are still necessary to verify that evaluation.

6.6.2. Corporate indemnification for managerial liability from third parties

The following will briefly outline the corporate indemnification for managerial liability against third parties, by country.

The USA – The considerations about the internal *ex ante* indemnification also apply to the external relationship. Payments involved to compensate the manager for potential liability may be made prior to an actual claim "*as authorized by the board of directors in the specific case upon receipt of an undertaking by or on behalf of such director of officer to repay such amount unless it shall ultimately be determined that he is entitled to be indemnified.*"[774]

Regarding third party relationships, a permissive *ex post* indemnification (authorization on a case by case basis) is allowed when the director "*acted in good faith and in a manner he reasonably believed to be in or not opposed to the best interests of the corporation.*"[775]

The UK – A breach of a duty against a creditor will most likely also constitute a breach of duty against the corporation or shareholder. The rules on indemnification are the same as just explained, taking into account section 310 of the Companies Act 1985. Generally, external liability falls in the scope of the vicarious liability of the corporation. The corporation might in turn be willing to recover the loss from the director as a second step by way of internal liability. Indemnification of internal liability is prohibited pursuant to section 310 Companies Act 1985 and already outlined above.[776]

773 Thümmel 1998, pp. 124–125; §93(4):3 AktG; §276(2) BGB.
774 Moskowitz and Effross 1992, p. 911; Delaware Code, title 8, §145(e).
775 Delaware Code, title 8, §145(a).
776 Baxter 1995, pp. 539, 543–546; also compare to Kraakman 2008, p. 144; Stone 1980, p. 17.

The Netherlands – A *vrijwaring* (roughly translated: to safeguard), being external and *ex ante*, is more commonly accepted in the legal literature than a *vrijtekening*. The corporation promises the manager to cover any personal losses that result from a liability claim lodged against him by external parties. The corporation agrees to compensate the manager *ex post* for remedies and accompanying legal costs. The *vrijwaring* can be included in a contract or in the articles of association. The *vrijwaring* is limited by the principle of *ordre public* and the *bonos mores*. A *vrijwaring* that includes intentionally or grossly negligent misconduct is void. Furthermore, a *vrijwaring* that would also cover an internal action ex art. 2:9 BW is void.[777]

When the corporation is in bankruptcy proceedings, a *vrijwaring* is regarded as having only limited effect in practice. According to the *vrijwaring*, the manager may claim to be covered by the corporation. The corporation, however, is insolvent. The Dutch legal system provides that all corporate liabilities are on hold, except those that are secured. The manager who is liable will thus have to file the claim to be indemnified with the bankruptcy administrator and his claim has the same priority as all other unsecured claims. The recovery rate of the claim will be negligible. In this regard, the *vrijwaring* only has limited effect on his wealth.[778]

Germany – A *Freistellung* (roughly translated: exemption or indemnification) can be structured according to one of two alternatives. First, the corporation agrees to fulfil the obligations of the manager arising from an external liability directly. Secondly, the manager fulfils the claim but is reimbursed by the corporation later on. The difference between the two manners of compensation materializes when the corporation declares bankruptcy. When the manager makes an advance payment (which relates to the second manner), he will seek to be reimbursed by the corporation. Because the corporation is bankrupt, he will have to lodge his claim with the bankruptcy administrator. Because the manager is one of many creditors that lodged their claims, the manager is likely to recover only a small fraction of the original claim.[779] When the corporation agreed to pay the liability claimant directly (the first manner of compensation), the manager is not obliged to fulfil the liability claim at any time. He will not have an unenforceable claim to be indemnified against the corporation.[780]

The *Freistellung* must not include cover for internal liability claims. External claims that are based on §823 section 1 and 2 or §826 BGB have usually an internal angle as well. Thus, the *Freistellung* is only valid when a *Verzicht* also would have been.[781]

777 Hendrikse and Van den Heuvel 2009, p. 130; Eesthuis et al 2011, pp. 36–37.

778 Hendrikse and Van den Heuvel 2009, p. 130.

779 This consideration does not take into account potential possibilities to set-off the claim of the manager against the corporation (to receive the insurance compensation) with the debt of the manager owed to the corporation (pursuant to bankruptcy liability). The effectiveness of such a strategy is subject to the specific conditions and requirements of the national bankruptcy law with respect to setting-off. See: Kraakman et al. 2009, p. 141–142.

780 Thümmel 1998, p. 157.

781 Thümmel 1998, pp. 157–159.

External liability, without an internal angle to it and without foreseeable bankruptcy, is very rare. In such rare cases, literature suggests that the manager has a legal right to be indemnified by the corporation, according to §§670, 257 Sentence 1 BGB.[782]

Comparison – In the USA and the UK, the indemnification for external liability has limited importance due to the external party's inability to bring a claim. In Germany and the Netherlands, such indemnities might well be important to avoid external liability risk.

The indemnification of external liability becomes most important when the corporation is in bankruptcy proceedings / almost insolvent (in the vicinity of insolvency). However, in bankruptcy the corporate assets are frozen. Reimbursement by the corporation for external liability claims is virtually impossible, when a corporate payment of debts is suspended. The manager is probably unlikely to retrieve the amount due from the insolvent corporation. To circumvent this problem, the corporation might choose to transfer an amount to the manager before bankruptcy for the purposes of potential reimbursement.[783]

6.7. Corporate demand for D&O insurance

This section will analyse how far the four legal systems regulate managerial indemnification and apply the hypotheses of Chapter 5 to the regulations observed.

Subsection 5.3.2 argued that a firm, when it is risk neutral, has a comparative advantage to bear risk over a risk-averse manager.[784] Furthermore, the shareholders would indemnify the manager, when the shareholders think that the scope of internal liability is too harsh to incentivize managerial risk taking.[785]

In the four legal systems observed, *ex post* indemnification is usually linked to the verification of the yearly financial statements. With their verification, the manager is indemnified by the end of the financial year for all acts that could have been revealed when (carefully) scrutinizing the statements. When the majority of shareholders are in favour of indemnification *ex post*, the manager does not need to fear internal liability after the end of the financial year.

At first sight, the shareholders that indemnify *ex post* appear to not be exposed to any risk provided that they carefully scrutinize the financial statements. Yet, one could argue that there may be circumstances in which the managerial actions that may qualify for a suit and the occurrence of the damage are far apart in time. Under these circumstances, the manager may be held liable long after the shareholders indemnified the manager from a decision rendered previously. In this regard, it could be argued that even with respect to *ex post* indemnification, the shareholders may bear a risk.

782 Thümmel 1998, pp. 157–159; Schlechtriem 1991, pp. 73–75.

783 This transaction may be voidable *ex post* in bankruptcy proceedings pursuant to *actio pauliana* / claw back provisions. See: Thümmel 1998, p. 157; Kraakman et al. 2009, p. 141–142.

784 Fischel and Bradley 1985, p. 285; Sykes 1948, pp. 1235–1236.

785 Marks 1999, p. 704; Kraakman 1984, p. 859.

Ex ante indemnification is only authorized with respect to the German GmbH and for corporations established under Delaware law. In particular, the Delaware Code allows for substantial indemnifications, even *ex ante*. The rules governing the German AG harshly regulate such indemnification. In the Netherlands and the UK, an *ex ante* indemnification is (probably) forbidden.

These observations demonstrate that the legal limitations on indemnification differ to a high degree among countries and that indemnification is harshly regulated in the legal systems. In line with the previous considerations of section 5.5, when indemnification is prohibited, the firm seems to have no choice but to compensate the manager for the liability risk in the form of an increased salary or, alternatively, to insure internal liability.[786] According to the reasoning explained in subsection 5.3.2, it would have been cheaper for a firm to indemnify the manager than to raise his salary. The legal systems seem to rather agree with the scholars that argue that indemnification increases agency costs.[787]

Instead of a prohibition of indemnification Kraakman et al. propose to award attorney fees only when the suit would increase corporate value.[788] Furthermore, subsections 5.5.1 and 5.6.2 propose to incentivize insurance for the risk borne by the corporation to indemnify the liable manager, rather than prohibiting indemnification. Chapter 8 will outline to what extent a market of insurance for the indemnification risk exists.

The indemnification of external liability has limited importance when an external party cannot bring a claim in the first place (which is the case in the USA and the UK). In Germany and the Netherlands, indemnification is (probably) authorized. Subsection 5.5.1 argued that when the voluntary creditor knows that indemnification is used to increase managerial risk-taking to his detriment, the effect of indemnification are already part of the costs of debt capital.[789]

In bankruptcy, the corporate assets are frozen in all observed countries. Re-imbursement by the corporation for external liability claims is virtually impossible, when a corporate payment of debts is suspended. The manager is probably unlikely to retrieve the due and payable amount from the insolvent corporation. In line with the expectations of subsection 5.4.3, the manager is likely to desire no indemnification for the bankruptcy risk and instead desires insurance or a salary increase.[790] The relationship between insurance and a salary increase with respect to this liability risk will be outlined in Chapter 7.

786 Bishop 1964, p. 839; Bishop 1966, p. 96; Polinsky and Shavell 1993, p. 241; Fischel and Bradley 1985, p. 285.

787 Bishop 1964, p. 844; Bishop 1966, p. 97. Kraakman 1984 advocates the opposite at p. 865.

788 Kraakman et al. 1993, pp. 1762–1766. They further suggest possibilities of calculating the increase of corporate value. For a more general discussion of the effect of fees, see: Harrington and Danzon 2000, p. 304.

789 An argumentation based on the illustrations of Marks 1999, p. 704; Kraakman et al. 2009, pp. 116–117 and MacMinn and Garven 2000, pp. 541–544.

790 Kraakman 2008, p. 144; Kraakman 1984, pp. 868–869.

Section 5.5 argued that indemnification should be prohibited, when the expected loss that would have been borne by the manager is externalized through indemnification to a judgement-proof firm. Being judgement-proof, the firm's incentives to take care are limited to the expected loss of its assets. Any remaining damage is ignored by the firm.[791] The observed restrictions pursuant to the national bankruptcy laws seem to prevent the corporation from indemnifying its manager, which effectively means that indemnification is useless when the corporation is insolvent (or has become judgement-proof). In this regard, the observed regulations could be explained by the theory on firm delicts outlined in section 5.5. Chapter 9 will analyse, whether the national bankruptcy laws have a similar effect on insurance for the bankruptcy liability risk.

6.8. Conclusion

This chapter provided an overview of the managerial liability rules and the regulation of indemnification in the USA, the UK, the Netherlands, and Germany. This chapter applied the hypotheses of Chapter 5 to these rules and regulations. This conclusion will summarize (i) the different liability rules, (ii) the risk aversion of the manager and (iii) the regulation of indemnification.

(i) Liability rules encompass internal liability, tort liability and bankruptcy liability.

Subsections 5.2.1 and 5.4.4 argued that internal liability increases corporate value when either the prospect of the suit deters misconduct or the suit yields a net return. Subsection 5.5.2 argued that when the prospect of filing does not relate to misconduct but to expected benefit and the manager does not bear the costs of liability (he is compensated for it), the manager does not link the claim to his misconduct. The additional condition in the UK and Germany, pursuant to which a claimant has to show that it is in the interests of the corporation to file a claim, may establish the necessary link between misconduct and the prospect of filing. A claim under US securities law is not subject to similar conditions. The Dutch corporate governance tool to file an internal liability claim is very restricted in the first place.

Tort liability is absent in the USA and the UK, and has only limited application in the Netherlands and Germany. Such observation supports the argument that vicarious liability is more likely than external liability of the manager. Vicarious liability may not be sufficient when the firm cannot monitor the manager or is judgement-proof.

Possibly because the firm may not sufficiently monitor the manager, the Netherlands imposes tax liability rules. The UK adopts criminal liability against fraudulent/wrongful trading and the USA only criminally punishes managers to deter large one-shot frauds (cf. Enron).

Furthermore, in the vicinity of insolvency, additional bankruptcy liability to vicarious liability can be observed in all countries. Where bankruptcy liability does not deter enough, one can introduce criminal liability, for instance Germany resorts to criminal liability, possibly leading to imprisonment.

791 Kraakman 1984, p. 868.

(ii) The chapter has shown that the conditions and standards imposed by the liability rules differ considerably by country. The duty of loyalty is much stricter in the USA and the UK than in Germany and the Netherlands. External liability only exists in Germany and the Netherlands. The standard of care with respect to bankruptcy liability is lenient in the USA and the UK and very strict in Germany (aggravated by criminal sanctions).

When the manager loses sight of all liability rules or the court mistakenly holds the manager liable, the standard of care corresponding to the rules may be uncertain. Uncertainty creates risk. Subsection 5.2.4 suggested that a risk-averse manager desires compensation in the form of insurance, indemnification or a salary increase, when he has to bear risk.

(iii) Indemnification should be effective for internal liability and external liability. However, indemnification with respect to internal liability is harshly regulated in the four legal systems. *Ex post* indemnification is subject to the verification of the yearly financial statements. *Ex ante* indemnification is (probably) forbidden for the German AG, in the Netherlands and in the UK.

When indemnification is prohibited, the firm seems to have no choice but to compensate the manager for the liability risk in the form of an increased salary or, alternatively, to insure internal liability (indemnification would have been cheaper provided that the firm is risk neutral).

Indemnification with respect to external liability is (probably) authorized in Germany and the Netherlands. UK and US corporations do not have to indemnify their manager for external liability because external liability without a distress angle to it appears to be absent.

The observed restrictions pursuant to the national bankruptcy laws seem to prevent the corporation from indemnifying its manager, which effectively means that indemnification is prohibited when the corporation is insolvent (or has become judgement-proof). Chapters 8 and 9 will analyse whether the national bankruptcy laws have a similar effect on insurance for bankruptcy liability.

Chapter 7

EMPIRICAL EVIDENCE ON THE EFFECT OF D&O INSURANCE

7.1. Introduction

To understand the D&O insurer's role in managerial risk taking, Chapter 5 developed hypotheses on the demand for and supply of D&O insurance. Chapter 6 explained to what extent the legal environments in the USA, the UK, the Netherlands and Germany create demand for D&O insurance.

This chapter will analyse what kinds of corporations desire D&O insurance, to what extent the D&O insurance policies differ from corporate characteristics and how far the insurer is able to control managerial risk taking. To answer these questions, this chapter will review empirical studies. These studies more or less suggest that the demand for insurance indeed differs due to a high range of factors and that the insurer responds to these factors.

The empirical studies are mainly based on D&O insurance purchased by public Canadian firms because in Canada the D&O insurance data is public. Although our focus lies with other countries and will be applicable to private corporations alike, the empirical studies indicate factors that could be essential to understanding the context of D&O insurance.

When analysing the empirical findings, some caveats are in order. First, when comparing these studies, the problem arises that the data set, the variables and regressions do not perfectly correspond. Each study has its own methodology and thus the outcome stands by itself.

Secondly, these studies show correlations with D&O insurance. They are unable to show any causal link between D&O insurance and other factors. Furthermore, a correlation with D&O insurance does not necessarily mean that the insurer knows of that correlation and adapted its policy intentionally to the factors.

The studies rely on statistical methods: A mean constitutes what is known by average in normal language. The median is the integral that is closest to the mean. When an event correlates (highly) significantly at the 5% (1%)-level, it means that 95% (99%) of the observed corporations behaved that way. The remaining group behaved differently. Intuitively, the smaller the number of corporations behaving differently (deviation), the better the finding is. The p-level is just another way of indicating the percentage of deviations by ways of a decimal. For example, a 5% level corresponds to a p-value of 0.05.

In this regard, it must be kept in mind that there has been no evaluation of how far these studies are subject to statistical errors that may render the empirical findings inconclusive.[792]

With these caveats in mind, this chapter is structured as follows. Section 7.2 will outline the seminal study of Bhagat et al. in 1987 that also takes into account indemnification. Section 7.3 will look at the possibilities for the insurer to imperfectly observe the insured. It will analyse whether premiums and limits work independently from each other. Such finding would imply that the insurer knows more about the insured than just his desired insurance policy. Section 7.4 will apply the hypotheses of Chapter 5 to the findings of section 7.3. Section 7.5 will turn to the particular demand patterns for D&O insurance. Section 7.6 will again apply the hypotheses of Chapter 5 to the findings of section 7.5. Section 7.7 will outline the relationship between premiums and correlating factors. Section 7.8 will analyse whether these factors have one effect on limits but another effect on premiums. If so, this might suggest an information advantage for the insurer. Section 7.9 will turn to possible inefficiencies in the market. Section 7.10 will evaluate the findings of section 7.9.

Once the empirical evidence is outlined, the following Chapter 8 will analyse whether the demand and supply patterns introduced in Chapter 5 can be observed with respect to the insurance policies of the USA, the UK, the Netherlands, and Germany. To do so, it will interpret polls on demand and supply and scrutinize insurance contracts.

7.2. Correlations with indemnification

This section will present the result from a study of Bhagat et al. in 1987 that looks at indemnification, D&O insurance and share value.[793]

During the mid- and late 1980s in the US, the scope and limitation of the D&O insurance relating to shareholder derivative suits slowly crystallized as a result of court decisions. Against this discussion, Bhagat et al. in 1987 contributed to the controversy by providing empirical evidence. They based their model on the assumption that a drop in share value corresponds to shareholder dissatisfaction. With this assumption in mind, they looked at how far certain events lead to a drop or increase of share value. Such a finding would suggest how far such an event relates to the firm's performance in the interest of the shareholders.[794]

To receive evidence, the authors first used the null hypothesis that some to-be-defined events do not affect shareholder wealth. Secondly, they sought to prove the hypothesis that the events negatively affect shareholder wealth. The events being tested were the

792 De Groot 1975, pp. 419–421; Doane and Seward 2011, pp. 15–17, 551–552; Bain and Engelhardt 2014, pp. 358–359. For more information on errors with respect to the approval or rejection of the null-hypothesis, see: Doane and Seward 2011, pp. 344–347. For background information on errors generally, see: Doane and Seward 2011, pp. 15–17.

793 Bhagat et al. 1987, pp. 721–723.

794 Bhagat et al. 1987, pp. 721–722.

adoption of D&O insurance, broadening indemnification, and the New York state law in 1941 that authorized indemnification clauses. On average, the adoption of D&O insurance rejects the null hypothesis and suggests that it increases shareholder wealth. The two latter events do not have a significant effect on shareholder wealth and confirm the null hypothesis.[795]

The authors suggest not regulating the D&O insurance market, because they could not prove no effect or a negative effect on shareholder wealth. Furthermore, a regulation for indemnification would be senseless because the process of regulating is probably more costly than the potential costs related to unregulated indemnification. According to them, this finding suggests an alignment of interests between shareholders and managers due to insurance.[796]

However, this contribution must be considered carefully. First, the sample used by Bhagat et al. was very small, 28 respondents for the question of D&O insurance and 112 respondents for indemnification. The authors defended their study by showing the statistical significance of their outcome.[797]

Secondly, the study of Bhagat et al. was conducted in the 1980s, where no periods of un-insurability had taken place.

Thirdly, the positive view on insurance is also subject to the assumption that the social efficiency goal can be limited to shareholder wealth. This Chicago type shareholder model that is usually applied in the context of corporations having a dispersed ownership structure largely ignores interests of other stakeholders, such as the environment, suppliers, consumers, banks, or society in general.

Finally and maybe most importantly, the insurance market and liability system was structured differently. Deductibles for Side-A and Side-B[798] were comparably high, the coverage was co-insured by the insured with a 5% intake, and the coverage had a lower upper limit than is currently the norm in the US. The coverage excluded obvious conflicts of interest between shareholders and managers.[799] Furthermore, the liability system did not include securities liability actions until 1995 that currently amount to the major part of suits. During the time of the contributions, the derivative claim was used the most.[800]

7.3. Insurer's imperfect knowledge

Before looking at common characteristics of corporations requiring insurance, the question is first whether the insurer knows about the different characteristics of corporations which request this, and is able to adapt its policy to it. Section 4.5 outlined

795 Bhagat et al. 1987, pp. 728–733.

796 Bhagat et al 1987, p. 733.

797 Bhagat et al. 1987, p. 728–730, also see: Holderness 1990, p. 127.

798 For more information on Side-A and Side-B coverage, see subsection 8.4.1.

799 Managerial deductibles were between $ 5,000 and $25,000. Corporate deductibles were between $50,000 and $100,000, and quickly more, up to $2 million. The corporation often pays less than 100% of the premiums, leaving the remaining amount to the managers. See: Bhagat et al. 1987, p. 724.

800 Bhagat et al. 1987, p. 733; Holderness 1990, p. 117.

the insurer's tools of adaptation. This section distinguishes between the adaptation of the premium and the limitation of the coverage.

The observation of such characteristics grants us the insight that the insurer has imperfect knowledge and is able to differentiate.

The study of Gupta and Prakash in 2012 sheds more light on firms performance.[801] They use a panel data set of 93 firms in the years 1998, 2000 and 2002. They heavily rely on the model by Core in 2000.[802]

Gupta and Prakash 2012 focus on information asymmetry between manager and insurer. They seek to find evidence regarding the insurer's attempt to avoid adverse selection. To do so, they sought to observe factors that correlate with premiums and limits.[803]

Whereas the regression model is very similar to Core's,[804] one specific variable is included, the manager's excess control. It is defined as voting rights by the manager not to be explained by his share ownership. They argue that this variable is not only a reliable proxy for bad governance but moreover a good measure to quantify information asymmetry between manager and others. The variable should include managerial insider knowledge and unobserved managerial risk-taking.[805]

Premiums and limits sometimes correlate. In some cases, the same proxies lead to similar correlations. This is the case for firm size and US exchange listing. 10%-shareholders, managerial ownership and managerial share option compensation have the same effect on premium and limit. This result is intuitive. Higher exposure of the risk by the insurer leads to a higher asking price for exposure. However, prior litigation affects premiums, but not limits.[806]

Limits are related to some but not all governance proxies. Everything else being equal, managerial excess control correlates negatively with coverage limits. Managerial ownership and one external 10%-shareholder,[807] also correspond negatively to limits. These findings are significant at the 5%-level. Managerial stock option compensation plans significantly increase the limit.[808]

The premium very significantly and negatively correlates with the proportion of managerial share ownership and the existence of 10%-shareholders. Firm size and US-exchange listing are positively and significantly related.[809] Prior litigation

801 Gupta and Prakash 2012, pp. 1–7.

802 Core 2000, pp. 449–451.

803 Section 4.4.

804 Core 2000, p. 449–451.

805 Gupta and Prakash 2012, p. 12.

806 Gupta and Prakash 2012, p. 12.

807 This variable indicates whether certain groups of majority shareholders own the corporation and how far the corporate ownership is dispersed. Also see section 7.6.

808 Corporate size and listing on the US-exchange highly significantly (p-value of 0.00) and positively affect the limit. Gupta and Prakash 2012, p. 18–20.

809 Incentive compensation is insignificantly positively related to premiums. Gupta and Prakash 2012, pp. 18–21.

significantly increases premiums. The premium does not correlate with managerial excess control.[810]

7.4. Discussion of the insurer's ability to observe

As outlined in subsection 4.5.2, the insurer may be able to observe a change in the consumption of correlative products. If so, the insurer can adapt the premium accordingly.[811] An enhanced risk categorization (of correlative products) can contribute to the correct adaptation of the premium. The excessive use of partial coverage as an inferior solution can be limited to cases where risk categorization does not deliver the possibility of classifying risks.[812]

The outcome of the above mentioned study suggests that the insurer is able to categorize risks. Some correlative products bear enough information for the insurer to adapt the premium. Other correlative products are less informative, where the insurer resorts to the inferior solution of partial coverage.

The next section will look at partial coverage. Consequently, section 7.7 will deal with correlations with respect to D&O premiums.

7.5. Demand for insurance and partial coverage

Previously Chapter 5 made several suggestions about the demand for insurance. Against these theoretical suggestions, this section will introduce some empirical studies on the demand for D&O insurance.

These studies look at two features of D&O insurance. First, they look at the existence of D&O insurance. The comparison between firms having a D&O coverage and those which do not, provides a clear picture about demand.

Secondly, they look at financial limitations. The choice of the corporation for a certain financial limitation reveals their risk class, considering the theory of self-selection.

The remainder of this section follows a chronological order, including studies by Mayers and Smith 1990 on re-insurance, O'Sullivan 1997, Core 1997 and O'Sullivan 2002, Kaltchev 2006, and Warning 2008.

810 Gupta and Prakash 2012, p. 19–21. Some of these considerations are hotly disputed. For example, Boubakri and Ghalleb 2008 suggest that the insurer pools risks and is not able to differentiate at all. This assertion is interestingly enough in clear opposition to a prior study of the same authors including Boyer 2008, six months earlier. In that contribution, they conclude that insurers are indeed asking a higher premium for corporations with poor long-term performance and a smaller premium for corporations that ask for a limit that is unexplainable by their corporate governance quality and business risk. See: Boubakri and Ghalleb September 2008, p. 27; Boubakri, Ghalleb and Boyer March 2008, p. 26.

811 Bond and Crocker 1991, pp. 178, 179.

812 Bond and Crocker 1991, pp. 178, 179; Dionne et al. 2000, pp. 233–234.

7.5.1. Evidence from re-insurance: Mayers and Smith 1990

In 1990, a study by Mayers and Smith sought to outline the D&O purchasing behaviour of firms in the USA. Because no data was publicly available, the authors turned to the re-insurance market. Although the re-insurance market does not distinguish between insurance policies, it might grant limited observations on the corporate demand for D&O insurance.[813]

The data is based on property/casualty re-insurance and includes 1,276 insurers. The authors are particularly interested in the following features of the covered insurer: (1) corporate size (affecting taxes, expected bankruptcy costs, under-investment, and real-service efficiencies[814]), (2) business concentration[815] (affecting real-service efficiencies), (3) ownership structure[816] (referring to risk aversion), (4) rating on default risk (affecting expected bankruptcy costs and under-investment), (5) geographic concentration (which might increase volatility of taxes and firm value and also might hamper the real-service efficiencies), and (6) lines of business[817] (to better understand the outcome of means and ranges for the sample). In turn, the authors hold one of the aspects constant and look at the development of the other five factors.[818]

The following findings were observed. According to ownership structure, subsidiaries are more likely to purchase re-insurance than non-subsidiaries. The same goes for private corporations in relation to public corporations. Furthermore, there is weak evidence that dispersed-ownership corporations purchase less re-insurance than controlled-ownership corporations.[819]

The study suggests that size, the rating on default risk, geographic concentration, and lines of business concentration reduce the demand for re-insurance. The study further implies that the real-service efficiencies argument might be the most important argument.[820]

7.5.2. Corporate governance and demand: O'Sullivan 1997

O'Sullivan's study is based on a UK sample of 366 corporations. Costs and limits of D&O insurance are not included in the sample. Only the very existence of a D&O policy is considered. He seeks to find out in how far D&O insurance influences these monitoring

813 Mayers and Smith 1990, p. 19–20.

814 *"Insurance firms develop a comparative advantage in processing claims because of scale economies and gains from specialization. [They] are low-cost suppliers of these services."* See: Mayers and Smith 1990, p. 23.

815 Business concentration refers to a degree of specialization of the insurer, in for example low-volatility claims. See: Mayers and Smith 1990, p. 25.

816 The variable ownership structure has three variations: more than 50% owned by one family, closely held (100 shareholders or less), or publicly held (more than 100 shareholders). See: Mayers and Smith 1990, p. 27.

817 Lines of business relate to the number of insurance policies. For example, some insurers only cover car accidents, other also include aircraft insurance. See: Mayers and Smith 1990, p. 25, 29.

818 Mayers and Smith 1990, pp. 23–29.

819 Mayers and Smith 1990, pp. 29–38.

820 Mayers and Smith 1990, pp. 38–39.

mechanisms. To do so, he looks at shareholders, board composition and executive share ownership.[821]

Relating this to D&O insurance, insured corporations have a significantly higher proportion of outside directors[822] than uninsured corporations.[823] The separation of the chairman position and the CEO position does not have an impact.[824]

Regarding the size[825] aspect discussed before, the proportion of outside directors and the likelihood of an existing D&O policy increase with corporate size. Such correlation has been observed by many and their relationship has been hotly disputed.[826] There is no significant correlation between D&O purchase and the number of (at least) 3% shareholders. Managerial shareholding correlates negatively with the D&O purchase decision.[827] Latter observation suggests, according to O'Sullivan, a substituting role between managerial shareholding and D&O insurance.[828]

7.5.3. Response to Mayers and Smith: Core 1997 and O'Sullivan 2002

In 1997, Core examined the purchasing behaviour of Canadian firms in response to the findings of Mayers and Smith 1990. The data could be gathered because Canadian law requires listed corporations to publish information about the existence of D&O coverage and the upper cap (limit).[829] Similarly in 2002, O'Sullivan was able to gather data from big UK firms to analyse D&O purchasing practice. In this study, only the existence of D&O coverage was available.[830] This subsection follows Core's model. Specifications by O'Sullivan 2002 are indicated as such.

Excess pay[831] positively correlates with D&O limit and likelihood for D&O insurance.

Litigation risk[832] highly correlates with D&O insurance and the size of corporate deductible. Corporations with prior or pending litigations are more likely to purchase insurance, pending or prior litigations increase their limit, but do not affect their deductibles.[833] O'Sullivan found that a high beta corresponds to a higher probability of

821 O'Sullivan 1997, pp. 545–546, 550.

822 Outside directors are directors that do not emerge from within the corporation but are instead appointed as an outsider of the firm, not having any previous relations to the firm. See: O'Sullivan 1997, p. 548.

823 With a significance of the 1% level. See: O'Sullivan 1997, p. 548.

824 O'Sullivan 1997, p. 552.

825 Size is measured by a logarithm of market capitalization at the 1991 financial year end. See: O'Sullivan 1997, p. 550.

826 The reader is referred to the studies outlined below: Kaltchev 2004, p. 50; Core 1997, p. 82.

827 O'Sullivan 1997, pp. 551–554.

828 O'Sullivan 1997, pp. 545–556.

829 Core 1997, pp. 63–65.

830 O'Sullivan 2002, pp. 574–575.

831 The logarithm for excess pay incorporates managerial shareholding and a dummy (yes or no, binary option, no scale) for stock option plans. Although the study speaks of cash, the logarithm attempts an approximation. The study does not resort to actual cash payments. See: Core 1997, pp. 74–75.

832 Litigation risk is the outcome of a logarithm incorporating volatility, ROA, pending or prior litigations, assets in the US, exchange listing in the US, acquisitions, and divesting. See: Core 1997, pp. 71–73.

833 Core 1997, p. 81.

purchased D&O insurance in the UK.[834] Such a finding is intuitive, because volatility is associated with liability risk.[835] Volatility might lead to distress, take-overs and most importantly shareholder's lack of sympathy. These events argue for measures of recourse, managerial liability being one of them. Anticipating this, corporations might want to insure against increased managerial liability risk due to volatility.

Operations in the USA correlate with the decision to purchase insurance but not with the upper limit of insurance.[836] Similar to this, O'Sullivan in 2002 found that UK firms with operations in the USA are more likely to be insured than those without operations in the USA. O'Sullivan thinks that such correlation is based on the expectation of increased litigation risk in the USA.[837]

Divesting corporations buy significantly more insurance and are significantly more likely to have insurance. So do corporations with higher distress probabilities.[838] Furthermore, O'Sullivan detected that corporations that have a higher ratio of debt capital are more likely to have D&O insurance.[839] However, there is no significant correlation between M&A (mergers and acquisitions) activity and D&O limit or D&O purchase.[840] O'Sullivan found the same result to be true in the UK.[841]

The correlations to size are dubious. Size may be measured as market value of all outstanding shares or as the value of all corporate assets.[842] Taken together, size does not have an effect on D&O insurance purchase. It is argued that size has offsetting effects. It leads either to a higher risk of litigation, or to less likelihood of bankruptcy.

Comparing the correlations of the two variables, asset value positively correlates with limits, according to Core. Interestingly, greater share value (which might lead to more litigation risk) did not affect D&O upper limits.[843] Share value does have a positive impact on D&O purchase in the UK, according to O'Sullivan.[844]

In this regard, a consideration of shareholding is essential. A controlling shareholder significantly contributes to a lower insurance limit and less likely purchase. The same goes for managerial voting control. That suggests that corporations having a more dispersed ownership structure desire more insurance.[845]

834 High volatility of corporate shares compared to the entire market is called a high BETA in finance. For more information on the BETA, see: Berk & De Marzo 2013, Chapter 11: Optimal Portfolio Choice and the Capital Asset Pricing Model.

835 O'Sullivan 2002, p. 579.

836 Core 1997, p. 81.

837 O'Sullivan 2002, p. 579.

838 Core 1997, p. 81. This variable is -log (market value of total assets / total liabilities) / 10 * standard deviation of the firm's ROA for the prior three years. See: Core 1997, p. 73.

839 O'Sullivan 2002, p. 579.

840 Core 1997, p. 81.

841 O'Sullivan 2002, p. 579.

842 One aspect of size is the amount of corporate assets. Here, all assets that are owned by the corporation are added up. Another aspect to incorporate size is the measurement of market value of equity (MVE). In this method, one adds up the market value (read: the price of shares on the publicly traded exchange) of all equity (read: outstanding shares). See: Kaltchev 2004, p. 23.

843 Core 1997, p. 82.

844 O'Sullivan 2002, p. 579.

845 Core 1997, p. 82. However, although O'Sullivan detected the same correlation in the UK, it was not significantly so. Thus, this factor may still be a controversial one. See: O'Sullivan 2002, p. 581.

In this regard, O'Sullivan turns to the presence of non-executive board members and D&O insurance. O'Sullivan detects that a higher amount of non-executive board members correlates with the likelihood of D&O purchase.[846]

Corporations that have a strong growth prediction[847] are hypothesized to purchase more D&O insurance because it will improve decision making and deter under-investment. This result could not be found. O'Sullivan sought to observe whether insured firms have higher growth expectations. However, such evidence was absent.[848] Core interpreted that such corporations have strong cash-flow constraints. Thus, they incentivize their managers by way of stock option plans instead of insurance.[849]

7.5.4. A model on D&O insurance demand: Kaltchev 2006

As a response to this controversy, Kaltchev 2004 and other authors[850] sought to build a descriptive model to prove and reject some of these theories. Kaltchev attempts to prove one primary and five subsidiary hypotheses. (1) First, his primary hypothesis is that a corporation with more return demands less insurance. Return is measured by raw stock returns and returns on assets.[851] (2) Secondly, corporate governance influences the D&O insurance demand. (3) Thirdly, financial risk influences insurance limits. (4) Fourthly, smaller corporations demand more insurance due to real-service efficiencies[852] and expected bankruptcy costs. Furthermore, the higher the market value of corporate equity, the higher the limit. (5) Fifthly, insurance mitigates the under-investment problem.[853]

He further splits the samples to reflect some of the liability crises in 2001, referring to the advent of liability claims during the DotCom crisis. Thus, the first sample is between 1997–2000, the second one between 2000–2002. The results he found are highly correlating, which means that they have a predictive value of 99%.

(1) The first hypothesis is approved. More return (return on assets) correlates with less insurance. The approval suggests that higher returns are associated with an alignment of interest between shareholders and the manager or, in other words, lower agency costs. Aligned interests between the two suggest less litigation, rendering D&O insurance meaningless.

846 O'Sullivan 2002, p. 579.

847 Growth is defined as the ratio of the sum of market value and book value of liabilities divided by the book value of the firm's assets. See: Core 1997, p. 73.

848 O'Sullivan 2002, p. 579.

849 Core 1997, pp. 81, 82.

850 Chen and Li 2008, Warning 2008, Fier et al. 2012. These contributions may be less reliable, however, because of their small sample set that is based on surveys and less advanced models.

851 This hypothesis is retrieved from Gutiérrez-Urtiaga 2000.

852 Kaltchev uses the same definition as Mayers and Smith 1990. "*Insurance firms develop a comparative advantage in processing claims because of scale economies and gains from specialization. [They] are low-cost suppliers of these services.*" See: Mayers and Smith 1990, p. 23.

853 Kaltchev 2004, pp. 22–24.

Subsequently, he puts his findings relative to MVE size, making all corporations the 'same size', to better compare the remaining variables to purchasing behavior. Still, higher return on assets correlates to less insurance.

(2) An increased amount of board members slightly negatively correlates with the desire to purchase insurance.[854] Kaltchev thinks that an increased amount of managers leads to better monitoring. However, an increased amount of outside managers[855] has a slightly positive correlation (similar to O'Sullivan 1997).[856] In a second sample just looking at a time period between 2000–2002, the positive correlation regarding outside managers increased.[857]

Katchev could not find one-sided evidence that controlling shareholders demand more insurance.[858] Such a correlation is, however, suggested by Warning in Germany, though Warning used a less anticipated model and a smaller sample.[859]

Regarding corporate governance, monitoring mechanisms do not seem to prominently influence the D&O insurance decision. Kaltchev interprets that "*[t]he role of D&O insurance in mitigating the agency problems between manager and shareholders is dubious.*"[860]

Similar considerations have been brought forward by Fier et al. in 2012.[861] New to their study is the observation of demand patterns relative to time and industry. They regarded certain types of industries that were strongly affected by the corporate scandals in 1990s and 2000s and those who were not. Those industries directly affected by the scandals had a higher demand in D&O insurance. Furthermore, the industries that were most associated with the scandals also purchased higher limits. They suggest that an increase of a real or perceived likelihood of managerial liability exposure aggregates the limit amounts of already insured corporations.[862]

(3) Leverage, as a sign of distress, and volatility increase the desired protection. This observation corresponds to hypothesis three. A similar observation was made in Taiwan.[863]

854 However, an increased amount of board members does not correlate with the size of limit. Chen and Li observed a similar pattern in Taiwan. See: Kaltchev 2004, pp. 35–36; Chen and Li 2008, p. 13.

855 Outside directors are directors that do not emerge from within the corporation but are instead appointed as an outsider of the firm, not having any previous relations to the firm. See: Kaltchev 2004, pp. 35–36.

856 O'Sullivan 1997, p. 548.

857 Kaltchev 2004, pp. 35–36. He argued that such a finding contributes to the second hypothesis, also being influenced by the coming into force of the Sarbanes-Oxley Act in 2002 that incentivized securities claims. See: Kaltchev 2004, p. 48.

858 Kaltchev 2004, pp. 43–45. He detected that the number of controlling shareholders correlates positively and the relative amount of controlling shareholders in the firm correlates negatively with insurance.

859 Warning 2008, pp. 19–20.

860 Kaltchev 2004, p. 53.

861 Fier et al. 2012, pp.1–5.

862 Fier et al. 2012, pp. 16–23.

863 Chen and Li 2008, pp. 14–15.

Insurance might be able to mitigate bankruptcy risk. Kaltchev's found correlation of D&O limits provides a definite signal about the financial health of the corporation. The amount of limit can be interpreted as to show bankruptcy risk.[864]

(4) Size is a valuable co-efficient to predict liability damages and thus demanded coverage. The bigger the size based on MVE the higher is the limit.[865]

Cancelling MVE from the regressions, the amount of assets negatively correlates with demand for insurance. According to Kaltchev, this finding confirms that smaller corporations are willing to make use of the insurer's specific knowledge to decrease the risk. Furthermore, D&O insurance might limit the risk of default. Kaltchev argues that big corporations might have a greater ability to self-insure.[866]

(5) According to growth, the correlation to insurance is slightly negative. That means that hypothesis 5 is not confirmed. Insurance is not regarded as a way to mitigate under-investment. Kaltchev thinks that growth corporations are more tolerant of risk, with less risk-averse managers.[867]

Finally, Kaltchev remarks that findings and essential variables change over time. He emphasizes that changing environments and circumstances may lead to a different appreciation or at least corporate evaluation for D&O insurance. This consideration could turn the focus to biases and behavioural economics, not yet subject to the discussion of the D&O insurance market.

7.5.5. *Corporate governance and size of deductibles: Warning 2008*

Another German study by Warning 2008 shows that a far-reaching compliance of the German Corporate Governance Code negatively correlates with the size of deductibles.[868]

When assuming that the insured self-selects the D&O policy,[869] this finding makes sense. A choice for a higher deductible implies that the corporation runs a smaller D&O risk. D&O risk is closely related to the alignment of interests between shareholder and manager. Compliance with the Corporate Governance Code suggests a well functioning alignment. Because the D&O risk is smaller for corporations that comply to the Code, they choose to insure less.

Furthermore, she shows that the existence of shareholder concentration relates to a stronger likelihood of D&O insurance without a deductible. Furthermore, if the

864 Kaltchev 2004, pp. 49–50.

865 Kaltchev 2004, p. 48. However, this is the opposite regarding assets, when subject to a certain time period. Between 1997 and 2000, corporations with bigger assets bought less insurance. See: Kaltchev 2004, pp. 47–48.

866 Kaltchev 2004, pp. 51–52.

867 Kaltchev 2004, p. 45. Although the finding is similar with O'Sullivan 2002, p. 579 and Core 1997, pp. 81, 82, the interpretations differ.

868 Warning 2008, pp. 1–5.

869 On partial coverage see: section 5.10 and Dionne et al. 2000, p. 193; Ehrlich and Becker 1972, pp. 634–643; Loubergé 2000, p. 162.

controlling shareholder is either individual or a government agency, this relationship is even more pronounced.[870]

Peculiar to her study in Germany is that she finds no significant correlation of D&O deductibles with return on assets, leverage, volatility, proportion of employee representatives in the board, or average managerial compensation.[871]

7.6. Comparison between hypotheses on demand and actual demand

The variables tested can be loosely grouped into four kinds of factors, (1) firm performance, (2) litigation risk/corporate governance quality, (3) managerial compensation, and (4) business risk. The studies looked at the very existence of D&O insurance (D&O purchase), the size of the limit and the size of deductibles.

(1) With respect to firm performance, the variables share value, return on assets (ROA), growth, and volatility have been observed. Greater share value does not correlate with limits or D&O purchase (Core 1997) or positively correlates with limits (Kaltchev 2006). ROA negatively correlates with limits. According to Warning, ROA does not correlate with deductibles. There is a slightly negative (Katchev 2006) or no correlation (Core 1997, O'Sullivan 1997 and 2002) between growth and limits. Volatility positively correlates with the existence of D&O insurance and limits. Such a finding suggests that D&O insurance does not incentivize managers to maximize corporate utility. However, the findings may also be misleading (noisy) due to unobserved correlating factors. For example, many studies seemed to not consider indemnification of the manager. The following chapter will further consider a possible relationship between D&O insurance and firm performance.

(2) Regarding corporate governance, the factors of number of outside directors, majority shareholders, dispersed shareholding, US operations, litigation risk and litigation history were observed. The number of outside directors positively correlates with D&O purchase and limits. O'Sullivan suggested that (i) either D&O insurers might require the corporation to hire outside directors before underwriting, (ii) D&O insured corporations might be more attractive to non-executive board members, or (iii) non-executive board members may be much more risk averse and thus would have a higher demand for D&O insurance.[872]

Some, but not all studies observe a correlation between majority shareholders and D&O purchase or limits. Indeed, it has been argued that the liability system could empower individual shareholders to influence the corporate strategy. The prospect of being held liable could induce the manager to publish more information about the corporation.[873]

870 Warning 2008, p. 20.

871 Warning 2008, p. 20.

872 O'Sullivan 2002, p. 581.

873 Marks 1999, pp. 696, 698–709; Kraakman 2009, pp. 36, 39, 115; Lawless et al. 1997, p. 112. By way of the liability system, a minority shareholder may be able to control the corporation against the will of majority shareholders and management. See: Marks 1999, pp. 708–709.

Warning observes a negative correlation between the concentration of shareholding and the size of the deductible. It has been suggested that corporations that have a more dispersed ownership structure desire more insurance.[874] According to Warning 2008, the compliance with the Corporate Governance Code positively correlates with the deductible. Similarly, O'Sullivan and Bhagat et al. 1987 suggest that diversified shareholders have an increased cost of monitoring because of their great investment portfolio. Yet, on the basis of these findings the validity of the monitoring hypotheses outlined in section 5.6 remains dubious.[875]

US operations positively correlate with D&O purchase but not with limits. The previous section 6.5 pointed to the great ability of shareholders to successfully bring a claim under American securities law. Thus the positive correlation of the US operations with D&O purchase confirms the hypothesis that the liability rule under American securities law creates uncertainty which in turn creates risk. The manager demands compensation for that risk, such as insurance.

Litigation risk has the same relationship with D&O insurance as the factor of US operations. The correlation of litigation risk might indicate that corporations with internal power struggles indeed ask for more D&O insurance.[876] Such a consideration would confirm the hypotheses of 5.6.2 on the mediating role of the insurer.

Litigation history has a positive relationship with D&O purchase and limits. Litigation history has no correlation with deductibles, however.

(3) Regarding managerial compensation, the studies looked at excess pay and at shareholding (including stock option compensation plans). Excess pay has a positive correlation with D&O purchase and limits. Managerial shareholding negatively correlates with D&O purchase and limits. Warning finds no correlation between the deductible and managerial compensation. This ambivalent finding is remarkable. It shows that compensation via shares has the opposite effect on D&O insurance from excess cash payments. According to Core 1997, excess pay is a complement to insurance and stock option compensation plans are a substitute to insurance. Core argues that "*these results are more consistent with compensation components becoming complements because they are bundled together by an insider who does not internalize their cost, or because little attention is given to designing director compensation plans*"[877] Further, firms with greater growth opportunities and consequently greater cash constraints provide the manager with stock option plans rather than with D&O insurance.[878]

874 This finding would approve the hypotheses of subsection 5.6.1. Core 1997, p. 82. However, although O'Sullivan detected the same correlation in the UK, it was not significantly so. Thus, this factor may still be a controversial one. See: O'Sullivan 2002, p. 581.

875 Compare to section 6.5.

876 It has to be kept in mind that the factor litigation risk refers to a logarithm that includes the factor US operations. In this regard, the mutual relationship of US operations and litigation with D&O insurance is less surprising. See: Core 1997, pp. 71–73.

877 Core 1997, p. 81.

878 First, "*firms with higher excess director pay are more likely to carry D&O insurance ... and purchase higher limits. These results are in contrast ... to the common assumption that various compensation components are substitutes.*" Secondly, "*firms with greater growth opportunities tend to be cash constrained, and, as part of an overall strategy to conserve cash, the firms may substitute noncash*

(4) Regarding business risk, size, divesting, distress risk, and leverage were observed. Size is defined differently in the studies, it either means market value of equity, or value of assets. According to Core 1997, neither of the size variables correlates to D&O purchase, but the asset value has a positive relationship with limits,[879] and the market value has no correlation to the limit. According to Kaltchev, market value correlates with D&O purchase and limits (similar O'Sullivan who only tested D&O purchase). The value of assets negatively correlates with limits, according to Kaltchev.[880] Supposedly, the corporate size has off-setting effects.

Divesting positively correlates with D&O purchase and limits. Distress risk positively correlates with D&O purchase and limits. Leverage positively correlates with D&O purchase and limits. There is no correlation between leverage and deductible.

In this regard, three considerations can be made.

First, subsection 5.4.3 argued that bankruptcy liability gives rise to demand for insurance irrespective of the corporate indemnification efforts. When the indemnifying corporation is close to insolvency (in the vicinity of insolvency), the indemnified manager remains subject to damage arising from liability. To eliminate the remainder of the liability risk, the manager is likely to desire insurance. The empirical findings do not relate the demand for insurance to whether the purchasing corporation is close to insolvency, but they do show that D&O insurance is desired more when the corporation is in financial trouble.[881]

Secondly, section 5.3 argued that the manager is more likely to be indemnified than insured.[882] Further, it is cheaper for a firm to indemnify the manager than to raise his salary. Chapter 5 did not establish a preference when confronted with the alternative of having insurance or a salary raise. Core suggests that *"firms with higher excess director pay are more likely to carry D&O insurance ... and purchase higher limits. These results are in contrast ... to the common assumption that various compensation components are substitutes."*[883]

In this context, the following observation can be made. D&O insurance has no correlation with firm performance[884] and a positive correlation to business risk.[885] An empirical study by Bloom and Milkovich 1998 suggests that managerial incentive pay has a negative correlation to firm performance and a negative correlation to business risk.[886] In this regard, the studies' outcome could be extrapolated to argue that, under

compensation (such as stock options) for an otherwise optimal amount of insurance." See: Core 1997, pp. 81, 82.

879 Core 1997, p. 82.

880 Kaltchev 2004, p. 50.

881 Alternatively, it can be argued that the size of the limit indicates the financial health or stability of the corporation.

882 e.g. a similar reasoning by Oesterle 1983, p. 570, 572; Pillai and Tractenberg 1981, p. 105.

883 Core 1997, pp. 81, 82.

884 Chen and Li 2008, p. 1–5; Gupta and Prakash 2012, p. 22–23.

885 Kaltchev 2004, pp. 49–50.

886 *"Higher levels of risk and greater use of incentive pay may be associated with lower firm performance."* Further: *"The data suggest that organizations facing higher risk do not place greater emphasis on short-term incentive pay-indeed, they place less emphasis on it."* See: Bloom and Milkovich 1998, pp. 291, 292.

financial distress, insurance is preferable to a salary increase.[887] D&O insurance may be a valuable alternative to excess pay in times of financial instability when the level of firm performance will remain the same.[888]

Thirdly, the hypothesis on the beneficial signalling effects of D&O insurance for the creditor seem to be partly approved. The hypothesis of signalling introduced in subsection 5.6.3 is subject to three heavy qualifications, being (i) the insurer is able to differentiate risks, (ii) the insurance policy is publicly available to function as a signal and (iii) the creditor makes effective use of that signal. The outlined correlations suggest that the first assumption holds. The second assumption holds, at least in Canada, where the information on D&O insurance coverage is public. Sections 7.9 and 7.10 will evaluate whether the third assumption holds as well.

7.7. Risk differentiation and premium adaptation

Having said that the insurer is able to imperfectly differentiate the risk, this section looks at the characteristics that publicly correlate with the premium.

In this regard, the study of Core 2000, and Boyer and Stern 2012 will consider corporate governance quality and correlating risks, such as business risks.

7.7.1. Corporate governance and business risk: Core 2000

Core's study reflects a sample of 110 Canadian firms in the time period between 1993 and 1994.[889] Core seeks to prove the following hypothesis: The D&O insurance premium reflects the business risk and the inefficiency of corporate governance. The higher the business risk and corporate governance inefficiency, the higher is the D&O premium.

To do so, Core defines terms first. First, the D&O premium is equal to the actuarially fair premium, plus supplementary costs, such as administration. The actuarially fair value is computed from the frequency of litigation claims times the expected damage arising from the claims. Core names the actuarially fair value *ex ante* litigation risk because it measures the risk of litigation before it has crystallized.[890] Secondly, corporate governance is the ability of shareholders to impose tight constraints on the manager. Thirdly, business risk is an accumulation of risks that include firm size, profitability, operations in the USA.[891]

The negative link between incentive pay and firm performance has been somewhat weakened by studies such as: Hutchinson and Gul 2004, pp. 609–610.

887 Such an argument ignores other forms of salary increase, such as a payment in the form of corporate shares, e.g. the already outlined correlation of managerial shareholding with growth opportunities. See: Core 1997, p. 81, 82.

888 Furthermore, one could argue that insurance is more practical than compensation in the form of shares because the share value of financially distressed firms usually remains depressed for some time.

889 Core 2000, pp. 449–451.

890 Core 2000, p. 450. This reasoning is based on the study of Romano 1991. She finds some evidence that the corporate governance inefficiency correlates with *ex post* litigation risk. For more information see: Romano 1991, pp. 55–56.

891 Core 2000, p. 450.

He needs to proxy these general terms to make a model. First, corporate governance is measured by nine variables, being (1) the proportion of managerial voting control, (2) the proportion of managerial share ownership, (3) the amount of shareholder's share ownership that exceed 10%, (4) the proportion of outside directors appointed by the CEO, (5) the proportion of outside directors in relation to the board, (6) whether the CEO is also board chair, (7) whether the managers have employment contracts, (8) whether the managers have golden parachutes, and (9) whether the corporation has takeover deterrents.[892]

Secondly, business risk is formulated through six variables, which are (10) a logarithm of the number of years the CEO has been on the board, (11) return on equity, (12) a logarithm of total assets to measure size, (13) prior and pending litigation, (14) operations in the US, and (15) listing on the US exchange.[893]

These variables were tested against the D&O insurance premium. First, let us consider the corporate governance variables. There is a significantly positive correlation to (1) managerial voting control and a significantly negative correlation with (2) managerial share ownership. The amount of (3) shareholder ownership above 10% does not have an impact on D&O insurance. It is explained that this aspect has offsetting effects, on the one hand strengthening corporate governance, whereas on the other hand increasing the likelihood of liability suits. There is a positive significant relationship with (4) proportion of outside directors appointed by the CEO and no relationship with (5) proportion of outside directors. Further, there is a highly significant positive relationship to (7) the existence of a manager employment contracts.[894]

Secondly, all of the business risk variables have a significant impact on D&O premiums. More specifically, (10) the number of years the CEO has been on the board and (11) the return on equity has a highly significant negative effect on the D&O premiums. The variables (12) size based on corporate assets, (13) litigation, (14) US operations and (15) listing in the US all have a significantly positive relationship to D&O premiums.[895]

So far he knows that the D&O premium is dependent on business risk and corporate governance. As a next step, he wants to find out how far corporate governance quality alone is reflected in the D&O premium. Thus, he makes his findings comparable, taking business risk out of the equation. He finds evidence in his sample that when corporate governance (being the sum of the nine variables) is one standard deviation weaker than the average, D&O premium rises to roughly 32% more than the average comparable firm.[896]

He does acknowledge a catch to this study, namely corporate governance inefficiencies corresponding to D&O premiums do not need to be bad for shareholders. Thus, he aims to show a relationship of high D&O premiums and worse off shareholders. He does so, by

892 Core 2000, pp. 457–461.

893 Core 2000, p. 462.

894 Core 2000, pp. 462–467.

895 Core 2000, pp. 462–467.

896 Core 2000, p. 469.

demonstrating that weak governance correlates with excess CEO compensation.[897] Excess CEO compensation is shown to be to the detriment of shareholders due to a decrease of share value.[898] He shows that, everything else being equal, a corporation with one standard deviation less in the average corporate governance variable correlates to a compensation that is 26% higher. Further, he looks at the relationship between excess pay and D&O insurance. He hypothesizes that if D&O insurance indeed substitutes the monitoring role, the size of the premium relates to the excess CEO compensation. Indeed, he finds evidence for this relationship. CEO compensation significantly positively correlates with the D&O premium. This relationship is sustained, when accounting for size of limits and the part of the premium's size relating to business risk.[899]

He concludes that "*the finding provides indirect evidence that D&O insurance charges higher premiums when hav[ing] governance structures that make shareholders worse off.*" The "worse off" does not refer to share performance however, but to CEO compensation.[900]

The findings of business risk and outside directors have also been observed in China by Zou et al. in 2008.[901] Furthermore, Core's finding has been applied and developed by Kang in 2011.[902] Her sample uses 92 US corporations that are listed in Canada between 1 June 2009 and 31 May 2010. Due to this environment, these corporations are subject to US-American legal liability rules and at the same are required to disclose D&O insurance data in Canada.[903]

Kang uses and develops Core's model. For the proxies on CEO power (4) to (6), there was a significant negative relationship for (4) proportion of outside directors appointed by the CEO and (5) the CEO being also the board chair. Plus, there was an insignificant positive relationship with the (6) proportion of outside directors on the board. According to Kang, this evidence might suggest that the skills of the CEO to appoint outside directors is a positive sign for the insurer as board conformity might be likely to lead to less litigation risk.[904]

Furthermore, she replaces (3) the amount of shareholder's share ownership that exceeds 10% and (8) whether the managers have golden parachutes with (3NEW) the percentage of total CEO compensation that consists of short term incentive payments. One standard deviation increase aggregates D&O premium by, roughly, a factor of two.

897 "*CEO compensation is the sum of the base salary, annual incentive payments, the value of option grants, and the value of long-term incentive plans, and the value of any benefits and perquisits.*" See: Core 2000, p. 471–472.

898 Core 2000, p. 471. For more information, please refer to: Borokovich et al. 1997; Hallock 1997; Core et al. 1999. For information on the relationship between incentive pay and firm performance, see Bloom and Milkovich 1998, pp. 291, 292. The negative link between incentive pay and firm performance has been somewhat weakened by studies such as: Hutchinson and Gul 2004, pp. 609–610.

899 Core 2000, pp. 471–475.

900 Core 2000, p. 475.

901 Zou et al. 2008, pp. 2636–2638, 2642–2644.

902 Kang 2011, pp. 3–9.

903 Kang 2011, pp. 38–40.

904 Kang 2011, pp. 42–43.

Other proxies and sensitivity tests led to a similar result for the cross-national firms as the pure Canadian sample of Core, confirming his findings.[905]

7.7.2. Corporate structure: Boyer and Stern in 2012

Their study is based on a Canadian sample of 200 firms.[906] In contrast with prior studies, they explicitly focused on the firm's legal personality and in how far that would affect the D&O policy. They distinguish between public corporations and income trusts. Whereas the legal structure of corporations has been explained, income trusts have not been. In a trust, there are no exact rules on corporate governance. Thus, the individuals that grant the capital do not, *per se*, have controlling rights to incentivize or deter the manager for certain actions. The trust is used to manage static capital flows.[907]

The authors observed that income trusts pay by far a higher D&O premium than corporations. Everything else being equal, income trusts pay a 80% higher premium than a corporation. Furthermore, they confirm the findings of Chalmers et al. 2002 (outlined below) that insurers are able to predict share price performance *ex ante* (a strong indicator for potential claims) and this knowledge is reflected in the premium.[908]

A similar study by Boyer in 2007, mentioned below, suggests comparable results.[909] Additionally to his observations on D&O demand, he makes two other statements. First, he finds a negative correlation between unit price (premium divided by coverage limit) and market return, namely, the more significant the larger the corporation. In other words, when the corporation pays low premiums for a big coverage limit, they will make more return than a corporation that pays high premiums for a small coverage limit. This finding is based on the idea that the insurer has more information about the corporation than an outside investor. When using the premium price as a signal the investor could apply the insurer's insider information for his investment strategy.

There is a second finding, which is not entirely applicable to the case of D&O insurance of corporations. In this observation, Boyer looks at the performance of income

905 Kang 2011, pp. 49–50. Similar results were found by Lin et al. 2013, pp. 50–52. Turning to managerial risk taking, they consider total risk (of the corporation) and systemic risk (of the market). They control for business risk (outlined above) and managerial compensation packages. They show that, indeed, an increased D&O coverage ratio correlates with increased risk taking. It suggests that D&O insurance leads to more risk taking.
Furthermore, another study to link compensation with D&O insurance has been conducted by Egger et al. 2011, pp. 1–3.

906 Boyer and Stern 2012, p. 356.

907 Boyer and Stern 2012, pp. 354–355.

908 Boyer and Stern 2012, p. 366. Similar to previous studies, in their study of market to book ratio, market value, return on assets, leverage and age do not seem to have any significant impact on the price per dollar D&O coverage limit. Furthermore, the proportion of outside managers positively correlates with the D&O premium. See: Boyer and Stern 2012, p. 369.

909 Boyer 2007, pp. 80–81.

trusts. For income trusts only, he depicts a negative correlation between D&O coverage limit and trust performance.[910]

7.8. Discussion about the relationship of limits and premiums

As explained in subsection 3.2.1, the size of premiums relates to the actuarially fair value and additional costs. The actuarially fair premium refers to the multiplication of magnitude and probability of the risk. Previous sections showed that the magnitude is usually pre-defined by way of setting an upper D&O insurance limit. The actuarially fair premium is thus related to the chosen limit (by the insured) times the perceived probability (by the insurer).

The correlation to premiums might indicate the insurer's ability to categorize risks. This section will outline how far D&O limits and D&O premiums do not or negatively correlate with the same corporate feature. Such a finding might suggest that the insurer has an information advantage over the corporation. The following will first look at the business risk and secondly turn to the governance quality.

Regarding firm performance and business risk, there are four factors, being the return on equity, the value of corporate assets, litigation, and US operations. Return on equity has a negative effect on premiums. Return on assets also has a negative correlation to limits. The value of corporate assets negatively correlates with limits (at least according to Kaltchev), but positively correlates with premiums. Section 7.6 already outlined that corporate size has offsetting effects on corporate demand. Yet, corporate size seems to increase the premium. D&O insurers seem to categorize the D&O risk by looking at the corporate size. In this regard, an empirical study of Kim and Skinner suggests that the litigation risk with respect to claims under the American securities law correlates positively with size.[911]

Litigation has a positive correlation to limits and premiums. US operations do not correlate with limits but positively with premiums (and D&O purchase). Based on these

[910] According to a study by Zou et al. 2008, at p. 2637, D&O insurance in China has similar effects on business and litigation risks China's legal framework leads to a situation, in which controlling shareholders are able to receive the shares of minority shareholders. According to them, controlling shareholders first initiate a public offer of shares to get outside capital from minority shareholders. When enough capital is raised through share issuance, they take the shares back. As a result, money is made opportunistically.
Zou et al. 2008 argue at p. 2644 that "*the announcement of D&O insurance decisions seems to have a negative effect on shareholder wealth.*" They interpret this finding as result from the controlling shareholders' right (often state-owned enterprises) to assume the shares of minority shareholders. To be safe from litigation of expropriated minority shareholders, controlling shareholders plus the managers demand D&O insurance, according to them. They recommend protection rights for the minority shareholder, who has to be granted approval rights for the purchase of D&O insurance. However, their finding needs to be considered against the background of a small sample. They used 53 firms with D&O insurance and another 53 firms as a control sample. Furthermore, most of their results have a 10% deviation, which means that their correlations may not be regarded as significant as those of other introduced studies in this chapter. See: Zou et al. 2008, pp. 2641–2644, 2644.

[911] Kim and Skinner 2012, pp. 296, 300.

correlations, one might argue at first sight that the variable US operation is considered highly risky by the insurer.

When looking at the governance quality, there are also five factors, being managerial share ownership, managerial excess control, majority shareholders, proportion of outside directors, and CEO compensation. Managerial share ownership has a negative correlation to limits and premiums. Managerial excess control correlates negatively with limits, but has no[912] (or a positive)[913] correlation to premiums. The amount of majority shareholders does not have a correlation to premiums or limits. According to Gupta and Prakash, the existence of 10% shareholders has a negative impact on premiums. The number of outside directors has a positive correlation to limits and no correlation to premiums. In other words, the more outside directors there are, the higher the insurance limits become. CEO compensation positively correlates with the limit and the D&O premium.

The existence of 10% shareholders correlates negatively with premiums. In line with subsection 5.4.4, it could be argued that when fewer claims are brought, the liability risk decreases and in turn the premium to insure that risk would fall. Supposedly, the 10% shareholders are represented by constitutional investors, interested in the stability of assets and who withdraw from any corporate governance. In other words, they abstain from the tool of managerial liability.

Furthermore, the correlation with the number of outside directors is peculiar but has suggestive power. The outside directors seem to demand a higher limit. The insurer, however, does not regard the outside directors as a detriment (or advantage) to the probability of the D&O risk. In this regard, managerial excess control also seems not to be punished by insurers (by way of increased premiums).

7.9. (In)efficient D&O market

The previous sections suggested that the insurer is able to differentiate the risks and price accordingly. Such a finding implies that the insurer is able to observe the risk. To control the risk, the insurer also has to be able to change the insured's behaviour. When this change can be induced by way of premium adaptation, the question arises, whether the premium adaptations are high enough to change the insured's behaviour. More generally, if moral hazard cannot be controlled, one must ask whether the risk is insurable.

The following studies suggest that the D&O insurance market is either inefficient or successful. Regarding market inefficiency, there is one study on irrational behaviour and three studies on moral hazard.

A study by Boyer 2007 suggests behavioural, less rational purposes behind the question whether to purchase D&O insurance (subsection 7.9.1). Regarding moral hazard, a study by Chalmers et al. 2002 shows a correlation between IPO over-evaluation and D&O insurance (subsection 7.9.2). Similarly, a study by Lin et al. in 2011 looks at

912 Gupta and Prakash 2012, p. 20.

913 Core 2000, pp. 462–467. In the study of Core 2000, managerial excess control refers to the voting control of the manager. The study of Gupta and Prakash 2012 is based on Core's model, but enhances the model. As a result, when conflicting, the thesis bases its argument on the latter, more advanced model by Gupta and Prakash 2012.

empire building (subsection 7.9.3). Finally, a study by Chung and Wynn in 2008 and other studies outline the correlation between D&O insurance and aggressive earning forecasts (subsection 7.9.4).

On the other hand, some studies suggest, that D&O insurance has no effect or a positive effect on the market. Regarding no effect, one study by Boubakri and Ghalleb 2008 shows that D&O premiums can be used as a signal, though investors seem to ignore that information (subsection 7.9.5). Furthermore, a study by Chen and Li 2008 shows that D&O insurance does not have such a big impact on the manager after all (subsection 7.9.6).

Moreover, other studies show a correlation between loan spreads and D&O insurance, being the study by Bradley and Chen 2011 (subsection 7.9.7) and the study by Lin et al. 2013 (subsection 7.9.8).

A third set of studies by Gupta and Prakash in 2012 (subsection 7.9.9, parts of the study were already outlined section 7.2 on the insurer's imperfect knowledge) and Lin et al. 2013 (subsection 7.9.10, parts of the study which will already have been mentioned in subsection 7.9.8) observe a better firm performance of insured managers, provided that they function in a competitive environment. These studies will be outlined below.

7.9.1. D&O insurance due to behavioural aspects: Boyer 2007

In a study based on data between 1993 and 1998 and published in 2007 by Boyer,[914] the author reflected on these prior studies. His sample included 354 Canadian corporations, where he exempts financial institutions, mining and natural resources.[915] He suggested that corporate risk management and other governance factors seem to be of no or negligible effect to the D&O insurance demand. The main question corporations ask, when they purchase D&O insurance, is: "*What did we do last year?*"[916] The corporation is thus subject to inertia. Inertia means that the individual is "*unwilling to change ex post what it did ex ante.*"[917] Firms that have D&O insurance purchase it for the next year, whereas firms that do not have it, do not purchase it. Boyer argued that this is the case because of the 'claims-made' principle of D&O insurance. Such a system deters cancellation of the policy. Firms that reject insurance do so because it might arguably reduce incentives for the managers to work for share value increase.[918]

Similarly, deductibles and policy limits also seem to be particularly dependent on the insurance history. Inertia better explains D&O insurance than managerial risk aversion, asset substitution, under-investment, real-service efficiencies, expected default risk, or taxes. The latter aspects were used to explain a policy change by prior studies of Core,

914 Boyer 2007, p. 75–77. Also compare to: Boyer 2003.

915 It remains unclear what the definition and scope of 'financial institutions' is. Their exemption seems peculiar, since financial institutions (here defined as: Financial Services, including Insurance) usually purchase high D&O limits and are most likely of all industries to purchase insurance. Compare to: Racioppo 2013, pp. 4–10. Furthermore, in the reviewed literature, only O'Sullivan 2009, stated below, explicitly exempts this industry also. See: O'Sullivan 2009, p. 150.

916 Boyer 2007, p. 80.

917 Boyer 2007, p. 86.

918 Boyer 2007, pp. 86–87.

O'Sullivan, and Mayers and Smith. Boyer interprets these findings as a result of the market structure. A small number of insurers and brokers sell the majority of policies.[919]

Kaltchev confirms Boyer's statement. Last year's purchase decision affects this year's decision. Moreover, this aspect increases in relevance, when comparing sample 1997–2000 with sample 2000–2002. However, in Kaltchev's opinion there are other factors that significantly affect purchase as well.[920]

7.9.2. IPO over-evaluation: Chalmers et al. 2002

Another seminal contribution is 'Managerial Opportunism? Evidence from Directors' and Officers' Insurance Purchases'. Chalmers et al. observed a sample of 72 US firms. Whereas O'Sullivan's study was not able to gather information about premiums and limits, this contribution had such resources. Their aim was to find a relationship between the Initial Public Offering (IPO) and D&O coverage. Such a relationship would suggest opportunistic behavior of the manager. The reasoning goes as follows.[921]

First, assume that a manager has inside information about a corporation. Further, he wants to maximize the amount of capital he receives from the capital markets through an IPO. To do so, he waits for a period in time to offer shares to the public (IPO), when the corporate shares are more highly valued on the market than they are actually worth. It is thus very likely that shares offered in such a way will lose their value in the long run.[922]

Secondly, assume that the manager thinks *ex ante* that the loss of share value will strongly correspond to managerial liability claims.[923] Although this assumption gained recognition due to the concept of litigation risk,[924] it does not seem to be very robust in the sample that Chalmers et al. observed; Chalmers et al. could not show a correlation. However, Chalmers et al. argue that the correlation does not have to actually exist, but only to be so perceived by the manager.[925]

Thus, Chalmers et al. hypothesize that the manager wants to hedge the increased litigation risk due to an overvalued IPO with D&O insurance. If he knows that the IPO evaluation is very much over-rated, he will seek a grand limit and premium. Similarly, when the evaluation is only slightly over-rated, the D&O limit and premium will be less. The use of superior information about corporate under-performance *ex ante* suggests opportunistic behaviour of the manager.[926]

919 Boyer 2007, p. 87.

920 Kaltchev 2004, p. 42–43, 46. The reader is also referred to the study by Fier et al. 2012. According to their findings at pp. 17–18, demand increased after managers of competitive firms were held liable. Such demand might suggest availability heuristics of the D&O purchaser.

921 Chalmers et al. 2002, pp. 609–613, 615.

922 Chalmers et al. 2002, pp. 609–610.

923 This assumption is based on former literature and interviews from D&O insurers. Compare to: Chalmers et al. 2002, p. 623.

924 For more information on the correlation between litigation risk and D&O insurance (also taking into consideration volatility), the reader is referred to O'Sullivan 2002 and Core 1997.

925 Chalmers et al. 2002, pp. 622–625.

926 Chalmers et al. 2002, pp. 625–629.

Chalmers et al., indeed, observed such a negative relationship for the small sample of 72 firms. The share value three years after the IPO corresponded negatively with the amount of D&O insurance limit and premium. Thus, the amount of limit and premium might *ex ante* predict the share value development and corresponding bad firm value. The D&O insurance information would be highly valuable for the investor to adapt share value predictions.[927]

Very similar to Chalmers et al. is the study of Boyer 2012. In this study, the author looks at the US American market and finds comparable results. Moreover, he finds that the D&O insurance premium contains information about volatility and share returns for the first year after the IPO. This means that the higher the premium per dollar of coverage limits are, the more volatile and the lower the returns are. This correlation only holds for the first year, however.[928]

7.9.3. Empire building: Lin et al. in 2011

The study of Lin, Officer and Zou is also based on data granted from Canadian corporations due to their legal notification requirements. They seek to find a correlation between M&A outcomes and D&O insurance.[929]

Their variable of D&O coverage takes into account the ratio of the limit to the share market value of the corporation.[930] To acquire cohesive M&A data, they filter on whether the purchaser is a Canadian firm, the deal is completed, and the purchaser has sufficient (primary issue) stock price data.[931]

To find evidence for empire building, the value of the acquisition must be based on certain factors. They observe the short-term and long-term horizons. Regarding the short-term, they look at (1) the cumulative abnormal return to the purchaser (CAR) and (2) acquisition premiums. Regarding the long term, they look at the synergy effect of the acquisition by turning to (3) the value creation and operating performance of the purchaser. Finally, they look at (4) the robustness of their observations.

(1) Regarding CAR, abnormal return relates to the difference between actual return and expected return of an investment. The cumulative abnormal return is the sum of all daily abnormal returns, in this case 211 days before announcement up to 11 days before announcement. When CAR is low, the deal is not regarded as profitable by the market. When CAR is high, the market perceives the deal as profitable. The study found a significantly negative correlation between CAR and D&O coverage.[932]

927 Chalmers et al. 2002, pp. 629–632. Also compare this finding to: Fier et al. 2012, pp.1–5.
928 Boyer 2012, pp. 3, 30–31.
929 Lin et al. 2011, pp. 507–510.
930 The second variable is calculated as limit divided by market value of equity. See: Lin et al. 2011, p. 511.
931 The number of acquisitions of the sample is fairly distributed between 118 and 86 throughout the years of empirical analysis, being 2002–2008. See: Lin et al. 2011, p. 510.
932 Lin et al. 2011, pp. 513–514.

(2) Acquisition premiums are the ratio of the offer price to buy the target against the target's stock price four weeks prior to acquisition announcement. The observations regarding acquisition premiums are twofold. First, the existence of D&O insurance does not correlate with acquisition premiums. Secondly, the size of D&O coverage significantly and positively correlates with acquisition premiums.[933]

(3) Regarding the long-term observation on synergies, they use the measure of value creation and operating performance. Value creation looks at the combined CAR of target firm and purchaser. In this calculation, the value creation is significantly lower for insured corporations than for uninsured corporations.[934]

To measure operating performance, they observe return on assets and asset turnover.[935] They experience significant worsening of operating performance for corporations of high coverage limits. However, no such worsening is to be found for corporations with low coverage limits. These correlations become worse over the last years.[936]

(4) To look at the robustness of these observations, they control for factors that seemed to affect M&A substantially.[937] These are methods of payment, relative deal size, industry relatedness of the acquisition, and target type. Also related are factors of the purchaser such as size of purchasing firm, market to book ratio, leverage, free cash flow, and volatility. Looking at the existence of D&O insurance, insured corporations are more likely to purchase unrelated corporations, are more likely to pay cash, and make more deals with targets that are subsidiaries.[938]

Similar to this study, Chi et al. 2013 show in their study how far excessive D&O insurance correlates with acquisitions that are unrelated to the original business. Such findings correspond to the empire building hypothesis. Furthermore, they show that the increased M&A activities correlate with share value decrease. Together these findings strongly suggest opportunistic behaviour of the manager, when D&O insurance is excessive.[939]

7.9.4. *Earning statements: Chung and Wynn & Cao and Narayanamoorthy*

In their study, Chung and Wynn seek to find a relationship between managerial liability coverage limit and less conservative (aggressive) earnings forecasts. Furthermore, they want to show that this relationship is more pronounced in the US than in Canada, supposedly because US corporations face a bigger litigation risk. They use a sample of 224 firms.[940]

933 See: Lin et al. 2011, pp. 520–521. This variable could only be used for 160 deals, because the other M&As were privately owned corporations and no data was available. See: Lin et al. 2011, p. 512.

934 Lin et al. 2011, pp. 521–523.

935 Asset turnover refers to the ratio revenue divided by total assets. See: Lin et al. 2011, p. 519.

936 Lin et al. 2011, pp. 523–523.

937 Lin et al. refers to Masulis, Wang and Xie 2007.

938 Lin et al. 2011, pp. 522–523.

939 Chi et al. 2013, pp. 5, 24.

940 Chung and Wynn 2008, pp. 135–136, 143.

To calculate the managerial liability coverage limit, they add D&O insurance variables, such as premium, coverage limit and deductible and D&O indemnification. Indemnification is measured as excess cash of the corporation solely held for the purpose of compensating the manager.[941] To account for business risk, they use similar variables as previous studies.[942] Earning forecasts describe the mainly quarterly reporting of the predicted accounting income of the last time period. They can be positive or negative. The observation of Chung and Wynn deals with the forecasts of negative earnings. Late (which is also called aggressive) negative earning statements are associated with the short term advantage of the manager. During the time that he does not report, he still benefits from bonus payments, avoids debt covenant violations and prevents an increase of the cost of capital. On the other hand, late earnings forecasts lead to greater litigation risk than earlier (conservative) earning forecasts.[943]

Chung and Wynn find that the D&O coverage limit is negatively related to earnings conservatism. That means that managers are slower to report negative news, when they are well covered for litigation risk.[944]

Similar results have been observed by Kim in 2006. According to her, excess coverage limits positively and significantly correlate with a likelihood of restatements.[945]

Kim's definition of excess coverage differs from that of studies which have already been discussed. Her calculation of excess coverage is driven by the calculation of "expected" coverage. "Expected" coverage is the insurance of litigation and business risk. To define litigation risk and business risk, she uses proxies that are similar to previous studies, such as size, market value of equity, debt to equity ratio. A coverage limit that surpasses these risks is excess coverage.[946]

941 Proxies are firm size, growth opportunities, cash flows, financial distress, net working capital, governance quality. See: Chung and Wynn 2008, pp. 144–145.

942 These are firm size, market to book ratio, member in high tech industry, cross listing status and CEO ownership. See: Chung and Wynn 2008, p. 145.

943 Chung and Wynn 2008, pp. 138. Studies have shown that managers seek to find a balance between aggressive and conservative earnings forecasts. Furthermore, scholars have shown that legal systems or legal persons that entail greater litigation risks, such as the USA or public corporations, have more conservative earnings than systems that have less litigation risk, such as the UK or private corporations. Conservatism is also more distinct in common law countries than in civil law countries. Same goes with rules on taxation and securities.
See: Chung and Wynn 2008, p. 138.

944 Chung and Wynn 2008, p. 140. For more information: cf. Chi et al. 2011, pp. 147–149. In their model, they also seem to find wrong statements. They show that the higher the excess coverage limit the more likely it is that the corporation re-stated its earnings. This correlation is significant at the 1% level. The correlation is even higher for the excess cash than for the excess insurance. They explain this difference by arguing that excess cash is not subject to conditions. In the end, indemnification may be paid more timely and for the entire damage. Furthermore, indemnification might even apply for more cases than insurance does.

945 Kim 2006, pp. 1–3. Similarly Lin et al. 2013 at pp. 52–53, find that the D&O coverage ratio is positively and significantly associated with the existence of earnings re-statements.

946 Kim 2006, p. 2.

Re-statements refer to published earning forecasts that have to be restated after their publication. Re-statements may result from negative and aggressive earning forecasts, misuses of fact, wrong application of accounting rules, or fraud.[947]

When controlling for these proxies, she finds a positive and significant correlation between excess limits and the likelihood of restatements. A limit that is smaller than "expected" does not correlate with restatements.[948]

Another study by Cao and Narayanamoorthy in 2011 is concerned with earnings forecasts. They hypothesize and find evidence that there is a relationship between earnings forecasts and the D&O insurance premium. As opposed to previous studies, they also include positive earnings forecasts in the analysis.[949]

The premium significantly positively correlates with the likelihood, precision, and earliness of a publication of bad earnings. The amount of information of bad news does not correlate with the premium. Regarding good news, the likelihood, precision, timing and amount of information has no significant correlation with the premium.[950]

7.9.5. No use of D&O insurance as signal: Boubakri and Ghalleb 2008

Boubakri and Ghalleb use that call for public disclosure of D&O insurance as a hypothesis. They find a positive correlation of the likelihood of existing D&O insurance with larger revenue and less volatility. They suggest that the information about D&O insurance limits can be used to predict stock price performance, but investors do not seem to use this measure.[951]

7.9.6. No effective measure: Chen and Li 2008

Chen and Li in 2008 attempt to find a correlation between D&O insurance and firm performance. Firm performance is measured by a proxy incorporating ROA, ROE, and share price development. They did not find a significant correlation between firm performance and D&O insurance.[952]

They go as far as to conclude from their findings that D&O insurance does not have a significant impact to deter or incentivize managerial behaviour. In their opinion, litigation costs, on which the D&O insurance is based, is too small to make a dent. Other costs and rewards, such as reputation, compensation, and external competition are more essential to firm performance than D&O insurance.[953]

947 Kim 2006, pp. 2–3.
948 Kim 2006, p. 22.
949 Cao and Narayanamoorthy 2011, pp. 125–128.
950 Cao and Narayanamoorthy 2011, pp. 127–128.
951 Boubakri and Ghalleb 2008, pp. 29–30.
952 Chen and Li 2008, pp. 1–5.
953 Chen and Li 2008, p. 17.

7.9.7. *Loan spreads and credit rating: Bradley and Chen 2011*

The outcomes of the study of Bradley and Chen in 2011 are counter-intuitive. They find evidence that indemnification correlates with lower spreads and a better credit rating.[954] Furthermore, they seek to find a correlation between indemnification and managerial-risk taking.[955]

Risk-taking is divided into R&D expenditures, capital expenditures, the number of diversifying acquisitions, and share volatility. There is a highly significant negative correlation of indemnification with capital expenditures and equity volatility. The correlation with R&D expenditure is *positive*, but insignificant. These correlations, ignoring the insignificant correlation of the R&D expenditure suggest less managerial risk-taking. However, less volatility also indicates more corporate stability. Stability is in turn associated with continuity, the latter factor being regarded as a feature of quality by long term investors.[956]

Further, there is a significant negative correlation with the number of diversifying acquisitions. The latter observation suggests empire building. The authors argue that indemnification does not lead to more, but less, self-operating risk-taking of the manager. Such a correlation suggests less growth of corporations that indemnify their manager.[957]

The lesser amount of risk taking is awarded by the bondholders, asking for a smaller spread. Such observation might be explained by the bondholder's fear of the manager's acceptance of very risky projects.[958] With self-serving, but less risky actions of the manager, the bondholder regards the agency costs between corporation and creditor as smaller. The result of smaller agency costs translates to smaller spreads.

Furthermore, they provide evidence that a positive correlation between indemnification and attraction (or retention) of the most competent managers is non-existent. Instead, they find a negative (though insignificant) correlation. Competence is defined as the number of outside directors and the number of directors that are also executives of other firms.[959]

7.9.8. *Loan spreads: Lin et al. 2013*

The study of Lin et al. in 2013 draws attention to the effects of D&O insurance on a particular external party, namely a bank granting loans. They seek to find a correlation

954 The proxies for indemnification are threefold, (i) the existence of limited liability clauses in the articles of association, (ii) the indemnifying amount provided by the articles of association, and (iii) the existence of indemnification contracts with the manager. See: Bradley and Chen 2011, p. 84.

955 Bradley and Chen 2011, pp. 82–85.

956 Bradley and Chen 2011, p. 92 and Table 3.

957 Bradley and Chen 2011, p. 92 and Table 3.

958 Compare to subsection 2.3.3.

959 Bradley and Chen 2011, pp. 92, 100. Please note that the proxies for competence do not seem very comprehensive. Outside directors are usually used to describe monitoring ability among managers. The number of positions of one manager does not necessarily mean that he does his job well. One might even say that the increased numbers of positions hamper a sufficient focus on each position. As a result, the validity of this finding seems questionable.

between D&O coverage and loan spreads. Their sample is based on 615 loans by 186 Canadian corporations. To define D&O coverage, they divided the coverage limit by the market value of equity. The average coverage ratio is 6.5%. The loan spread is defined as the spread that exceeds the LIBOR (London Interbank Offered Rate) plus origination fees.[960]

Control factors include already introduced proxies on business risk[961] and corporate governance quality.[962] They include proxies for product market competition.[963]

In their regressions, the insured group is related to positively and significantly higher loan spreads. However, corporations with moderate insurance behave like those without any coverage. A one standard deviation increase of the coverage ratio increases loan spreads by approximately 10%. These findings are unaffected by an abnormal pricing of the premium, suggesting that the excess payment does not lead to a changed corporate appearance. Furthermore, the correlation stays unchanged over the years, suggesting that economic crises, like a recession, do not have an effect. Moreover, corporate bonds are similarly affected as loans.[964]

The stated correlation is absent for short maturity rate loans. D&O insurance has a greater impact on loans that are subject to terms or acquisition purposes.[965]

Subsequently, Lin et al. compare found relationships with corporate governance proxies. They looked at the existence of 10%-shareholders, number of analysts that follow the corporation, and the existence of prior lending relations. Fewer analysts (than median), no 10% shareholder, and no relations, have a significant and positive impact on D&O insurance coverage ratio. Especially, fewer analysts correlates strongly with a D&O coverage ratio rise. More analysts (equal or greater than median), existence of 10% shareholders and prior relations, still have a positive impact, though the impact is mitigated dramatically. Especially, more analysts make a correlation with a D&O ratio rise insignificant, which means that the D&O ratio can be indirectly fixed, when enough outside analysts follow the corporation.[966]

To consider the endogeneity of these findings, they look at how far an exogenous event affects the D&O coverage ratio. This event is the coming into force of the Ontario Bill 198 that expanded civil liability. As expected the enactment of the bill aggravated the correlation between D&O coverage ratio and loan spreads. *"Lenders appear to care much*

960 Lin et al. 2013, pp. 37–39, 40.

961 These are industry, year, size, market to book ratio, asset tangibility, cash flow volatility, leverage. See: Lin et al. 2013, p. 40.

962 These are CEO-chairman duality, proportion of outside directors, manager share ownership, 10% shareholders, excess managerial control. See: Lin et al. 2013, p. 41.

963 Market competition has a twofold effect on corporations. On the one hand, it mitigates agency costs and improves firm performance. On the other hand, less competition might lead to less default risk, because there is no other corporation to face the demand. The proxies are among others, loan size, presence of a performance pricing clause, loan type, purpose, S&P credit rating. See: Lin et al. 2013, pp. 54–55.

964 Lin et al. 2013, pp. 43–44, 58. Naturally, the loan spreads increase in recessions because of higher risk aversion of banks. However, this increase is solely dependent on the economic environment and not the D&O insurance. See: See: Lin et al. 2013, p. 58.

965 Lin et al. 2013, pp. 45–46.

966 Lin et al. 2013, p. 47.

more about the loan pricing (moral hazard) implication of D&O insurance coverage after [the] Ontario Bill 198."[967] Uninsured corporations do not experience a significant correlation between enactment and loan spreads. These results suggest moral hazard of the insured manager.

Changing the regressions of the independent variables, they notice that loan spreads on a subsequent loan are higher, when the D&O coverage ratio is higher than the last time they negotiated the first loan.[968]

In 2012, Chen et al. observed that D&O insurance correlates with the cost of equity. An increase of D&O insurance limit by one standard deviation raises the cost of equity by 7% of the mean. Furthermore, insured corporations conduct seasoned equity offerings less frequently and raise less capital. They conclude that shareholders require insured corporations to make a higher than expected return than uninsured corporations.[969]

Their study controls for business risk variables. Furthermore, their study shows that the cost of equity follows, which means that it is affected by the D&O limit.[970]

The study suggests that shareholders punish the corporation for purchasing D&O insurance. If insured, they expect higher returns.[971] It seems that shareholders regard D&O insurance as creating a moral hazard for which they want to be compensated.

7.9.9. Firm performance: Gupta and Prakash in 2012

The previously discussed contribution of Gupta and Prakash briefly examines treatment possibilities for their observed obstacles. The discussion above came to the conclusion that managerial excess control correlates with lower D&O insurance limits. So they seek a relationship between firm performance and managerial excess control. Firm performance is measured as return on assets (ROA) and operating profit ratio (EBITDA). When governance, business risk and leverage are held equal, ROA and EBITDA positively and highly significantly correlate with excess control.[972]

Thus, the joint application of the correlations between limits and excess control on the one hand, and firm performance and excess control on the other hand, show that higher firm performance correlates with lower coverage limits. This deduction does not hold for firm performance and premiums however, because premiums do not correlate with excess control. This finding is robust to changes in leverage and industry type.[973]

They summarize their findings by pledging in favour of a public disclosure of D&O insurance in the big markets like the USA because it contains useful information. In

967 Lin et al. 2013, p. 48.
968 Lin et al. 2013, p. 49.
969 Chen et al. 2012, p. 3.
970 The definition of cost of equity is not very clear, though. Making reference to other models, they derive the cost of equity from stock price performance and analyst's earnings forecasts. Furthermore, they refrain from using 'realized returns' as a measure because it is supposed to be affected by cash flows and discount rates. See: Chen et al. 2012, pp. 9–10.
971 Chen et al. September 2012, p. 18.
972 Gupta and Prakash 2012, pp. 20–21.
973 Gupta and Prakash 2012, pp. 20–21.

particular, it may signal firm performance (due to managerial control) to the public.[974] A similar pledge was made by Baker and Griffith 2010.[975]

7.9.10. Firm performance: Lin et al. 2013

To answer the question, whether D&O insurance is necessary to enable corporations to hire risk-averse managers that raise share value, Lin et al. look at the relationship between D&O coverage ratio on the one hand, and firm performance as well as corporate governance on the other hand. For corporate governance quality the correlations found in prior studies are confirmed. For firm performance, Lin et al. surprisingly show that the marginal value of investment decisions improve with D&O coverage ratio, as long as the corporation is active in a highly competitive market. If the market is not competitive this positive effect of D&O insurance is not observable. Lin et al. conclude "*while firms with a high level of D&O insurance on average exhibit lower excess returns, strong monitoring afforded by independent directors and competition in product markets seems to lead to increased investment efficiency.*"[976]

7.10. Discussion of the findings about the market's status

The previous section outlined studies that showed correlations between D&O insurance and opportunistic behaviour. The studies sketched a multifaceted picture on the opportunistic behaviour of the manager.

On the one hand, the section showed behavioural attitudes of the manager, IPO over-evaluation, empire building, and aggressive earnings. On the other hand, it showed no or positive signs of, D&O insurance on performance or loan spreads. Let us highlight the most important findings.

The study of Chalmers et al. showed that the limit and premium correlate with lower returns and more volatility. Kaltchev also showed a similar correlation between returns and limit. In Boyer's study, this correlation only holds for the first year, however. It is questionable, whether it is not observable in the later years due to possible adaptive policies of the insurer. In this regard, the insurer might indeed be able to apply the tool of experience rating to those corporations.

Furthermore, Lin et al. showed that highly insured firms pay more for acquisitions, the acquisitions are less appreciated by the market, and the synergy effects are less pronounced. However, when the D&O coverage (ratio of limit divided by share market value) is lower than average, the insured purchaser does not overpay the target shareholders and also does not perform worse afterwards. Such a finding may indicate that the insurer is able to apply the tools of self-selection outlined in subsection 5.8.1. The insurer is able to differentiate between good risks and bad risks by offering policies with different limits. Those who demand a higher limit are identified as bad risks.

974 Gupta and Prakash 2012, pp. 22–23.
975 Baker and Griffith 2010, pp. 203–204.
976 Lin et al. 2013, p. 55.

Another set of studies focused on earning forecasts. The studies suggest that, at first sight, there is no significant correlation between earnings forecasts and D&O insurance. When looking closer, Kim observes a positive correlation between D&O limit and likelihood of re-statements.[977] Furthermore, Cao and Narayanamorrthy find a positive correlation between premium and likelihood, precision, and earliness of the publication of bad earnings. Cao and Narayanamorrthy do not find a correlation between premium and the publication of good news.

When comparing the studies, Chung and Wynn and Kim look at limits and argue that increased coverage might indicate sloppy forecasts. The study of Cao and Narayanamoorthy looks at premiums and shows that they correlate with thorough forecasts. Together these studies suggest that the insurer first differentiates the risk types by ways of self-selection and consequently adapts the premium to incentivize publication of negative earnings forecasts.

Boabakri and Ghalleb observe that public disclosure of the D&O insurance data provides valuable information for the investor, but the data is not used.

Similarly, Chen and Li argue that there is no significant correlation between D&O insurance and firm performance. Chen and Li believe that the benefits of insurance are too small (managers fear reputation costs much more) and that the controlling abilities of the insurer via the premium adaptation is negligible (because the size of the premium is too small to have an effect).

The study of Lin et al. observed a number of differentiating correlations between D&O insurance and loan spreads. Basically, creditors seem to rely on the information inherent to the coverage limit but ignore the information inherent to the premium.

When the D&O coverage ratio is higher than average, there is a positive correlation with loan spreads. However, there is no correlation between average coverage ratio and loan spreads. These findings suggest that the creditor is certain about the insurers' ability to classify the risk types into two groups due to self-selection, whereas the group asking for higher limits represents the bad risk type.

Consequently, creditors apply their knowledge about the D&O insurance as a signal and apply it to the cost of debt. However, when a corporation having a high insurance coverage has many analysts following it, the positive correlation to the loan spreads evaporates. The creditor seems to appreciate the proxy 'number of analysts' as a signal rather than a high amount of D&O coverage. This finding seems to suggest that creditors have more faith in the analysis of analysts. That is understandable since analysts incorporate all factors to measure default risk and insurers only look at the D&O risk.

These findings are essential regarding the creditor signalling hypothesis of subsection 5.6.3 which was subject to three heavy qualifications, namely (i) the insurer is able to differentiate risks, (ii) the insurance policy is publicly available to function as a signal and (iii) the creditor makes effective use of that signal. Section 7.6 suggested that assumption one and two hold. The consideration of this paragraph suggests that the third assumption holds to a certain degree. Note, however, that these considerations only

977 Re-statements refers to a practice that published earning forecasts have to be re-stated after their publication. See above: earning statements, Chung and Wynn 2008; Cao and Narayanamoorthy 2011.

apply to the market in Canada, because in Canada information on D&O insurance is public.

In line with this, Chen et al. suggest that a high D&O limit positively correlates with the cost of equity. Shareholders of well covered corporations expect higher returns from their shareholding. This finding might indicate that the shareholders seem to insure for managerial liability due to their belief that the insurer is the more cost-effective D&O risk carrier. As a result, when insured, they expect higher returns. The question is whether the insurer is indeed able to mitigate the D&O risk more efficiently than the shareholders.

Gupta and Prakash observe two correlations. First, there is a negative correlation between managerial excess control and D&O limit. Secondly, they notice a positive relationship between excess control and firm performance. Linking these two observations, firm performance correlates with fewer limits. This observation is similar to Kaltchev and others. Premiums do not correlate with excess control. Still, Lin et al. shows that there is indeed a positive correlation between the value of investment decisions and the D&O coverage ratio, provided that the corporation works in a highly competitive market.

When comparing these findings to the study on indemnifications,[978] three mutual factors were tested: growth, volatility, and outside directors. D&O purchase and indemnification have the same negative correlation with growth. Volatility has a positive correlation with D&O purchase but a negative correlation with indemnification. Outside directors positively correlate with D&O purchase and indemnification.

Without more findings on the relationship between indemnification and D&O insurance, these correlations neither refute nor support the hypothesis of section 5.6.2 that insurers that insure the risk to indemnify a liable manager could mediate internal corporate conflicts.

7.11. Conclusion

This chapter based on the review of empirical studies showed (i) that D&O insurance is able to provide information on the demand for D&O insurance, (ii) that the insurer probably has an information advantage over the insured and (iii) to what extent the D&O insurance market affects the corporation and the manager.

(i) The studies approached demand, (a) either by looking at whether or not a corporation purchased insurance (called D&O purchase) or (b) by determining the size of the purchased coverage limit (called limit). The factors that correlate with demand can be grouped in firm performance, corporate governance, managerial compensation, and business risk.

It is unclear whether D&O insurance hampers, boosts or does not correlate with firm performance. Regarding corporate governance and in contrast to the hypotheses of

978 See above: Bradley and Chen 2011; Bhagat et al. 1987.

subsection 5.6.1, the number or concentration of majority shareholders seems to have no correlation with the D&O purchase or the size of the limit. However, building on the monitoring and mediating hypothesis in section 5.6, corporations with dispersed ownership (incorporating supposedly well-diversified shareholders) seem to desire higher limits. The validity of the monitoring hypothesis remains dubious. Litigation history and dealings in the USA correlate positively, as expected, with the D&O purchase decision, as does the number of outside directors. Furthermore, managerial cash compensation positively and managerial shareholding negatively correlates with limits. The reason could be that managerial shareholding (in contrast to cash compensation) indeed mitigates the D&O risk. Regarding business risk, corporate size measured by market value positively correlates with D&O purchase and limits. However, corporate size measured by the value of assets negatively correlates with limits. Divesting, distress, and leverage increase D&O purchase and limits. This finding suggests that D&O insurance is desired more when the corporation is in financial trouble. Furthermore, in times of financial instability D&O insurance may be a valuable alternative to excess pay when the level of firm performance remains the same.

(ii) The limits and premiums do not perfectly correlate. Such a finding suggests that the insurer has an information advantage and makes use of, but is not limited to self-selection. It further may resort to experience rating and, more generally, risk categorization.

The legal environment, such as operations in the USA, changes the premium. Furthermore, the corporate size increases the premium. The level of corporate governance, such as the number of 10%-shareholders decreases the premium. Managerial excess control and the number of outside directors does not have an effect on the premium.

(iii) The answers to the question, whether the insurer is able to control the insured corporation and manager is unclear. The studies could show that highly insured firms are rather prone to managerial empire building. The positive correlation of premiums with earning forecasts may suggest that the insurer incentivizes the publication of negative earnings forecasts. However, investors in Canada seem to ignore the information that is contained in the D&O insurance data. Such ignorance might be explained by the fact that studies such as Chen and Li find it difficult to observe a correlation between D&O insurance and firm performance. Firm performance is the essential factor that drives the investor. Although a direct link to firm performance is difficult to draw, the value of investment decisions seem to rise with D&O coverage as long as the competitive pressure is high enough.

Creditors, in contrast to equity investors, seem to use the D&O information as a signal. Higher than average limits correlate with a higher spread.

Chapter 8

QUALITATIVE ANALYSIS OF THE D&O INSURANCE

8.1. Introduction

The previous chapter showed that the D&O insurance policy differs with respect to the features of a purchasing corporation. It further provided evidence to what extent D&O insurance has an effect on managerial risk taking.

This chapter will answer the question of how the D&O insurer can control the manager and which tools it uses to do so. It will also analyse the current status of the D&O insurance market in the four countries.

It will analyse several reports and general views of practitioners, insurers, and brokers, as well as policy designs in the USA, the UK, the Netherlands, and Germany. Moreover, this chapter refers to the field research of Baker and Griffith.[979]

Before turning to the structure of this chapter, some caveats are in order. All of these sources lack an empirical validation with respect to the European D&O insurance market. The research of Baker and Griffith is based on the US market and rather qualitative. The other documents are based on polls and limited to a small data set.

This chapter will be structured as follows. Section 8.2 will outline the D&O insurance industry. As will be shown, the D&O insurance policy is drafted cooperatively by the corporation, the broker and the insurer. The involvement of the insured manager is less pronounced.

The next sections will turn to the demand for (8.3) and supply of (8.4) D&O insurance, as well as the observed obstacles of D&O insurance (8.4). These sections build on the previous findings.

Consequently, this chapter will discuss the tools that are applied, in order to raise capacity (8.5), combat imperfect observation (8.6) and control the insured (8.7). Section 8.8 will analyse the use of partial coverage. The D&O insurance policy incorporates limits, deductibles, and content exclusions.

Having discussed the insurer's tools to cope with the D&O risk (which means collectively, the liability risk and the indemnification risk), this chapter will analyse to

979 Baker and Griffith 2007, 'Predicting Corporate Governance Risk', pp. 487–490; Baker and Griffith 2007, 'The Missing Monitor', pp. 1795–1801; Baker and Griffith 2009, 'How the Merits matter', pp. 755–763.

what extent the insurer is able to monitor the manager (8.9) and how far the proposed mediating ability of the insurer with respect to the corporation is observable (8.10).

The next chapter will analyse the extent to which the liability risk is insurable and to what extent the D&O insurer may be unable to control managerial risk. It will further recommend changes to enhance the benefits of the D&O insurance on managerial risk taking.

8.2. D&O insurance industry – General overview

According to section 5.11, the pricing of D&O insurance is highly affected by the level of competition. With high competitive pressure, the price of the premium approximates to the actuarially fair premium. Similarly, the distribution of D&O insurance is related to the complexity of the underlying risk. This thesis showed in section 6.5 that the managerial liability rules are very complex indeed.

Furthermore, the insurance policy is affected by an ever-returning cycle of hard and soft markets. When the cycle is placed in a hard market situation, the premiums are high and coverage very limited. When there are soft market conditions, the premiums are low and the scope of coverage is high. These conditions alternate because each preceding situation over-stimulates the market, which leads to the opposing situation. No exhaustive explanation or model is yet existent to predict the cycle.[980]

This section will first outline the players of the market and the premiums in the USA, the UK, the Netherlands, and Germany. Subsection 8.2.2 will turn to the existence of an insurance cycle in these four countries and the current state of their markets, considering the cycle.

8.2.1. *Market players and prices*

This subsection will deal with the market players and the prices of D&O insurance. It will enable a general comprehension of the market and the competitive pressures in each country. This subsection will discuss each country in turn.

The USA – The insurance market has four main players, the corporate buyer, the insurance seller, the insurance broker, and the re-insurer. The existence of the broker seems to be necessary because of the complexity of the liability risk outlined in section 6.5.

The corporate buyer is represented by the risk manager, a position that reports to the treasury or Chief Financial Officer. In the course of negotiation, the manager himself and the legal department also become involved. The coverage usually has a cap. The amount that is usually insured correlates to the size of the corporation (measured by market capitalization). The industries that mostly purchase D&O insurance are agriculture, mining and construction, manufacturing, insurance, energy, and health

980 Compare to subsection 4.6.2 and see Priest 1987, pp. 1529–1532; Cooter and Ulen 2012, pp. 239–240; Harrington and Danzon 2000, pp. 297–300.

care excluding pharmaceuticals. 43% of the insurer's revenue was made with purchasers having a size (market capitalization) of $1 billion to $4.9 billion. Compared to earlier surveys of 2006 the limits, but also the premiums, keep increasing up to 2013.[981]

Regarding the insurers, 90% of the premiums and limits written derive from 20 insurers. Approximately 40% of the policies are underwritten by the top three, two of those three being Chubb and AIG, and the third one alternatively XL, ACE or Allied World. The top three can not to be pinpointed precisely, as the exposure and profit from these policies vary greatly on a yearly basis.[982]

Some studies suggest that the D&O risk arising from securities law for an average public corporation amounts to 2% per year. The usual procedure regarding such a claim goes as follows: (1) the filing of the claim in court, (2) the motion to dismiss, (3a) settlement talks or alternatively (3b) a possible judgement.[983]

Most of the claims are settled. Regarding the first stage, studies that analyse claims between 1991 and 2007 reported the filing of more than 3000 claims. Around 30% of the filed claims were dismissed by the court (motion to dismiss). In other words,, about one third of the claims cannot show on a *prima facie* basis that they have merit.[984] 37 of the 3000 claims were tried to judgement (the final stage).[985] The remaining claims were settled in the period between the motion to dismiss and the judgement.

The average settlement amount was $24 million in 2005. This seems to refer to a remarkable increase of settlement amounts. Between 1993 and 2003, the average settlement amount still ranged between a minor $4 and $6 million. The difference between $6 million and $24 million, amounts to an increase by a factor of four.[986]

Private corporations with an annual revenue of up to $50 million pay an average premium of $15,851 for a limit of $2.6 million. Above a revenue of $ 50 million, the policy becomes dependent on the industry. Corporations with a revenue between $50 and $100 million, pay an average of $50,000 for a $5 million limit.[987]

The UK – The industries that mostly demand D&O insurance are the financial sector (almost 100%), oil/chemicals and pharmaceuticals (75%), and general manufacturing (50%). The financial sector on average pays the highest premium.

In 1994, 83% of the D&O insurance policies were supplied by 4 insurers, being AIG, Chubb, Lloyd's, and Sun Alliance. Zurich International also was a big player, regarding accrued revenues from D&O insurance. Whereas brokers seem essential to structure the

[981] Racioppo 2013, p. 4; A market capitalization of $ 999 million relates to $57.2 million of coverage, one of $9.9 billion relates to $149.8 million, and one that exceeds $10 billion purchases on average $ 199.1 million. Compare to: Tillinghast Towers Perrin 2006, p. 6; Advisen Report 2013, p. 10.

[982] Advisen Report 2013, p. 7.

[983] Baker and Griffith 2009, pp. 776–778.

[984] In the US, the claim has to meet certain formal pleading requirements before the court evaluates the merits of the case. If these requirements are not met, the claim is dismissed. Baker and Griffith 2009, p. 775.

[985] Baker and Griffith 2009, pp. 776–778, citing Black et al. 2006, p. 1064.

[986] Baker and Griffith 2007, 'Predicting Corporate Governance Risk', p. 498; Baker and Griffith 2007, 'The Missing Monitor', p. 1801; Cornerstone Research 2013, p. 4; Racioppo 2013, p. 16–18.

[987] Advisen Report 2013, pp. 10–11.

insurance policy in smaller corporations, the risk management of big corporations is done internally by their risk department.[988]

In 1994, the price of premiums ranged between GBP 3,000 and 4,000 for a coverage limit to GBP 1 million. For GBP 5 million, the premium cost around GBP 5,000 to 7,000. The mean average was GBP 127,693. 35% of the corporations in 2010 responded to have a coverage limit of GBP 51 to 100 million. The Airmic report suggested similar pricing in 2010. Approximately 45% of the responding private corporations in 2010 paid a premium of GBP 100,000 or less.[989] Claims were virtually always settled.[990]

The Netherlands – The corporations that seek insurance seem to be in the industry of semi-conductors, IT, pharmacy, and corporations that conduct business with North America.[991]

In 2001, the market leader of D&O insurers was BCA-pool. The pool was an alliance between numerous insurers. Primary insurer of the pool was Bloemers & Co. Assuradeuren B.V. According to the US example, the primary insurer is responsible for the management, administration, marketing, eligibility, and legal procedures.[992] On 1 January 2007, the BCA-pool was wound up.[993] Around this time, new players from the Anglo-Saxon region and also other from continental European countries entered the market, raising the competition between insurers.[994]

In 2008, the premium of the top 500 enterprises (having a revenue of more than EUR 500 million) was between EUR 10,000 and EUR 100,000 per year for a coverage limit between EUR 100 and 200 million. For SMEs, the premium corresponded to EUR 1,000 to EUR 10,000 with a coverage of EUR 1 to 10 million. If the enterprise conducted business in North America, the premium was above EUR 100,000. The average was a premium of approximately EUR 2,800 with a coverage of EUR 4 million.[995]

988 The Wyatt Co 1993/94, para. 4.3. The survey has been criticized because of its low response rate: Out of 4,000 questionnaires 123 responded. Compare to: Finch 1994, p. 897–905; Baxter 1995, p. 546–556; Airmic Research 2010, p. 3; Marsh Insurance Market Report 2013, p. 29.

989 The Wyatt Co (1993/94), para. 4.3; Airmic Research 2010, p. 17; Marsh Insurance 2013, p. 29.

990 Finch 1994, p. 901; Baxter 1995, p. 554–555. Also compare to Airmic Research 2010, p. 25.

991 Weterings 2010, p. 165.

992 Participants were AEGON Schadeverzekering N.V., Delta Lloyd Schadeverzekering N.V., Fortis Corporate Insurance N.V., Generali Schadeverzekering Maatschappij N.V., Goudse Schadeverzekering Maatschappij N.V., Hooge Huys Schadeverzekeringsmaatschappij N.V., N.V. Interpolis Schade, Nassau Verkering Maatschappij N.V., Nationale-Nederlanden Schadeverzekering Maatschappij N.V., N.V. Maatschappij van Assurantie, Discontering en Beleening der Stad Rotterdam Anno 1720. See: Vroom 2001, p. 37, 43.

993 Hendrikse and Van den Heuvel 2009, p. 127. Since 18 November 2011, Bloemers & Co. Assuradeuren B.V., which is affiliated with Nassau Verzekering Maatschappij N.V., merged with HDI Gerling. See: HDI Gerling website.

994 Marsh Insurance 2013, p. 16.

995 Hendrikse and Van den Heuvel 2009, pp. 128–132; Vroom 2001, pp. 40–43; Weterings 2010, p. 165. The increased amount of external liability claims made by the bankruptcy administrator and the increased competition in the Dutch insurance market seem to be important for the rise in coverage. The limit includes legal costs and relates to the entire board. It has been suggested that such inclusion might have the potential to lead to opportunistic behaviour of one manager to the disadvantage of others. He

In the end, 80% of the claims are not admissible in court. Of the admissible claims, 70% end in a settlement. The amount of claims covered by the insurer increased by 30% in 2009 in relation to 2008. Three quarters of these claims are external liability claims, whereas the majority of claims that are finally admitted to the court are internal liability cases. According to Weterings, bankruptcy administrators are more likely to hold the manager liable, when they know that the managers are insured against it.[996]

Germany – The reports mentioned did not give a clear indication whether some industries especially demand D&O insurance. Generally, similar branches as those outlined in other countries are likely to be the primary demanding corporations in Germany as well. In this regard, insurers view the industries of financial services and construction as highly risky.[997]

According to the comparison website KuV24 Manager, the group of important insurers counts 14 firms, most of them being of Anglo-Saxon origin. The usual suspects, such as Chubb, AIG, XL, and Zurich are listed. Other prominent insurers are HDI Gerling and VuR Versicherungen.[998] In 2004, Hendricks stated that the market at that time was still very competitive and diversified. Big corporations usually had a coverage of EUR 300 million, covered by multiple international insurers. The premium for SMEs was usually EUR 1000. For big multinationals, the premium corresponded between 0.1 and 0.3% of the coverage.[999]

Comparison and analysis – This paragraph will compare and analyse the involvement of particular parties, being (1) corporations who request cover, (2) insurers and brokers, and (3) turn to the analysis of the prices.

(1) The corporations seem to have similar characteristics such as industry type and size. It is remarkable, however, that the corporations are generally quite big. Section 6.5 explained that many managers desire to insure the bankruptcy liability risk. Furthermore, section 7.6 suggested that size has off-setting effects with D&O insurance. This outcome will be analysed in section 9.2.

(2) Furthermore, the number of insurers that offer D&O insurance seem to be smaller in the USA and the UK, moderate in Germany, and high in the Netherlands after the fall of the market leader 'BCA-pool'. The main players in those four countries originate from the Anglo-Saxon area. Still, the competition seems to be fierce among the top players, as will be outlined in the next subsection.

would consume most of the coverage for himself. Hendriksen and Kalff thus suggest a coverage limit per legal entity and per manager. See: Hendriksen and Kalff 2008, p. 109.

996 Weterings 2010, pp. 169–170.

997 Thümmel 1998, pp. 165, 161–165.

998 KuV Manager website, Versicherungsvergleich zur D&O Managerhaftpflicht.

999 Hendricks 2004, p. 9–11. Also compare to: kuv24 Manager website, D&O coverage.

(3) The premium prices seem to suggest a coverage to premium ratio of 0.07–0.1% in the Netherlands, 0.1–0.3% in the UK, 0.1–0.3% in Germany and 0.6–1% in the USA. These great differences in prices already indicate the relative differences to be held liable in these countries.

Furthermore, they provide a very general indication about the probability of the D&O risk in these countries.[1000] Subsection 4.6.3 outlined that the actuarially fair premium refers to the multiplication of magnitude and probability, plus a certain loading. It further outlined that the loading decreases as the competitive pressure increases. From the above it can be asserted that the magnitude is limited considering that each D&O policy includes an upper limit. Thus, when dividing the premium by the amount of coverage, the resulting ratio should indicate the size of the insured D&O risk including a residual that refers to the loading.

Bearing in mind this consideration plus the competitive pressure in each country, the following conclusions can be drawn. In the Netherlands, the 0.09% (coverage limit divided by premium) closely resembles the probability of the D&O risk, as the residual for the loading is close to zero due to the competitive pressure.

In Germany, the UK and the USA, the coverage-to-premium ratios of 0.2%, 0.2% and 0.8% respectively, also somewhat resemble the probability of the D&O risk in those countries. However, the ratio also indicates the size of the loading residual. The premium loading is probably higher in Germany, the UK and the USA than in the Netherlands, because the competitive pressure is weaker. As a result, the ratios of Germany, the UK and the USA are less reliable to reflect the D&O risk's probability than the ratio of the Netherlands.

The ratio of the USA is the highest by far. This may be explained by the generally high liability risk. In the USA some studies suggest a probability of around 2%.[1001] Yet, the fact that the coverage to premium ratio is lower (0.8%) than the suggested liability risk could indicate the efficiency effects of D&O insurance. However, without more elaborate and developed calculations, this relationship is purely indicative and lacks conclusiveness.

8.2.2. *Insurance cycle*

The following will turn to the past and current states of the D&O insurance cycle in the USA, the UK, the Netherlands, and Germany.

The USA – The market cycle refers to the insurer's change in policy. The D&O insurance market experienced hard phases in the mid-1980s and between 2001 and 2003. Baker

1000 A similar ratio has already been outlined in subsection 7.7.2 is also applied by the empirical study of Boyer and Stern 2012, pp. 354–355. Please note, however, that these calculations are of an indicative nature. The outcomes of these calculations neither provide conclusive answers on the probability of the D&O risk nor do they provide evidence for the effect of D&O insurance on the risk. Still, a comparison of the coverage-to-premium ratio to the D&O risk may serve as a foundation for a more developed and balanced calculation.

1001 Baker and Griffith 2009, pp. 776–778.

suggests on the basis of interviews undertaken that the market began to soften by 2007.[1002] However, this phase might have been short because the financial crises and corresponding managerial liability cases indicate another hard phase.[1003]

According to the Advisen Report 2013, the pricing tendency must be differentiated in three groups of clients differing in their amount of revenues. Smaller corporations up to a revenue of $50 million and huge corporations with a revenue above $1 billion, experienced a flat premium rate since 2008 and 2003 respectively. Corporations between $50 – $1 billion faced somewhat more volatility with a high in 2009.[1004]

The UK – In 1994, Finch regarded the market as being fairly soft, with the exemption of the far reaching exclusions. She did not find many indications to assume a hard market in the upcoming years. However, she considered the English system to be quite similar to the US system, which might translate to cyclical market changes in the UK as well. According to the Marsh Insurance Report 2013, the soft market, in place for eight years, begins to stabilize to a healthier state. Most policies are renewed flat or a low premium reduction. Most insurers want to hold onto existing rates. Without shocks or new strong competition, the market is likely to stay the same.[1005]

The Netherlands – After the break up of the BCA-pool in 2007, competition between insurers in the D&O market has been increasing. Thus, no single insurer seems to dominate the market. That translates into a soft insurance market, with wide coverage and small premiums. In 2010, Weterings predicted a hardening of the market.[1006] Similarly, Hendriksen and Van den Heuvel in 2009 regarded the insurance coverage as utterly wide. They also predicted further limitations and exclusions.[1007] However, according to forecasts provided in the Marsh Report 2013, the market rates will stay the same or might even decrease by 10%. These findings suggest that the year of 2014 should resemble a soft market as well.[1008]

Germany – The markets were soft in the 1990s, hard in 2002 to 2004 and seemed to soften again in 2006 onwards. The Marsh Insurance Report regarded the D&O insurance market as stable in 2012. On the one hand, demand of SMEs was increasing and insurance competition continues to be strong. On the other hand, contract renewals stayed the same.[1009] According to the AON Report 2013, the market is relatively soft. It experienced an all time low in 2013 and the premium is likely to have stayed flat (in other

1002 Baker and Griffith 2007, 'Predicting Corporate Governance Risk', pp. 506–508.

1003 Willis 2013, p. 10; Baker and Griffith 2010, p. 55. For an explanation and different view on the insurance crisis in the 1980s see: Priest 1987, pp. 1529–1532, 1550–1590.

1004 Advisen Report 2013, p. 26.

1005 Marsh Insurance 2013, p. 29; The Wyatt Co (1993/94), para. 4.3. The survey has been criticized because of its low response rate: Out of 4,000 questionnaires 123 responded. Compare to: Finch 1994, p. 897–905.

1006 Weterings 2010, pp. 167–168; Hendrikse and Van den Heuvel 2009, p. 128.

1007 Hendrikse and Van den Heuvel 2009, p. 132.

1008 Marsh Report 2013, p. 16.

1009 Marsh Report 2013, p. 12.

words: no change) in 2014. Furthermore, competition also from UK insurers remains fierce.[1010]

Moreover, new products enter the market. These are so-called sidecars, such as personal managerial insurance, D&O insurance for retired managers, and insurance for the required deductible of managers in public corporations (AG).[1011]

Comparison and analysis – The price developments seem to stay flat in all countries. Furthermore, competition in the Netherlands and Germany remains high and new products are being developed.

The absence of the potential impact of the sub-prime mortgage crisis, the financial crisis, and the Euro crisis on the D&O risk is remarkable.[1012] One might have argued that these crises would lead to drastic actions of holding the manager accountable for their alleged participation in these crises or even being a possible cause for these crises. Furthermore, some polls suggest that managers and insurers are increasingly aware of the liability potential due to the crises.[1013] To explain the difference between theory and practice, there are several considerations to make.

First, apparently, insurers seem to not consider it necessary to restrict the distribution of policies or to increase prices.[1014] If the coverage-to-premium ratio indeed signals the D&O probability as sketched in this subsection, one would come to the conclusion that the D&O probability risk has not increased.

Secondly, the competitive pressure and the complex system of risk distribution may off-set any changes to the price. On the one hand, more corporations ask for insurance and purchase higher limits. On the other hand, new insurers keep entering the market, the offered products keep developing, and insurers anticipate an increase in claiming.[1015] Without more comprehensive research,[1016] the crises do not seem to have affected the D&O market much. Such a finding may also indicate that insurers can control the insured manager. Section 9.3 will turn to this consideration more thoroughly.

Thirdly, regulation and policy exclusions may play a big role. To explain, suppose that the crises led to liability claims that are not insurable (such as criminal liability in Germany or intentional conduct). The insurance price would not take into account these liability claims because they are not covered. The increased liability risk would not translate into higher prices. The scope of the policy exclusions will be analysed in section 8.8.

1010 AON Risk Solutions 2013, p. 3, 6–8.

1011 AON Risk Solutions 2013, p. 8; Gurochkina 2014.

1012 Eling and Schmeiser 2010, p. 13; Baluch et al. 2011, p. 130.

1013 Eling and Schmeiser 2010, p. 13.

1014 Although insurers expected a high amount of liability claims after the crisis, this fear has not been met. See: Eling and Schmeiser 2010, p. 13; Baluch et al. 2011, p. 130.

1015 Eling and Schmeiser 2010, p. 13.

1016 In this regard, see: Holt 2011, pp. 589–560; Eling and Schmeiser 2010, pp. 10–11, 13, 25; Baluch et al. 2011, pp. 126–127.

Fourthly, the situation of the D&O insurance market needs to be distinguished from the D&O re-insurance market. As will be outlined below, the D&O re-insurance market may have experienced a higher pressure originating from the crises mentioned.[1017]

8.3. Demand for D&O insurance

The following will shortly review the desire of the manager and corporation to cover for the liability risk and the risk to indemnify the liable manager.

8.3.1. Managerial demand

Risk aversion – The previous discussion in section 6.5 suggests that the scope of the rules is highly complex. The complexity is likely to create risk.[1018] The manager may be averse or even be chilled to take risks.[1019] In this regard, the risk to be held liable should be allocated to a more efficient risk bearer, such as the corporation or an insurer. The manager will seek compensation by a combination of an increased salary, indemnification or insurance.[1020] Subsection 5.3.3 argued that except for bankruptcy liability, indemnification is more likely than insurance when indemnification saves transaction costs (finding and negotiating the insurance policy) and litigation costs (simplified settlements).[1021] To eliminate the remainder of the bankruptcy liability risk, the managers are likely to desire insurance instead of indemnification.[1022] Section 7.6 argued that in times of financial instability D&O insurance may be a valuable alternative to excess pay when the level of firm performance remains the same.

Capacity – As predicted, the liability risk has a low probability and a high magnitude.[1023] The manager is likely to be judgement-proof.[1024] He probably also faces disastrous reputation costs.[1025] With regards to the findings of section 6.5, one may suggest that self-insurance of the manager is unlikely.[1026]

1017 Alwis et al. 2005, p. 1; Baluch et al. 2011, p. 130.

1018 Shavell 2004, p. 265; Polinsky and Shavell 1993, p. 254.

1019 The chilling effect was related to the increased liability risk under the Sarbanes-Oxley Act in the USA and describes an attitude where the manager refrains from taking any risks. See: Bargeron et al. 2010, pp. 34–35.

1020 Bishop 1964, p. 839; Bishop 1966, p. 96; Polinsky and Shavell 1993, p. 241; Fischel and Bradley 1985, p. 285.

1021 Similar arguments have made by Kraakman 1984, p. 865; Fischel and Bradley 1985, p. 291; Oesterle 1983, p. 570, 572.

1022 Kraakman 2008, p. 144; Kraakman 1984, p. 868–869.

1023 Bishop 1966, p. 95; Pillai and Tractenberg 1981, p. 102; Baker and Griffith 2007, 'Predicting Corporate Governance Risk', pp. 494–496; Bishop 1964, p. 834.

1024 Subsection 3.2.4 and Shavell 2004, p. 275; Wagner 2009, p. 395.

1025 Paetzmann 2008, p. 192.

1026 Paetzmann 2008, p. 188.

8.3.2. *Salary increase and indemnification*

In accordance with the manager's desire to be compensated, the corporation assembles a combination of indemnification, insurance and a salary premium. The compensation in the form of a salary increase may be expensive (when the manager is risk averse)[1027] and may weaken firm performance.[1028]

Indemnification is harshly regulated in the legal systems but with the exception of Delaware law, as analysed in section 6.7. According to Baker and Griffith, virtually all corporations incorporated under Delaware law indemnify their managers.[1029] When indemnification is prohibited, the firm seems to have no choice but to compensate the manager for the liability risk in the form of an increased salary or, alternatively, to insure internal liability.

Section 7.5 analysed the corporate demand for D&O insurance. The studies did not distinguish between the insured liability risk and the indemnification risk. In this regard, this thesis could not find any evidence to confirm or refute the hypotheses on the mediation ability of the D&O insurer outlined in section 5.6.

8.3.3. *Corporate demand for D&O insurance*

Risk aversion – Whatever the original reason for indemnification,[1030] the shareholder may develop risk aversion to the D&O risk (which means collectively, the liability risk and the indemnification risk). Although demand due to shareholders' risk aversion is not particularly prominent in mainstream literature,[1031] risk aversion may indeed be a justifiable reason for indemnification in private and/or family owned businesses. An *a contrario* argument on risk averse shareholders would infer that well-diversified shareholders do not demand D&O insurance. However, section 5.6 and the observations of Baker and Griffith advocates the opposite. Virtually all public corporations have D&O insurance.[1032] Moreover, on the basis of the empirical findings, it has been suggested that corporations that have a more dispersed ownership structure desire more insurance.[1033]

Increase of return on investment – Some shareholders might desire insurance to compensate for a share value loss. The insurance could increase the solvency of the (indemnified) manager (deep-pocket problem).[1034] Although such a practice is suggested by the observations of Baker and Griffith, the feasibility of this strategy is questionable.

1027 Cf.. Fischel and Bradley 1985, p. 285; Kraakman 1984, pp. 864, 865.

1028 Bloom and Milkovich 1998, pp. 291,292. The negative link between incentive pay and firm performance has been somewhat weakened by studies such as: Hutchinson and Gul 2004, pp. 609–610.

1029 Baker and Griffith 2007, 'The Missing Monitor', p. 1803.

1030 Reasons of indemnification were suggested in section 5.3.

1031 Baker and Griffith 2007, 'The Missing Monitor', p. 1823; Paetzmann 2008, p. 185.

1032 Baker and Griffith 2007, 'Predicting Corporate Governance Risk', p. 487.

1033 Core 1997, p. 82. However, although O'Sullivan detected the same correlation in the UK, it was not significantly so. Thus, this factor may still be a controversial one. See: O'Sullivan 2002, p. 581.

1034 Bhagat et al. 1987, p. 276; Baker and Griffith 2009, p. 797, citing an interviewee: "*Other people's money is easy money*".

After all, the insurer knows about such a strategy as well and will adapt its policy to it. The adapted policy amount denotes a negative net present value project.[1035]

Signalling – Section 5.6 proposed that shareholders and creditors would like to know about the D&O insurance. The size of the coverage could serve as a signal about the corporate financial status and corporate governance. This proposition is partially observable as sections 7.6 and 7.10 outlined. In general, creditors do not punish insured corporations, provided the limit is average. Equity investors seem to ignore D&O insurance information,[1036] even though, under high competitive pressure, insured corporations seem to make more valuable investment decisions.[1037] Furthermore, a study of O'Sullivan 2009 suggests that auditors, supposedly external gatekeepers, sanction a corporation that is insured against the D&O risk.[1038]

Real-service efficiencies/monitoring – The monitoring-hypothesis by Holderness has had overwhelming responses in literature. Baker and Griffith and others believe that this hypothesis lays the foundation of corporate demand for D&O insurance.[1039] However, the empirical studies above could neither refute nor support the monitoring hypothesis.[1040]

The subsequent question is, whether the insurer has a greater ability to monitor the manager's risk taking than the shareholders. When analysing this question, it is worth mentioning that the national law maker (drafting the liability rule) may have had different thoughts on optimal managerial risk taking than the insurer. The national lawmaker may be led by public opinion to change managerial liability rules. The insurer on the other hand may rather seek to maximize its utility.

The following sections will analyse how the D&O insurer insures the D&O risk and which tools the insurer uses to do so. Section 9.5 will outline how the insurer affects managerial risk taking.

8.4. Supply of D&O insurance

This section will first outline the general insurance coverage of D&O insurance and secondly turn to obstacles to insurance.

8.4.1. Supply to the manager and the corporation

The following subsection will discuss the wording of the coverage and its general scope in the four countries.

1035 Paetzmann 2008, p. 188; Kraakman et al. 1993, p. 1746.

1036 Boubakri and Ghalleb 2008, pp. 29–30.

1037 Lin et al. 2013, p. 55.

1038 In this context, the existence of D&O insurance positively and significantly correlates with audit fees. See: O'Sullivan 2009, pp. 153–154. In his words, *"this finding suggests that the reduced liability exposure expected from the audit of insured companies is more than counterbalanced by the other characteristics of insured companies expected to have a positive impact on audit fees."*

1039 Baker and Griffith 2007, 'The Missing Monitor', pp. 1828–1829; Paetzmann 2008, pp. 188–190.

1040 Compare to section 7.6.

The USA – The D&O insurance coverage is based on three types of coverage. The first type covers loss of the manager that arose from the shareholder derivative suit, called Side-A coverage. Furthermore, it covers personal liability claims, when the corporation is unable to do so, because of bankruptcy or insolvency. A typical example for Side-A coverage is (derived from AIG):

> "The Insurer will: (i) pay the Loss of each Insured Person arising from a Claim against that Insured Person except to the extent that the Insured Person has been indemnified by the Company for the Loss;"[1041]

The second type of coverage compensates the corporation for its indemnification payments to the manager, called Side-B. A typical example is:

> "The Insurer will: (ii) reimburse the Company for any Loss arising from a Claim against an Insured Person for which it has indemnified an Insured Person."[1042]

The third type covers the corporation for losses it has to bear because of shareholder litigation, called Side-C. A typical example is:

> "The Insurer will pay the Loss of each Company arising from a Securities Claim brought against a Company."[1043]

The policies in the US seem to be tailor made, without standardizations existing. Prices of premiums, coverage limits, and exclusions are subject to timely negotiation.[1044]

The UK – Finch distinguishes between the Corporate Re-imbursement Coverage and the Personal Coverage. Corporate Re-imbursement Coverage entails Side-B coverage plus compensation for legal costs borne by the corporation. Personal Coverage translates to Side-A coverage. A Side-A coverage usually covers "*a claim based on any actual or alleged breach of duty, breach of trust or neglect, plus errors, omissions, misstatements and breaches of warranty of authority, ...*",[1045] as long as it does not fall within one of the exceptions.[1046]

The policy is mostly tailor-made and standardization is rare. Thus, a purchaser has to be very careful to read everything. Comparison will be difficult because the structure of the policies is highly individualized. When the corporation grows bigger, the insurance

1041 AIG Policy Wording 2013, clause 1.1(i).

1042 AIG Policy Wording 2013, clause 1.1(ii).

1043 AIG Policy Wording 2013, clause 1.4.

1044 Baker and Griffith 2007, 'Predicting Corporate Governance Risk', p. 499–501. See for example: Chubb Specimen Policy (Nov 2002); The Hartford, Directors Officers and Company Liability Policy.

1045 Baxter 1995, p. 549–550; Finch 1994, p. 898.

1046 Also see O'Sullivan 2009, pp. 147–149. O'Sullivan 2009 provides a general description of the structure of D&O insurance in the UK citing Finch 1994. The references of O'Sullivan suggest in this regard that there is no recent literature on the structure of D&O insurance in the UK. Compare to section 10.4.

contract tends to be more tailored to the particular needs, whereas the broker has an essential role to produce first documents.[1047]

Generally, the insurance covers legal costs and compensation of damage. The insurer will usually want to gain the right to undertake legal actions on behalf of the corporation/ manager. It will further insist that the corporation may not incur any legal costs without the consent of the insurer. Although, in general, these provisions seem theoretically sound, they might be less useful when speed or a response to an unreasonable threat is at stake. Furthermore, when there is a potential to mitigate huge damages by way of a quick reaction, the question of responsibility is difficult to answer. Subsequently, if not having reacted quickly leads to more damage, the question arises, whether that increased amount is covered.[1048]

The Netherlands – The insured is usually the employer of the manager, being the corporation. It also pays the premium. The insurance covers globally all forms of managers, either formal directors or officers, or the actual informal manager. Generally, also actions or omissions relating to subsidiaries, with a 50% and higher participation, are within the scope of coverage. Moreover, the insurance covers the corporation for losses that result from indemnification. No deductible is included in the coverage. As long as the premiums are paid and the insurance contract is still ongoing. Also an individual that used to work as a manager for the corporation is insured at the time that he retired from the position.[1049]

The insurance compensates for the loss of the manager, but also covers any associated legal costs. The latter is also done, when the claim seems inadmissible. Here the insurers know two practices that might overlap. They either have their own legal experts and cover upfront, or they let the corporation decide which lawyer to use and let the corporation pay at first. The legal support might include representation in criminal proceedings.[1050]

The coverage for the legal costs seems to be essential for the manager, because he not only fears pecuniary loss, but also fatal damage to his reputation. Discretion, efficiency and expertise are thus utterly important. Furthermore, the claimant's interest might only be to put pressure on the corporation, using the often complex facts of the case to his advantage. The insurer's coverage and management of legal proceedings loosen that tension.[1051]

Germany – Some insurers deny any coverage upfront, others pay first and deal with coverage later. This is especially problematic for the manager, who is already damaged existentially by the legal costs.[1052]

1047 Baxter 1995, p. 549–550; Finch 1994, pp. 898–890.
1048 Baxter 1995, p. 549–550; Finch 1994, pp. 889, 898–890.
1049 Hendrikse and Van den Heuvel 2009, p. 128; Vroom 2001, pp. 37–38.
1050 Hendrikse and Van den Heuvel 2009, p. 128; Vroom 2001, p. 40.
1051 Hendrikse and Van den Heuvel 2009, p. 128; Vroom 2001, p. 42.
1052 Küpper-Dirks 2002, p. 66.

The D&O insurance is organized similar to the US system. External claims are covered. Internal claims might be subject to limitations. The formal board is covered and the corporation pays the premium. Furthermore, formal managers and supervisors are covered. Top executives that are not formal managers can be excluded from the coverage. According to Thümmel, inclusion of that group is not necessary because they have less risk to be held liable under the current regime. Many insurers do cover informal managers, however. Past managers are covered.[1053]

The policy coverage is twofold, compensating for damages and legal costs. Also legal costs that arise from formal expert reports (*Sachverständigengutachten*) and attorney fees are covered. Actions done to mitigate the damage of eligible actions are included. All costs consume the coverage cap that has been agreed upon during the negotiations on a first come first served basis.[1054]

Side-B insurance, called company re-imbursement, is existent. However, it is limited to situations, where the indemnification is legally valid.[1055] It is limited for the corporation only, subsidiaries of the corporation are not entitled. However, some insurers do include coverage for subsidies, for example RUV Versicherungen.[1056]

Comparison and analysis – The D&O insurers primarily offer D&O insurance to the corporation. Personal insurance comparable to professional liability insurance (sought by lawyers or doctors) is not very common in the observed countries. Such a finding approves the hypothesis of subsection 5.4.3 that D&O insurance is part of the managerial compensation package, next to salary and indemnification.[1057] The manager and the firm mutually agree on the risks and rewards attached to taking the job, one of which is the size of the liability risk.[1058]

Further, subsection 5.3.3 argued that it is cheaper for a firm to indemnify the risk-averse manager than to raise his salary[1059] or insure him.[1060] The manager approves indemnification of the liability risk, except with respect to the bankruptcy liability risk. Bankruptcy liability is likely to be insured.[1061]

These findings suggest that the corporation may resort to D&O insurance due to two reasons.

First, insurance is sought when indemnification is ineffective, such as for the bankruptcy liability. To compensate for bankruptcy liability, it has been argued that D&O insurance is a better alternative to a salary increase when the firm is in financial

1053 Hendricks 2004, pp. 9–12; Thümmel 1998, pp. 165, 161–164; Küpper-Dirks 2002, p. 72.

1054 Küpper-Dirks 2002, pp. 64–65.

1055 Koch 2010, p. 98. As outlined in section 6.6, indemnifications are regulated in Germany.

1056 RUV Versicherungen 2012, clause A.1.4. Furthermore, new products such as the *D&O Vermögensschutzversicherung* or *persönliche D&O Versicherung* slowly enter the market. See e.g.: kuv24 Manager website, persönliche D&O Versicherung.

1057 Bishop 1964, p. 839; Bishop 1966, p. 96; Polinsky and Shavell 1993, p. 241; Fischel and Bradley 1985, p. 285.

1058 Bishop 1966, p. 101.

1059 Cf.. Fischel and Bradley 1985, p. 285; Kraakman 1984, pp. 864, 865.

1060 Similar arguments have made by Kraakman 1984, p. 865; Fischel and Bradley 1985, p. 291; Oesterle 1983, p. 570, 572.

1061 Kraakman 2008, in: Faure 2009, p. 144; Kraakman 1984, p. 868–869.

distress.[1062] In accordance with this argument, empirical studies show that factors associated with business risk such as divesting, financial distress, and leverage aggravate D&O purchase and limits.[1063] In a situation without financial distress in which indemnification remains ineffective, the corporation buys insurance when a salary increase (or similar compensations such as managerial shareholding) is more expensive than insurance.[1064] However, as section 9.2 will outline, the market of insurance for bankruptcy liability does not appear to be that developed.

Secondly, insurance is desired because the corporation values the insurer's monitoring and mediating abilities.[1065]

The coverage of the D&O risk is structured in two layers. First, it covers costs that arise from damages to be paid by the manager or the corporation. Secondly, it covers the costs that are associated with legal proceedings. Generally, the second layer has a wider scope, as it is also triggered in situations, in which coverage by ways of the first layer is regarded to be illegal. To illustrate, the manager is covered for legal costs associated with criminal proceedings by the insurer. The insurer does not cover for criminal sanctions, as will be outlined in the section on exclusions.

The definition of manager differs in the countries; the Dutch insurers seem to insure a wider scope of leading management personnel than the insurers in the other countries. However, such a finding has limited applicability, because the considerations are based on a small number of scrutinized general terms and conditions.

8.4.2. Obstacles to supply

This subsection will briefly reconsider the findings of prior chapters in relation to the obstacles to D&O insurance.

Insurer uncertainty – Although not observed in the findings, subsection 5.7.2 suggests that the insurer might be unable to entirely insure the risk due to uncertainty.[1066] Indeed, as will be outlined in section 9.2, there is limited accessibility of insurance for smaller corporations.

Insurer's capacity – The insurer might face a capacity issue due to the D&O risk's high magnitude or the uncertainties about the risk.[1067] These capacity issues should, in principle, be cured by a well functioning insurance system. If the capital structure of the insurer is not sufficient to carry a particular risk, subsection 4.3.8 described the possibilities of third party intervention or partial coverage.

1062 Section 7.6 indeed argued that D&O insurance is a better alternative to a salary increase when the firm is in financial distress. Also compare to: Core 1997, pp. 81, 82.

1063 Kaltchev 2004, pp. 49–50.

1064 Bishop 1964, p. 839; Bishop 1966, p. 97; Kraakman et al. 1993, p. 1746. As outlined in section 7.6, the form of managerial salary affects the D&O insurance purchase decision significantly. See: Core 1997, p. 81, 82.

1065 Please refer to section 5.6. For the monitoring hypothesis, see: Holderness 1990, pp. 118–123.

1066 e.g. Küpper-Dirks 2002, p. 74.

1067 Baker and Griffith 2007, 'Predicting Corporate Governance Risk', pp. 494–496.

Adverse selection – section 5.8 suggested the potential of adverse selection in the market. In this regard, the level of competition may indicate the extent of adverse selection. In this environment, the insurer attempts to discriminate in risk and price as much as possible to build a competitive edge. When numerous insurers are able to insure, the issue of adverse selection cannot be so dramatic. Some observe the D&O insurance market to revolve, at least in the US, around a small number of insurers.[1068] Still, the overwhelming majority regards the D&O insurance market, especially in discussed European countries, as highly competitive.[1069] Still, competition does not preclude adverse selection. However, the practice of highly advanced risk differentiation pursued by D&O insurers should overcome adverse selection.

Moral hazard – Implicit in the monitoring-hypothesis is the issue of moral hazard. If the monitoring is impossible or too expensive, the insurer is able to partially cover the insured, in order to avoid moral hazard.

The following sections will outline the insurer's responses.

8.5. Tools to raise the capacity

As previously shown, the insurer desires to pass on part of the risk. The insurer does so because the D&O risk is uncertain and has a great magnitude feature.[1070] The insurance industry resorts to towering, co-insurance and pooling, and re-insurance.

Towering – Towering means that insurers co-operate with each other to be able to offer a higher limit. If the insured wants to purchase more coverage than an insurer could offer, the corporation can approach another (secondary) insurer that offers another layer of insurance between the amount already provided by the first insurer and the secondary insurer's own upper limit. When the coverage of the first layer is fully consumed, the subsequent layer is used.

Because single insurers in the USA have trouble in covering large risks in excess of $10 to 25 million, towering is common. The corporate insurance is towered, with different layers of insurance coverage by different insurers, in which the primary insurer, offering the first D&O policy retains most relevance. The compensation to the corporation by the insurer is executed layer by layer. When the coverage of the first layer is fully consumed, the subsequent layer is used. The primary insurer, the insurer of the bottom layer, has the closest relationship to the corporation. The primary insurer asks for a surplus on the premium because that insurer is asked to pay first, whenever an eligible claim arises. The main market players in the USA for primary insurers are AIG and Chubb, controlling 53% of the market. The scope and content of the coverage layers stay the same, which is

[1068] Baker and Griffith 2007, 'Predicting Corporate Governance Risk', p. 505.

[1069] Marsh Insurance Report 2013, p. 16; Hendricks 2004, p. 9–11.

[1070] Interestingly, the respondents of the Advisen Report 2013 do not actually experience that many claims. *"The majority of companies received only one claim during the three-year period, while some noted receiving 6 claims and one 'a dozen or so'."* See: Advisen Report 2013, p. 16.

called 'following-form' basis. It goes without saying that the probability of compensating the insured decreases with the insurer's location in the tower's layers.[1071]

The layers that amount to the final coverage limitation seem to have a sticky point, as observed by Boyer. He detected that corporations cover for an amount that builds up in steps of $5 million, with no corporation asking for coverage in between these steps. So policy limits often correspond to $5 million, $10 million, $15 million, $20 million, $25 million and then a big jump to $50 million.[1072] It has been suggested that the claimant's knowledge about the cap leads to a situation in which the claimant will only sue for the amount that is covered. Thus, the activity of the claimant changes because of insurance, referring to the deep-pocket problem.[1073] This issue indicates the mediating role of the insurer and will return in the section on imperfect control.

The individual creating the tower to the conditions of the insurer and corporation is the broker. He is the trusted intermediary between the two parties. In the US, big brokerage firms are Marsh, AON, Willis.[1074]

Co-insurance and pooling – The limit for insurers is EUR 10 million. To cover for higher amounts, the insurers resort to one of two options in the Netherlands. The first possibility is a *pro rata* co-insurance. Every participating insurer covers the same proportional amount of the damage. A second possibility is the towering, explained in the section on the US market. Pooling has been done in the Netherlands in the past, until the winding-up of BCA-pool.[1075]

Re-insurance – Re-insurers are common in the US. They spread the risk and enable smaller insurers to enter the D&O insurance market. Re-insurers cover with limits of $15 million, the maximum being $25 million. Most re-insurance treaties include limitations to coverage, either a loss ratio cap[1076] or limited re-instatements.[1077] Moreover, deductibles are demanded by re-insurers between $5 and $10 million.[1078]

Some argue that the D&O crunch between 1997 and 2001 hit harder on the re-insurance market than on the primary D&O insurers.[1079] This issue will return in section 9.3.

1071 Baker and Griffith 2007a, p. 504–505; Baker and Griffith 2010, p. 53.

1072 Boyer 2007, p. 87.

1073 Baker and Griffith 2010, p. 169; Bhagat et al. 1987, p. 276; Baker and Griffith 2009, p. 797, citing an interviewee: "*Other people's money is easy money*".

1074 Baker and Griffith 2007a, p. 504–505; Baker and Griffith 2010, p. 53. It can be argued that this essential role in the D&O market and its unmonitored practice might easily lead to an abuse of the role. See: Baker and Griffith 2007, 'Predicting Corporate Governance Risk', p. 505.

1075 Weterings 2010, p. 165.

1076 This ratio measures losses and loss adjustment expenses against earned premiums and reflects the percentage of premiums being consumed by losses. See: American Institute For Chartered Property Casualty Underwriters 2013, p. 1.

1077 "*[T]he total number of losses to be paid by the reinsurer is limited.*" See: Mata 2000, p. 349.

1078 Baker and Griffith 2007, 'Predicting Corporate Governance Risk', pp. 505–506.

1079 Alwis et al. 2005, p. 1; Baluch et al. 2011, p. 130; Finch 1994, p. 896.

8.6. Tools to combat imperfect observation

To overcome the outlined obstacles to insurance, the insurer needs to be able to observe and control the insured. This section will turn to the tools of the insurer to enable observation of the insured.

8.6.1. *Extensions of the policy (self-selection)*

This subsection will outline some of the most important clauses in the D&O insurance policy that may be purchased in exchange for a higher premium.

Additional coverage for grossly negligent acts – In the Netherlands, if desired, the insurer may also cover gross negligence. In this regard, the insurance might have a wider scope than indemnification. Such widening also comes in useful in a situation of bankruptcy, where the manager only has an unprotected claim against an insolvent corporation.[1080]

Coverage for punitive damages – In the Netherlands, cover is usually excluded for punitive damages and those damages that have punitive characteristics. The latter refers to administrative penalties, contractual provisions, and environmental damage. These limitations enable the insurer to better define the actual risk of managerial liability. Some insurers do include damages of a punitive character (except criminal sanctions) for an increased premium, however.[1081]

The final adjudication coverage – In the USA, the policy usually exempts intentional or fraudulent acts of the managers. However, as an extension to that exemption, many insurers offer the 'final adjudication' extension. The extension provides compensation for legal costs regarding the D&O claim until the claim has been finally adjudicated. Because most claims settle, the damage rarely is finally adjudicated in court.[1082]

In Germany, Hendricks & Co. GmbH, according to their website the leading broker for D&O insurance,[1083] distinguishes between three policies of coverage for mid-sized corporations. Regarding the first policy, the insurer checks, whether the claim is covered by the insurance. If so, the insurer assumes the legal process and cover damages, when they occur. If not, the second policy may be bought. The insurer assumes the legal process anyway and defends the insured. If successful, the issue is solved. If not, the third policy can be purchased, which involves the insurer negotiating a settlement with the claimant.[1084]

The severability clause – In the USA, in the absence of a policy extension, the insurer will not cover when the insurance deal is negotiated on the basis of material misrepresentation

1080 Vroom 2001, pp. 40–43; Hendrikse and Van den Heuvel 2009, pp. 128–132.
1081 Vroom 2001, pp. 40–42; Hendrikse and Van den Heuvel 2009, pp. 128–132.
1082 Baker and Griffith 2007, 'Predicting Corporate Governance Risk', pp. 500–501.
1083 Hendricks & Co. GmbH website.
1084 Hendricks & Co. GmbH 2014, Der Rundumschutz für den Mittelstand, pp. 1–2.

or a wrongful act to the insured corporation. With full severability, these situations will not lead to a cancellation of coverage. With limited severability, these situations will only lead to a cancellation, when the signatory or relevant executive knew of the false information in the insurance application.[1085]

The extension for the claims-made principle (UK) – In the UK, the insurance coverage lasts on the principle of 'claims-made', already described. Here, the actual reporting of the claim is essential for potential coverage. Requirements as to the procedure to report and the transition for the beginning and the end of the contractual period are to be scrutinized.[1086]

The corporation can also buy an extension for claims that arise after the policy has been terminated provided that the claim is based on actions that the manager engaged in during the term of the policy (prolongation of the policy). According to Baxter, the conditions of prolongation are often disadvantageous to the corporation.[1087]

The extension for the claims-made principle (Netherlands) – In the Netherlands, most contracts exclude coverage for actions that are made before or after underwriting. It will limit the risk of the insurer to compensate for actions that have their origin prior to the insurance contract, called '*inlooprisico*'. To cover actions prior to the contract, the insurer asks in an application form, whether the insured knows of circumstances or actions that might lead to a claim within the scope of the insurance. When answered in the affirmative, the insurance will only cover those actions that happened after the insurance contract entered into force.

The coverage ends with the opening of formal bankruptcy proceedings of the insured corporation. Claims that are based on actions that were made before the opening of the proceedings are covered. Because claims for actions before bankruptcy could be filed long after the opening of bankruptcy proceedings, the insurer provides to cover these claims up to five years after the opening of the bankruptcy, called *uitloopregeling*.

If promptly reported by the bankruptcy administrator, the *uitloop* can also be bought from some insurers shortly after the opening of the bankruptcy proceedings. Insurers might even have the duty to offer such *uitloopregeling* when the corporation becomes bankrupt.[1088] According to Koburg, the time frame is up to three months after the opening of the bankruptcy proceedings.[1089] The bankruptcy administrator may also, on behalf of the corporation, be entitled to use the coverage within that time-frame for external claims, in order to raise the bankruptcy estate.[1090]

Note, however, that the administrator or manager needs to be careful to fulfil the premium-payment obligations, when the corporation is in distress. If premiums are not entirely paid, the coverage is absent. Furthermore, these considerations are of the utmost

1085 Baker and Griffith 2007, 'The Missing Monitor', pp. 1805–1806.

1086 Finch 1994, pp. 898–899; Baxter 1995, p. 549; Airmic Research 2010, p. 25.

1087 Finch 1994, pp. 898–899; Baxter 1995, p. 549.

1088 Rb. ECLI:NL:RBMNE:2014:507.

1089 Koburg 2009, pp. 83–85.

1090 In this case, he may have priority over other corporate creditors to receive the insurance coverage. Compare to: Hendriksen and Kalff 2008, pp. 105, 107.

importance to past managers that can still be held liable. In this regard, it is important whether the insurer or the manager/corporation pays upfront. The first situation protects the manager/corporation. The second situation favours the bankruptcy administrator.[1091] This consideration will return in section 9.2.

Furthermore, claims are covered for an additional amount, when they are made after the contract was terminated, but the facts of the claim are based on circumstances that were sufficiently known in detail by the insurer at the time of the contractual relationship. This is called *omstandighedendekking*. Reports by the insured to the insurers on the basis of that provision have been increasing due to the financial crises.[1092]

The extension for the claims-made principle (Germany) – In Germany, the coverage is also based on the claims-made principle. The insurer offers a *Rückwärtsdeckung*. The *Rückwärtsdeckung* covers claims that are based on actions prior to underwriting, as long as they were not known by the insured. In this regard, the insured is required to report any circumstances that might lead to a claim.[1093]

Furthermore, German insurers offer a *Nachhaftungsfrist* or *Nachmeldefrist*, which covers for claims that are filed after termination of the insurance contract for actions that arose during the insurance contract. Usually, the *Nachhaftungsfrist* has to be purchased within one to two years after termination of the contract. Regarding the RUV Versicherungen, the *Nachhaftungsfrist* is without temporal limitation and is thus always covered, as long as the claim is based on actions during the insurance coverage.[1094]

Additional coverage when operating in the USA – In the UK, because affiliations with the USA or Canada, such as assets, subsidiaries or activities, are regarded as highly risky by the insurer, liability that is based on anything relating to North-America is often excluded. Big corporations often specifically seek international coverage and pay accordingly. The corporation often underwrites for local D&O insurance to cover for damages that are not caught by the international coverage.[1095]

Coverage for internal conflicts – In the UK, the insurance only covers when a claim is made against past or present directors, whereas the claimant has no control over the present office holders. This exclusion will limit a situation in which internal warfare is financed by the insurer. As a result, claims of shareholders that have a substantial participation in the corporation, family members or trusts might not be covered. To cover claims that fall within this exclusion another insurance policy is offered, called 'directors' professional liability policy'.[1096]

1091 Furthermore, the right of the administrator to freeze the available coverage may be in conflict of the manager's right to be compensated for legal costs arising from liability cases against him. Compare to: Hendriksen and Kalff 2008, p. 107.

1092 Hendriksen and Kalff 2008, p. 107.

1093 Brand 2010, pp. 82–83.

1094 Brand 2010, pp. 83–84. RUV Versicherungen 2012, para. A.3.2.

1095 Finch 1994, p. 901; Baxter 1995, p. 550.

1096 Baxter 1995, pp. 552–553; Finch 1994, p. 899.

Subsection 5.6.2 hypothesized that the insurer can mediate internal corporate conflicts. The existence of this extension may indicate the insurer's appreciation of internal conflicts. Based on this extension, insurers seem to ask for a mark-up, when conflicts among shareholders seem likely.

Coverage for change of control – In the Netherlands, another additional coverage is concerned with change of control/material change. These cases relate to third parties or the state attempting a financial recovery, structural changes in the business, or a reorganization. Generally, the occurrence of these situations leads to the automatic termination of the insurance contract. However, additional coverage outlives these cases.[1097]

Comparison and analysis – The existence of these extensions points to certain aspects. First, the D&O underwriting process requires timely negotiations and skilled parties on both sides. Secondly, the insurer is able to offer individualized policies that satisfy the desires of the insured corporation. Thirdly, the extensions of the policies allow the insurer to apply the tool of self-selection. Through the use of self-selection, the insurer is able to build up private information about the features of the D&O risk. When holding enough private information, the insurer can categorize the risk. These considerations will be further developed in section 8.9.

The extensions to the claims-made principle seem popular in the EU countries. The final adjudication coverage is offered by insurers in Germany and the USA. Coverage for internal conflicts or a change of control is offered by UK or Dutch insurers respectively. The other extensions seem to be offered in one legal system only. One may expect, however, that extensions that turn out to be lucrative in one country will be adopted by insurers of other countries as well.

8.6.2. Risk categorization

This subsection will further outline the insurer's use of the tool of risk categorization.

USA – The issue of risk categorization is researched by Baker and Griffith 2007 at length.[1098] One interview with a D&O underwriting officer clearly explains, what factors are important for D&O insurers. According to him:

> "We look at the industry that the company operates in trying to figure out if we are in a mature industry, a growth industry, a start up section of the industry, whatever. Are we working with proven technology, new technology, proven consumer goods, new consumer goods?
>
> We look at the history of the company and see if M&A is a prominent part of their planning process for the future or not. We look if there are takeover risks. We look if there is a restructuring perhaps necessary in the future of the company. We examine the type of

1097 Hendrikse and Van den Heuvel 2009, pp. 130–131.

1098 Baker and Griffith 2007, 'Predicting Corporate Governance Risk', pp. 508–512.

securities filings they did at the [SEC]... We look at any SPEs, SPVs, joint ventures that they are using to grow strategically.

Then we dive into the corporate governance. We examine who the directors and officers are, their applicable experience. We look at interlocking board relationships. We actually keep a separate database here. Since 1996 we can run our database and tell you if any one director or officer was a defendant in a securities class action or derivative action.

[W]e record which company they were serving in when they were sued, but what we can then do is go back and look to see if the folks that we are underwriting now were sued in what was a fender bender or if it was a complete corporate meltdown. So we have a driving record in this.

We look at the organization of the corporate governance committees and independence of those committees and how active they are and then we look at insider ownership [and] compensation packages. Then we move into a broader understanding of the entire ownership of the company and... what conflicts may or may not exist within the ownership interest.

We take a serious look at the equity trend of the company over recent years and what made its price earnings multiple what it is. We examine insider trades. We look at any intellectual property that the company may be relying upon. We look at the regulatory structure and who the regulators may be and how the history with the regulatory relationships were *[sic]*. We look at both former existing director and officer litigation as well as general litigation that the corporation may be involved in that could be a threat to the future value of the company. We look at how they handle corporate investor communications. We look at how they are handling legislative or environmental issues that may face the company. We look at how they may handle employment practices and bankruptcy of course. We have an entire dedicated review of the bankruptcy and potential emergency or liquidation.

Then we go into a very meticulous breakdown of the financials of both the balance sheet and the cash flow statement and profit and loss statement. You know, your typical ratio analysis is supported by about 55 or so different ratios. Underneath those ratios we look meticulously at who the auditors are, what the revenue recognition policies are, how they manage accounts receivable, inventory, payables, valuing intangibles, you know, formulating debt and appreciation, capital expenditures, pension obligations, and we look even at vendor financing if it exists. Then we take all that stuff and we rate it for risk."[1099]

Furthermore, they not only base their categorization on the financial statements, but also consider the corporate compliance culture and the character of the manager. Regarding the culture, insurers analyse the constraints on the manager, such as the process for M&A activity, the structure of executive compensation, the dealing with bad news.[1100] The manager's character is evaluated, as to whether he is risk taking above the norm and in how far he reacts to corporate problems.[1101]

1099 Baker and Griffith 2007, 'Predicting Corporate Governance Risk', pp. 512–514, citing: Underwriter #2 at pp. 3–6.

1100 Baker and Griffith 2007, 'Predicting Corporate Governance Risk', pp. 517–523.

1101 Baker and Griffith 2007, 'Predicting Corporate Governance Risk', pp. 523–525.

The UK – To fix the price of the premium, insurers mostly take into account public information. Financial statements seem to receive the greatest attention, such as annual reports and the like. Furthermore, some insurers research news articles and press reports of the past years to estimate activities, industry and level of risk taking. Thirdly, the corporation will have to disclose the following, most of the time in a form of a list of questions: legal personality, age of business, corporate activities and activities of its subsidiaries, names of the managers, shareholder structure, subsidiary structure, mergers and acquisitions, change of the corporate name, sale of subsidiaries, change of the capital structure, expected mergers and acquisitions, expected IPOs or other offers, and previous D&O claims. Although insurers do not assess individual board members, the existence of seemingly risk-taking types will correspond to higher premiums. Most of these disclosures are repeated on a yearly basis. In bigger corporations, the manager also actively asks his insurer for information that the insurer has on the manager in order to understand his D&O risk exposure.[1102]

Generally, insurers regard some activities as highly risky, which translates to higher premiums. Among them is the involvement in North America, mergers and acquisitions, divestment, and a recent pre-tax loss. The latter relates to possible conflicts of interests that might return in the near future. Furthermore, the increasing claim culture already mentioned affects the UK as well. In this regard, the financial crisis, and also the BP oil spill have led to an increased perception of D&O risk exposure.[1103]

The Netherlands – The price of the premium depends on numerous variables. These variables include the age of the corporation and the underlying business, the corporate size, the kind of industry, the financial corporate situation, activities in foreign countries, majority shareholding, and the quality of the manager. Also expected merger/acquisitions, change in profitability, IPOs, accountant reports and its insurance history are essential. A rise in the premium seems to correlate to corporate affiliation with the US market, because their liability regime is regarded as stricter than in the Netherlands. Furthermore, in big multinational concerns, interviews with the managers are conducted. The organization and structure of the concern is of relevance, too.[1104]

Furthermore, the risk estimation of managerial liability takes place yearly and leads to renegotiation of the terms. The insurer is to be informed about changes in the board structure, new board members, payment problems, change in activities, change of the articles of association, solvability ratios, financial statements, and new mergers and acquisitions. It is essential that the corporation does not have more debt than equity. If that is the case, the insurer is likely to deny coverage because of the increased likelihood of bankruptcy.[1105]

Germany – Information must be granted to insurers in cases of indemnification clauses; clauses to compensate for deductibles; essential information before underwriting;

1102 Finch 1994, p. 901; Marsh Insurance Market Report 2013, p. 29; Airmic Report 2010, p. 11.

1103 Baxter 1995, p. 547–548; Airmic Research 2010, p. 3.

1104 Weterings 2010, p. 164–165; Vroom 2001, p. 42.

1105 Weterings 2010, p. 165; Vroom 2001, p. 42.

information about eligible circumstances; material change, decrease or increase in business; change in business structure or corporate structure; participations of more than 10%; liquidation or reorganization of the corporation and its subsidies; and yearly financial statements, revenues, profits, and ratios. During the negotiations, the insurer demands a filled out form that is also signed by at least one formal manager. Further, warranty statements are requested.[1106]

Comparison and analysis – The tool of risk categorization seems highly advanced for the liability risk and the risk to indemnify. The insurer's observations should enable a sufficient differentiation of risks. The next section will turn to the insurer's capabilities of controlling the insured.

In all the four countries observed, the insurer considers the corporate financials, categorizing the risk by applying ratios. In the Netherlands, the insurer may deny coverage when the corporation has more debt than equity. In the USA, insurers take into account the identity of the auditor and support their financial analysis by about 55 ratios. In the EU countries, insurers ask whether the concern operates in the USA. The risk of bankruptcy is particularly analysed by insurers in the USA and the Netherlands.

Furthermore, insurers in all countries consider corporate governance. The identity of the manager and his managerial qualities are assessed in the USA, the UK and the Netherlands. Such assessment is particularly common, when the insured manager runs a multinational concern. In Germany, insurers ask for information on indemnification and the corporate compensation on insurance deductibles. In the UK, managers may ask the insurer to communicate its D&O risk assessment, possibly to limit their exposure themselves.

In all countries, insurers tend to ask for the group structure and corporate shareholding. In the USA, the Netherlands and Germany, insurers seek to know whether the corporate shares are held by majority shareholders. Insurers in all countries are interested in the corporate M&A activities and the change of the business or corporate structures.

However, the manner of risk categorization may differ between insurers rather than between countries. In the end, the observed policies are offered by globally operating insurers. If an insurer values a certain set of indicators in one country, it is safe to assume that the insurer does so in other countries as well, provided that it is legally possible and feasible.

8.7. Tools to enhance control

To guarantee sufficient monitoring, the insurer has to be capable of controlling the insured next to observing corporate risk taking. In this regard, the dualistic role of D&O insurance must be kept in mind. The insurer needs to control the manager, but also mediate internal corporate conflicts. The following will outline tools that are usually used to control the insured (being the manager and the corporation). These tools refer to yearly adaptations and settlements.

1106 Hendricks 2004, p. 10; Paetzmann 2008, p. 189.

8.7.1. *Yearly adaptations and cancellations*

The USA – The insurance coverage usually lasts for a year. Each year will be negotiated anew.[1107]

The UK – Cancellation of the policy is often permitted without cause and potentially leads to dramatic effects on the corporation. To mitigate these dramatic effects, the corporation can buy a policy prolongation extension. According to Baxter, the conditions of prolongation are often disadvantageous to the corporation.[1108]

The Netherlands – The yearly termination has not been applied in the past. Whenever neither the insured nor the insurer cancel the contract, it is presumed to be valid. It is very difficult for the insurer to cancel the contract other than once a year. According to Vroom in 2001, termination on behalf of the insurer took place rarely, and only in cases where the insured refused to provide information about a claim and corresponding circumstances.[1109] According to Weterings in 2010, this practice had changed dramatically. Every year, the risk and conditions are negotiated anew.[1110]

Germany – The negotiations are conducted yearly. The corresponding form will be substantially smaller with regards to the form to be filled out when the corporation first bought coverage, though. The RuV Versicherungen has an automatic prolongation of coverage as long as neither contractual party terminates the contract.[1111]

According to Hendricks, the insurer often denies coverage on the basis of alleged timing. In this regard, the claims-made principle and its associated provisions are of utmost relevance in practice.[1112] For example, Hendricks & Co. GmbH makes use of this confusing market by offering an insurance policy that insures against the risk that the claim is not covered by the D&O insurance policy.[1113]

8.7.2. *Settlements*

In the US, the parties start the settlement talks with an amount that roughly equals two to six percent of the claimed damages. The claimed damages more or less correspond to the alleged drop in share price multiplied by the outstanding shares of the corporate defendant.[1114]

1107 Baker and Griffith 2007, 'The Missing Monitor', p. 1820.

1108 Finch 1994, p. 893; Baxter 1995, p. 549.

1109 Vroom 2001, p. 42.

1110 Weterings 2010, p. 165.

1111 RUV Versicherungen 2012, para. A.3.4.

1112 Hendricks 2004, p. 10.

1113 Website Hendricks & Co. GmbH 2014, HPDR.

1114 For example, the alleged share price dropped by $5. The corporation has one million shares outstanding. The claimed damage is $5 million. The settlement would revolve around 4% (the median of 2–6%) of $5 million, which is $200.000. Cf.. Baker and Griffith 2009, pp. 792–794.

This approximate amount is subsequently mediated. When the case has "sex-appeal", the claimant has leverage to raise the settlement. "Sex-appeal" relates to actions that add an emotional and personal side to the infringement of securities law. These are news-type aspects, such as SEC investigations, criminal charges, suspicious stock re-purchase programs, defendants pointing fingers at each other, the resignation of board members, whistle-blowers, termination of senior officers, or bad documents.[1115]

Furthermore, the amount is related to similar settlements, the available insurance, and the defendant's ability to cover excess amounts.[1116]

The insurer is able to relate to similar settlements.[1117] Because this information is likely to be private, the insurer enjoys an information advantage over the other parties. It is reasonable to assume that the insurer uses this advantage to its own benefit.

The availability of insurance refers to limits and the towering structure.[1118] The settlement amount usually consumes the coverage up to the limit. The "sticky" points are the layers of insurances. For insurers, it is sensible to include many layers, in order to mitigate the settlement amount.[1119] To better understand that practice, consider the following example. The insurers could build a tower of 10 policies where each policy includes an amount of $10 million. The "sticky" point refers to the amounts of $10, $20, $30, up to $100 million. As argued above, the parties usually settle for an amount that equals a "sticky" point. So, regarding this example, it is difficult to settle for an amount equal to say $15 million because the "sticky" point is either $10 or $20 million. To be able to settle for an amount that would approximate to $15 million, the insurers could simply introduce more layers for the same maximum amount.

In this regard, insurers build a tower of 20 policies where each policy equals an amount of $5 million. When the damage is more likely to be in the area of $15 million and assuming that the settlement amount will equal a "sticky" point, the insurers may be more likely to settle when having more layers, say 3 policies that equal $15 million, instead of fewer layers, say 2 policies that equal $20 million (original "sticky" point).

Furthermore, many layers enable the insurer to use the "sticky" point to its own advantage. The insurer could pay an amount that most closely resembles the wrongdoing of the manager. Similar to the reasoning of Kraakman et al.,[1120] the insurer could pay higher settlement amounts whenever the claim has a high likelihood of adequately deterring the manager. When more "sticky" points are included in the tower, the insurer's ability to influence settlement payments is sophisticated.

Especially in Germany,[1121] but supposedly in other countries too,[1122] the insurer tries to invoke a limitation or exclusion in order to prevent an otherwise obligatory compensation payment. Still, the claimant is careful to plead the facts of the case in such

1115 Baker and Griffith 2009, p. 786–791.
1116 Baker and Griffith 2009, p. 796.
1117 Baker and Griffith 2009, p. 822.
1118 Baker and Griffith 2009, p. 804.
1119 Baker and Griffith 2009, p. 809–815.
1120 This argumentation has been inspired by the proposal provided by Kraakman et al. 1993, p. 1763.
1121 Hendricks 2004, p. 10.
1122 For example, see: Finch 1994, p. 893; Baxter 1995, p. 549; Vroom 2001, p. 38 that discuss the insurer's effort to deny coverage.

a way that it falls within the scope of the coverage. For instance, the claimant rarely asserts that the defendant acted intentionally, because intentional behaviour is not covered by the insurance.[1123]

8.8. Partial coverage

This section will outline how far insurers limit their coverage. Partial coverage refers to financial limitations and policy exclusions.

8.8.1. Financial limitations

In the USA, whereas insurers do not include deductibles or co-insurance for Side-A insurance, the insurers do so for Side-B and Side-C. The caps for the three policies are synthesized as one. Either policy consumes the capital of the corporate limit. The sum of costs has to be below the cap.[1124]

The UK insurers also use deductibles. Deductibles for public corporations and corporations with a US listing are the highest.[1125]

In the Netherlands, side-A coverage usually has no deductible. Side-B coverage has a deductible. In comparison to Germany, the deductible is very small in the Netherlands.[1126]

In Germany, a deductible regarding the AG is regulated by law. According to §93 Abs. 2 AktG, the manager is required to proportionally contribute to the compensation of the damage. The deductible is set between two minimum amounts from at least 10% of the damage to at least 1.5 times his yearly salary.[1127] The manager of the GmbH is not legally required to pay a deductible. It is not common to include a deductible. Sometimes the corporation on behalf of the shareholders desires a deductible to deter the manager from risky conduct.[1128] Deductibles are promoted by the German Corporate Governance Code, but only 50% of the listed corporations (that are not required to do so legally) adopted it.[1129]

1123 Baker and Griffith 2009, pp. 821–822.

1124 Baker and Griffith 2010, p. 46.

1125 Baxter 1995, pp. 553–554; Finch 1994, pp. 893, 900, 902. Also see O'Sullivan 2009, pp. 147–149. As mentioned above, the references of O'Sullivan suggest that there is no recent literature on the structure of D&O insurance in the UK. Compare to section 10.4. According to Finch 1994, in 1994 the Side-A average deductible in 1991 was GBP 1,656 per person. The average increased to GBP 4,873. One third of policies in the UK included deductibles. The Side-B deductible was within the range of GBP 680,000. Here, 70% of the insurers applied deductibles. Both kinds of deductibles experienced a threefold increase between 1991 and 1994.

1126 Weterings 2010, pp. 166–167.

1127 Salary relates to his fixed compensation. Bonus payments seem to be excluded from the calculation of the deductible. Compare to: §93(2) AktG.

1128 Paetzmann 2010, pp. 184, 191–193. RUV Versicherungen, email on 22 November 2012.

1129 Werder and Bartz 2013, p. 888.

8.8.2. *Policy exclusions*

The USA – The policies have three basic exclusions. First, they exclude fraud and personal enrichment. It entails any action or omission that intentionally breached duties or rules. There are differences in the policies, some only excluding actual fraud and others widening the scope of exclusion. Furthermore, the fraud exemption is subject to the final adjudication clause. As long as fraud is not finally adjudicated in the legal proceedings, the insurer will cover all legal costs. Because settlement is very likely, which means that no final adjudication has taken place, the fraud exclusion loses applicability.[1130]

Secondly, there is the market segmentation exclusion. Whenever another insurance policy would cover the damage, the D&O insurer will not cover for the loss. Those are claims relating to the environment, Employee Retirement Income Security Act claims, or bodily injury or emotional distress.[1131]

Thirdly, the policy excludes litigation, in which both parties to the dispute are regarded as one by the insurer. An example would be, when one manager sues another. The UK insurers offer extensions to that exclusion.[1132]

The UK – The exclusions can be distinguished between four basic categories, according to Finch. First, there are acts that are either uninsurable or against the public order. Dishonesty, fraud or any other illegal or criminal act fall within this category. This exclusion entails intentional conduct. However, some insurers cover the costs for legal representation until the court considers it proven that the manager is held blameworthy for have engaged in a criminal act. Fines, other than civil damages will not be covered by the insurer. This might lead to difficulties in deciding, what amount is purely compensatory and which part is punitive. This is especially true, when considering the important role law in equity plays for these claims.[1133]

Secondly, exclusions refer to acts that are usually covered by more specific insurance. This category relates to bodily injury, property damage, libel, slander, warranties and guarantees. In this regard, close attention must be given to the specification of 'acts of the director'. Some insurers apply such a narrow description to these acts, that the manager is not covered. Cover might only be provided for decisions made during board meetings or the like.[1134]

Thirdly, there are risks that seem very difficult to estimate and thus impossible to cover. In this regard, environmental or pollution liability is excluded.[1135]

Furthermore, there might be specific exclusions relating to the structure or specific circumstances of the potential insured corporation. Finch considers the exclusion of particular shareholders that have a peculiar stake to the corporation, which is likely to

1130 Baker and Griffith 2010, p. 49. This is also known as the deep pocket phenomenon. Compare to: Hendriksen and Kalff 2008, p. 111; Bhagat et al. 1987, p. 276; Baker and Griffith 2009, p. 797, citing an interviewee: *"Other people's money is easy money"*.

1131 Baker and Griffith 2010, p. 49.

1132 Baxter 1995, p. 552; Baker and Griffith 2010, p. 49.

1133 Finch 1994, p. 899; Baxter 1995, p. 551.

1134 Finch 1994, p. 899; Baxter 1995, pp. 550–551.

1135 Finch 1994, p. 899; Baxter 1995, p. 550.

leads to a derivative suit initiated by them. Moreover, previous cases, statements or risks faced by the corporation could be excluded.[1136]

The Netherlands – First, intentional behaviour is excluded.[1137] This exclusion is legally demanded, coverage is held to be against *ordre public* and *bonos mores*, according to the *Bierglas* case.[1138] According to Wachter, insurance may also not cover the liability, when the manager is blameworthy for applying the fault standard of criminal liability.[1139]

Secondly, cover is excluded for criminal sanctions or sanctions with a penalizing character.[1140]

Thirdly, damage is excluded if it falls within the scope of a coverage that is or should have been underwritten by another insurer. The question of what should have been is to be answered by looking at the usual conduct in the particular industry.[1141] In any case and irrespective of the previous sentence, damage that arises due to an initial public offering or share issuance is likely to be excluded.[1142]

Fourthly, the claim has to be reported in due time to the insurer. Overdue reporting may lead to the exclusion of coverage for a particular claim, especially when the delay results in damages for the interests of the insurer.[1143]

Fifthly, the insurance forbids the insured corporation and manager to publicly comment on the covered claims. In the insurer's view such a remark might impede the legal proceedings. This prohibition is especially important, when the manager wants to confess (limited) fault.[1144]

Germany – The *Durchgriffshaftung* (piercing the corporate veil) is not covered. Intentional misconduct is excluded. The coverage includes gross negligence. It has been questioned whether an *Eventualvorsatz* (roughly translated: the potential to have acted intentionally), a less serious form of intentional misconduct, is excluded. The condition for *Eventualvorsatz* is that the manager either knew that the actions might be eligible for liability or ignored the eligible circumstances, and he is indifferent about the potential damage.[1145] Hendricks qualifies coverage as adequate, when the insurer defends the insured until intent is proven.[1146]

In practice, administrative claims might also be covered. Criminal sanctions are not covered.[1147] Furthermore, only pecuniary damages are covered. Any damage to the person or object is excluded. That means that environmental claims and product liability

1136 Finch 1994, p. 899; Baxter 1995, pp. 552–553.
1137 Vroom 2001, p. 41; Weterings 2010, p. 169.
1138 Weterings 2010, p. 162; HR NJ 1976/572.
1139 Note of Wachter below the case of HR NJ 1976/572, para. 2.
1140 Vroom 2001, p. 48; Weterings 2010, pp. 163, 169; Hendrikse and Van den Heuvel 2009, p. 128.
1141 Weterings 2010, p. 163. However, some insurers cover managerial liability with respect to environmental law as well. See: Vroom 2001, p. 48.
1142 Hendrikse and Van den Heuvel 2009, p. 128.
1143 Vroom 2001, p. 48; Weterings 2010, p. 163; Hendrikse and Van den Heuvel 2009, p. 128.
1144 Hendrikse and Van den Heuvel Juni 2009, pp. 130–131.
1145 Paetzmann 2008, p. 192; Schilling 2013, p. 39.
1146 Hendricks 2004, p. 10.
1147 Schilling 2013, p. 52.

are likely to be excluded. If the corporation covers these claims and wants to recover the loss of its manager, the manager is likely to be unable to be covered by D&O insurance. Thümmel suggests, however, that many insurers do cover for some environmental liabilities, for example §22 Abs. 1 *Wasserhaushaltsgesetz* (roughly translated: Water Act).[1148] Furthermore, according to Hendricks, especially American insurers cover damage to the person or object, when they are the result of the originally just pecuniary damage.[1149]

The insurance often excludes international conduct. When a foreign court holds the manager liable, or he breaches foreign law, or any of his actions took place in foreign territory, coverage is excluded. Thümmel regrets the exclusion because it hampers international business.[1150]

Further exclusions entail the following: no coverage, when another insurer covers; delayed reporting, failure to mitigate damage; dealing with the claimant without consultation with the insurer; damage to the reputation; fraud; and speculation.[1151]

Comparison and analysis – These exclusions can be loosely grouped under two general headings.

First, the insurance excludes criminal sanctions and intentional behaviour. More specifically, in the USA and the UK, insurers exclude fraud and intentionally breached duties. In the Netherlands, the exclusion of intentional breaches is legally required and insurers also exclude coverage for criminal sanctions. In Germany, insurers do not cover criminal sanctions. It remains controversial whether *Eventualvorsatz*, a less serious form of intent, may be covered by an insurer.

Section 6.6 analysed that indemnification, if allowed, does not encompass intentional behaviour or criminal liability.[1152] Section 5.5 argued that risk shifting, such as insurance or indemnification should be prohibited when the personal liability of the manager is essential to induce an optimal level of care.[1153] Kraakman argues that indemnification or insurance should be prohibited when the sanction that corresponds to the liability rule is unable to sufficiently deter firm delicts.[1154] More generally Shavell argues that intentional behavior represents a non-ambiguous and certain action that will not be insured. The manager should be able to avoid intentional misconduct and to take care. In this regard, intentional actions do not create a risk that has to be insured.[1155]

1148 Thümmel 1998, p. 175.
1149 Hendricks 2004, p. 10.
1150 Thümmel 1998, p. 176.
1151 Hendricks 2004, p. 10; Schilling 2013, pp. 40–43.
1152 With respect to Dutch indemnification see: HR NJ 1967, 261; Eesthuis et al 2011, p. 36–37. with respect to the Delaware indemnification see: Moskowitz and Effros 1992, p. 915. With respect to the German indemnification see: Thümmel 1998, p. 122–124; §397 BGB; §93(4):3 AktG; BGH WM 1968, 114; BGH GmbHR 1998, 278. Great Britain generally prohibits indemnification. See: Companies Act 1985, s 310; Ellington and Fletcher 1988, p. 496.
1153 It has been argued that absolute liability is likely to serve as an effective control over organizational conduct. See: Kraakman 1984, p. 859. A similar reasoning is provided by Privileggi et al. 2001, pp. 181–195.
1154 Kraakman 1984, p. 868.
1155 Shavell 2004, p. 264–265.

Secondly, insurers exclude specific characteristics of individual insurers. In the USA, insurers exclude coverage when one manager wishes to sue another manager of the same corporation. In the UK, insurers exclude coverage when previously identified shareholders bring the particular liability claim. In the Netherlands, insurers do not cover when the defendant manager publicly announces his involvement in the case. In Germany, insurers may deny coverage in cases in which foreign courts hold the manager liable.

This set of exclusions could support the second Holderness' hypothesis, as the next section 8.9 will outline.

8.9. Insurer's ability to monitor the manager

According to Holderness, the insurer is able to monitor the manager through the use of (i) an extensive underwriting process, (ii) an adaptation of the coverage during the period of insurance, and (iii) the insurer's active participation in the settlements.[1156]

The above outlined tools confirm the hypotheses of Holderness. In accordance with the first hypothesis, section 8.6 showed that the insurer performs an extensive underwriting process. Regarding the second hypothesis, section 8.6 and 8.8 showed that the insurer tailors and prices the coverage according to the respective individual circumstances. These observations may indicate a practice where the insurer tends to exclude any action that corresponds to a factor which, the insurer knows, will increase the liability risk. Consequently, it offers extensions to the corporation that would in turn incorporate the originally excluded action. Probably the extensions are priced to take into account a corresponding increase of the liability risk. If such argumentation holds, the insurer is able to self-select and categorize the risk. Considering the third hypothesis, section 8.7 outlined that the insurer makes use of private information advantage in settlements.

Baker and Griffith strongly doubt whether these practices sufficiently control the manager. They make three objections to the current D&O insurance practice, being that the insurer (i) inappropriately discriminates in pricing at underwriting,[1157] (ii) is unable to monitor during the policy period,[1158] and (iii) does not actively engage in settlements.[1159] The arguments of Baker and Griffith will receive closer attention in section 9.4.

8.10. Insurer's ability to mediate

In the USA, the vast amount of insurance sold is Side-B coverage, being coverage for the risk to indemnify the liable manager.[1160]

It remains questionable how far the insurer is able to mediate between a claiming shareholder and a defendant corporation, once the insurer has sold insurance for the indemnification risk. In analogy with the Holderness hypotheses that he formulated in

1156 Compare to subsection 5.6.1, section 5.10 and Holderness 1990, p. 118–123.
1157 Baker and Griffith 2007, 'Predicting Corporate Governance Risk', pp. 533–537.
1158 Baker and Griffith 2007, 'The Missing Monitor', pp. 1808–1813.
1159 Baker and Griffith 2007, 'The Missing Monitor', pp. 1813–1817; Baker and Griffith 2009, pp. 820–827.
1160 Compare to section 8.4.

relation to the manager,[1161] the insurer seems to be able to apply the tool of self-selection before underwriting and the tool of risk categorization during underwriting; also in relation to disputes among shareholders. In accordance with this argumentation, empirical studies show that in the USA, the premium to coverage ratio is materially lower than the average probability of a corporation faced with a securities law claim. Secondly, limits correlate with the litigation history of the corporation.

The offer of coverage extensions that this thesis has already outlined in relation to managers in section 8.7 may also be available in relation to the indemnification risk. For instance, in the UK, an extension can be purchased that explicitly covers internal disputes among shareholders. In the Netherlands, one may purchase an extension for coverage when the corporation is faced with a change of control.

Furthermore, in analogy to the third Holderness hypothesis, it is likely that the insurer can mediate effectively internal corporate conflicts in settlements. A settlement is faster and more discrete than open court proceedings.

8.11. Conclusion

This chapter analysed the current status of the D&O insurance market in the four countries. This chapter further answered the question of how the D&O insurer can control the manager and which tools it uses to do so. This conclusion will turn to these two aspects in turn.

Viewing the key figures of the D&O insurance market, four aspects attract attention, which are (1) the corporate size, (2) competition, (3) the coverage-to-premium ratio and (4) cycles. (1) Corporate size is associated with a higher amount of coverage, a better access to insurance and a higher price. The polls suggest that small corporations have little coverage and pay a higher coverage-to-premium ratio. The question of whether D&O insurance is unavailable to small corporations will be answered in section 9.2. (2) The number of, and the competitive pressure among, secondary insurers is high. Market entry for new secondary insurers is rather simple because of the re-insurance possibilities. Although the number of primary insurers is much smaller (e.g. in the USA), competition to offer the best policy for the lowest price remains high. Generally, competition is associated with a healthy market, capable of regulating itself. The competitive pressure is smaller in the USA and the UK, moderate in Germany, and high in the Netherlands. (3) The coverage to premium ratio is an illustrative indication that enables a comparison between the countries. The ratio is very high in the USA, followed by Germany, then the UK, and the lowest in the Netherlands. This ranking re-inforces the findings of section 6.5 that the managerial liability risk is high in the USA. (4) The past market crises did not have a strong impact on D&O insurance, suggesting a robust market. However, the re-insurance market may have been hit harder by the crises. A section on the re-insurance market is included in section 9.3.

1161 Compare to section 8.9.

The insurer may turn to third parties, such as other insurers (towering and co-insurance) and re-insurers, in order to increase capacity and pass on some of the uncertain risk.

The monitoring tools of the D&O insurer are very similar to Holderness' expectations. First, the insurer applies an extensive underwriting process. To boost its observation abilities, the insurer makes use of self-selection by ways of extended policy offers and categorizes the individual risk beyond a simple scrutiny of the firm financials (including psychological evaluations of the manager). Secondly, the insurer tailors the policy to the risk type of the insured. The categorizations described are ongoing and adaptations usually take place once a year. The insurer adapts the size of the coverage (referring to limits and deductibles) and alters the exclusions to the policy. As hypothesized, premium adaptations play an inferior role. Thirdly, the insurer is likely to make use of its information advantage in settlements.

In all the four observed countries, the insurer considers the corporate financials, categorizing the risk by applying ratios, taking into account corporate governance and tending to ask for the existence and identity of majority shareholders. Insurers in all countries are interested in the corporate M&A activities and the change of the business or corporate structures. In the EU countries, insurers ask whether the concern operates in the USA. The risk of bankruptcy is particularly analysed by insurers in the USA and the Netherlands. In the UK, managers may ask the insurer to communicate its D&O risk assessment, possibly to limit their exposure themselves. These findings generally confirm the empirical data outlined in Chapter 7 and suggest that the empirical observations summarized in Chapter 7 can be of use for insurers in the four observed countries as well.

It remains unclear, however, how far the insurer adapts its policy according to the indemnification risk (cf. mediation role).

The question as to whether the insurer's controlling abilities of the insurer sufficiently incentivize efficient managerial risk-taking will be analysed in section 9.5.

Chapter 9

OBSTACLES TO D&O INSURANCE AND RECOMMENDATIONS

9.1. Introduction

The previous chapter raised questions about the availability of insurance, the availability of re-insurance, and the insurer's ability to control the manager. This chapter seeks to answer these questions and analyse how far D&O insurers affect managerial risk taking.

First, D&O insurance may not be available to small corporations. Although managers fear the liability risk, small corporations do not carry the desired coverage. The small corporations may be uninsured because (i) either the manager is otherwise compensated, for example by means of a salary increase or indemnification, (ii) insurance is desired but not available, or (iii) the manager is not compensated at all for the risk. Section 9.2 will deal with this issue.

Secondly, the past crises may have hit hard on the D&O re-insurance market. Sections 8.2 and 8.5 outlined how far re-insurance is essential to guarantee sufficient competition. Section 9.3 will be devoted to this issue.

Thirdly, the extensive studies of Baker and Griffith suggest that the insurer is unable to deter improper managerial behaviour. Their arguments will be outlined and discussed in section 9.4.

Comprehending the current D&O market and its obstacles, section 9.5 will analyse whether D&O insurance affects the risk taking of the manager and if so, whether the D&O insurer contributes to efficient managerial risk taking. In this regard, it has to be kept in mind that managers are hired because they are (perceived to be) the experts of assessing and taking the relevant business risk. To do so, section 9.5 will take a step back and place D&O insurance in the context of overall social desirability. It will analyse the arguments of Baker and Griffith and answer the research question on how D&O insurance affects managerial risk taking.

Section 9.6 will point to some recommendations that could enhance the positive effect of D&O insurance on managerial risk taking and point to future research possibilities.

9.2. Limited access to D&O insurance

This subsection will deal with access to D&O insurance or rather the apparent absence of supply to the small and medium sized businesses. This subsection will analyse the four countries: the USA, the UK, the Netherlands, and Germany.

The USA – According to the Advisen report 2013, more than half of the corporations having a revenue above $300 million owned D&O insurance. A third of the corporations with a revenue between $10 – $300 million and those having a revenue below $500.000 received D&O coverage. The corporations with revenues between $500.000 and $10 million were not as likely covered by D&O insurance.[1162]

In the Towers Perrin Survey of 2012, 43% of the respondent managers indicated that the additional protection next to indemnification was sought in order to be protected in bankruptcy proceedings. In 2010, it was just 28%.[1163] It has been suggested by Baker and Griffith on the basis of their interviews that no individual would accept a board position, when his personal liability is not insured.[1164]

According to Baker and Griffith, the vast majority of claims are in the scope of Side-B and Side-C coverage, thus directed towards the corporation. However, according to Carpenter, many corporations only purchase Side-A insurance, because of price and availability issues. 41% of the D&O policies purchased included Side-A coverage in 2012, compared to only 34% in 2011.[1165] The current trend indicates a change of the D&O insurance market.

The UK – In 1994, Finch regarded D&O liability insurance as widely accepted for bigger businesses, whereas SMEs seemed to be willing to take the risk of having to compensate a liable manager.[1166] However, interviews with insiders in 2010 suggested that the market for SMEs is growing. As a result, some niche insurers offered Side-A insurance explicitly excluding any Side-B or Side-C coverage in order to have more competitive prices.[1167]

In 2010, insurers very often denied coverage to SMEs' managers and the policy exclusions were far reaching. From top level management, 25% of the non-executive directors were concerned with respect to managerial liability and desired coverage. For CEO's, it was 8%.[1168]

1162 Advisen Report 2013, p. 9.

1163 Racioppo 2013, p. 15.

1164 Baker and Griffith 2010, p. 45.

1165 Baker and Griffith 2007, 'Predicting Corporate Governance Risk', pp. 499–501; LaLone 2004, p. 2; Racioppo 2013, p. 3.

1166 Compare to the three forms of compensation, being indemnification, salary increase and insurance, outlined in section 5.3.

1167 Finch 1994, p. 900; Airmic Research 2010, p. 7. Compare to subsection 8.4.1.

1168 Airmic Research 2010, p. 19. According to Finch 1994, pp. 899–900, one in four D&O claims fell outside the scope of coverage in 1994. This might also explain the general dissatisfaction about the D&O insurance market from the point of view of the insured, in 1994. As mentioned above, the references of O'Sullivan 2009 suggest that there is no recent literature on the D&O insurance in the UK. Compare to section 10.4.

The Netherlands – Vroom estimates that approximately 95% of big corporations have D&O insurance. 50% of businesses that have a size between big corporations and SMEs have insurance, according to Vroom. SMEs rarely purchase D&O insurance.[1169] 40% of all managers are not insured. On the insurer's side, the refusal to cover a small corporation is relatively high; 50% according to Weterings. Big multinational concerns are very welcome, however.[1170]

Germany – Whereas big multinationals are mostly covered, any enterprise that is smaller will be even less likely to have D&O insurance than in the Netherlands or the US. Small enterprises are viewed suspiciously.[1171]

Analysis – The observations in these countries suggest that the small corporations in the UK, the Netherlands and Germany carry little or no D&O insurance. Similarly, only a minority of the mid-revenue corporations in the USA seem to have D&O insurance.

However, according to the outlined surveys, managers of small corporations seem to desire insurance. On a similar note, subsection 7.5.4 outlined that smaller corporations (and highly leveraged corporations) have higher D&O insurance limits.[1172]

The manager's desire of insurance is understandable given the hypothesis of subsection 5.2.4 that D&O insurance is one aspect of the total managerial compensation package. When small corporations have less funding to indemnify the manager, D&O insurance should be a valuable alternative.

Considering that these corporations rarely have insurance, one might argue that, as stated above, (i) either the manager is otherwise compensated, for example by means of a salary increase or indemnification, (ii) insurance is desired but not available, or (iii) the corporation that would purchase the insurance does not desire it. Let us turn to these three alternatives.

Regarding alternative one, the empirical evidence showed that excess pay has a positive correlation with D&O purchase and limits. In this regard, excess pay is a complement to insurance rather than a substitute.[1173] However, stock option compensation plans remain a substitute to insurance.[1174]

In this regard, incentive pay as an alternative can be ruled out and indemnification remains as an alternative means to D&O insurance. However, when the indemnifying corporation is close to insolvency, the indemnified manager remains subject to damage

1169 Vroom 2001, p. 37.

1170 Weterings 2010, p. 165, 169.

1171 Thümmel 1998, pp. 161–165.

1172 However, as repeatedly held, size seems to have offsetting effects in relation to the decision to purchase D&O insurance and the size of the D&O insurance limit. In some studies, smaller corporations do not have higher D&O insurance limits. Compare to section 7.6.

1173 Further, section 7.6 argued that if under financial distress, D&O insurance should be preferred to salary premiums which would lower a firm's performance.

1174 Core 1997, p. 81.

arising from liability. To eliminate the remainder of the liability risk, the manager is likely to desire insurance.[1175]

In other words, indemnification is a feasible alternative provided that the small corporation is sufficiently solvent. In turn, when small corporations have insufficient assets (which is often the case as small corporations have limited assets by definition) or when the compensation package aims at protecting the manager from bankruptcy liability, the indemnification does not properly protect the manager.

Existing research suggests that stock option compensation plans are a substitute to D&O insurance. It merits future research into how such a substitution affects managerial performance and, more specifically, whether D&O insurance may be a valuable alternative to stock option compensation plans in times of financial instability.

Regarding alternative two, insurance may not be available, when the risk is uninsurable or insurance is prohibited. Let us discuss both in turn.

First, subsection 4.3.8 outlined the concept of subdividing the risk as a solution to uninsurability. Indeed, sections 8.5 and 8.8 explained how far the D&O insurer is able to increase capacity and provide partial coverage. These findings suggest that the D&O risk borne by smaller corporations is indeed insurable.[1176] In this regard, the claim of uninsurability seems less convincing.

Secondly, the nature of bankruptcy law may complicate the effectiveness of D&O insurance. When the corporation is bankrupt, the corporate payment of debts is suspended. Any claim against the firm has to be lodged with the bankruptcy administrator.[1177] The observed restrictions pursuant to the national bankruptcy laws

1175 Section 7.6.

1176 However, sections 8.5 and 8.8 provided a general discussion on insurability that may not perfectly correspond to the status of insurability of the D&O risk borne by smaller corporations.

1177 Bowers 1999, pp. 94–95.
In this regard, one can distinguish the effects of bankruptcy proceedings on insurance between external liability and internal liability.
When an insured manager is held liable by a creditor and the insurer pays the insured losses to the corporation, the money that should have compensated the creditor cannot be recovered. The manager's or creditor's only possibility is to lodge a claim with the bankruptcy administrator in order to be provided with the money. Because the manager or creditor is one of many creditors that lodged their claims, the manager or creditor probably recovers only a small fraction of the original claim. In effect, the liable manager has to pay the damages because he does not have access to the insurance money. On first sight, this problem could be circumvented when the insurer agrees to pay the creditor or manager directly, removing the involvement of the corporate estate. This transaction may be voidable *ex post* in bankruptcy proceedings pursuant to *actio pauliana* / claw back provisions. See: Thümmel 1998, p. 157; Kraakman et al. 2009, p. 141–142. Also compare to: Hendriksen and Kalff 2008, p. 108.
In cases where the insured manager is held liable by (a proxy of) the corporate estate, the manager would be better off if the insurer would make the payment to the corporate estate. Making the payment to the corporate estate, the claim of the manager against the insurer evaporates and a new claim of the manager emerges against the corporate estate. In this regard, the debt of the manager owed to the corporate estate (pursuant to internal liability) and the claim of the manager against the corporate estate (pursuant to the insurance contract) could be set-off. The effectiveness of this strategy is subject to the specific conditions and requirements of the national bankruptcy law with respect to setting-off and claw backs. See: Kraakman et al. 2009, p. 141–142.

seem to hamper the effect of insurance when the corporation is insolvent (or has become judgement-proof). In this regard, D&O insurance faces a *de facto* prohibition.

As to alternative three (the manager is not compensated at all for the risk), there are two lines of arguments. First, the smaller corporations may not carry D&O insurance because the manager does not desire compensation for this liability risk at all. The corporation and the manager may choose to ignore the prospect of liability. The manager might live in the hope that 'It won't happen to me', similar to car drivers explained in subsection 4.3.3.[1178] Such an approach may guarantee effective decision-making to the detriment of the corporate risk management. Such reasoning does not take into account the manager's desire to be insured as outlined by the surveys. In this regard, this argument is less convincing.

Secondly, an important side effect and possibly another reason to go without insurance, is the cash constraint many smaller corporations face. When being small and possibly having the potential to grow, cash is limited.[1179] To have maximum impact, the manager might decide to use most of the cash for investment in projects. As a result, little or nothing is left for issues like insurance. In this regard, an indemnifying corporation becomes judgement-proof with respect to the liability claims.[1180]

From the above, one can conclude that (i) either the manager is compensated by stock option plans, (ii) the insurance is ineffective in bankruptcy and thus not desired, or (iii) an asset constrained (i.e. judgement-proof) corporation has no amounts left for D&O insurance. The absence of D&O insurance may be socially undesirable, which will be further considered in subsection 9.6.1.

9.3. Pressure on the re-insurance market?

The D&O crunch between 1997 and 2001 may have hit harder on the re-insurance market than on the primary D&O insurers.[1181] Yet, despite worries,[1182] the D&O insurance market remained strong in the recent financial crises.[1183]

This fact may suggest that the D&O re-insurance market sometimes faces problems in providing re-insurance to insurers. First, the re-insurer may be ambiguous about the risk. In this regard, the re-insurer may not know how much of the insurance policy amounts to underwriting risk (the corporate specific risk) and which part is systemic risk (the risk that the entire market bears).[1184] In theory, the former risk is borne by the insurer and the latter risk can be assumed by re-insurers. When failing to distinguish

1178 Cf. section 4.3 and Hogarth and Kunreuther 1989, p. 27–29.

1179 Cf. section 7.6 and Core 1997, p. 81, 82.

1180 Cf. Shavell 2004, pp. 275–276. Compare also: Cooter and Ulen 2012, pp. 240–241; Harrington and Danzon 2000, p. 290.

1181 Alwis et al. 2005, p. 1; Baluch et al. 2011, p. 130; Finch 1994, p. 896.

1182 Eling and Schmeiser 2010, p. 13.

1183 Baluch et al. 2011, p. 130.

1184 In this regard, see: Harrington and Danzon 2000, p. 291. They describe to what extent the liability risks correlate because liability losses depend on social norms and legal standards.

these risks, the re-insurer may carry some of the underwriting risk. To take into account the insurer's ambiguity as to what risk the re-insurer actually assumed, the re-insurance premium has to be increased.[1185]

This may lead to a second problem, namely that the re-insurance premiums might be perceived as too high by the insurer, which could lead to uninsurability.[1186]

Thirdly, even if the risk is not regarded as uninsurable, the inability to distinguish systemic from underwriting risk makes simplified categorization of claims impossible. In this regard, the insurer may carry high costs of monitoring and assessment costs to evaluate the eligibility of each individual claim. This problem might create moral hazard.[1187]

Fourthly, there is the long tail issue. The obligation to compensate the insured could arise much later than when the insurer underwrote the risk. The capacity of the re-insurer is not essential at the time of underwriting, but at the time when the claim to compensate the policyholder must be paid. When underwriting, the insurer assumes the risk that the re-insurer has insufficient capacity at the time the claim must be paid, known as credit risk.[1188]

9.4. Baker and Griffith: The (in)ability to deter bad corporate conduct

Baker and Griffith interviewed several practitioners, D&O insurer personnel, insured corporations, mediators, brokers and other parties involved. From their interviews, they concluded that D&O insurance for securities law claims bought by public corporations in the USA does not deter bad corporate conduct.[1189] The problems they observe seem closely related to the monitoring hypotheses outlined by Holderness. According to Holderness, the insurer may be able to monitor the insured when underwriting, during the policy period, and in settlements.[1190] Baker and Griffith suggest (1) an inappropriately small price discrimination at the time of underwriting, (2) lack of monitoring during the policy period, and (3) an absence of settlement oversight. These findings will be outlined first and subsequently analysed.

(1) Baker and Griffith acknowledge a highly advanced method of risk categorization of the underwritten D&O risk. The insurers are able to distinguish bad risks from good risks, possibly capable of eliminating adverse selection. However, the scholars fear that the difference of premium prices between good and bad risks is too small. They wonder whether good firms subsidize bad firms. Furthermore, they are doubtful whether a

1185 Grundfest 28-03-2013; Berger et al. 1992, pp. 264, 269–270.

1186 Grundfest 28-03-2013; Baluch et al. believe that the risk is not un-insurable. See: Baluch et al. 2011, p. 130.

1187 Grundfest 28-03-2013; Doherty and Smetters 2005, pp. 375–378.

1188 Grundfest 28-03-2013; Baluch et al. 2011, pp. 130–132; Harrington and Danzon 2000, p. 291. However, the long tail could also work to the advantage to the insurer. Because the claims would not arise all at once (due to the long tail), the insurer can gradually respond to unexpected claims when they arise. See: Harrington and Danzon 2000, p. 292.

1189 Baker and Griffith 2009, p. 831.

1190 Holderness 1990, pp. 115–116, 118–123.

change in the premium can influence the behaviour of the insured. They argue that the publication of D&O insurance data would enable a signal for the capital market participants. The market participant's response to the signal might properly influence the corporation.[1191]

(2) Once insured, the communication between insured and insurer ceases until a claim is filed, the policy is terminated, or re-negotiated. The insurer has been willing to give more guidance to the corporation, in order to mitigate the insured D&O risk. For instance, in the 1990s, an insurer published a loss prevention guide to communicate their observations of the risk to the insured corporation and offer best practices. However, the guide was a genuine failure. Among other reasons, the insurer was not able to grant complying corporations a discount. In other words, the guide was not economically feasible.[1192]

(3) When a claim is filed, the insurer takes an active role to settle. Although insurers negotiate on the settlement amount, they seem quite passive regarding the choice of the defendant's lawyers and corresponding costs. Insurers simply re-imburse the defendant corporation for all defence costs *ex post*.[1193]

Furthermore, Baker and Griffith fear that the unregulated settlement practice has the potential of not contributing to the intended deterrence effect of the securities law liability rule. Instead, the players involved seem to weigh different aspects than the pure facts of the case, such as "sex-appeal",[1194] to arrive at a settlement.[1195]

Some general remarks on these studies need to be raised.

First, the studies neither provide empirical evidence, nor discuss managerial liability of private corporations, nor discuss managerial tort liability or bankruptcy liability. The authors limit their discussion to securities class actions against public corporations in the USA. The reason for doing so is clear: the vast majority of claims are based on this rule. However, the UK, the Netherlands, and Germany do not have a comparable liability rule.[1196] Furthermore, in the USA, legal limitations on indemnification are virtually absent and the shareholder's ability to sue on the basis of securities law is far-reaching.[1197]

Secondly, their finding focuses on the deterrence of the manager, but seems to ignore the mediating role of insurers between claimants and the defendant corporation, outlined in subsection 5.6.2.

Thirdly, an internal liability claim brought by shareholders is not the only tool to incentivize proper managerial behaviour. Indeed, it has been suggested that other

1191 Baker and Griffith 2007, 'Predicting Corporate Governance Risk', pp. 533–537.

1192 Baker and Griffith 2007, 'The Missing Monitor', pp. 1808–1813.

1193 Baker and Griffith 2007, 'The Missing Monitor', pp. 1813–1817. Also compare to: Harrington and Danzon 2000, p. 286.

1194 Subsection 8.7.2.

1195 Baker and Griffith 2009, pp. 820–827.

1196 Compare to subsection 6.3.2.

1197 Compare to subsection 6.5.1; section 6.7.

corporate governance measures, such as appointment and dismissal are much more effective than liability.[1198]

Still, the in-depth analysis and great insight of the actual D&O market make this study highly valuable. Bearing these topics in mind, the next sections will sketch the current status of D&O insurance.

9.5. The effect of D&O insurance on managerial risk taking

Sections 8.6 through to 8.8 showed how far the manager and the corporation seek to partially insure the D&O risk and how far D&O insurers are able to offer partial insurance. The aim of this section is to discuss the research question, of how D&O insurance affects managerial risk taking. It will answer this research question by analysing whether D&O insurance affects the risk taking of the manager and in turn whether the D&O insurer contributes to efficient managerial risk taking.

This section will be structured as follows. Subsection 9.5.1 will set D&O insurance in the context of managerial liability and other corporate governance and creditor protection mechanisms. Subsection 9.5.2 will analyse the tools of the insurer to insure the liability risk. Subsection 9.5.3 will discuss to what extent D&O insurance affects managerial risk taking. Subsection 9.5.4 will extrapolate these findings and consider what effect D&O insurance seems to have on society.

9.5.1. *D&O insurance in context*

Managerial liability and D&O insurance needs to be placed in the bigger picture of corporate governance and stakeholder protection.[1199] Managerial risk taking is affected by a whole range of external and internal factors. D&O insurance is only one of many pieces of a mosaic picture. The following will identify where D&O insurance comes into contact with managerial risk-taking. This discussion will provide an understanding of which parts of managerial risk taking could be affected by D&O insurance and which parts of managerial risk-taking are beyond the scope of D&O insurer's potential influence.

According to economic theory, managerial liability will deter the manager from taking excessive risks.[1200]

Next to internal liability, other mechanisms incentivize and deter the manager, to name but a few, business failure, the market for corporate control, direct managerial financial incentives, or reputation costs.[1201] These mechanisms have a greater effect on a manager's risk taking than internal liability.[1202]

1198 Compare to section 2.4 and Kraakman 2009, p. 78; Pacces 2011, p. 314–316.

1199 Compare to section 2.5.

1200 Compare to section 2.2.

1201 Paetzmann 2008, p. 192; Posner 1974, p. 178–181; Kraakman 2009, p. 35.

1202 Kraakman 2009, p. 78; Pacces 2011, p. 314–316; Fischel and Bradley 1985, p. 283.

Managerial external liability is an exception to the general rule of vicarious liability of the firm.[1203] Only when the firm has insufficient assets or cannot monitor the manager, additional managerial liability is desirable. The state sometimes prohibits removing the liability risk when the personal (absolute) liability of the manager is essential to induce sufficient solvency of the firm[1204] or an optimal level of care.[1205] In this regard, the Netherlands and Germany, and to a lesser extent the USA and the UK, enforce (absolute) public sanctions against the manager.[1206]

The manager is in principle compensated by the firm for any liability risk he bears.[1207] Where it cannot indemnify (because of legal restrictions or because it is insolvent), the corporation will purchase insurance for the manager or pay a salary premium.[1208] Although some D&O insurers also sell insurance to the manager personally, the D&O insurance is mostly sold to the corporation.[1209]

Because, except in Delaware law, indemnification is harshly regulated in the legal systems, the firm seems to have no choice but to compensate the manager for the liability risk in the form of an increased salary or, alternatively, to insure liability.[1210] It merits future research in how far the harsh regulations of indemnification are economically justified.

Within this described scope, D&O insurers could in principle affect managerial risk taking. These findings suggest that D&O insurance insures internal liability and corresponding indemnification payments rather than the other D&O risks. Tort liability is often not insured because it is either absent (e.g. in the USA and UK) or absolute (e.g. public uninsurable sanctions). Furthermore, bankruptcy liability is not likely to be effectively insured because the observed restrictions pursuant to the national bankruptcy laws seem to hamper the effect of insurance when the corporation is insolvent (or has become judgement-proof).[1211]

9.5.2. *The tools used to insure the liability risk*

The process of insuring the liability risk is very similar to Holderness' expectations. First, the insurer applies an extensive underwriting process. To boost its observation abilities, the insurer makes use of self-selection by ways of extended policy offers and categorizes the individual risk beyond simple scrutiny of the firm's financials (including psychological

1203 Shavell 2004, p. 232.

1204 Polinsky and Shavell 1993, p. 240.

1205 Kraakman 1984, p. 859. A similar argument is made by Privileggi et al. 2001, pp. 181–185.

1206 Compare to subsection 6.5.1.

1207 Bishop 1964, p. 839; Bishop 1966, p. 96; Polinsky and Shavell 1993, p. 241; Fischel and Bradley 1985, p. 285.

1208 Compare to section 9.2. There are other compensation possibilities as well (such as managerial shareholding, bonus payments). Compare to: Kraakman 2009, p. 14–16; Posner 1974, p. 184, 185; Marks 1999, p. 707–708.

1209 Compare to subsection 8.2.1.

1210 Bishop 1964, p. 839; Bishop 1966, p. 96; Polinsky and Shavell 1993, p. 241; Fischel and Bradley 1985, p. 285.

1211 Compare to section 9.2.

evaluations of the manager).[1212] Secondly, the insurer tailors the policy to the risk type of the insured. The categorizations described are ongoing and adaptations usually take place once a year. No adaptation takes place during the yearly policy period.[1213] The insurer adapts the size of the coverage (referring to limits and deductibles) and alters the exclusions to the policy. As hypothesized, premium adaptations play an inferior role.[1214] Thirdly, the insurer is likely to make use of its information advantage in settlements.[1215] However, some argue that insurers fail to exercise sufficient oversight during settlement.[1216]

To overcome the obstacles of uncertainty, the insurer may turn to third parties, such as other insurers (towering and co-insurance) and re-insurers, in order to increase capacity and pass on some of the uncertain risk. However, some observations suggest that the D&O re-insurance market may face some problems in providing re-insurance to insurers in times of financial crises.

9.5.3. *The level of impact of insurers on managerial risk taking*

Having established that the insurer's tools are more or less effective in coping with the liability risk, the following question is to what extent the insurer's activity influences managerial risk taking. To this effect, this thesis has reviewed empirical studies of the Canadian D&O insurance market.[1217]

The empirical evidence on Canadian D&O insurance can be summarized in four points. First, some authors do not observe any clear relationship between the D&O insurance and efficient risk taking of the manager.[1218] In this regard the general comment could be made that many observations on clusters or tendencies that researchers seek to find are actually random.[1219]

Secondly, there are correlations that suggest IPO over-evaluations and empire building of the manager, especially when the limits are above average.[1220]

Thirdly, there are also observations that associate D&O insurance with (i) better investment decisions, provided that the corporation operates under high competitive pressure[1221] and (ii) no change on the costs of debt capital, provided that the corporation purchases an average insurance coverage.[1222]

Fourthly, the correlations of D&O insurance data with a vast amount of proxies illustrate the power of D&O insurance to signal a great variety of factors.

1212 Compare to Section 8.9.
1213 Baker and Griffith 2007, 'The Missing Monitor', pp. 1808–1813.
1214 Baker and Griffith 2007, 'Predicting Corporate Governance Risk', pp. 533–537.
1215 Compare to Section 8.9.
1216 Baker and Griffith 2007, 'The Missing Monitor', pp. 1813–1817; Baker and Griffith 2009, pp. 820–827.
1217 It must be reiterated that the studies may not reflect the status of the US-American, British, Dutch or German D&O insurance market, as most of the empirical studies looked at the Canadian market.
1218 Chen and Li 2008, pp. 1–5.
1219 Feller 1967, p. 161.
1220 Chalmers et al. 2002, pp. 629–632. Also compare this finding to: Fier et al. 2012, pp.1–5.
1221 Lin et al. 2013, p. 55.
1222 Lin et al. 2013, pp. 43–44, 58.

The empirical studies suggest that the insurer's practice has an impact on managerial risk taking.

9.5.4. *The effect of D&O insurance on society*

The remaining question is whether this impact on managerial risk taking is indeed socially desirable. Baker and Griffith paint a fairly pessimistic picture with respect to the contribution of D&O insurance to managerial risk taking in the USA. They conclude that the D&O insurance market covering securities class actions for public corporations in the USA does not deter bad corporate conduct.[1223] The empirical evidence on the Canadian D&O insurance as outlined in detail in sections 7.9 and 7.10 approved but also disproved such a finding. In this regard, the question of desirability has to take into account (i) the potential signalling effect of published corporate D&O insurance information, (ii) the observed correlations, and (iii) the manner in which the insurer handles settlements.

First, the empirical studies show that D&O insurance provides useful signals to the market. This finding supports the proposal of Baker and Griffith to publish D&O insurance information.

D&O insurance has a role that has not been entirely appreciated by market participants, such as equity investors.[1224] As argued in the previous section, D&O insurance may contribute to efficient managerial risk taking. Some suggest that D&O insurance provides a similar signal to the public as external auditing.[1225] In this regard, the D&O insurer could assume the role of a gatekeeper.[1226]

Viewing D&O insurers as gatekeepers strengthens the argument for publishing the D&O insurance data. Such data may efficiently signal managerial behaviour, business risk, and corporate governance quality. It grants capital market participants and other parties a more detailed picture of the corporation.[1227] It also deters the insurer from having the adverse incentive to monitor less. The argument goes as follows. When it can be assumed that the insurer settles anyway, the insurer might be induced to not ask questions and settle quickly. After all, the answers to these questions might lead to more damage, which the insurer would have to cover.[1228]

1223 Baker and Griffith 2009, p. 831.

1224 Compare to section 7.9; Boubakri and Ghalleb 2008, pp. 29–30.

1225 Paetzmann 2008, pp. 192–194.

1226 Ben-Shahar and Logue 2012, p. 245, who compare gatekeeping to the role of insurers to monitor risk taking. Also compare to Baker and Griffith 2010, p. 216.

1227 Cf. Ben-Shahar and Logue 2012, p. 246; Ronen 2002, pp. 57–58. Ronen 2002 introduces a system in which firms are held strictly liable for misrepresentation of financial statements and have to insure for this liability. Such insurance would be called financial statement insurance. When the information of that insurance is public, investors can interpret the insurance coverage as a signal that enables more informative investment decisions.

1228 This argument is based on an argument on vicarious liability by Marks 1999, p. 696; Kraakman 2008, in: Faure 2009, pp. 137–138.

The arguments in favour of publication have been summarized well by Baker and Griffith and have already been outlined above. Adding to their comments, the least intrusive measure to require publication may be to ask corporations to publish the D&O insurance data with their corporate governance reports. Similar to other aspects of the national corporate governance codes, the corporation either has to comply with the publication or explain the absence of publication.[1229]

There are also arguments against over-detailed publication. As subsection 4.4.8 outlined, experience rating and risk categorization are only possible when the revealed information remains confidential with the insurer. If the insured came to know of that information and the insurance market is competitive, the insured would simply switch to an insurer that had not accrued the relevant information yet. In other words, under a competitive environment, some private information of the insurer should be protected.[1230] Thus when requiring a too extensive publication of the coverage, the insurer may be unable to properly rate on experience, settle, or enable self-selection.[1231] As shown in subsection 4.4.8, without the ability to apply these tools, the insurance market could be exposed to the problems of adverse selection.

Secondly, insuring the manager on first sight serves the interests of creditors rather than those of shareholders provided that the coverage which is bought does not surpass the average of bought D&O insurance coverage.[1232] Yet, D&O insurance may also enhance the value of investment decisions provided that the corporation operates under high competitive pressure.[1233] There are also correlations that suggest a relationship between IPO over-evaluation[1234] and empire building of the manager,[1235] especially when the limits are above average.

The incentivization of the manager to act more on behalf of creditors (voluntary and involuntary) to the (short-term) detriment of shareholders might be advantageous to society.[1236] Under the conditions just outlined, D&O insurance may yet be another (and possibly desired) mechanism to weaken the detrimental effects that firms have on (voluntary and involuntary) creditors.[1237]

Thirdly, Baker and Griffith argued that the insurer, claimant and insured (the manager and corporation) do not take into account the intended deterrence effect of the liability rule. Instead, the players involved seem to weigh different aspects than the pure facts of

1229 e.g. MacNeil and Li 2006, pp. 486–487; Arcot et al. 2010, pp. 193–194.
1230 Nilssen 1990, pp. 641–645; Dionne et al. 2000, pp. 216–217, 235–236.
1231 Compare to subsection 4.4.8.
1232 Lin et al. 2013, pp. 43–44, 58. Also see on increased costs of equity: Chen et al. 2012, p. 3.
1233 Lin et al. 2013, p. 55.
1234 Chalmers et al. 2002, pp. 629–632. Also compare this finding to: Fier et al. 2012, pp. 1–5.
1235 Lin et al. 2011, pp. 522–523.
1236 When the alignment of interests between managers and shareholders is under-developed (for example in large corporations), the manager is less likely to harm creditors. See: Kraakman et al. 2009, p. 135; Posner 2007, pp. 440–443.
1237 Compare to sections 2.2 and 2.3.

the case, such as "sex-appeal",[1238] to arrive at a settlement.[1239] In this regard, general liability insurance theory has to be kept in mind that tells us that the insurer settles claims that are difficult to audit and fully compensates claims that would be simple to audit.[1240] The insurer may take into account more practical issues of auditing cost than simply considering whether the due standard of care, as required by the law, is met.

Some argue that insurers are indeed much better regulators of socially efficient risk taking than the state.[1241] However, scholars might expect too much from insurers. After all, insurers only use proxies that imperfectly, and sometimes even adversely, reflect the actual insured risk. The better these proxies reflect the insured risk, the more insurance contributes to the efficient risk-taking of the manager.

Arguing from another angle, a court could function as an impartial agency.[1242] A court also seems to be a better forum to publicly discuss how society appreciates the managerial action in question.[1243] Indeed, one should find a balance between the beneficial effects of a settlement and those of a court trial.[1244] On a similar note, discussing independent directors, instead of D&O insurers, about their role in settlements, Kraakman et al. argue "*on one hand, screening by independent directors is likely to be cheaper and better informed as to the facts...; on the other hand, screening by courts is likely to be better informed about the law and less prone to structural bias...*"[1245]

Without more evidence, the slightly positive effect of D&O insurance on creditors to the cost of shareholders and the insurer diverging from the legally established due level of care when settling (the insurer settles on the basis of other facts) do not make the current market necessarily inefficient. In the end, the nature of liability is precisely to enable the parties to agree among each other how to allocate the risks.[1246]

9.6. The way ahead

The outcomes of the previous section point to three possibilities for future research. These three aspects entail (i) how D&O (re)insurance can further penetrate the market, (ii) how insurance for the indemnification risk affects the firm, and (iii) to what extent the observed effect of D&O insurance on the manager is socially desirable. This section will turn to these three issues.

1238 Subsection 8.7.2.

1239 Baker and Griffith 2009, pp. 820–827.

1240 Compare to subsection 4.5.6. For more information: Townsend 1979, p. 266; Bond and Crocker 1997, p. 240.

1241 Ben-Shahar and Logue 2012, pp. 247–248. The managerial liability system may also be exposed to high administration costs, where the victim starts a liability action too soon or not soon enough. A well-functioning insurance system and the insurer's ability to settle may mitigate these costs. See: Shavell 2004, pp. 286–287; Cooter and Ulen 2012, pp. 242–243; Harrington and Danzon 2000, p. 285.

1242 Bishop 1964, p. 843.

1243 Kuykendall 1998, p. 574.

1244 Bishop 1964, p. 843; Oesterle 1983, p. 581; Kraakman et al. 1994, p. 1769; Kuykendall 1998, p. 574.

1245 Kraakman et al. 1994, p. 1769.

1246 Calabresi and Melamed 1972, p. 1127.

9.6.1. *Insurability of the D&O risk*

The observations of this chapter indicate that under some circumstances insurance and/or re-insurance may be unavailable. Smaller corporations usually lack D&O insurance and previously written D&O insurance appears to be difficult to re-insure in times of crises.

First, small corporations rarely have insurance. It may be socially undesirable that (i) insurance may be ineffective in bankruptcy and is thus not desired, or that (ii) an asset constrained (i.e. judgement-proof) corporation has no amounts left for D&O insurance.[1247]

The effect of bankruptcy or the fact the corporation is judgement-proof externalize costs, originally borne by the corporation, on the manager.[1248] In this regard, the corporation may exploit the effect of bankruptcy or the asset limitation to the detriment of the manager.[1249] In line with subsection 3.2.5, requiring smaller corporations to insure may deter corporations from externalizing costs on the manager. However, insurance is only effective, when insurers can monitor the judgement-proof insured corporation.[1250] Section 9.5 analysed how far the insurer is able to monitor the corporation. Furthermore, this thesis argues that D&O insurance may be a valuable alternative over other compensation alternatives to guarantee firm performance in times of financial distress.[1251] These considerations suggest the benefits of requiring smaller corporations to carry D&O insurance and ask for further research.

In accordance with the promotion of entrepreneurship in the EU by reforming bankruptcy law,[1252] it merits further research (i) in how far an adaptation of bankruptcy law could contribute to a better availability of D&O insurance for smaller corporations and (ii) whether the compensation mechanism (insurance, indemnification, salary) must be regulated to deter smaller corporations to externalize costs to the manager.

Secondly, the supply of re-insurance may be limited in times of crises. Possibly new products strengthen the supply of re-insurance. In this regard, new technology may be able to differentiate between the systemic and the firm-specific risk of the liability risk.[1253] Future research will show to what extent such differentiation may mitigate the re-insurers uncertainty about the underwritten risk and accompanying obstacles (such as moral hazard).

1247 Another alternative was that smaller corporations lack D&O insurance because the managers are compensated by stock option plans. It merits future research whether D&O insurance may be a valuable alternative to stock option compensation plans.

1248 Kraakman 1984, p. 870.

1249 Also compare the concept of asset dilution in subsection 2.3.3.

1250 Pillai and Tractenberg 1981, p. 106; Polinsky and Shavell 1993, p. 254. A similar argument has been provided by Kraakman 1984, p. 866.

1251 Such an argument ignores other forms of salary increase, such as a payment in the form of corporate shares. For example, see the already outlined correlation of managerial shareholding with growth opportunities. See: Core 1997, pp. 81, 82.

1252 European Commission 2011, pp. 5–6.

1253 See for example a patent that will enable the distinction between systemic D&O risk and firm-specific D&O risk. See: Grundfest 28-03-2013. Authors such as Alwis pointed to new D&O pricing models. See: Alwis et al. 2005, p. 1.

9.6.2. *Insurance of the risk to indemnify*

Subsection 5.5.1 hypothesized that when insurers are able to sufficiently monitor the judgement-proof firm, insurance for the risk to indemnify may be less intrusive than a prohibition of indemnification.[1254] With the exception of Delaware law,[1255] indemnification is harshly regulated in the observed countries. The empirical studies did not distinguish between insurance for the liability risk and indemnification risk and thus could not provide indications as to whether the hypotheses of section 5.5 hold. In any case, section 8.10 showed that the indemnification risk is covered provided that the indemnification is legally authorized. In this regard, a market seems to exist where corporations desire insurance for the indemnification risk and insurers are willing to underwrite the risk.

It merits future research to understand the actual role of D&O insurers to mediate between the claiming shareholder and the defendant corporation.[1256]

9.6.3. *Effect on managerial risk taking*

This subsection will return to three effects of D&O insurance, being (i) the signalling effect, (ii) the benefit of creditors, (iii) the insurer's settlement practice. The following will consider these three effects in turn.

First, a publication of the individual corporate D&O policy may signal valuable information to market participants. In this regard, this thesis, along with the work of other scholars in the field, proposes a limited publication of these policies.[1257] The various tools to encourage or even require publication (such as a comply-or-explain approach pursuant to corporate governance codes)[1258] will have to be compared and evaluated.

Secondly, this thesis suggested that D&O insurers may encourage the manager to take into account other interests than shareholder's interests.[1259] If these considerations hold true, future research could show how far the D&O insurance system should be subsidized or regulated for public policy reasons.[1260]

1254 For background information, see: Oesterle 1983, p. 570; Shavell 2004, pp. 276, 278.

1255 Moskowitz and Effros 1992, p. 915.

1256 Maybe the mediation practice contributes to a more efficient trading of securities in the USA, where the possibilities to indemnify and subsequently insure the risk attached to it are far-reaching. On the efficiency of the security trading in the USA, see Kraakman et al. 2009, p. 300–301.

1257 Baker and Griffith 2007, 'Predicting Corporate Governance Risk', pp. 533–537; Gupta and Prakash 2012, p. 22; Chalmers et al. 2002, p. 633; Boyer 2007, p. 104.

1258 e.g. MacNeil and Li 2006, pp. 486–487; Arcot et al. 2010, pp. 193–194.

1259 Subsection 9.5.4.

1260 Maybe a strategy to purchase D&O insurance could reflect a prisoner's dilemma. Insurance may protect the manager from myopic and short-term oriented shareholder behaviour, where the shareholders strive for quick money. In this regard, insurance could encourage managers to take into account the long-term continuity of the firm (and indeed, managers are expected to do precisely that). For more information, on the prisoner's dilemma with respect to the relationship between shareholder and manager: Marks 1999, pp. 699–703.

Thirdly, this chapter analysed the insurer's settlement practice. It was argued that the insurer takes into account more practical issues of auditing cost than simply considering whether the due standard of care as required by the law is met. Future research could show to what extent the interplay between full compensation, settlement and auditing effectively controls the manager and how far the insurer's settlement practice meets public policy considerations or is socially desirable from an economic perspective.

9.7. Conclusion

This chapter has analysed (i) three possible divergences from the hypotheses outlined in Chapter 5, (ii) discussed the effect of D&O insurance on the manager and (iii) sketched possibilities for future research.

The practice seems to differ from the theory of Chapter 5 in three aspects. First, smaller corporations are often not insured. Still, managers of these corporations claim to desire D&O insurance. The reason may be that (i) either the manager is otherwise compensated, (ii) insurance is desired but not available, or (iii) the manager is not compensated at all for the risk. However, if a smaller corporation bears higher business risks than bigger ones, D&O insurance should be preferred over other compensation mechanisms (such as indemnification and salary premiums). In this regard, alternative (i) is ineffective. As to alternative (ii) and (iii), national bankruptcy laws seem to restrict the effect of insurance when the corporation is insolvent (or has become judgement-proof). A restriction may be desirable in accordance to subsection 3.2.5, when smaller corporations are (or become) rather judgement-proof than bigger corporations. However, also in line with subsection 3.2.5, requiring insurance may be more effective than restricting insurance, when insurers can monitor the judgement-proof insured firm.

Secondly, D&O re-insurance may sometimes be difficult to provide. Some believe that re-insurers charge excessive premiums for re-insurance, which may lead to uninsurability. Such a situation could be explained by uncertainty about the size of the liability risk and/or a general fear with respect to moral hazard.

Thirdly, Baker and Griffith argue that D&O insurance for securities class actions in the USA does not deter bad managerial conduct in public corporations. They argue that the insurer (1) discriminates insufficiently in pricing, (2) is unable to mitigate the D&O risk, and (3) does not take into account how much the corporation spends on legal expenses and whether the legally required due standard of care has been met by managers.

To assess the validity of these arguments, D&O insurance needs to be set in context with all the corporate governance and creditor protection tools. Internal liability is one of the tools of corporate governance (and probably a less important one) that seeks to limit agency costs. Managerial external liability is an exception to the general rule of vicarious liability of the firm and even if adopted, external liability is sometimes uninsurable (or more generally the underlying risk is absolute and cannot be shifted). The manager is in principle compensated by the firm for any liability risk he bears. Where the corporation cannot indemnify him (because of legal restrictions or because it is insolvent), the corporation will purchase insurance for the manager.

As bankruptcy law hampers the insurance of bankruptcy liability and external liability often cannot be insured because it is an absolute liability rule, D&O insurance primarily appears to cover internal liability and corresponding indemnification.

In accordance with the Holderness hypotheses, the insurer applies an extensive underwriting process and tailors the policy to the risk type of the insured. When settling, the insurer probably considers other issues than whether the due standard of care as established by the law is met. Yet, the supply side may face the problem that insurance is unavailable for smaller corporations and/or is difficult to re-insure, as already discussed above.

The empirical studies further suggest that the insurer's practice has an impact on managerial risk taking. First, the empirical studies show that D&O insurance provides useful signals to the market. In this regard, some basic information on D&O insurance should be published. When the insurance market is competitive, a required publication of insurance information has to respect the necessary and desired information advantage of the insurer. Without retaining some private information on the insured, the insurer that is under competitive pressure is unable to sufficiently categorize the risk that the insured faces. In that case the insurance prices would dramatically increase and may even become uninsurable.

Secondly, insuring the manager on first sight benefits the creditors rather than the shareholders subject to the condition that the D&O coverage which is bought reflects the average. D&O insurance may also enhance the value of investment decisions provided that the corporation operates under high competitive pressure. Under the conditions just outlined, D&O insurance may yet be another (and possibly desired) mechanism to weaken the detrimental effects of firms on (voluntary and involuntary) creditors, which were outlined in Chapter 2.

Thirdly, as outlined above the insurer may weigh different aspects than the pure facts of the case, such as "sex-appeal", to arrive at a settlement, maybe also bearing in mind auditing costs. "Sex-appeal" relates to actions that add an emotional and personal side to the infringement of the relevant liability rule (e.g. fraud, media coverage or whistle-blowers). Some argue that insurers are indeed much better regulators of socially efficient risk taking than the state. However, a court could represent an impartial forum where all involved parties can openly exchange their views on whether the managerial act in question was desirable.

These outcomes point to three aspects where further research could enhance the positive effects of D&O insurance. First, it merits further research (i) on the extent to which the effect of bankruptcy law on D&O insurance is socially desirable, (ii) whether D&O insurance should be made compulsory for judgement-proof corporations, and (iii) whether new technology effectively encourages re-insurance.

Secondly, it was argued in subsection 5.6.2 that insurance for the indemnification risk may be socially desirable. A market of insurance for the indemnification risk seems to exist and future research could analyse the effects of that insurance on the firm.

Thirdly, returning to the effect of D&O insurance on managerial risk taking, future research could clarify (i) which specific tool to use to stimulate publication, (ii) whether D&O insurance should be subsidized to encourage managers to take into account stakeholder interests, and (iii) to what extent the insurer's settlement practice is socially desirable.

Chapter 10

CONCLUSION

The nature of risk taking in business appears to be like a two-edged sword. Excessive risk taking by managers may harm society. Still, without any risk takers innovation could be hampered. One may even argue that the best managers are those who take (efficient) risks.

Law and economics scholars argue that liability insurance is in the position to influence risk taking. In this regard, insurance for a manager's liability (also called Directors' & Officers' insurance or D&O insurance) may either elegantly contribute to efficient risk taking or instead may adversely encourage opportunistic behaviour. In this context, this thesis sought to answer the following research question: *How does D&O insurance affect managerial risk taking?*

This thesis answered this question by showing that the D&O insurer (i) signals managerial risk taking behaviour to the market, (ii) potentially influences the manager to the benefit of creditors and (iii) settles on the basis of other standards than those applied in court trials.

Moreover, the thesis pointed to issues of potential availability to provide D&O (re) insurance. This thesis also formulated hypotheses as to what extent corporate insurance for the risk to having to indemnify a liable manager influences the corporation and the manager.

As to the methodology, this thesis developed hypotheses on the D&O insurance market from a law and economics perspective. It consequently applied these hypotheses to the actual D&O insurance market in the USA, the UK, the Netherlands and Germany. The effect of D&O insurance was illustrated by a review of existing empirical studies.

This conclusion is structured as follows. Sections 10.1 and 10.2 summarize the observations about the demand for and supply of D&O insurance respectively. Section 10.3 summarizes the answer to the research question. Sections 10.4 and 10.5 indicate limitations of this thesis and point to future research possibilities.

10.1. Analysis of D&O demand

Classic theory of insurance explains the demand for insurance by analysing the risk attitude of humans. A person that bears a risk could develop an aversion to that risk. In order to be freed from that burden, he desires insurance.

This section outlines the risk that is associated with managerial liability in subsection 10.1.1. Subsection 10.1.2 analyses to what extent a manager would develop an aversion against the liability risk. Subsection 10.1.3 outlines how the liability risk can be allocated so that the risk averse manager does not have to bear the risk. Next to insurance, the risk could be allocated to the corporation of the manager. In the latter case, the corporation would bear the liability risk on behalf of the manager. Subsection 10.1.4 discusses, to what extent the corporation desires insurance for bearing that risk. It outlines other reasons next to risk aversion that could explain the corporate demand for D&O insurance.

10.1.1. The liability risk

The manager bears the risk to be held personally liable, called liability risk. Managerial liability refers to the right of a shareholder or creditor to be compensated by the manager for harm that the manager caused on behalf of his corporation. In principle, liability rules incentivize the injurer to reduce harm by taking care. Liability allocates (some of) the costs of damage to the manager. The manager takes precautionary measures (also called care). This thesis outlined three liability rules, tort liability, bankruptcy liability and internal liability.

Tort liability is generally refused when the manager's acts are to be attributed to his firm. For the scope of this thesis the most important reason for such refusal is that the manager does not have enough assets to entirely pay the expected loss. Damage collection would cause his insolvency. In this regard, his incentive to reduce risk by taking care is limited to the expected loss of his personal assets. Any remaining expected damage is ignored by the manager (the judgement-proof problem). As a solution to the judgement-proof problem, scholars suggested vicarious liability. Under vicarious liability another party – generally the manager's firm – is held liable for the misconduct of the manager – its agent. Usually the firm can induce the agent to behave. However, when the firm has problems in monitoring the manager, managerial liability of the manager as additional liability to vicarious liability was proposed (tort liability). In accordance to this theory, vicarious liability could be observed in all four countries and tort liability as an additional liability rule was restricted to the Dutch and German legal system.

Bankruptcy liability will compensate firm creditors in cases in which they are unable to recover the entire damage because the firm does not have enough assets to entirely fulfil the expected losses. In other words, bankruptcy liability as additional action to firm liability, solves the problem that the corporation is (also) judgement-proof or insolvent. In accordance with this theory, the manager can be held liable when the corporation is (in the vicinity of being) insolvent in all observed countries.

Internal liability is one (and probably less important) tool of corporate governance. Internal liability should deter the manager from "*shirking*" or "*stealing*" from his shareholders. The duty of care should ensure managerial competence ("*shirking*") and the duty of loyalty should prevent conflicts of interests ("*stealing*"). It is argued that when the prospect of filing does not relate to misconduct but to the claimant's expected benefit and the manager does not bear the costs of liability (he is compensated for it), the manager does not link the claim to his misconduct. The additional condition in the UK and Germany pursuant to which a claimant has to show that it is in the interest of the corporation to file a claim, may establish the necessary link between misconduct and the prospect of filing. In these countries, internal liability could again signal a level of risk taking that is in the interest of the corporation. A claim under US securities law is not subject to similar conditions. The Dutch corporate governance tool to file an internal liability claim is very restricted in the first place.

Scholars suggest the imposition of fines (or possibly imprisonment) when the incentive to take due care should be enhanced. This thesis observed that the Netherlands presumes managerial liability when wage taxes and revenue taxes are not paid or when the financial statements were not disclosed on time. Germany holds the manager criminally liable, possibly leading to imprisonment, for a failure to publish corporate documents, acting in bad faith or over-leveraging the corporation. The UK adopts criminal liability against fraudulent/wrongful trading and the USA only criminally punishes managers for serious cases of fraud or self-dealing to deter large one-shot frauds (cf. Enron).

10.1.2. Managerial risk aversion

Risk aversion describes an attitude of dislike of risk. Generally, human beings are risk averse to a varying degree. The degree of risk aversion depends on the size of the expected loss and the size of the private assets. Risk aversion can only exist when a person bears a risk. Similarly, the manager cannot develop a risk aversion, when he does not bear a risk to be held liable.

Simplified, there are two methods to hold a manager liable. Under the negligence rule, the manager is only liable when he does not take sufficient care. Thus, under negligence liability, the manager does not bear a liability risk as long as he takes due care. Under strict liability, the manager is always held liable when damage occurs. Thus, the manager bears the entire risk for the occurrence of loss.

So when the manager takes due care, he can only be exposed to risk aversion under strict liability. In this regard, a negligence rule is preferable when the manager is highly risk averse.

However, there is a chance that the due level of care is incorrectly established by the court (error) or the manager is unable to take the required level of due care (inability). If that is the case, one speaks of an uncertain level of care. The uncertainty whether to be held liable creates a risk. A manager that bears the risk of uncertainty could develop an aversion to that risk.

It has been suggested that the liability rules in the observed countries are uncertain. The scope of the precise level of care is difficult to deduce from the national rules also having to take into account changes established by courts (e.g. Germany and the Netherlands with respect to external liability) and by the state (e.g. Dutch proposals to impose criminal sanctions).

Further, the national rules also differ to a high degree. For instance, the duty of loyalty is strict in the UK and Delaware but lenient in Germany and the Netherlands. The standard of care with respect to bankruptcy liability is lenient in Delaware and the UK, strict in Germany (aggravated by criminal sanctions), and moderate in the Netherlands. A manager of a multinational concern is probably ambiguous about the extent of these differences.

When the rules are uncertain, the manager could develop an aversion to the risk of uncertainty. In this regard, managerial liability may undesirably deter the manager from taking beneficial but risky decisions. The manager may even be chilled to take any risks. Especially, dealings in the USA could chill the manager, as the US-legal system is associated with an increased liability risk arising from securities class actions. In line with this thought, empirical studies observed that dealings in the USA correlate positively with the D&O purchase decision.

10.1.3. Compensation of the manager

When the manager is risk averse, the risk of uncertain liability rules should be allocated to a more efficient risk bearer.

Next to insurance, the risk could be allocated to the corporation of the manager. A firm when risk neutral, has a comparative advantage to bear risk over a risk averse manager. Firms are risk neutral when the shareholders are able to diversify their investment.

When the corporation and the manager negotiate on the terms of employment, a risk-averse manager is likely to seek compensation for the uncertainty attached to the liability rules. This compensation takes the form of a combination of an increased salary, and indemnification or insurance. In this regard, D&O insurance is part of the compensation package. In line with this hypothesis, D&O insurance is sold to the corporation rather than directly to the manager in most cases.

The subsequent question is to what extent the compensation measures relate to each other.

Because of the differences in risk attitude, it is cheaper for a firm to indemnify the manager than to raise his salary. Indemnification can encompass tort liability, bankruptcy liability and internal liability.

Scholars consider that indemnification with respect to tort liability should be allowed provided that the sum of managerial liability and firm liability equal the harm. Indeed, indemnification with respect to tort liability is (probably) authorized in Germany and the Netherlands. Indemnification in Delaware and the UK is not required, because tort liability without a distress angle to it appears to be absent.

Indemnification of bankruptcy liability should be prohibited, when the expected loss that would have been borne by the manager is externalized through indemnification to a judgement-proof firm. Being judgement-proof, the firm's incentives to take care are limited to the expected loss of its assets. Any remaining damage is ignored by the firm. In accordance with this view, the national bankruptcy laws of the observed countries seem to prevent the corporation from indemnifying his manager, which effectively means that indemnification is prohibited when the corporation is insolvent (or judgement-proof).

Indemnification of internal liability may endanger the original goal of promoting firm performance and corporate value. Accordingly, it has been observed that indemnification is harshly regulated. *Ex ante* indemnification is only authorized regarding the German GmbH and for corporations incorporated under Delaware law. In the Netherlands and the UK, an *ex ante* indemnification is probably forbidden. Only *ex post* indemnification is authorized but such indemnification is usually subject to the condition that the shareholders must also approve the corporate financial statements of the previous year.

This thesis argued that insurance for the risk to indemnify may be less intrusive than regulation of indemnification. Insurance should be effective, as long as the insurer is able to monitor the risk-taking of the manager and the firm. Yet, as outlined above, the UK, the Netherlands and Germany with respect to the AG rather opt for the more intrusive measure of harsh regulations.

10.1.4. Corporate demand for D&O insurance

Next to indemnification, the firm can compensate the manager in the form of insurance or a salary increase. In general, a risk neutral corporation would not desire insurance. It can bear the risk itself. It is argued that the corporation nevertheless desires D&O insurance because of three reasons.

First, insurance is sought when indemnification proves to be ineffective. Indemnification could be ineffective because it is prohibited or because the assets of the firm are insufficient to fully indemnify the manager. Instead of insurance, the firm could also compensate the manager in the form of a salary increase in these cases. However, the empirical studies show that salary compensation and D&O insurance are not substitutes for each other. Managerial cash compensation positively correlates with limits.

It has been argued that D&O insurance is a better alternative to a salary increase when the firm is in financial distress. In accordance with this argument, empirical studies show that the demand for D&O insurance increases with factors associated with business risk such as divesting, financial distress, and leverage.

Secondly, insurance for the liability risk may also be desired when the insurer is in a better position to monitor the manager than the corporation or corporate well-diversified shareholders. When the insurer can decrease corporate specific costs associated with liability, such as litigation costs, insurance should be desired. Although many scholars highlight this monitoring-hypothesis, the empirical findings were not conclusive with respect to this theory.

Thirdly, the corporation may desire insurance for the risk of having to indemnify the liable manager (indemnification risk), when the insurer is in a better position to mediate between the claiming shareholder and the defendant corporation. The empirical studies indeed show that the corporate litigation history and litigation risk increase the demand for D&O insurance.

10.2. Analysis of D&O supply

In exchange for assuming the liability risk and the indemnification risk (collectively called the D&O risk), the insurer asks the corporation to pay an actuarially fair premium. The actuarially fair premium equals the multiplication of the probability times the magnitude of the D&O risk. When the insurer is uncertain about the D&O risk, the insurer compensates for the uncertainty by asking for a safety loading on top of the actuarially fair premium. This thesis identified that smaller corporations carry less D&O insurance and that re-insurance may be difficult to provide. These two problems are discussed in subsection 10.2.1 and 10.2.2 respectively.

More generally, supply of insurance is explained by the law of large numbers. The law of large numbers enables a spreading of risks. Spreading only functions properly when there is a large number of risks that are similar but independent of each other. When the risks are different from each other, the insurer needs to adapt its policy to each individual risk. Failure to classify the different risks may lead to adverse selection as outlined in subsection 10.2.3.

Once insured, insurance may change the insured manager's incentive to take care. Because the corporation does not have to pay for damages any-more in the form of increased managerial compensation (indemnification costs and salary costs), the corporation may monitor the manager less carefully and encourage more dangerous activity of the manager. To maintain the original level of care and activity, the insurer will have to do the monitoring itself. This issue is discussed in section 10.3.

10.2.1. D&O insurance unavailable for smaller corporations

It has been observed that smaller corporations carry less D&O insurance, though their managers claim to desire D&O insurance. This thesis suggested two reasons for this divergence, being insurer ambiguity and/or a judgement-proof problem.

First, the insurer may be ambiguous to what extent the risk of bankruptcy affects the D&O risk. When probability and/or magnitude is uncertain, the insurer asks for a safety loading. The premium may be so high that the risk bearing individual is unwilling to pay for it.

One possibility to overcome uncertainty is a subdivision of the risk that mitigates the exposure to the uncertainty. Indeed, the D&O insurance policy has an upper limit below which the insurer compensates for the damage. Above that limit the underwritten corporation is not insured. Less often D&O insurance has a deductible as well.

Secondly, when the expected loss arising from managerial liability surpasses the assets of a corporation, the uncovered part of the loss could be ignored by the corporation. The incentives of the corporation to buy insurance for the entire damage are dulled. It is cheaper for the corporation to externalize some of the risk than to insure for it. In this regard, scholars argue that the corporation may exploit the effect of managerial liability (and deny compensation to the manager) in order to externalize costs on the manager.

This argument may explain why smaller corporations carry less D&O insurance, though their managers claim to desire it.

To guarantee that the entire risk is covered and to incentivize the corporation to take care, the lawmaker may choose to either make insurance compulsory or prohibit insurance. Prohibition of insurance becomes socially desirable when the insurer is unable to monitor the judgement-proof corporation. Indeed, this thesis observed that national bankruptcy laws seem to restrict the effect of insurance when the corporation is insolvent (or has become judgement-proof). The nature of bankruptcy law rather tends to prohibit effective D&O insurance for smaller corporations.

Yet, empirical evidence suggests that, in times of financial instability, D&O insurance should be desired over other compensation measures to safeguard firm performance. Further, the monitoring of insurers is not entirely absent as will be outlined below. In this regard, prohibition may not be socially desirable. These findings raise the interesting questions as to what extent the effect of current bankruptcy law is socially desirable and whether D&O insurance should be made compulsory for smaller corporations.

10.2.2. Re-insurance for D&O insurance difficult to provide

The insurer may turn to third parties, such as other insurers (towering and co-insurance) or re-insurers, to increase capacity and pass on some of the uncertain risk.

However, D&O re-insurance may sometimes be difficult to provide. Some believe that re-insurers charge excessive premiums for re-insurance, which may lead to uninsurability. Excessive re-insurance premiums could be explained by uncertainty about the size of the re-insured risk and/or ambiguity of re-insurers with respect to their exposure to moral hazard. Possibly, new technology may be able to distinguish between the systemic part and the firm-specific part inherent to the liability risk. Such technology could mitigate the uncertainty and ambiguity of re-insurers.

10.2.3. Overcoming adverse selection

Adverse selection deals with the issue that good risks self-insure and bad risks pay a premium that is lower than it should be. To treat adverse selection, the insurer has several tools at his disposal. Either (i) the individual reveals his risk class himself when selecting his policy, (ii) the insurer is able to classify the risk on the basis of past experience, and/or (iii) the insurer is able to categorize the risk class according to correlating factors. Some may disapprove of risk categorization because of equality concerns (e.g. discrimination based on sex).

Empirical findings suggest that the corporation reveals its size of D&O risk when selecting the policy (self-selection). The insurer seems to categorize the insured corporation (risk categorization) by considering the corporate legal environment, the corporate size and the amount of 10%-shareholders. The corporate size increases the premium whereas the amount of 10%-shareholders decreases the premium. In contrast to arguments raised by scholars, managerial excess control and the number of outside directors do not have an effect on the premium.

10.3. Effect of D&O insurance on managerial risk taking

On first sight, the research question as to how D&O insurance affects managerial risk has already been covered with respect to the US D&O insurance market by Baker and Griffith. Baker and Griffith argue that D&O insurance for securities law claims for public corporations in the USA do not deter bad corporate conduct. They argue that (1) insurers discriminate insufficiently in pricing, (2) the insurer is unable to mitigate the D&O risk, and (3) when settling, the insurer does not take into account how much the corporation spends on legal expenses and whether the legally established due standard of care has been met.

Indeed, the insurer usually cannot control the manager by adapting the premium to his risk-taking because the premium is borne by the corporation. The manager would not be directly affected by an adaptation of the premium. Yet, subsection 10.3.1 analyses other tools than premium adaptations to control the manager.

Even if these other tools are unable to perfectly control the manager and mitigate D&O risk, subsection 10.3.2 demonstrates to what extent managerial performance is signalled by D&O insurance. Furthermore, it appears that such a signal is used by creditors as subsection 10.3.3 summarizes.

Subsection 10.3.4 turns to the issue whether the current settlement practice of D&O insurers is desirable.

10.3.1. Controlling the manager other than through premium adaptations

Holderness proposed additional measures when premium adaptations are ineffective. The insurer is able to monitor the manager through the use of an extensive underwriting process and an adaptation of the coverage during the period of insurance.

In this regard, the findings of Baker and Griffith and the empirical research suggest that the insurer takes into account a vast variety of corporate factors. To enhance the underwriting process, the insurer seems to make use of self-selection by way of extended policy offers and categorizes the individual risk beyond simple scrutiny of the firm financials (including psychological evaluations of the manager). Secondly, insurers in all observed countries tailor the policy to the risk type of the insured. The described categorizations are ongoing and adaptations usually take place once a year. The insurer adapts the size of the coverage (referring to limits and deductibles) and alters the exclusions to the policy (excluding intention and differentiating among corporations). As hypothesized, premium adaptations appear to play an inferior role.

10.3.2. Signalling the D&O risk instead of actively mitigating it

The correlations of D&O insurance data with a vast amount of proxies illustrate the power of D&O insurance as a signal.

Although a direct link to firm performance is difficult to draw, the value of investment decisions seems to rise with D&O coverage as long as the competitive pressure is high enough. Furthermore, creditors do not punish insured corporations with higher costs of debt capital, provided that the corporation purchases an average insurance coverage. There are also correlations that suggest a relationship between IPO over-evaluation and empire building of the manager, especially when the limits are above average.

However, investors in Canada seem to ignore the information that is contained in the D&O insurance data. The reason may be that the empirical evidence could not show that D&O insurance hampers or boosts firm performance.

One can conclude that D&O insurance provides useful signals to the market. Some basic information on D&O insurance should be published.

However, too extensive publication requirements may be disastrous to the D&O insurance market, when the D&O insurance market is competitive. When the entire information about D&O insurance is published, the corporation would always know when it is categorized as a bad risk class and could leave the insurer for another one. In that case, the insurer is unable to induce bad risks to pay higher premiums. Such a situation could lead to adverse selection. To avoid such a situation, the insurer must retain some private information on the insured corporation.

10.3.3. Creditor's appreciation of D&O insurance

It could be argued that corporate insurance can provide a signal about the firm's asset sufficiency and/or monitoring ability to the voluntary creditor. In accordance with this hypothesis, creditors, other than the equity investors, seem to use the D&O information as a signal. Higher than average limits correlate with higher spread.

In this regard, the signal would contribute to incentivizing the manager to act on behalf of creditors. This might be advantageous to society. D&O insurance may yet be another (and possibly desired) mechanism to reduce indirectly the harm that firms cause.

10.3.4. The desirability of the current settlement practices

It has been argued that a well-functioning system of settlements can administer sufficient claiming behaviour of the shareholder or creditor. However, the process of settling may be different to a court proceeding.

In line with this thought, Baker and Griffith argued that the insurer, claimant, manager and corporation do not take into account the intended deterrence effect of the liability rule. Instead, the involved players seem to evaluate different aspects than the pure facts of the case, such as the degree of bad publicity in the media, to arrive at a settlement.

To understand why the insurer evaluates other aspects, general liability insurance theory has to be kept in mind. It tells us that when audits are costly and the insured entity is likely to under-report, the insurer incentivizes proper reporting by entirely covering losses that are cheap to audit and by settling the losses that are costly to audit. In this regard, the insurer may evaluate the facts of the case by bearing in mind the attached auditing costs.

The question remains whether it is socially desirable that the involved players do not entirely take into account the merits of the case. In this regard, scholars disagree as to whether the insurer's settlement practice is more desirable than a court trial. On the one hand, the insurer may resolve the dispute at a lower price and may be better informed as to facts of the case at hand. On the other hand, a court is an impartial forum where all involved parties can openly exchange their views on whether the managerial act in question was desirable.

10.4. Limitations of this thesis

It must be kept in mind that the findings of the empirical studies, the polls, the statistics and the interviews of Baker and Griffith have to be used with caution. These observations are only comparable to a certain extent because their methodologies differ. The empirical research is based on the Canadian D&O insurance market. These findings probably do not perfectly correspond to the US-American, British, Dutch and German D&O insurance market.

Further, the legal framework of the four countries that were outlined is illustrative only, and cannot be substitute for consultation with national practitioners trained in the field of managerial liability and D&O insurance. In this context, some of the sources appear old and their applicability to the current D&O market remains questionable (i.e. the data on the UK D&O insurance market).

Furthermore, own field-research of qualitative or quantitative nature have not been conducted with respect to the four countries. Empirical studies or comprehensive interviews on the D&O insurance market in the USA, the UK, the Netherlands and Germany are yet to be published.

10.5. Future research

The above outlined the demand side and supply side of D&O insurance. It identified three possibilities for future research. These three aspects entail (i) how insurance for the indemnification risk affects the firm, (ii) how D&O (re)insurance can further penetrate the market, and (iii) to what extent the observed effect of D&O insurance on the manager is socially desirable.

First, insurance for the indemnification risk may be socially desirable. A market of insurance for the indemnification risk seems to exist and future research could analyse the societal effects of that insurance.

Secondly, it merits further research (i) to what extent the effect of bankruptcy law on D&O insurance is socially desirable, (ii) whether D&O insurance should be made compulsory for judgement-proof corporations, and (iii) whether new technology effectively encourages re-insurance.

Thirdly, returning to the effect of D&O insurance on managerial risk taking, future research could clarify (i) which specific tool to use to stimulate publication, (ii) whether D&O insurance should be subsidized to encourage managers to take into account stakeholder interests, and (iii) to what extent the insurer's settlement practice is socially desirable.

SUMMARY

Risk taking in business contributes towards innovation. Yet, excessive risk taking is associated with corporate failure. In other words, risk taking can affect society positively as well as negatively. The possibility to hold managers liable for alleged wrongful acts functions as a deterrence to excessive risk taking. Insurance of managerial liability (D&O insurance) may influence managerial risk taking. In this context, this thesis answers the research question of how D&O insurance affects managerial risk taking.

In order to answer this question, this thesis analyses the D&O insurance market in the USA, the UK, the Netherlands and Germany. Furthermore, the effect of D&O insurance is illustrated by empirical studies from the Canadian D&O insurance market.

There are three main effects of D&O insurance on managerial risk taking.

Firstly, D&O insurance signals managerial risk taking behaviour to the market. The value of investment decisions seems to rise with D&O coverage as long as competitive pressure is high enough. Furthermore, creditors do not punish insured corporations with higher costs of debt capital, provided that the corporation purchases an average insurance coverage. D&O insurance can also signal an IPO over-evaluation and empire building of the manager. In this regard, this thesis advocates that some basic, but not all, information on D&O insurance should be published in the USA, the UK, the Netherlands and Germany to publicly show this signal.

Secondly, D&O insurance potentially affects the manager to act in the benefit of third parties such as creditors, provided that the corporation purchases an average insurance coverage.

Thirdly, the D&O insurer seems to apply other standards than those applied in court trials, such as taking into account the degree of bad publicity in the media. In this context, the insurer may evaluate the facts of the case by bearing in mind the attached auditing costs. All in all, it remains controversial whether the insurer's settlement practice is more desirable than a court trial.

Furthermore, the thesis points to potential availability issues in the provision of D&O insurance. This thesis shows that the nature of national bankruptcy laws tend to prohibit effective D&O insurance for smaller corporations. Yet, empirical evidence suggests that, in times of financial instability, D&O insurance functions better than other compensation measures in safeguarding firm performance. This raises questions as to what extent the effect of current bankruptcy law is socially desirable and whether D&O insurance should be made compulsory for smaller corporations.

Finally, this thesis advocates that the corporation should indemnify its manager for managerial liability and subsequently insure the risk to indemnify. However, indemnification is harshly regulated in the UK, the Netherlands and to a lesser extent in Germany. Only corporations in Delaware, where indemnification is allowed, mostly insure the indemnification risk.

SAMENVATTING

Door het nemen van risico's levert de manager een bijdrage tot innovatie. Echter, het nemen van excessieve risico's kan leiden tot een faillissement. Het gedrag van managers kan een samenleving dus zowel positief als negatief beïnvloeden. Het concept van bestuurdersaansprakelijkheid geeft prikkels aan managers om zich met de nodige zorgvuldigheid te gedragen. Een verzekering voor bestuurdersaansprakelijkheid (D&O verzekering) zou de manager in beginsel kunnen beïnvloeden bij het nemen van risico's. Tegen deze achtergrond wordt in dit proefschrift de onderzoeksvraag beantwoord welke invloed de D&O verzekering op de manager heeft bij het nemen van risico's.

Dit proefschrift beschrijft de D&O verzekeringsmarkt van de Verenigde Staten, het Verenigd Koninkrijk, Nederland en Duitsland. Verder worden de effecten van D&O verzekeringen beschreven, zoals die uit eerder empirisch onderzoek blijken.

De D&O verzekering lijkt drie effecten te hebben op het nemen van risico's.

Ten eerste geeft de omvang van de D&O verzekering een indicatie omtrent het risicogedrag van de manager. De waarde van investeringsbeslissingen neemt toe met de verzekeringslimiet, onder de voorwaarde dat de betreffende onderneming in een sterke competitieve markt actief is. Verder blijven de kosten om vreemd vermogen aan te trekken constant, indien de vennootschap een verzekeringslimiet koopt die niet bovengemiddeld hoog is. De D&O verzekering kan ook een signaal zijn van te hoog gewaardeerde emissiebesluiten en "empire building". Dit proefschrift pleit dan ook voor een beperkte, maar niet volledige, publicatie van D&O informatie in de Verenigde Staten, het Verenigd Koninkrijk, Nederland en Duitsland, om dit signaal aan derden kenbaar te maken.

Ten tweede lijkt de D&O verzekering de manager zodanig te beïnvloeden, dat hij, onder de voorwaarde dat de verzekeringslimiet gemiddeld is, de belangen van derden, zoals crediteuren, eerder behartigt dan een onverzekerde manager.

Ten derde lijkt de verzekeraar andere feiten te beoordelen dan een rechter, onder andere door op de vraag te letten in hoeverre de betreffende zaak in de media is voorgekomen. Schrijvers verschillen van mening of het schikkingsgedrag van de verzekeraar maatschappelijk gezien eerder gewenst is dan een gerechtelijke procedure.

Voorts gaat dit proefschrift in op het feit dat managers van kleine vennootschappen vaak niet gedekt zijn. Hierbij lijkt het nationale faillissementsrecht de effectiviteit van de D&O verzekering te belemmeren. De empirische analyse wekt echter de suggestie dat een verzekeringsdekking voor vennootschappen die in financieel slecht weer verkeren meerwaarde biedt. In dat verband rijzen de vragen in hoeverre het effect van het faillissementsrecht maatschappelijk gewenst is, en of een D&O verzekering verplicht gesteld zou moeten worden voor kleine vennootschappen.

Dit proefschrift beschrijft ook dat de mogelijkheden voor vrijwaring zeer beperkt zijn in Nederland, het Verenigd Koninkrijk en Duitsland. Enkel vennootschappen gevestigd in Delaware kunnen volledig gebruik maken van vrijwaring. Dit proefschrift pleit er dan ook voor om meer mogelijkheden in het recht te scheppen om vrijwaringen mogelijk te maken en de verzekering voor het vrijwaringsrisico te gedogen.

ZUSAMMENFASSUNG

Es ist allgemein bekannt, dass sich die Risikobereitschaft von Managern positiv auf das Wirtschaftswachstum auswirkt. Dennoch wird eine exzessive Risikobereitschaft mit unternehmerischem Scheitern in Zusammenhang gebracht. Dementsprechend hat die Risikobereitschaft sowohl positive als auch negative Folgen für die Gesellschaft. Die Haftung von Managern soll als Abschreckung gegen exzessive Risikobereitschaft wirken. Eine Versicherung gegen Manager-Haftung (D&O Versicherung) könnte zu einer optimalen Risikobereitschaft des Managers beitragen. Vor diesem Hintergrund ist die Fragestellung dieser These, wie sich die D&O Versicherung auf die Risikobereitschaft des Managers auswirkt.

Es werden die D&O Versicherungsmärkte in den USA, dem Vereinigten Königreich, den Niederlanden und Deutschland analysiert. Der Effekt der D&O Versicherung wird anhand von empirischen Studien illustriert.

Es konnten allgemein drei Auswirkungen beobachtet werden.

Zum ersten signalisiert die D&O Versicherung die Risikobereitschaft von Managern. Die Anlageentscheidungen steigen an Wert, wenn eine D&O Versicherung vorliegt, solange die jeweilige Gesellschaft in einem konkurrenzstarken Umfeld agiert. Auch bestrafen Gläubiger die versicherte Gesellschaft nicht mit höheren Kreditkosten, wenn die Versicherungssumme durchschnittlich ist. Allerdings korreliert die D&O Versicherung mit überbewerteten Börseneinführungen und dem sogenannten „*Empire Building*". Um diese Korrelation auch in den USA, dem Vereinigten Königreich, den Niederlanden und Deutschland als Signal beobachten zu können, wird eine beschränkte, aber nicht vollständige, Veröffentlichung der D&O Versicherungsinformationen gefordert.

Zweitens scheint die D&O Versicherung den Manager so zu beeinflussen, dass er eher im Interesse anderer Stakeholder, sowie Gläubiger, handelt, solange die Versicherungssumme durchschnittlich ist.

Drittens scheint der Versicherer andere Fakten zu beurteilen, wie zum Beispiel den Grad der öffentlichen Schuldzuweisungen, als das ein Richter täte. Es bleibt umstritten, ob das Anstreben von Vergleichen durch den Versicherer gesellschaftlich eher wünschenswert ist als ein gerichtliches Verfahren.

Außerdem wurde die Abwesenheit einer D&O Versicherung bei kleineren Gesellschaften beobachtet. Das nationale Insolvenzrecht scheint eine effektive

Versicherbarkeit von kleinen Gesellschaften zu beeinträchtigen. Hierbei ist bemerkenswert, dass mit der D&O Versicherung bei finanziell angeschlagenen Gesellschaften eine höhere Unternehmensleistung erzielt werden könnte. Es ist demnach fraglich, inwiefern der Effekt des Insolvenzrechts wünschenswert ist, und ob kleinere Gesellschaften verpflichtet werden sollten eine D&O Versicherung abzuschließen.

Letztlich wird gefordert, dass Gesellschaften ihren haftenden Manager schadlos stellen sollten und das damit entstandene Zahlungsrisiko zu versichern. Allerdings ist solch eine Haftungsfreistellung im Vereinigten Königreich, den Niederlanden und Deutschland nur eingeschränkt möglich. Nur Delaware-Gesellschaften, bei denen die Haftungsfreistellung erlaubt ist, versichern sich umfassend gegen das Haftungsfreistellungsrisiko.

LIST OF REFERENCES

1. Literature

Acharya 2013, 'Caught between Scylla and Charybdis? Regulating Bank Leverage when there is Rent Seeking and Risk Shifting', Federal Reserve Bank of New York Staff Reports, working paper, pp. 1–50, available at: http://hdl.handle.net/10419/60757, retrieved at: 03-01-2015.

Altman and Raju 2005, 'Delaware Alternative Entities and the Implied Contractual Covenant of Good Faith and Fair Dealing Under Delaware Law', *The Business Lawyer*, 60, pp. 1469–1486.

Anderson 2009, 'Directors' Liability for Corporate Faults and Defaults – An International Comparison', *Pacific Rim Law & Policy Journal Association*, 18:1, pp. 1–51.

Akerlof 1970, 'Market for Lemons: Quality Uncertainty and the Market Mechanism', *The Quarterly Journal of Economics*, 84:3, pp. 488–500.

Allais 1953, 'Le Comportement de l'Homme Rationnel devant le Risque: Critique des Postulats et Axiomes de l'Ecole Americaine', *Econometrica*, 21, pp. 503–546.

Alwis et al. 2005, 'D&O Reinsurance Pricing – A Financial Market Approach', working paper, p. 1–22, available at: casualtyactuarialsociety.com/pubs/forum/05wforum/05wf001.pdf, retrieved at: 05-01-2015.

Arcot et al. 2010, 'Corporate Governance in the UK: Is the comply or explain approach working?', *International Review of Law and Economics*, 30, pp. 193–201.

Arrow 1963, 'Uncertainty and the welfare economics of medical care', *American Economic Review*, 53, pp. 941–973.

Arrow 1971, *Essays in the Theory of Risk Bearing*, North-Holland Publishing Company, 278 pages.

Bain and Engelhardt 2014, *Introduction to Probability and Mathematical Statistics*, Custom Cengage Learning, 656 pages.

Bainbridge 1999, 'Insider Trading', in: Bouckaert and De Geest (eds.) 2000, *Encyclopedia of Law and Economics*, Volume III, *The Regulation of Contracts*, Edward Elgar, pp. 772–812.

Bainbridge 2006, 'Much Ado About Little? Directors' Fiduciary Duties in the Vicinity of Insolvency', *Journal of Business and Technology Law*, 1:2, pp. 335–370.

Baker and Griffith 2007, 'Predicting Corporate Governance Risk: Evidence from the Directors' and Officers' Liability Insurance Market', *The University of Chicago Law Review*, 74, pp. 487–544.

Baker and Griffith 2007, 'The Missing Monitor in Corporate Governance: The Directors' and Officers' Liability Insurance', *The Georgetown Law Journal*, 95, pp. 1795–1842.

Baker and Griffith 2009, 'How the Merits matter: Directors' and Officers' Insurance and Securities Settlements', *University of Pennsylvania Law Review*, 157:3, pp. 755–832.

Baker and Griffith 2010, *Ensuring Corporate Misconduct*, The University of Chicago Press, 285 pages.

Baluch et al. 2011, 'Insurance, Systemic Risk, and the Financial Crisis', *The Geneva Papers*, 36, pp. 126–163.

Bargeron et al. 2010, 'Sarbanes-Oxley and corporate risk-taking', *Journal of Accounting and Economics*, 49, pp. 34–52.

Barron and Leider 2010, 'The role of experience in the gambler's fallacy', *Journal of Behavioral Decision Making*, 23, pp. 117–129.

Baxter 1995, 'Demystifying D&O Insurance', *Oxford Journal of Legal Studies*, 15:4, pp. 537–564.

Bebchuk 1989, 'Limiting Contractual Freedom in Corporate Law: The Desirable Constraints on Charter Amendments', *Harvard Law Review*, 102:8, pp. 1820–1860.

Bendremer 2005, 'Delaware LLCs and Veil Piercing: Limited Liability has its limitations', *Fordham Journal of Corporate and Financial Law*, 10:2, pp. 385–406.

Ben-Shahar and Logue 2012, 'Outsourcing Regulation: How Insurance Reduces Moral Hazard', *Michigan Law Review*, 111:2, pp. 197–248.

Berger et al. 1992, 'Reinsurance and the Liability Insurance Crisis', *Journal of Risk and Uncertainty*, 5, pp. 253–272.

Berk & De Marzo 2013, *Corporate Finance*, 3rd ed., Pearson, 1104 pages.

Berliner 1985, 'Large Risks and Limits of Insurability', *The Geneva Papers on Risk and Insurance*, 10:37, pp. 313–329.

Bhagat et al. 1987, 'Managerial Indemnification and Liability Insurance: The Effect on Shareholder Wealth', *The Journal on Risk and Insurance*, 54:4, pp. 721–736.

Binder et al. June 2005, 'Distinct Brain Concepts for using concrete and abstract words', *Journal of Cognitive Neuroscience*, 17:6, pp. 905–917.

Bishop 1964, 'Indemnification of Corporate Directors, Officers and Employees', *Business Lawyer*, 20, pp. 833–844.

Bishop 1966, 'New Cure to an old Ailment: Insurance against Directors' and Officers' Liability', *Business Lawyer*, 22, pp. 92–141.

Black et al. 2006, 'Outside Director Liability', *Stanford Law Review*, 58, pp. 1055–1159.

Bloom and Milkovich 1998, 'Relationships among Risk, Incentive Pay, and Organisational Performance', *The Academy of Management Journal*, 41:3, pp. 283–297.

Blumberg 1985, 'Limited Liability and Corporate Groups', *The Journal of Corporation Law*, 11, pp. 573–631.

Bond and Crocker 1991, 'Smoking, Skydiving, and Knitting: The Endogenous Categorization of Risks in Insurance Markets with Asymmetric Information', *Journal of Political Economy*, 99:1, pp. 177–200.

Bond and Crocker 1997, 'Hardball and the soft touch: The economics of optimal insurance contracts with costly state verification and endogenous monitoring costs', *Journal of Public Economics*, 63, pp. 239–264.

Borch 1960, 'The safety loading of reinsurance premiums', *Scandinavian Actuarial Journal*, 3–4, pp. 163–184.

Borch 1962, 'Equilibrium in the Reinsurance Market', *Econometrica*, 30:3, pp. 424–444.

Border and Sobel 1987, 'Samurai Accountant: A Theory on Auditing and Plunder', *Review of Economic Studies*, 54:4, pp. 525–540.

Borokovich et al. 1997, 'CEO Contracting and Antitakeover Amendments', *Journal of Finance*, 52, pp. 1495–1517.

Boubakri and Ghalleb September 2008, 'Does Mandatory Disclosure of Directors' and Officers' Liability Insurance curb managerial opportunism? Evidence from the Canadian Secondary Market', working paper, pp. 1–49, available at: www.fma.org/Reno/Papers/Does_Mandatory_Disclosure_Curb_Managerial_Opportunism.pdf, retrieved at: 05–01–2015.

Boubakri et al. (Ghalleb and Boyer) March 2008, 'Managerial Opportunism in accounting choice: Evidence from Directors' and Officers' Liability Insurance Purchases', working paper, pp. 1–50, available at: http://papers.ssrn.com/sol3/papers.cfm?abstract_id=1109254, retrieved at: 05–01–2015.

Bowers 1999, 'Security Interests, Creditors' Priorities and Bankruptcy', in: Bouckaert and De Geest (eds.) 2000, *Encyclopedia of Law and Economics*, Volume II, *Civil Law and Economics*, Edward Elgar, pp. 90–128.

Boyd and Ingberman 1994, 'Non-compensatory Damages and Potential Insolvency', *The Journal of Legal Studies*, 23:2, pp. 895–910.

Boyer 2003, 'Is the Demand for Corporate Insurance habit driven? Evidence from directors' and officers' insurance', working paper, pp. 1–51, available at: www.cirano.qc.ca/pdf/publication/2003s-42.pdf, retrieved at: 05–01–2015.

Boyer 2007, 'Three Insights from the Canadian D&O Insurance Market: Inertia, Information and Insiders', *Connecticut Insurance Law Journal*, 14:1, pp. 75–106.

Boyer 2012, 'Insurer Information, Insiders and Initial Public Offering', working paper, pp. 1–54, available at: http://papers.ssrn.com/sol3/papers.cfm?abstract_id=2019167&download=yes, retrieved at: 05–01–2015.

Boyer and Stern 2012, 'Is Corporate Governance Risk valued? Evidence from Directors' and Officers' insurance', *Journal of Corporate Finance*, 18, pp. 349–372.

Bradley and Chen 2011, 'Corporate governance and the cost of debt: Evidence from director limited liability and indemnification provisions', *Journal of Corporate Finance*, 17, pp. 83–107.

Brand 2010, 'Das Lauterkeitsrecht der Versicherungswirtschaft nach den Reformen 2008–2009', in: Looschelders and Michael (eds.) 2010, *Düsseldorfer Vorträge zum Versicherungsrecht 2009*, Verlag Versicherungswirtschaft, 3rd ed., pp. 49–96.

Braun and Latham 2009, 'Managerial Risk, Innovation, and Organizational Decline', *Journal of Management*, 35:2, pp. 258–281.

Bucy 1990, 'Indemnification of Corporate Executives who have been convicted of crimes', *Indiana Law Review*, 24, pp. 279–356.

Brough 2005, *Private Limited Companies: Formation and Management*, Sweet & Maxwell, 217 pages.

Cabrillo and Depoorter 1999, 'Bankruptcy Proceedings', in: Bouckaert and De Geest (eds.) 2000, *Encyclopedia of Law and Economics*, Volume V, *The Economics of Crime and Litigation*, Edward Elgar, p. 261–289.

Cahn and Donald 2010, *Comparative Company Law*, Cambridge University Press, 927 pages.

Calabresi 1961, 'Some thoughts on Risk Distribution and the Law of Torts', *Yale Law Journal*, 70, pp. 499–553.

Calabresi 1970, *The Costs of Accidents: A legal and Economic Analysis*, Yale University Press, 840 pages.

Calabresi and Melamed 1972, 'Property Rules, Liability Rules, and Inalienability: One view of the Cathedral', *Havard Law Review*, 85:6, pp. 1089–1128.

Cao and Narayanamoorthy 2011, 'The Effect of Litigation Risk on Management Earnings Forecasts', *Contemporary Accounting Research*, 28:1, pp. 125–173.

Caracciolo di Torella 2011, 'On Lies and Statistics: the Relationship between Gender Equality and Insurance', *ERA Forum*, 12, pp. 59–70.

Carney 1999, 'Limited Liability', in: Bouckaert and De Geest (eds.) 2000, *Encyclopedia of Law and Economics*, Volume III, *The Regulation of Contracts*, Edward Elgar, pp. 659–691.

Chalmers et al. 2002, 'Managerial Opportunism? Evidence from Directors' and Officers' Insurance Purchases', *The Journal of Finance*, 57:2, pp. 609–636.

Chung and Wynn 2008, 'Managerial legal liability coverage and earnings conservatism', *Journal of Accounting and Economics*, 46:1, pp. 135–153.

Chen & Li 2010, 'Directors' and Officers' Insurance and Corporate Governance and Firm Performance', *International Journal of Disclosure and Governance*, 7, pp. 244–261. A 2008 working paper with the title 'Directors' and Officers' Insurance and Corporate Governance', pp. 1–22, available at: http://portal.business.colostate.edu/projects/ARIA/Shared%20Documents/1a_Chen_DO%20Insurance%20%20Corporate%20Governance.pdf, retrieved at: 05–01–2015.

Chen et al. 2012, 'Directors' and Officers' Liability Insurance and the Cost of Equity', working paper, p. 1–50, available at: http://papers.ssrn.com/sol3/papers.cfm?abstract_id=1837912, retrieved at: 07–01–2015.

Chi et al. 2011, 'Accounting Restatements and Managerial Legal Liability Coverage', *Procedia – Social and Behavioural Sciences*, 25, pp. 147–158.

Chi et al. 2013, 'Effects of Director Equity Compensation and Liability Insurance on Corporate Diversification and Performance', working paper, pp. 1–47, available at: http://papers.ssrn.com/sol3/papers.cfm?abstract_id=2312952, retrieved at: 05–01–2015.

Coase 1960, 'The Problem of Social Cost', *Journal of Law and Economics*, 3, pp. 1–44.

Cohen 2001, 'Directors' Negligence Liability to Creditors: A Comparative and Critical View', *Journal of Corporate Law*, 26, pp. 351–391.

Cooper and Hayes 1987, 'Multi-Period Insurance Contracts', *International Journal of Industrial Organization*, 5, pp. 211–231.

Cooter and Ulen 2012, *Law & Economics*, Pearson Education International, 6th ed., 555 pages.

Core 1997, 'On the Corporate Demand for Directors' and Officers' Insurance', *The Journal of Risk and Insurance*, 64:1, pp. 83–87.

Core et al. 1999, 'Corporate Governance, Chief Executive Officer Compensation, and Firm Performance', *Journal of Financial Economics* 51, pp. 371–406.

Core 2000, 'The Directors' and Officers' Insurance Premium: An Outside Assessment of the Quality of Corporate Governance', *Journal of Law, Economics, and Organization*, 16:2, pp. 449–477.

Culp and O'Donnell 2009, 'Catastrophe reinsurance and risk capital in the wake of the credit crisis', *The Journal of Risk Finance*, 10:5, pp. 430–459.

Curley et al. 1986, 'Psychological Sources of Ambiguity Avoidance', *Organizational Behavior and Human Decision Processes*, 38, pp. 230–256.

Crocker and Snow 1986, 'The Efficiency of Categorical Discrimination in the Insurance Industry', *Journal of Political Economy*, 94:2, pp. 321–344.

Crocker and Snow 2000, 'The Theory of Risk Classification', in: Dionne (eds.) 2000, *Handbook of Insurance*, Kluwer Academic Publishers, pp. 245–276.

D'Arcy and Doherty 1990, 'Adverse Selection, Private Information, and Lowballing in Insurance Markets', *The Journal of Business*, 63:2, pp. 145–164.

D'Arcy 1994, 'The Dark Side of Insurance', in: Gustavson and Harrington (eds.) 1994, *Insurance, Risk Management, and Public Policy*, Springer Netherlands, pp. 163–181.

De Baere and Goessens 2011, 'Gender Differentiation in Insurance Contracts after the Judgment in Case C-236/09', *Columbia Journal of European Law*, 18, pp. 339–367.

De Geest 2012, 'Who should be immune from Tort Liability?', *The Journal of Legal Studies*, 41:2, pp. 291–319.

De Groot 1975, *Probability and Statistics*, Addison-Wesley Publishing, 607 pages.

Doane and Seward 2011, *Applied Statistics in Business & Economics*, McGraw-Hill, 3rd ed., 864 pages.

Dionne et al. 2000, 'Adverse Selection in Insurance Markets', in: Dionne (eds.) 2000, *Handbook of Insurance*, Kluwer Academic Publishers, pp. 185–244.

Doherty 1980, 'A Portfolio Theory of Insurance Capacity', *The Journal of Risk and Insurance*, 47:3, pp. 405–420.

Doherty and Smetters 2005, 'Moral Hazard in Reinsurance Markets', *The Journal of Risk and Insurance*, 72:3, pp. 375–391.

Easterbrook 1990, 'Is corporate bankruptcy efficient?', *Journal of Financial Economics*, 27, pp. 411–417.

Egger et al. 2011, 'D&O Insurance, Corporate Governance and Managerial Incentives', working paper, pp. 1–36, available at: www.iew.uni-osnabrueck.de/Radulescu.pdf, retrieved at: 05–01–2015.

Ehrlich and Becker 1972, 'Market Insurance, self insurance and self protection', *Journal of Political Economy*, 80:4, pp. 623–648.

Einhorn and Hogarth 1986, 'Decision-making under Ambiguity', *The Journal of Business under Ambiguity* 59:4, Part 2: The Behavioral Foundations of Economic Theory, pp. 225–250.

Eling and Schmeiser 2010, 'Insurance and the Credit Crisis: Impact and Ten Consequences for Risk Management and Supervision', *The Geneva Papers*, 35, pp. 9–34.

Ellington and Fletcher 1988, '1. Responsibilities and Liabilities of Directors and Officers of Insolvent Corporations in the UK', *International Business Law*, 16, pp. 491–498.

Ellsberg 1961, 'Risk, Ambiguity, and Savage Axioms', *Quarterly Journal of Economics*, 75, pp. 643–669.

Fahlenbrach and Stulz 2011, 'Bank CEO incentives and the credit crisis', *Journal of Financial Economics*, 99:1, pp. 11–26.

Faure 2004, 'Alternative Compensation Mechansisms as Remedies for Uninsurability of Liability', *Geneva Papers on Risk and Insurance*, 29:3, pp. 455–489.

Faure and Fiore 2008, 'The Coverage of the Nuclear Risk in Europe: Which Alternative?', *The Geneva Papers*, 33, pp. 288–322.

Faure and Heine 2011, 'Insurance against financial crisis?', *NYU Journal of Law and Economics*, 8, pp. 117–150.

Feller 1967, *Introduction to Probability Theory*, Wiley, Volume 1, 498 pages.

Fier et al. 2012, 'Probability Updating and the Market for Directors' and Officers' Insurance', working paper, pp. 1–27, available at: http://dx.doi.org/10.2139/ssrn.1524063, retrieved at: 05–01–2015.

Finch 1994, 'Personal Accountability and Corporate Control: The Role of Directors' and Officers' Liability Insurance', *The Modern Law Review*, 57:6, pp. 880–915.

Fischel and Bradley 1985, 'The Role of Liability Rules and the Derivative Suit in Corporate Law: A Theoretical and Empirical Analysis', *Cornell Law Review*, 71, pp. 261–297.

Foss et al. 1999, 'The Theory of the Firm', in: Bouckaert and De Geest (eds.) 2000, *Encyclopedia of Law and Economics*, Volume III, *The Regulation of Contracts*, Edward Elgar, pp. 631–658.

Friedman and Savage 1948, 'The Utility Analysis of Choices involving Risks', *The Journal of Political Economy*, 56:4, p. 279–304.

Fudenberg and Tirole 1990, 'Moral Hazard and Renegotiation in Agency Contracts', *Econometrica*, 85:6, pp. 1279–1319.

Gärdenfors and Sahlin 1982, 'Unreliable Probabilities, risk taking, and decision making', *Synthese* 53, pp. 361–386.

Gärtner 2013, 'BGH: Umfang der Garantpflicht von Gesellschaftsführern gegenüber außenstehenden Dritten', *Compliance-Berater*, 08–04–2013, pp. 37–40.

Gietl 2010, *Handbuch des Fachanwalts Insolvenzrecht*, Luchterhand, 4th ed., 2080 pages.

Golobardes and Pomar 2009, 'Contributory and comparative negligence in the law and economics literature', in: Faure (eds.) 2009, *Encyclopedia of Law and Economics*, Edward Elgar, 2nd ed., pp. 46–79.

Gutiérrez-Urtiaga 2000, 'An Economic Analysis of Corporate Directors' Fiduciary Duties', working paper, EFA 2001 Barcelona Meetings; CEMFI Working Paper No. 0014, pp. 1–30, available at: http://papers.ssrn.com/sol3/papers.cfm?abstract_id=257594, retrieved at: 05–01–2015.

Gupta and Prakash 2012, 'Information Embedded in Directors and Officers Insurance Purchases', *Geneva Papers on Risk and Insurance*, 37, pp. 429–451. A 2012 working paper, pp. 1–34, available at: http://papers.ssrn.com/sol3/papers.cfm?abstract_id=1968571, retrieved at: 05–01–2015.

Hagendorff and Vallascas 2011, 'CEO pay incentives and risk-taking: Evidence from bank acquisitions', *Journal of Corporate Finance*, 17, pp. 1078–1095.
Hallock 1997, 'Reciprocally Interlocking Board of Directors and Board Compensation', *Journal of Finance and Quantative Analysis*, 32, pp. 331–344.
Harrington and Danzon 2000, 'The Economics of Liability Insurance', in: Dionne (eds.) 2000, *Handbook of Insurance*, Kluwer Academic Publishers, pp. 277–314.
Harrington and Niehaus 2000, 'Volatility and Underwriting Cycles', in: Dionne (eds.) 2000, *Handbook of Insurance*, Kluwer Academic Publishers, pp. 657–686.
Heath and Tversky 1991, 'Preference and Belief: Ambiguity and Competence', *Journal of Risk and Uncertainty*, 4, pp. 5–28.
Hemmer and Wüst 2012, *Zivilrecht V – Handels- und Gesellschaftsrecht*, Hemmer/Wüst Verlagsgesellschaft, 6th ed., 231 pages.
Hendricks 2004, 'Der D&O Versicherungsmarkt im Jahr 2004', *Der Aufsichtsrat* 7/8, pp. 9–11.
Hendriksen and Kalff 2008, 'D&O verzekering en faillissement', in: van Solinge et al. (eds.) 2008, *Geschriften vanwege de Vereniging Corporate Litigation 2007–2008*, Kluwer, pp. 103–112.
Hendrikse and Van den Heuvel 2009, 'Bescherming tegen bestuurdersaansprakelijkheid in tijden van crisis', *Tijdschrift voor de Ondernemingsrechtpraktijk*, 4, pp. 127–131.
Hirano et al. 2012, 'Insights from review and analysis of the Fukushima Dai-ichi accident', *Journal of Nuclear Science and Technology*, 49:1, pp. 1–17.
Hogarth and Kunreuther 1989, 'Risk, Ambiguity, and Insurance', *Journal of Risk and Uncertainty*, 2:1, pp. 2–35.
Holderness 1990, 'Liability Insurers as Corporate Monitors', *International Review of Law and Economics*, 10, pp. 115–129.
Hölmstrom 1979, 'Moral hazard and observability', *The Bell Journal of Economics*, 10:1, pp. 74–91.
Holt 2011, 'Subprime and Credit Crisis Investigations: What constitutes a claim for the Purpose of Professional Liablity Insurance', *Connecticut Insurance Law Journal*, 18:2, pp. 585–610.
Hoy 1982, 'Categorizing risks in the insurance industry', *The Quarterly Journal of Economics*, 97:2, pp. 321–336.
Hutchinson and Gul 2004, 'Investment opportunity set, corporate governance practices and firm performance', *Journal of Corporate Finance*, 10, pp. 595–614.
Jensen and Meckling 1976, 'Theory of the Firm: Managerial Behavior, Agency Costs and Ownership Structure', *Journal of Financial Economics*, 3:4, pp. 305–360.
Joskow 1973, 'Cartels, Competition and regulation in the property-liability insurance industry', *Belt Journal of Economics and Management Science*, 4, pp. 327–427.
Kahneman and Tversky 1973, 'Availability: A heuristic for judging frequency and probability', *Cognitive Psychology*, 5:1, pp. 207–232.
Kahneman and Tversky 1981, 'The framing of Decisions and the Psychology of Choice', *Science*, 211:4481, pp. 453–458.
Kaltchev 2006, 'Chapter 14 Dynamic Panel Models with Directors' and Officers' Insurance Data', *Contributions to Economic Analysis*, 274, pp. 351–360. A 2004 working paper with the title 'The Demand for Directors' and Officers' Liability

Insurance by US Public Companies', available at: http://papers.ssrn.com/sol3/papers.cfm?abstract_id=565183, retrieved at: 05-01-2015.

Kang 2011, 'Directors and Officers Insurance: Ordinary Corporate Expense or Valuable Signaling Device', *Standford Honours Thesis*, p. 1-90, available at: https://economics.stanford.edu/files/Kang_HThesis2011.pdf, retrieved at: 05-01-2015.

Kim 2006, 'Directors' and Officers' Insurance and Opportunism in Accounting Choice', working paper, pp. 1-36, available at: www.fma.org/Texas/Papers/KimDirectorsandOfficersInsurance.pdf, retrieved at: 05-01-2015.

Kim and Skinner 2012, 'Measuring securities litigation risk', *Journal of Accounting and Economics*, 53, pp. 290-310.

Koburg 2009, 'Het einde van de Nederlandse D&O-verzekering bij faillissement van de vennootschap, een "complicatie" voor bestuurder en curator?', *Ondernemingsrecht*, 20, pp. 82-87.

Kunreuther et al. 1993, 'Insurer Ambiguity and Market Failure', *Journal of Risk and Uncertainty*, 7, pp. 71-87.

Kraakman 1984, 'Liability Strategies and the Costs of Legal Constraints', *The Yale Law Journal*, 93:5, pp. 857-898;

Kraakman et al. 1993, 'When are Shareholder Suits in Shareholder Interests?', *The Georgetown Law Journal*, 82, pp. 1733-1779;

Kraakman 2008, 'Vicarious and corporate civil liability', in: Faure (eds.) 2009, *Encyclopedia of Law and Economics*, Edward Elgar, 2nd ed., pp. 134-149.

Kraakman et al. 2009, *The Anatomy of Corporate Law: A Comparative and Functional Approach*, Oxford University Press, 2nd ed., 322 pages.

Kuchmann 2008, *Die Haftung des Geschäftsführers einer deutschen GmbH und des Gerente einer argentinischen SRL im Rechtsvergleich*, Peter Lang, 260 pages.

Küpper-Dirks 2002, *Managerhaftung und D&O Versicherung: Haftungssituation und Deckungskonzepte*, Verlag Versicherungswirtschaft, 176 pages.

Küssel 2006, *Praxishandbuch Unternehmensgründung*, Springer Gabler, 584 pages.

Kuykendall 1998, 'Symmetry and Dissonance in Corporate Law: Perfecting the Exoneration of Directors, Corrupting Indemnification and straining the framework of corporate law', *Columbia Business Law Review*, 1998, pp. 443-577.

Laeven and Levine 2009, 'Bank Governance, regulation and risk taking', *Journal of Financial Economics*, 93, pp. 259-275.

Lawless et al. 1997, 'Influence of Legal Liability on Corporate Financial Signaling', *The Journal of Corporate Law*, 23, pp. 210-243.

Leebron 1991, 'Limited Liability, Tort Victims, and Creditors', *Columbia Law Review*, 91:7, pp. 1565-1650.

Lin et al. 2011, 'Directors' and Officers' liability insurance and acquisition outcomes, *Journal of Financial Economics*, 102, pp. 507-525.

Lin et al. 2013, 'Directors and Officers Liability Insurance and loan spreads', *Journal of Financial Economics*, 110, pp. 36-60.

Lipman 2009, 'Corporate Criminal Liability', *American Criminal Liability Review*, 46, pp. 359-390.

Koch 2010, 'Der Selbstbehalt nach §93 Abs. 2 Satz 3 AktG in der D&O Versicherung', in: Looschelders and Michael (eds.) 2010, *Düsseldorfer Vorträge zum Versicherungsrecht 2009*, 3rd ed., pp. 97–112.

Loubergé 2000, 'Developments in Risk and Insurance Economics: The past 25 years', in: Dionne (eds.) 2000, *Handbook of Insurance*, Kluwer Academic Publishers, pp. 3–33.

Machina 2000, 'The Robustness of the Classical Insurance Paradigm', in: Dionne (eds.) 2000, *Handbook of Insurance*, Kluwer Academic Publishers, pp. 37–96.

MacMinn and Garven 2000, 'On Corporate Insurance', in: Dionne (eds.) 2000, *Handbook of Insurance*, Kluwer Academic Publishers, pp. 541–564.

MacNeil and Li 2006, '"Comply or Explain": market discipline and non-compliance with the Combined Code', *Corporate Governance*, 14:5, pp. 486–496.

Manne 2006, 'Insider Trading: Hayek, Virtual Markets, and the Dog that did not bark', *The Journal of Corporation Law*, 31, pp. 167–185.

Markowitz 1952, 'Portfolio Selection', *The Journal of Finance*, 7:1, pp. 77–91.

Marks 1999, 'Separation of Ownership and Control', in: Bouckaert and De Geest (eds.) 2000, *Encyclopedia of Law and Economics*, Volume III, *The Regulation of Contracts*, Edward Elgar, pp. 692–724.

Masulis, Wang and Xie 2007, 'Corporate Governance and Acquirer returns', *Journal of Finance*, 62, pp. 1851–1889.

Mata 2000, 'Pricing Excess of Loss Reinsurance with Reinstatements', *Astin-Bulletin*, 30:2, pp. 349–368.

Mayers and Smith 1982, 'On the Corporate Demand for Insurance', *Journal of Business*, 55:2, pp. 281–296.

Mayers and Smith 1990, 'On the Corporate Demand for Insurance: Evidence from the Reinsurance Market', *Journal of Business*, 63:1(1), pp. 19–40.

Mookherjee and Png 1989, 'Optimal Auditing, Insurance and Redistribution', *The Quartely Journal of Economics*, 104:2, pp. 399–415.

Moskowitz and Effross 1992, 'Turning back the tide of director and officer liability', *Seton Hall Law Review*, 23, pp. 897–923.

Mossin 1968, 'Aspects of rational insurance purchasing', *The Journal of Political Economy*, 76:4, pp. 553–568.

Newman 1993, 'Beyond reasonable doubt', *New York University Law Review*, 68, pp. 979–1002.

Nilssen 1990, 'Consumer Lock-in with Asymmetric Information', *International Journal of Industrial Organization*, 18, pp. 641–666.

Oded 2011, 'Inducing Corporate Compliance: A compound corporate liability regime', *International Review of Law and Economics*, 31, pp. 272–283.

Oesterle 1983, 'Limits on a Corporation's Protection of its Directors and Officers from Personal Liability', *Wisconsin Law Review*, 1983, pp. 513–582.

O'Sullivan 1997, 'Insuring the Agents: The Role of Directors' and Officers' Insurance in Corporate Governance', *The Journal of Risk and Insurance*, 64:3, pp. 545–556.

O'Sullivan 2002, 'The Demand for Directors' and Officers' Insurance by Large UK Companies, *European Management Journal*, 20:5, pp. 574–583.

O'Sullivan 2009, 'The Impact of Directors' and Officers' insurance on audit pricing: Evidence from UK companies', *Accounting Forum*, 33:2, pp. 146–161.

Pacces 2011, 'How does Corporate Law matter? "Law and Finance" and beyond', in: Faure and Smits (eds.) 2011, *Does Law matter?, Ius Commune Europeanum*, Volume 100, pp. 297–329.
Paetzmann 2008, '"Insuring the Agents" – Managerdisziplinierung und Rolle der D&O-Versicherung als Instrument der Corporate Governance', *Zeitung für Versicherungswissenschaften*, 97, pp. 177–197.
Palandt 2010, *Kommentar zum Bürgerlichen Gesetzbuch*, Bassenge et al. (eds.), C.H. Beck, 69th ed., 3053 pages.
Pauly 1968, 'The Economics of Moral Hazard: Comment', *American Economic Review*, 58, pp. 531–537.
Pauly 1974, 'Overinsurance and Public Provision of Insurance: The Roles of Moral Hazard and Adverse Selection', *The Quarterly Journal of Economics*, 88:1, pp. 44–62.
Pillai and Tractenberg 1981, 'Corporate Indemnification of Directors and Officers: Time for a Reappraisal', *Journal of Law Reform*, 15:1, p. 101–128.
Plant and Prior 2000, 'Officers' and Directors' Liability in the Context of Insolvency', *International Business Lawyer*, 38, pp. 303–310.
Plück and Lattwein 2004, *Haftungsrisiken für Manager*, Springer, 300 pages.
Polak 2011, *Insolventierecht*, Kluwer, 12th ed., 469 pages.
Polinsky and Shavell 1993, 'Should Employees be subject to Fines and Imprisonment given the Existence of Corporate Liability', *International Review of Law and Economics*, 13, p. 239–257.
Posner 1974, *Economic Analysis of Law*, Little, Brown and Company, 2nd ed., 415 pages.
Posner 2007, *Economic Analysis of Law*, 7th ed., Aspen Publishers, 787 pp.
Priest 1987, 'The current Insurance Crisis in Modern Tort Law', *The Yale Law Journal*, 96:7, pp. 1521–1590.
Privileggi et al. 2001, 'Agent's liability versus principal's liability when attitudes toward risk differ', *International Review of Law and Economics*, 21, pp. 181–195.
Rao et al. 1996, 'Fiduciary duty a la Lyonnais: An economic perspective on corporate governance in a financially-distressed firm', *Journal of Corporate Law*, 22, pp. 53–78.
Regan and Tennyson 2000, 'Insurance Distribution Systems', in: Dionne (eds.) 2000, *Handbook of Insurance*, Kluwer Academic Publishers, pp. 709–748.
Romano 1991, 'The Shareholder Suit: Litigation without Foundation?', *Journal of Law, Economics, and Organization*, 7:1, pp. 55–87.
Ronen 2002, 'Post-Enron Reform: Financial Statement Insurance, and GAAP Re-Visited', *Stanford Journal of Law, Business & Finance*, 8, pp. 39–68.
Rothschild and Stiglitz 1976, 'Equilibrium in Competitive Insurance Markets', *The Quarterly Journal of Economics*, 90:4, pp. 629–649.
Rubinstein and Yaari 1983, 'Repeated Insurance Contracts and Moral Hazard', *Journal of Economic Theory*, 30, pp. 74–97.
Semadini 2008, 'Fight or Flight: Managing Stigma in Executive Careers', *Strategic Management Journal*, 29, p. 557–567.
Schäfer and Müller-Langer 2009, 'Strict liability versus Negligence', in: Faure (eds.) 2009, *Encyclopedia of Law and Economics*, Edward Elgar, 2nd ed., pp. 3–45.
Schauer 1978, 'Fear, Risk and the First Amendment: Unraveling the "Chilling Effect"', *Boston University Law Review*, 58, pp. 685–732.

Schilling 2013, *D&O-Versicherung und Managerhaftung für Unternehmensleiter und Aufsichtsräte: D&O – Straf-Rechtsschutz – Anstellungsvertrags-Rechtsschutz, Eine Übersicht für Praktiker*, Verlag Versicherungswirtschaft, 72 pages.

Schlechtriem 1991, 'Schadenersatzhaftung der Leitungsorgane von Kapitalgesellschaften', in: Kreuzer (eds.) 1991, *Die Haftung der Leitungsorgane von Kapitalgesellschaften*, Baden-Baden, pp. 9–78.

Shavell 1979, 'On Moral Hazard and Insurance', *The Quarterly Journal of Economics*, 93:4, pp. 541–562.

Shavell 1980, 'Strict Liability versus Negligence', *The Journal of Legal Studies*, 9:1, pp. 1–25.

Shavell 1982, 'On liability and insurance', *The Bell Journal of Economics*, 13:1, pp. 120–132.

Shavell 2004, *Foundations of the Economic Analysis of Law*, Belknap Press, Cambridge, 768 pages.

Skogh 1991, 'Insurance and the Institutional Economics of Financial Intermediation', *The Geneva Papers on Risk and Insurance*, 16:58, pp. 59–72.

Skogh 1999, 'Mandatory Insurance: Transaction Costs Analysis of Insurance', in: Bouckaert and De Geest (eds.) 2000, *Encyclopedia of Law and Economics*, Volume II, *Civil Law and Economics*, Edward Elgar, pp. 521–537.

Slovic 1999, 'Trust, Emotion, Sex, Politics, and Science: Surveying the Risk-Assessment Battlefield', *Risk Analysis*, 19:4, pp. 689–701.

Spence 1978, 'Product Differentiation and Performance in Insurance Markets', *Journal of Public Economics*, 10, pp. 427–447.

Spence and Zeckhauser 1971, 'Insurance, information and individual action', *American Economic Review*, 61:2, pp. 380–387.

Starmer 2000, 'Developments in Non-Expected Utility Theory: The Hunt for A Descriptive Theory of Choice under Risk', *Journal of Economic Literature*, 38, pp. 332–382.

Stone 1980, 'The Place of Enterprise Liability in the Control of Corporate Conduct', *The Yale Law Journal*, 90:1, pp. 1–77.

Suen 1995, 'Risk Avoidance under Limited Liability', *Journal of Economic Theory*, 65, pp. 627–634.

Sussman 2006, 'What is deepening insolvency', *Journal of Bankruptcy Law and Practice*, 15:6, pp. 793–799.

Sykes 1984, 'The Economics of Vicarious Liability', *The Yale Law Journal*, 93:7, pp. 1231–1280.

Syverud 1994, 'On the Demand for Liability Insurance', *Texas Law Review*, 72, pp. 1629–1654.

Thümmel 1998, *Persönliche Haftung von Managern und Aufsichtsräten*, Boorberg, 2nd ed., 244 pages.

Townsend 1979, 'Optimal Contracts and Competitive Markets with Costly State Verification', *Journal of Economic Theory*, 21, pp. 265–293.

Van Aalten 2003, 'D&O Insurance in the Age of Enron: Protecting Officers and Directors in Corporate Bankruptcies', *Annual Review of Banking and Finance Law*, 22, pp. 457–480.

Van Schilfgaarde 2006, *Van de BV en de NV*, Kluwer, 14th ed., 453 pages.

Vroom 2001, 'De aansprakelijkheidsverzekering voor bestuurders en commissarissen', *Onderneming & Financiering*, 48, pp. 37–43.
Wagner 2009, 'Tort law and Liability insurance', in: Faure (eds.) 2009, *Encyclopedia of Law and Economics*, Edward Elgar, 2nd ed., pp. 377–405.
Warner 1977, 'Bankruptcy Costs: Some evidence', *The Journal of Finance*, 32:2, pp. 337–347.
Warning 2008, 'D&O insurance and corporate governance quality – some empirical evidence', Institut für Arbeitsrecht und Arbeitsbeziehungen in der Europäischen Gemeinschaft, working paper, pp. 1–24, available at: http://ipersonal.univie.ac.at/fileadmin/user_upload/lehrstuhl_personalwirt/P%C3%96K_Papers/21_D_and_O_Insurance_Susanne_Warning_P%D0%A9K.pdf, retrieved at: 05–01–2015.
Werder and Bartz 2013, 'Corporate Governance Report 2013: Abweichungskultur und Unabhändigkeit im Licht der Akzeptanz und Anwendung des aktuellen DCGK', *Der Betrieb*, 17, pp. 885–895.
Weterings 2010, 'De aansprakelijkheidsverzekering voor bestuurders en commissarissen in de (verzekerings)praktijk', *Het Verzekerings-Archief*, 4, pp. 161–171.
Wilson 1977, 'A Model of Insurance Markets with Incomplete Information', *Journal of Economic Theory*, 16, pp. 167–207.
Winter 2000, 'Optimal Insurance under Moral Hazard', in: Dionne (eds.) 2000, *Handbook of Insurance*, Kluwer Academic Publishers, pp. 155–184.
Wittman 1977, 'Prior litigation versus Post Liability: The Choice between Input and Output Monitoring', *The Journal of Legal Studies*, 6:1, pp. 193–211.
Zou et al. 2008, 'Controlling-minority shareholder incentive conflicts and directors' and officers' liability insurance: Evidence from China', *Journal of Banking and Finance*, 32, pp. 2636–2645.

2. Case-law

2.1. USA

Guth v. Loft, Inc. (Delaware 1939) 5 A.2d, pp. 503–510.
Geyer v. Ingersoll Publ'n Co. (Delaware Ch. 1992) 621 A.2d, pp. 784–790.

2.2. European Union

CJEU 1 March 2011, Association belge des Consommateurs Test-Achats ASBL, Yann van Vugt, Charles Basselier v. Conseil des ministers, C-236/09.

2.3. UK

Re Patrick & Lyon Limited (1933) Ch 786.
Foss v. Harbottle (1843) 2 Hare 461.
Re Anglo French Co-Operative Society ex p Pelly (1882) 21 ChD 492, CA. 35.
Re D'Jan of London Limited (1993) BCLC 646 1993.

Re AMP International Limited (1996) 2 BCLC 9.
Mason v. Smith (1997) 140 N.H. 696.
Yukong Lines Limited v. Rendsburg Investment Corporation and Others (1997) [1998] 2 BCLC 485.
Facia Footwear v. Hinchcliffe [1998] 1 BCLC 218.
Colin Gwyer and Associates v. London Wharf (limehouse) [2002] EWHC 2748 (Ch) [2003] 2 BCLC 153.
Johnson v. Gore Wood and Co. [2002] 2 AC 1HL.

2.4. *The Netherlands*

HR 19 May 1967, NJ 1967, 261 (Saladin/HBU).
HR 30 May 1975, NJ 1976/572 (Bierglas) with note by Wachter.
HR 14 January 1983, NJ 1983, 597 (Peeters q.q./Gatzen).
HR 20 October 1989, NJ 1990, 308 (Ellem Beheer BV).
Note by J.M.M. Maeijer below HR 20 May 1997 NJ 1998, 170.
HR 10 January 1997, NJ 1997, 360 (Staleman/Van de Ven).
HR 7 November 1997, NJ 1998, 269 (Kandel).
HR 8 January 1999, NJ 1999, 318 (Pelco).
HR 10 December 1999, NJ 2000, 6 (Moonen).
HR 18 February 2000, NJ 2000, 295 (Oosterhof).
HR 21 December 2001, NJ 2005, 95 (Lunderstädt/De Kok I).
HR 8 December 2006, NJ 2006, 659 (Ontvanger/Roelofsen).
HR 30 November 2007, RvdW 2007, 1027 (Blue Tomato).
HR 20 June 2008, NJ 2009, 21 (NOM/Willemsen).
HR 25 June 2010, JOR 2010/227 with note by J.B. Wezeman.
Hof Amsterdam 17 January 2012, NJ 2012/355.
Rb. Midden-Nederland, 12 February 2014, JOR 2014/187 with note by mr. M.B. Esseling.
HR 5 September 2014, JOR 2014/296 with note by prof. dr. M.J. Kroeze (Tulip Air).

2.5. *Germany*

BGH NJW 30 October 1958, 1959, 192.
BGH WM 16 November 1967, 1968, 114.
BGH WM 19 January 1976, 1976, 736 f.
BGHSt 6 July 1990, 37, 106.
BGH 5 December 1989, 109, 297.
BGHZ 21 April 1986, 97, 382.
BGH 4 February 1997, DB 1997, 1068.
OLG München 26 April 1996, NJW-RR 1997, 544.
BGH 8 December 1997, GmbHR 1998, 278.
BGH 10 July 2012, VI ZR 341/10.

3. Official documents and reports

Advisen Report 2013, The Private Eye: Spotlight on the US private D&O market, Advisen Insurance Intelligence, August 2013, 37 pages, available at: https://www.advisen.com/pdf_files/us-private-d-o-market-spotlight-aig-2013-08.pdf, retrieved at: 03-01-2015.

AON Risk Solutions 2013, 'Market Report 2013: The German Insurance Market', Update August 2013, 14 pages, available at: www.aon.com/germany/publikationen/risk-solutions/marktreport2013/marketreport_082013.pdf, retrieved at: 05-01-2015.

Airmic Research 2010, Director's & Officer's Liability Insurance Benchmarking Report 2010, 29 pages, available at: www.acegroup.com/uk-en/assets/do_benchmarkingairmic.pdf, retrieved at: 07-01-2015.

Bradford and Bole 2013, Corner Advisen Report 2013, State of the European D&O Insurance Market, Zurich Insurance, 9 pages, available at: http://corner.advisen.com/pdf_files/2013_State_of_the_Euro_D&O_Insurance_Market_Report.pdf, retrieved at: 04-01-2015.

Cornerstone Research 2013, Securities Class Action Settlements, 37 pages, available at: https://www.cornerstone.com/Publications/Reports/Securities-Class-Action-Filings-2013-Year-in-Review, retrieved at: 04-01-2016.

Eesthuis et al. 2011, Het aansprakelijk stellen van bestuurders, Ministerie van Veiligheid & Justitie, 106 pages, available at: www.wodc.nl/images/ob303-volledige-tekst_tcm44-416916.pdf, retrieved at: 07-01-2015.

European Commission 2011, 'Report of the Expert Group – A second Chance for Entrepreneurs: Prevention of Bankruptcy, Simplification of Bankruptcy Procedures, and Support for a fresh start', D-G Enterprise and Industry, 13 pages, available at: http://ec.europa.eu/enterprise/policies/sme/business-environment/files/second_chance_final_report_en.pdf, retrieved at: 07-01-2015.

European Commission 2012/2013, 'Annual Report on SMEs 2012/2013', 99 pages, available at: http://ec.europa.eu/enterprise/policies/sme/facts-figures-analysis/performance-review/files/supporting-documents/2013/annual-report-smes-2013_en.pdf, retrieved at: 07-01-2015.

Faure and Hartlief 2001, 'Expanding systemic risks: The consequences for enterprises, insurers, and the role of governments', Study for the OECD, Metro Institute Maastricht, 243 pages.

Faure et al. 2013, 'Civil Liability and Financial Security for Offshore Oil and Gas Activities', Final Report for the European Commission, Maastricht European Institute for Transnational Legal Research, 351 pages.

Foster et al. 2007, 'BRO, Recent Trends 2007', NERA Economics Consulting, 16 pages, available at: https://www.mmc.com/knowledgecenter/BRO_Recent_Trends_SEC1288-final.pdf, retrieved at: 04-01-2015;

Gerner-Beuerle et al. 2013, 'Study on Directors' Duties and Liability', commissioned by the European Commission DG Markt, LSE Enterprise, 427 pages, available at: http://ec.europa.eu/internal_market/company/docs/board/2013-study-analysis_en.pdf, retrieved at: 03-01-2015.

United States Patent, no. US 8,452,620 B1, Grundfest 28-03-2013, Parametric Directors and Officers Insurance and Reinsurance Contracts and Related Financial Instruments, filed on 08-04-2009, available at: www.google.com/patents/US8452620, retrieved at: 07-01-2015.

Marsh Insurance 2013, Marsh Risk Management Research, Market Research - Europe, Middle East and Africa (EMEA), Insurance Market Report 2013, 36 pages, available at: http://deutschland.marsh.com/Portals/32/Documents/1302118_Marsh%20EMEA%20Insurance%20Market%20Report%202013.pdf, retrieved at: 07-01-2015.

Opstelten 27 June 2013, 'Wetgevingsprogramma Herrijking Faillissementswet', Letter of the Ministerie Veiligheid en Justitie to the Tweede Kamer, 9 pages, available at: www.vno-ncwmidden.nl/Downloads nieuwsberichten/VNO-NCW Den Haag/wetgevingsprogramma-herijking-faillissementsrecht[1].pdf, retrieved at: 04-01-2015.

Opstelten 16 July 2014, 'Voortgangsrapportage Wetgevingsprogramma Herijking Faillissementsrecht', Letter of Ministerie Veiligheid en Justitie to the Tweede Kamer, 9 pages, available at: www.rijksoverheid.nl/documenten-en-publicaties/brieven/2014/07/16/kamerbrief-voortgangsrapportage-wetgevingsprogramma-herijking-faillissementsrecht.html, retrieved at: 04-01-2015.

Racioppo 2013, Directors and Officers Liability: 2012 Survey of Insurance Purchasing Trends, Towers Watson, 44 pages, available at: www.towerswatson.com/en/Insights/IC-Types/Survey-Research-Results/2013/03/Directors-and-Officers-Liability-2012-Survey-of-Insurance-Purchasing-Trends, retrieved at: 04-01-2015.

Tillinghast Towers Perrin 2006, 2005 Directors and Officers Liability Survey, 15 pages.

Walters and Verhille 2009, 'A guide to Directors' and Officers' Liability in Europe, Strategic Risk', Chartis, 20 pages, available at: www.aig.co.uk/chartis/internet/uk/eni/A%20Guide%20to%20DirectorsOfficersLiability%20in%20Europe_tcm2538-379939.pdf, retrieved at: 04-01-2015.

Willis 2013, Willis Market Place Realities 2013, 25 pages, available at: www.willis.com/documents/publications/Marketplace_Realities/Marketplace_Realities_2013_v8.pdf, retrieved at: 07-01-2015.

Wyatt Company 1979, Directors' and Officers' Liability and Fiduciary Liability Survey 1979.

The Wyatt Company 1993/94, UK Directors' and Officers' Liability Survey 1993.

4. Miscellaneous references

AIG Policy Wording 2013, CorporateGuard 2013 Non-SEC Directors and Officers Liability Insurance, 27 pages, available at: www.aig.co.uk/chartis/internet/uk/eni/Clean - CorporateGuard for FI Non-SEC _UK_ Final _27 February 2013_ _lvl amended__tcm2538-477560.pdf, retrieved at: 05-01-2015.

American Institute For Chartered Property Casualty Underwriters 2013, Types of Reinsurance and Reinsurance Program Design 2.5, 4 pages, available at: www.theinstitutes.org/comet/programs/are/assets/docs/are144.pdf, retrieved at: 06-01-2015.

Chubb Specimen Policy Nov 2002, 18 pages, available at: www.chubb.com/businesses/csi/chubb2373.pdf, retrieved at: 05–01–2015.

Ferguson (director) 2010, 'Inside Job', Ferguson and Marrs (producer), USA, 105 min.

Gattuso and Proctor 2010, 'Reining in directors and officers in corporate America: In Delaware, the answer is not to expand their personal liability', Business Law Today, 19:3, available at: http://apps.americanbar.org/buslaw/blt/2010–01–02/gattuso-proctor.shtml, retrieved at: 04–01–2015.

Gurochkina 2014, 'Die D&O Versicherung', available at: www.markelinternational.de/regions/germany/products-and-expertise/Extra/Cover-stories/German-DandO-market-finding-your-way-through-the-liability-minefield/, retrieved at: 05–01–2015.

HDI Gerling website, available at: www.hdi-gerling.nl/nassau, retrieved at: 07–01–2015.

Hendricks & Co. GmbH website, available at: www.hendricks-gruppe.de/home.html, retrieved at: 06–01–2015.

Hendricks & Co. GmbH 2014, Der Rundumschutz für den Mittelstand, 2 pages, available at: www.hendricks-gruppe.de/fileadmin/webseite-download/h_co_multi_d_o.pdf, retrieved at: 06–01–2015.

The Hartford, Directors Officers and Company Liability Policy, Specimen DO 00 R292 00 0696, 10 pages, available at: www.hfpinsurance.com/forms/nj85.pdf, retrieved at: 05–01–2015.

The International Financial Reporting Standards Foundation, available at: www.ifrs.org/Pages/default.aspx, retrieved at: 04–01–2015.

Website Hendricks & Co. GmbH 2014, HPDR, available at: www.hendricks-gruppe.de/produkte.html, retrieved at: 06–01–2015.

KuV Manager website, Versicherungsvergleich zur D&O Managerhaftpflicht, available at: https://www.kuv24-manager.de/D%26O+Managerhaftpflicht/Versicherungsvergleich/Versicherungsanbieter/?pageid=1253, retrieved at: 07–01–2015.

kuv24 Manager website, D&O coverage, available at: https://www.kuv24-manager.de/Manager-Haftpflicht/Details+zur+D%26O-Versicherung/index.html?pageid=602&, retrieved at: 07–01–2015.

kuv24 Manager website, persönliche D&O Versicherung, available at: https://www.kuv24-manager.de/pers%C3%B6nliche+D%26O/Tarif%C3%BCbersicht+%28Preise%29/index.html?pageid=1614, retrieved at: 06–01–2015.

LaLone 2004, 'Current Conditions in the D&O Liability Insurance and Reinsurance Markets', Guy Carpenter Views, 8 pages, available at: http://gcportal.guycarp.com/portal/extranet/press/articles.html?vid=3, retrieved at: 06–01–2015.

Lipton 2007, 'Some thoughts for boards of directors in 2008', Memo of Watchell, Lipton Rosen & Katz, pp. 1–22, available at: http://blogs.law.harvard.edu/corpgov/files/2007/12/20071206-thoughts-for-boards-of-directors.pdf, retrieved at: 04–01–2015.

Marsh 2013, 'Risk-adjusted Benchmarking: D&O rates fall in second Quarter 2013', published on their website on: 24–09–2013, available at: http://usa.marsh.com/NewsInsights/MarshRiskManagementResearch/ID/33261/Risk-Adjusted-Benchmarking-DO-Rates-Fall-in-Second-Quarter.aspx, retrieved at: 04–01–2015.

RUV Versicherungen 2012, Allgemeine Versicherungsbedingungen für die Vermögensschaden-Haftpflichtversicherung von Unternehmensleitern und Leitenden Angestellten (ULLA), in: Vermögensschadenhaftpflicht – Unternehmens-D&O Versicherung, Tarif 07/2012, available at: https://online.ruv.de/uportal/content/portal/makler/produkte/komposit/haftpflicht/Vermoegensschaden/Tarife/400_allgemeiner_teil.pdf, retrieved at: 06-01-2015.

RuV Versicherungen, email regarding moral hazard in D&O insurances on 22 November 2012.

Sullivan and Durrant 2013, 'A Global Concern: The Rise of International Securities Litigation', Securities Regulation & Law Report, 45, pp. 628–632, available at: www.paulhastings.com/Resources/Upload/Publications/A_Global_Concern_-_The_Rise_of_International_Securities_Litigation.pdf, retrieved at: 04-01-2015.

The Economist 12 March 2010, A post mortem on Lehman Brothers, available at: www.economist.com/node/15695099, retrieved at: 03-01-2015.

Valukas 03-03-2010, Examiner's Report in re Lehman Brothers Holding Inc., et al. to the United States Bankruptcy Court Southern District of New York, Case No. 08, 13555 (JMP), Volume 1 of 9, 239 pages, available at: http://jenner.com/lehman/, retrieved at: 03-01-2015.

Wijnhoven 2009, 'Bestuurdersaansprakelijkheid in economisch slechte tijden', Chubb, 18, p. 28, available at: www.chubb.com/international/netherlands/chubb10580.pdf, retrieved at: 04-01-2015.

CURRICULUM VITAE

After finishing grammar school (*Gymnasium*) at the Sankt Thomas Kolleg in Vechta, Germany, in 2008, Maximilian Gaber studied European and International Law at the European Law School of Maastricht University. In this bachelor programme, Gaber took the *civiel effect* track that qualifies for access to the professional training phase of regulated legal professions in the Netherlands. He also participated in the Honours programme and was among the best 3% of law students during his first year.

After graduation from the bachelor course, Gaber acquired the LL.M. in Dutch law at Maastricht University. Because of the originality of his master thesis, Gaber was admitted to the Ph.D./doctor programme under the supervision of Prof. Michael Faure.

Next to researching for his Ph.D., Gaber worked as a legal counsel at the law firm RESOR NV in Amsterdam, which is specialized in corporate restructuring and insolvencies.

IUS COMMUNE EUROPAEUM

A peer-reviewed book series in which the common foundations of the legal systems of the Member States of the European Union are the central focus.

The *Ius Commune Europaeum* series includes horizontal comparative legal studies as well as studies on the effect of treaties within the national legal systems. All the classic fields of law are covered. The books are published in various European languages under the auspices of METRO, the Institute for Transnational Legal Research at Maastricht University.

Recently published:
Volume 127: *The Role of EU State Aid Law in Promoting a Pro-Innovation Policy. A Review from the Perspective of University-Industry R&D Cooperation*, M. Cisneros
Volume 128: *Tradition, Codification and Unification. Comparative – Historical Essays on Developments in Civil Law*, J.M. Milo, J.H.A. Lokin and J.M. Smits
Volume 129: *Nobody's Perfect. Comparative Essays on Appeals and Other Means of Recourse Against Judicial Decisions in Civil matters*, A. Uzelac and C.H. van Rhee (eds.)
Volume 130: *Legal Aid in the Low Countries*, B. Hubeau and A. Terlouw (eds.)
Volume 131: *State Aid and Public Procurement in the European Union*, S. Schoenmaekers, W. Devroe and N. Philipsen (eds.)
Volume 132: *Property Law Perspectives III*, A. Apers, S. Bouly et al. (eds.)
Volume 133: *Multi-Party Redress Mechanisms in Europe: Squeaking Mice?*, V. Harsági and C.H. van Rhee (eds.)
Volume 134: *Europe at the Edge of Pluralism*, D. Gozdecka and M. Kmak
Volume 135: *Cooperative Agreements between Public Authorities. The Influence of CJEU Case Law on National Legal Systems*, K. Wauters
Volume 136: *Common Core, PECL and DCFR: Could They Change Shipping and Transport Law?*, W. Verheyen, F.G.M. Smeele and M.A.I.H. Hoeks
Volume 137: *Who does What? On the Allocation of Competences in European Private Law*, B. Akkermans, J. Hage, N. Kornet and J.M. Smits
Volume 138: *The Nature of Mutual Recognition in European Law.* W. van Ballegooij
Volume 139: *Evidence in Contemporary Civil Procedure. Fundamental Issues in a Comparative Perspective*, C.H. van Rhee and A. Uzelac (eds.)

www.ingramcontent.com/pod-product-compliance
Ingram Content Group UK Ltd.
Pitfield, Milton Keynes, MK11 3LW, UK
UKHW051926100926
8556IPUK00022B/1405

9 781780 683485